Noel Coward once said:
'I adore England. It's in the very
marrow of my bones, but I do get the
most awful claustrophobia when I
can't get out of it.'

And so does Joy Packer. But this is
more of a blessing than a curse for
as wife of a naval man, she was
frequently having to 'pack and follow'
her husband, the late Admiral Sir
Herbert Packer, to wherever he had
been posted.

In this, the first volume of her
autobiography, Joy Packer relates her
travels – which are world-wide –
with a brilliant economy of words and
a fine sense of individual colour, and it
is a record of a life fully and bravely
lived.

Also by Joy Packer

Fiction
THE HIGH ROOF
NOR THE MOON BY NIGHT
THE GLASS BARRIER

Non-Fiction
GREY MISTRESS
APES AND IVORY

and published by Corgi Books

Joy Packer

Pack and Follow

One Person's Adventures in
Four Different Worlds

CORGI BOOKS
A DIVISION OF TRANSWORLD PUBLISHERS LTD

PACK AND FOLLOW

A CORGI BOOK 0 552 09448 X

Originally published in Great Britain
by Eyre & Spottiswoode (Publishers) Ltd.

PRINTING HISTORY

Eyre & Spottiswoode edition published 1945
Eyre & Spottiswoode edition reprinted eleven times
Corgi edition published 1974

This book is set in 10 on 10½pt Plantin

Corgi Books are published by
Transworld Publishers Ltd.,
Cavendish House, 57–59 Uxbridge Road,
Ealing, London W.5.
Made and printed in Great Britain by
Cox & Wyman Ltd., London, Reading and Fakenham

FOR MY MOTHER

CONTENTS

Part One
HOME IS WHERE THE HEART IS

Part Two
VARIETY SHOW

Part Three

THE DANGEROUS YEARS

Part Four

'DAY THAT I HAVE LOVED'

AUTHOR'S FOREWORD

Most of PACK AND FOLLOW was written in beleaguered London during the long night-blitzes of World War Two when I was living in England alone, my husband at sea, our young son – much against his will – an 'evacuee' in South Africa.

This book was my personal defence against fear and loneliness – an attempt to recapture the safe happiness of a youth sheltered by the affection that pervaded every aspect of my parental home in Cape Town.

In the South African sections of the book I have used the old spelling of words like Simonstown, kopje, Karroo and so on, as the modern Afrikaans spelling (Simon's Town, koppie, Karoo, etc.) evolved later, after World War Two, as the language became stabilized and official. In the chapter entitled 'On Tour with the Rebel Leaders' I witnessed the dramatic upsurge of the Nationalist Party which has remained in power for over a quarter of a century.

PACK AND FOLLOW re-lived too the adventures of a naval marriage which exchanged a predictable way of life for the uncertainty of never knowing 'what next?' or 'where next?' Partings and meetings were the essence of our existence, and, luckily for me, a resilient temperament and an insatiable interest in new places and people suited me to a roving life of infinite variety. I jotted down impressions in my diaries with the eagerness of a young reporter trained to extract the 'human interest' from every experience.

But, underlying the exotic pattern of those wandering years, there was always a strong thread of nostalgia for the land of my birth. Just plain homesickness for my own folk. It haunts the pages of PACK AND FOLLOW as it haunted the writer, like an unforgettable theme-song.

It was only when my husband's own brave island and its stoical people faced invasion and destruction that I began to understand the extent of my divided loyalty. It was then that I gradually came to realize that I loved his country as deeply as my own. The carefree attitude of PACK AND FOLLOW were, in

9

fact, the preparation for the testing time ahead when the 'grey mistress' was no longer 'showing the flag' in the distant friendly waters of a mighty empire, but sinking her fangs into the iron flesh of the enemy, defending and attacking.

It was then, when she had the right and the power to demand the ultimate sacrifice of those who sailed in her, that I learned to understand, respect and love her most.

JOY PACKER

Cape Peninsula,
1973.

Part One

HOME IS WHERE THE HEART IS

CHAPTER ONE

NO JORDAN-WATER FOR JOY

A LITTLE while ago, when Noel Coward was making the film 'In Which We Serve', he spent a week-end with us in our house near Portsmouth. We talked of many things – the war, the navy and England. Noel said: 'I adore England. It's in the very marrow of my bones, but I do get the most awful claustrophobia when I can't get out of it.'

So do I. That's why I am going travelling again – back to South Africa; the Mediterranean; Germany and France; the China Seas from Java to Japan; the Balkans and Greece; Turkey-in-Europe, Turkey-in-Asia; great oceans and rivers and the high skies over deserts, jungles, primeval forests and snow-capped equatorial volcanoes. That sounds like a travel book in the making. It is, in a way, but only in a small way, since it will be a book of people rather than places; of laughter and tears and kisses – my own and other people's. Kisses? Well, it may be Cape Town and German Nannie's rough lips on a child's cut finger 'kissing it well'; or Mustapha Kemal Atatürk forcing back a hiccough the better to kiss a white-haired old gentleman in the wintry dawn at Ankara; or pandemonium in a Japanese cinema at Formosa, where a Hollywood osculation had been inadvertently let loose upon the screen. I can still hear the manager's frenzied chattering and the word 'Keezu! Keezu! Keezu!' agitatedly repeated as the film was cut. What a disaster! The Japanese are forbidden to 'commit the Keezu' or even to witness a demonstration thereof. By my sainted ancestors! What next?

For me the laughter and tears and kisses all began in the beautiful Cape Peninsula.

Cape Town, the home of my childhood, is a shady white city,

sprawling at the foot of Table Mountain and tumbling into the bow-shaped bay. You can walk clean down the centre of it from the Mount Nelson Hotel to the end of the Pier, and then, if you are as absent-minded as my brother Norman once was, over the edge into the ice-cold waters of Table Bay. From the Mount Nelson Hotel as far as St. George's Cathedral and the Houses of Parliament you will be in Government Avenue, where no vehicular traffic is allowed, and the squirrels frisk about the oaks flinging nonchalant acorns at the coloured nursemaids gossiping on the benches while their charges play under the trees. Sometimes at night you may hear music and see rainbow lights festooning the branches in Government House garden, and then you will know that the Governor-General is giving a dance. After the dappled shadow of the avenue the white glare of Adderley Street hits the eyes a crack, but there is respite in the flower market, where fat coloured women pitch their camp in the shade of the Bank and call to passers-by, 'Missus! Missus! Ticky for a buns of painted ladies! Sixpence for de chincherinchees an' pig-lilies!' And every morning at eleven o'clock there is complete cessation of all activity while the entire town meets its friends in the cafés for tea. If you look for a South African in his office at eleven a.m. you are crazy. At noon a gun is fired from the fort. People set their watches by it and say, 'Heavens! Twelve o'clock! I must get back to the office!'

From November to March the Cape is swept by the South-Easter and warmed by the hot summer sun; in June, July and August it is washed by soft winter rains, and in spring and autumn the weather is unbelievably lovely. The suburbs of Cape Town trail round the hundred-mile coastline of the Peninsula, by way of Devil's Peak and Simonstown (the naval base) on the Indian Ocean seaboard, and Signal's Hill and Hout Bay on the Atlantic side. At Cape Point the two oceans meet in a wild trysting-place of turbulent waters and flying foam, beneath towering cliffs where baboons bark and scamper and sea-birds wheel with desolate cries.

The two coasts are as different as the two sides of a human profile, the one presenting stern, unyielding force of character and the other the gentler attributes of heart and mind. The Atlantic side is relentless. The Twelve Apostles loom above the hungry sea, the cliffs plunge headlong hundreds of feet, and the scenery is tremendous. One night two lovers in a motor-car stopped on that lonely road. The woman was another man's wife. An outraged Apostle heaved an avalanche of earth upon the sinners and buried them alive. So much for character.

The Indian Ocean seaboard is gentle and smiling, and the long rollers break upon the smooth white strands. Sometimes the waves somersault inexperienced surf-bathers on to the beach in a whirl of foam, and chuckle back, leaving the poor wretches spread-eagled in the shallows with a ton of sand down their bathing suits, a bath of water down their necks and some kind soul standing by saying, 'Here is your surf-board. You mustn't let yourself be put off. . . .'

Mimosa clothes the Flats, and in the Constantia Valley the vineyards glow and gracious gabled homesteads stand in the shade of ancient oaks. They belong to people with names like Cloete, Van der Byl and Hofmeyr, Dutch names of the first settlers, or to de Villiers, Jouberts and Marais, descendants of the French Huguenots who came afterwards.

My mother's father, Pieter Johannes Marais, was descended from those first French Huguenots who left their mother country after the repeal of the Edict of Nantes in 1685 and fled to Holland and thence to the Cape, where they intermarried with the Dutch and were absorbed into the life of the early settlers. He was born on a Stellenbosch fruit farm called 'Nectar', in the lee of a mountain. A stream ran through the property and later trout were imported from England and were bred there with great success.

My grandfather was a restless lad, and at the age of sixteen he set out in search of his fortune. He found the only part of it that really mattered in the little English settlement of Grahamstown, where he met and fell in love with steadfast Sarah Belfield, the daughter of English and Irish 1820 colonists. They were married, and in the course of a hazardous and precarious existence she bore him twelve children, nine of whom reached maturity, six boys and three girls. Towards the end of the century my grandfather, having made and lost and regained a fortune, bought Wheatfield, a beautiful house in the Cape Peninsula, and announced his intention of settling down for good. But he had not lived there for more than a few months before he said to his long-suffering wife: 'It's no good, hartje, we must inspan and trek again.'

She sighed. 'Where to this time?'

'Round the world, my darling. The whole world. We'll take Ellen. She's just the right age to appreciate a trip round the world.'

Ellen was my mother. But at that time she was a very young lady, as yet unattached, if not heart-whole. She was very lovely, with starry eyes and a golden voice. She had all the accomplishments of the gently nurtured Edwardian miss and a few to spare. To this day she cherishes a book of press cuttings, in which 'Miss Ellen Marais (and later Mrs. Julius Petersen) 'rendered a solo in the City Hall . . .' or in the Cathedral, or at this or that reception; and when she was not thus employed she was, according to the press cuttings, winning tennis tournaments with 'accurate lobbing and sly passing shots'. She drove her opponents demented with her 'accurate lobbing'. They said furiously as they staggered, hot and exhausted, from the scene of their undoing: 'But it isn't *tennis*; it's – it's pat-ball!' And their scarlet, baffled faces were filled with a strange bewilderment. Ellen was also a useful croquet player, no mean hand at billiards, and a better than average poker and bridge player. Her half-dozen handsome, amusing brothers said of her: 'Old Chips has a damn fine eye for a ball. She can put the blasted thing wherever she darn well likes.' My uncles used 'damns' and 'blasteds' as adjectives – sort of conversational jokers which could be taken to mean whatever the hearer fancied.

'Old Chips' also enjoyed a dance as much as the next pretty girl, and it was to the strains of 'The Blue Danube' that she and my father fell in love. She cannot hear it now without the 'damn fine eyes' becoming soft as starlight on the sea. Daddy was a good-looking young doctor with a fetching golden moustache, a mischievous twinkle, a well-established practice and a name highly respected in the medical world of the Cape. He was the son of a learned Dane named Petersen from Schleswig-Holstein, who had married a German girl from across the border and brought her to South Africa. They had settled in the Cape Peninsula on that remorseless Atlantic coast, and there gentle, unassuming Olga Petersen bore her academic Dane nine children. But for all her sweet simplicity there must have been a streak of the grandiose in her nature, since she named all her boys after emperors. There was Augustus, Julius, Anthony and (really letting herself go) Frederick-Ferdinand and Deidrich-

Maximillian. Poor Deidrich-Maximillian was struck dumb by this fearsome appelation and only pulled himself together at the age of five to make it clear that henceforth he would answer only to 'Dicky'. Daddy was Julius. He did his medical training in Edinburgh, while his elder brother Augustus did his in Heidelberg. When they both practised at the Cape they became known as 'Dr. August' and 'Dr. Julius', to distinguish them from one another. Many years later there was a brief period when there were four Drs. Petersen in the Peninsula – the two old ones and the two young ones. The young ones were my brothers Norman and Fred, both surgeons.

The romance between lovely Ellen Marais and Dr. Julius was ripening nicely – the swain had just presented the lady of his choice with an offering of an enormous snoek-fish he had caught 'specially for her' – when old P. J. Marais announced his intention of going round the world accompanied by his wife and his second daughter, Ellen. Lou, the eldest, was married and could look after Girlie, the youngest. Ellen was of a very suitable age – nineteen. And when old P. J. stated that a member of his family would do this or that there was never any argument. (Only once was he defied by any of his children, and with what disastrous results will be seen later.)

So Ellen sailed away. With a huge bouquet of carnations in her arms she watched Table Mountain and the Twelve Apostles recede into the mist of distance and tears. The carnations were from Dr. Julius. He thought they were 'her flower', for her beauty, like theirs, was orderly, fragrant, erect and enduring.

It was a year before she returned to Cape Town, her 'brown, delightful head' awhirl with a confused jumble of impressions – the snows of Everest, the smells of China, the thunder of Niagara, the nightingales of Italy, the pyramids of Egypt and the waters of Jordan. A pint of the last named she had thoughtfully brought back with her in a hermetically sealed bottle, much to the astonishment of her young sister Girlie. Spanish shawls, Indian silks, Chinese embroideries, Venetian beads and Persian miniatures – there was sense in those. But Jordan water! Champagne from France if you like, or red wine from Burgundy or Rhine wine from Germany, but why a bottle of rather off-colour water?

'What's the idea, Chips? There are taps in Cape Town.'

'It's sacred water, Girlie. From the holy River Jordan – a

muddy stream, if ever there was one! And one of these days I shall have my babies baptised with it. Then they'll be extra good always.'

'Your babies? Have you decided on a husband, then?'

'Well, not exactly. . . .' And Ellen thought of the fair-haired doctor with the merry blue eyes and wondered if he had remembered her.

He had. So, not long afterwards, there was a fashionable wedding in Cape Town Cathedral – at which Miss Ellen Marais for once rendered no solo, since she was otherwise engaged plighting her troth at the altar. The next thing she knew she was driving away on her honeymoon in a very smart buggy with Dr. Julius, proud and debonair, at her side; and a reasonable time after that Fred, the first-born, was yelling lustily as the waters of Jordan splashed upon his round bald head. Mother, ever thoughtful, had them poured back into the bottle, and seventeen months later it was uncorked again for Norman. Five years later the precious liquid did duty once more for Valerie, who died of pneumonia in infancy, and by the time the stop-gap came along in 1905 the sacred waters had been dissipated. Not one drop was left, and it was common or garden tap-water for Joy.

I doubt if my brothers have been 'extra good always', and I am very sure that I have not. My original sin, undiluted by the holy pint, has flourished like the green bay tree. But when Mother looks grieved and says, 'Darling, that was both wrong and foolish,' I cry out in contrition mingled with reproach: 'It's your fault, Mom. I'd never have behaved this way if you'd saved me just one sprinkle of that Jordan water.' She sighs and shrugs and gives in.

CHAPTER TWO

THE HOUSE UNDER THE MOUNTAIN

WHEN I think of home my mind does not flutter east or west to any of the scores of houses I have lived in since my marriage.

It flies straight as a homing pigeon to a gabled single-storied house slap up against the rugged violet face of Table Mountain.

Tees Lodge, which is the unaccountable name of this house, stands conspicuously back from Hope Street, as haughtily retiring as a tall fair woman in a room full of Japanese. There are two green lawns on either side of a flagged path, and a red hibiscus tree puts forth opulent blossoms in the centre of each. When anyone comes in the gate clicks and the dog barks. There are stoeps all round Tees Lodge, and french windows lead on to them from every room in the house. There is a tennis-court on one side and a fig orchard on the other. When the South-Easter blows and the tablecloth of cloud rolls over the gaunt straight summit of Table Mountain, its fringe falls just short of our rocking fig trees. The sound of the South-Easter tearing through the branches and rustling the scattered leaves along the paths is one of the voices of my home. The others are less violent. There is the mellifluous cooing of doves in the firs, the chirping of crickets, the diligent early-morning tinkle of a dozen different scales played on a dozen different pianos by a dozen different young ladies in the Good Hope Seminary opposite, the raucous trumpeting of the perambulating fishmonger, the resonant cries of the coloured strawberry seller – 'Starberreez! Starberreez!' – and the high voice of our little brown cook calling the equally brown chauffeur and gardener to their elevenses: 'Arend! Moses! Come fets your tea!'

Little old Cookie is as much a part of Tees Lodge as is my gracious mother. She was there before I was born or thought of, and I cannot picture a day when she will not be there. When at intervals of several years I go home she is always on the doorstep to greet me, laughing a little tearfully. 'Welcome home, Miss Yoy darling! Fie, Madam, Miss Yoy is too t'in. We mus' fatten her up!' And Mother agrees, so they set about fattening me up with those good Dutch dishes Cookie knows so well – sosaties, boboties, frikkadels, pigeon pies, konfyts and auflaufs – the latter being a pudding made with a dozen eggs! Cookie herself shrinks with the passage of time, and the years that have silvered my mother's chestnut hair have turned her frizzy mop to grey. Her sister Teena is mother's housemaid, and her daughter Chrissie is the parlourmaid. Her husband – a mild and amiable coloured man, known to us as the 'General' because his name happens to be Botha, like that of our late South African soldier-statesman, General Louis Botha – comes twice a week and sits on a wooden chair in the kitchen and drinks tea with his wife. For the rest of the week he lives with her relatives.

'The General' came into Cook's orbit rather late in life, and it was with amazement that Mother one day heard the news of her approaching nuptials, delivered by Cookie with deep petunia blushes and much fiddling with her apron.* Mother congratulated her and inquired, with some misgivings, what age the suitor might be. Cookie rolled large black orbs heavenward and pondered. At length she said: 'I t'ink he mus' be about ninety.'

'But surely that's very old!' gasped Mother.

Cook reconsidered. 'Well, den,' she said finally, 'if he's not ninety he might be nine*teen*.'

He was, in fact, somewhere in the early forties. The marriage has been a great success, and, apart from the lapse responsible for Chrissie, has consisted almost entirely of a bi-weekly cup of tea in the kitchen.

Teena, on the other hand, has been less fortunate in affairs of the heart, which have always cost her dear. She is blessed with a great many more than her reasonable share of teeth, a high-pitched voice, a heart of pure gold and a gait all her own. Mother says 'Teena galuphs about the house' and thereby says all. In her own brown world she is a goose for the plucking, a simple and affectionate virgin, no longer young. Fascinating coloured men-about-town make her acquaintance, swiftly discover that Teena does not know her onions, and very kindly offer to invest her savings for her. Somehow the investments always go wrong, and then Teena, who has never in her life harboured an evil thought of anyone, brings the whole sad tale to my mother. Mother implores her not to be so trusting and asks where the man-about-town can be found. Strange to say, he has vanished and left no address. Between her sobs Teena assures Mother that he was not a bad man, only misguided. 'He was resperkerbul, Madam. All de time he treated me like a yentleman.'

The dominant personality of my early childhood was Nannie.

* *Cookie's generation was illiterate. Today education for the coloured and Bantu people is free and compulsory.*

Nannie was a German from Dresden, homely, rough and tender. For punishment she pushed my face into a basin of water, and that piece of originality was the only indication she ever gave of having a latent disciplinarian somewhere in her make-up. I was not an easy child. I bit, scratched and kicked, and no doubt that ducking was merited. At any rate, Mother said we were both Tartars and left us to annihilate one another. In fact, however, we arrived at a compromise, and underneath the armed truce that is the chronic state of affairs between every nurse and her charge we were utterly devoted to one another. Once, after a particularly wicked bout of biting, scratching, kicking and vehement 'I *hate* yous', I was appalled to find her in tears with the snap-shots of her home in Dresden spread nostalgically all over the nursery table, and in her wet eyes such a yearning for the Vaterland as I have never seen before or since. I bellowed aloud in sympathy and swore never, *never* to be such a bad girl again.

'If you are,' she said in a stifled voice, 'I will go home and not come back.'

Dreadful threat! I flung my arms about her and we hugged mightily and swallowed each other's tears. Poor Nannie! I saw only the manifestation of a sentiment I did not understand. When, in due course, this malady of the soul became too much for her endurance, she went back to Dresden for seven months. I was about four years old and was temporarily cared for by a French nurse called Josephine. Josephine was sleek and dark, and the only kind thing she ever did to me was to stuff a chocolate down my throat when I had cut my arm to the bone and was about to have eleven stitches put in it on the dining-room table by my father. I brought the chocolate up into the chloroform mask, and my father was very angry with Josephine. I suppose she was competent, but I was wretched in her charge. She neither smacked me nor shoved my face into buckets of water, but nor did she ever take me on to her lap in a great, generous embrace and call me foolish love-names in her own language. 'Cherie', perhaps, in a little, stilted voice, and I didn't like that. The trouble with Josephine was that she had no comfort in her anywhere.

When Nannie returned I welcomed her with open arms and waved Josephine good-bye without a pang.

When my parents bought Tees Lodge the neighbourhood

was sparsely built up, and from the side stoep it was possible to see out across the bay, and then one day a little farther down our street (optimistically named Hope Street) there came into being a glaring white edifice. This was the Zionist Hall, and quite soon a deputation of Jewish gentlemen came to my parents and intimated a desire to buy Tees Lodge and convert it into a synagogue. My parents preferred it as it was.

The most exhilarating parts of Tees Lodge were the precincts of the backyard, a stone square in which the car was cleaned, the dog washed and chickens killed for the pot. The killing of these fowls terrified and fascinated me. Arend chopped off their heads and they ran headless round the yard in a blind, insane chase which threw me into a fever of fright lest they 'get' me.

Our yard was set about with enthralling excrescences. To begin with, there was the bottle rack outside the back door, where empty medicine and wine bottles reposed until a very old and filthy man arrived with a big sack, which he filled and somehow slung over his bowed shoulder and hobbled off. Then there was the 'outside room' which housed my brothers Fred and Norman and a number of far stranger objects. They kept fat green silkworms in cardboard shoe boxes filled with vine and mulberry leaves. I did not know about the silkworms, which were the same colour as the leaves, and one day Norman said, very suddenly opening the box: 'I'll give you a ticky if you lick these leaves – quickly, now this instant.' So young and green and avaricious was I that, suspecting no catch, I put out an impulsive tongue and was demented with horror and rage when it came in contact, not with a nice cool vine leaf, but with a soft, squirming monster with loathsome white eyes. My brothers were convulsed with merriment, but I, disillusioned at four years old, suffered thereafter from nightmares about caterpillars and still have a quite disproportionate fear of the creatures. My brothers also kept a Hottentot god and a tarantula to engage it in mortal combat, several fighting crickets and some white rats. The 'outside room' was the rendezvous, as well, for two stooges called Fatty and Hammy. My parents heartily disapproved of this pair and complained that 'the boys are always picking up queer friends'. But as fast as Mother hounded Fatty and Hammy out of the front gate they shuffled in again by way of the yard. The boys' door opened practically into the spacious home-made kennel of Jockie, a cynical Irish terrier who was forbidden 'to bring his fleas into the house'. He was, however, encouraged by my brothers to make free of their room, and on Saturday mornings he went to ground there under one of their beds. Not even the cry of 'Cats, boy! Sah!' would budge him. He knew that Saturday morning was zero hour for his fleas, and that Nannie would presently drag him forth with his collar over his ears and his tail between his legs and stand him in a tin bath stinking of disinfectant and there submit him to the lowest and chilliest indignities that can befall a self-respecting animal.

Next to the boys' room was the garage, and at right angles to that the woodshed, surmounted by the carpenter's shop. The carpenter's shop was really a loft approached by an ordinary outside ladder. Here my father and brothers hammered, sawed and banged on Sunday mornings, and were inordinately charmed and flattered when Mother gingerly negotiated the ladder in order to spur them on to greater efforts. Mother is a firm believer in encouraging people to do almost anything that 'keeps them out of mischief'. The boys often flew their kites from the roof, applauded by the stooges, who felt safe from Mother's wrath at that giddy height.

The woodshed below served more purposes than those for which it was primarily designed. There were bins containing corn for the chickens and pigeons, hooks for hanging game, which my father was often sent by grateful patients, and a maternity ward in the corner patronized by the Tees Lodge cats. Whenever one of them was ushered in and the door locked upon it, I knew that the next thing would be the arrival of several kittens, followed almost immediately by the mysterious disappearance of most of them and some unconvincing explanation from Mother. Only one Tees Lodge cat managed to evade the lying-in hospital so thoughtfully provided by my parents, and she was a sly puss named Tibby. Tibby was before my time, but her name has gone down to fame in our house for the quick one she pulled on Fred, then a poor greenhorn aged six. She beguiled the simple youth to such an extent that he was prevailed upon to conceal her one night at the foot of his bed under the blankets. He was not best pleased when he awoke next morning to find several purblind kittens attempting to suckle his toes.

Opposite the woodshed was the pigeon loft, where cosseted

homers and fantails fraternized with a crowd of common birds destined for the pot, and beneath their fluttering abode was a dingy outhouse covered by a vivid purple bougainvillea and known as Mahommed's room.

Mahommed was Moses' predecessor in our garden, and he came to a very bad end. He was a gruff, grey-bearded Indian with a wife and family in the Punjab and another in District Six. The Punjabi wife was a ridiculous extravagance, as Mahommed only revisited his homeland once in every seven years, and it was Aza, a too pretty Malay, who bore him the annual infant. Apart from his matrimonial commitments, he had a fruit shop, which was in every way a poor investment. While Mahommed tended my father's garden he employed a manager to run his shop. This fellow-countryman of our gardener's was a rascally type who cheated his customers and seduced his employer's wife. At length poor Mahommed found himself threatened with a gaol sentence for sharp practice (the manager's frauds) and about to have a bastard fathered upon him (likewise the manager's). For several days he behaved in a sullen, hostile manner, and Mother said to my father: 'Julie, there's something very wrong with Mahommed. I'm actually *afraid* of him.' She had every justification for her fears, as Mahommed was even then on the verge of that brainstorm which afflicts Malays and sometimes Indians. He ran amok and slit the pale, too lovely throat of flighty Aza. It was Sabela who told us of the tragedy. Sabela was our Malay laundrywoman and Aza's aunt. She was the fattest woman I have even seen anywhere in the world, and she sat in the kitchen and swayed back and forth like a mountain in labour, and wailed aloud, while Cookie sniffled and said: 'Cis tog, Sabela, how terrible! An' all dose poor chillun lef' behin'.'

Sometimes, when Mother had extra washing to be done, we went to Sabela's house in District Six to take it to her. District Six is marked on the police maps of Cape Town with a heavy red ring. It is the slums and worse. Poor whites, half-castes, Hottentots, Malays, Indians, Chinese and detribalized natives live there in unbelievable squalor and vice. The Chinese have their opium lairs in District Six, the coloureds smoke their dagga there (the hemp tobacco which drives men to a red madness in which no crime is beyond their capacity), the half-castes brew illicit liquor there in secret stills, and the prostitutes have a little trick of making men drunk, beating them up, robbing them and throwing them out on the street more dead than alive – and, in some instances, quite dead. District Six is the sailor's hell, and he is lured to his doom by the flabby, undulating hips of the coloured harlots who teeter down the narrow pavements between the mean, evil-smelling hovels on the lower slopes of Lion's Head.

I saw none of these things when Arend drove up to Sabela's house, navigating the alleys with skilful mauve-palmed hands. I only knew that our washerwoman's prodigious bulk, rippling beneath a silken tent of cyclamen hue, delighted me, and that her adopted daughter, a doll-like Chinese child, played quietly be herself on the high stone stoep, and that the Malays wore the gayest greens and purples and ice-cream pinks, and gold braid on the kerchiefs that covered their smooth dark hair, and that, if we were lucky, we might see one of their tinsel wedding processions.

When Mahommed came no more to Tees Lodge I was told he had gone home, and little dreamed that he had gone violently by way of 'the drop'. His place was taken by Moses, the most aboriginal little man I have ever seen. He must be the last of the Bushmen, so astonishing is his behind. In the Natural History Museum in the Avenue there is a waxwork group of Bushmen and women, little coffee-coloured folk with wedge-shaped faces and posteriors that shelve out abruptly in layers and layers of fat. Their sheep had the same peculiarity and were known as fat-tailed sheep. Very few Bushmen remain, and only their lively, primitive drawings on the rocks tell of the first hunters of South Africa – and sometimes one of their odd, freakish descendants like our Moses.

Moses's chief task was to care for my father's carnations. These rare blooms, which Daddy imported from all over the world, were grown in our fig orchard in rows and rows of two-gallon petrol tins split in half and painted green. There were carnations of every variety. Some were the colour of Ming *sang de boeuf*, others were sulphur-yellow or cardinal-red, and my favourites were little starched white ballet-dancers with threads of scarlet edging their frilly petals. Mother always had a bowl of 'Daddy's carnations' on the dining-room table (and still has, although my father is no longer there to enjoy them with her), but one morning, when I pranced in to breakfast in advance of the rest of the family, I was frozen in my tracks with dismay. Every lovely bloom had disappeared, nipped off at the head, and the decapitated stalks sprawled on the polished mahogany.

'Cookie!' I yelled. 'Hey, Cookie!'

The little brown woman pattered into the room, grinning at my flabbergasted face. She wagged her head sagely. 'Yes, Miss Yoy darling, I know about dose carnasons. I lef' dem like dat for your Mommie to see. I doan know what she goin' to say. If you arst *me*, it was a rat stole dem.'

Next day she put rat poison round the claw feet of the table. Three times the strange theft was repeated, and the fresh flowers that replenished the bowl vanished overnight. On the fourth day a terrible stench and a long line of ants across the kitchen floor bore out Cookie's theory, and when the floor boards were taken up a mammoth mother rat was discovered with half a dozen stillborn babies. They lay upon a patchwork quilt of prize carnations.

'Foei tog!' said Cookie. 'Yus' fancy dat!'

Nannie, Cookie, Arend, Teena, my brothers and Jockie were part and parcel of the everyday things of life. Daddy and Mother were apart. Daddy was always rushing off to see patients or going to his consulting-rooms, but when he was at home he was a mixture of kindliness, merriment and the sort of jokes that did not go down well – like his pressing offers of 'a nice dose of castor-oil' to my small friends. Mother had glamour. The nicest thing that could happen to me in those little-girl days was to be allowed to watch her dress to go to a dance. I had supper in her big bed on those evenings, and not one detail of her toilet escaped my notice. How lovely she was! Oh, how beautiful! Tall and firm, and yet somehow soft as well, with those shining grey eyes and that delicate little Marais nose. I have never seen her without her pearls about her throat, and my aunts used to say: 'Ellen's skin nourishes pearls.' It was a pleasant thought – the fragrant skin irradiating the double string of glowing pearls. There were always pearls or diamonds in the lobes of her ears, rather long lobes like those of a very high-class Buddha, and her tapering musical fingers were ringed with diamonds, emeralds and rubies. South African women love good jewellery. It is born out of the earth of their own land. All my aunts knew the value of each other's jewels

24

and compared notes about them, especially diamonds. Aunt May had a green and a yellow diamond of great worth and rarity. The green one had a milky opalescent light in its depths, and the yellow one was all sunshine and champagne.

When Mother washed her hands or played the piano she pulled off her rings. Her nails, polished but unvarnished, were kept rather short.

'I hate the click of long nails and rings on the keys,' she said.

'Rings on her fingers, and bells on her toes, she shall have music wherever she goes. . . .' Well, rings and music certainly, but bells on her toes? What a fantasy! No, it was corns, and I agonized over Mother's corns almost as much as she did. The joy of watching her dress was always embittered by that ugly moment when the lovely vain creature squeezed her feet into satin slippers too tight for her and winced and sighed, 'How can I dance tonight with these corns?' and Daddy answered heartlessly: 'Ach, Ellen, you'd have no corns if you'd wear your heels lower and your shoes bigger.' My father's medical training was in constant rebellion against any form of distortion. Tight lacing infuriated him, but, for all that, I found myself catching my breath in sympathy as Nannie pulled the laces of Mother's corset so that her brocade dress should cling tightly to her narrow waist and swelling bosom. I can still recall the gold embroidery of a certain blue gown penetrating my nostrils with a cool, metallic tang and the rough touch of it under my small exploring finger-tips. When she was ready Daddy invariably stood back to look at her, his blue eyes alight with admiration.

'Well, Ellen, you are a great swell tonight! Is that a new dress?'

'Now, Julie, how can you ask that? You've seen this dress for the past two years.' Her voice was long-suffering but resigned.

Mother disliked her old dresses being mistaken for new ones, and she disliked it even more when Daddy's sole comment on a new gown to which his attention had been forcibly drawn was: 'Well, old chap, I suppose it's all right, but give me the old one any day.'

I was a more satisfactory audience as I crouched in the big bed hugging my knees, intoxicated with her magnificence.

When they had gone I was left vibrating with second-hand excitement and praying ardently under my breath: 'Please, please, *please,* dear, *dear* God don't let Mommie's corns hurt too much. Amen.'

CHAPTER THREE

THAT TIGER AND THOSE BABOONS

I SOMETIMES wonder if little children are ever really consciously happy for more than two or three hours together. When I look back my early childhood seems to be unduly full of tears and tantrums interspersed with sincere and unsuccessful efforts to be good as Mother assured me that good children were always much happier than naughty ones. The reason for this she explained carefully (Mother took pains to explain everything) was that everybody *loved* good children. These mythical beings had only to skip into the room with radiant faces and all the grown-ups felt the better for seeing them and acted accordingly, plying them with sweets and invitations to 'go down town' with them and partake of ice-creams and all because it was such a pleasure to a grown-up to have a good child in its company. Good children spoke in soft voices, and when asked to fetch this or that they instantly put aside the childish thing absorbing their attention and scampered, whistling merrily, from the room to hunt high and low for whatever trifling object it was that the grown-up desired. When told that it was 'bedtime for Jumbo', these paragons did not pout and beg for 'just five more minutes', but leapt to their feet, kissed everybody happily, and ran cheerfully off with Nannie. And so on and so on.

Sometimes, exhausted by a particularly stormy passage, I tried it. But when I danced, beaming, into a room full of grown-ups the eager welcome I expected was replaced by a furtive 'Hush . . .' and somebody saying significantly: '. . . so the tiger went into the jungle.'

'What tiger, Mom?' (brightly).

'Oh, just a tiger Uncle Charlie was telling us about.'

'Please tell me, too.'

'Now, darling, never mind about the tiger. You run along and play out of doors. Little girls don't want to sit around with grown-up people on lovely days like this.'

But little girls did if the grown-up people were telling tiger stories. In time, however, I came to learn that this particular tiger's sole occupation was to synchronize his retirement into the jungle with my appearance. How he comported himself, either in or out of it, was a matter of total indifference to my elders, who were concerned only with this dull but timely transition from one milieu to the other.

A great trial to me was my map of Africa. This silhouette was (and still is) a British-pink continent of Africa, with an equally pink Madagascar off the wrong coast, rather oddly situated across the small of my back. Mother was, for some obscure reason, pleased with this birthmark and often showed it to my relations. 'Now, darling, turn round and pick up your dress and pull down your pants and show Auntie your map of Africa.' In later years I told this story, suitably embroidered, to an American naval officer in the Philippines. Soon afterwards he sent me a photograph of himself: 'To the girl with the map of Africa who put Africa on the map.' That was Frank Jack Fletcher, the Admiral who gave the Japanese their first real hiding in the Battle of the Coral Sea.

Another of my tribulations was Daddy's sneeze. Mother sneezed like a kitten, a polite and muffled explosion. 'Let yourself go, man!' Daddy would say (in South Africa everybody is 'man' from a boy of two to a grandmother of eighty). 'Really clear your passages and sneeze as if you meant it – like I do.' His sneeze was like an A.A. rocket shooting off at close range. And, perhaps because it made me jump, it amused him to come up behind me and practically blast me off my feet with a deafening 'Ah-tee-shoo!' When I turned round, white with fury, and stamped my foot, I would behold my father laughing his head off with that curious inner mirth of his. The result has been lasting. If anyone sneezes loudly near me I am seized with such a murderous impulse that I literally tingle from head to foot and long to burst into tears and strangle the sneezer. I have often told my husband about this, but he does not yet know I mean it. However, he always concedes an amused 'Sorry, darling. Really couldn't help it.' And I reply through a veil of sheer rage: 'Nothing like a good sneeze, as my dear father always used to say.'

Another of Daddy's bad habits, in my view, was a tendency to hold other boys and girls up to us as examples. These prodigies were usually as boring in our eyes as they were bright in my father's. But there were exceptions. For instance, there was 'Henny' Hofmeyr, for my brothers' edification, and Ena Burrill for mine. 'Henny' was an earnest, scholarly boy in spectacles, who passed all his exams brilliantly. 'Top o' the class,' said Daddy; 'not like our boys, who seem to think the middle good enough.' A criticism which riled Mother, who pointed out that Norman was entitled to be bottom if he liked, since he was usually about two years younger than the rest of his class. Well, they've all three got there now, each in his own way, and each in the way of his forbears. My brothers are established surgeons, in the Petersen tradition, and 'Henny', a descendant of J. H. Hofmeyr, is, like 'Ons Jan', a statesman to whom South Africa looks for guidance. He has never married, and he goes from strength to strength politically, with his mother, a dark little Dutchwoman, always at his side. While General Smuts was in London in 1942 and 1943 'Henry' Hofmeyr was acting Prime Minister.

Ena Burrill. What a contrast to that quiet man whose destiny may yet bring him to the fore as Prime Minister of South Africa and successor to General Smuts! Ena was a dazzling brunette with pearly teeth and considerable histrionic ability. Children in those days were supposed to possess parlour tricks, and my sole talent lay in an aptitude for recitation, but, as Daddy said, Ena could recite me out of countenance. 'Clever girl, Ena,' he would remark with approval. An echo of those days came to me in London in 1931, when I was working as a reporter on the staff of the *Daily Express*. One of my assignments was to interview C. B. Cochran about his latest review. The walls of his office were covered with photographs of his innumerable 'Young Ladies', and there, among them, was a far cry from my childhood at the Cape – a dark and glorious Bacchante.

'Ena Burrill!' I cried. 'She's South African!'

'Yes. Do you know her?' C. B. looked up with a smile in his grey eyes.

'Of course. She comes from the Cape. We all know each other at the Cape.'

'She's beautiful. She's one of my best show-girls.'

'I know she's beautiful. She was, even as a child.'

He said thoughtfully: 'Clever girl, Ena.' And there I was, back in Tees Lodge, with Daddy looking at me over his spectacles and saying reproachfully: 'Now Ena Burrill. Clever girl, Ena.'

Daddy's profession, like his sneeze, had its alarming implications. Our house was always full of patent medicines and tonics, and Daddy often tried these out on me. He would like to have experimented with Mother, too, only she was excessively healthy and nothing would induce her to touch any form of medicine. There was also a nightmare cupboard under the vast writing-desk in the study, with shelves of dreadful instruments which Cookie used to boil in the kitchen from time to time. There were knives, scissors, hedge-clippers, shears, niblicks, shoehorns, glove-stretchers and various other inquisitor's tools. There were dental forceps too, and when I had a loose tooth Daddy used to offer to operate with these. 'You don't want to swallow that tooth. How about letting me pull it out?'

'Oh no, please not!'

'Well, then, let's have a feel. Just to see how loose it is.'

'Only a *feel*,' I'd mutter, hostile and suspicious. 'Ow! You *promised* you'd only feel!'

'It came out in my hand, old chap.'

'You promised . . .'

'Here! What's all this chunking about? Take this little tooth and put it under the stone by the loquat tree and see if the Mouse doesn't bring you a ticky.'

That little silver threepenny bit was the only coinage in which the Tees Lodge Mouse trafficked. I believe English Mice give sixpence for a tooth. Perhaps mine was a humble coloured Mouse.

But if Daddy had a few exasperating ways, he had infinitely more that were entirely endearing. What an overgrown boy he was on a picnic; and how he loved a day by the sea! Sometimes, on Sundays, when he had finished his rounds and there was no patient too dangerously ill to be left for a day and no baby knocking on the door anywhere, we were able to drive down to Kommetje or Cape Point and shut out the world of work and clamour. Kommetje, between the river and the sea, with birds darting in the bulrushes, the sun on the brown-gold water of the vlei, a pink cloud of flamingoes, a colony of gulls on the dunes, and Daddy, hatless, his skin burning to bright lobster-red, laughing and chasing us about the beach like a schoolboy. Or Cape Point, high above that rendezvous of two great oceans, a lighthouse, solitary at the world's end and the wild sea and the wild cliffs. We used to pitch camp in the cove at their base, and my mother would sit in the shade of a rock, contentedly watching us play while Daddy grilled chops and boiled a kettle on the embers. Sometimes we collected winkles from the rocks and Daddy boiled these and ate them, and shook with laughter when Mother refused to share them. 'Your mother is a very conservative eater,' he used to say. He himself was quite an experimental eater and liked a number of things that didn't appeal to the rest of the family. Penguin eggs, for instance, which are like large plover's eggs, only coarser, with a slightly bitter taste of the sea about them. Occasionally a grateful patient sent Daddy a twelve hen-power ostrich egg, which we ate scrambled for supper, but it was rather rich. Afterwards I was given the papier-mâché shell to paint on. It made a grand Humpty Dumpty. Our picnic chops were always glorious. They had an ashy camp-fire flavour utterly unlike the humdrum home-grilled variety. We children always carried biltong in our pockets to gnaw as we ran about barefoot on the beach. Biltong is sun-dried buck or ostrich meat and looks and tastes rather like old shoe-leather.

Often there was a seal swimming up and down the long swells back of the breakers, or a school of porpoises, or even the evil fin of an over-bold shark. The surface water was not too cold when we dashed into waves, but there was an icy current deep down. The mild Indian Ocean and the biting Atlantic fought for dominance there.

The only disappointing part about Cape Point picnics was not being able to take Jockie with us. There was a troop of baboons there who would have killed him. They were shy of human beings, but merciless to dogs. Baboons are little brothers of the Bushmen, but whereas the humans have died out, the apes have survived and still hunt the kloofs and kranses of South African mountains. The Cape Point troop were bold fellows who used to scale the high cliffs gaily and gallop through the heather, the big males in the lead and the women

and children bringing up the rear, the new-born infants clinging under their mothers' bellies and the older ones astride the
backs of parents or relatives, impish and cute.

'See those chaps?' said Daddy, as a sea of blue behinds disappeared into a fold of the cliff. 'Your mother's cousin, Eugene
Marais, can speak their language. He lived with a troop of
baboons for three years in the Waterberg Mountains. He found
them more to his liking than human beings.' Daddy began to
chuckle. 'There's not much to choose, Joytje, but, if you ask me,
a baboon is the better man because he is not interested in
money.'

Eugene Marais was a sort of legend in the family. He, like
the baboons, was not interested in money. He was a doctor,
scientist, poet, naturalist and recluse. He studied the laws and
morals of the apes and the souls of termites. He was a hermit of
the wilderness, and his relations, the mundane Marais men,
always referred to him with a mixture of humorous bewilderment and awed respect. 'That blasted fellow's gone off
again,' they'd say. 'Buried himself in a damn ant-heap this
time!' When he died in 1937 his notes and books were discovered and hailed as the works of a genius. Methuen published
'The Soul of the White Ant' and 'My Friends the Baboons', and
the *Sunday Times* said of the writer, 'This was one of the
world's greatest naturalists and we ought to know more of him
. . .' and *John o' London's Weekly* went further and stated that
'Marais is far more convincing than Maeterlinck'. Marais, who
was no doubt probing the greater mysteries beyond the veil,
remained as unaware as 'his friends' of their appearance in
print, but the rest of us learned therefrom that the apes and
ourselves are even more alike than is apparent. They have a
form of government similar to our own, a democracy with a
president and council at its head, and Eugene observed that
in times of danger the council met and 'sat motionless
together' and 'there was a continuous soft mumbling among
them . . .' (only broken, I dare say, by the excited chattter of
some shrill Shinwell in their midst, hanging by his tail from the
branch of a tree). But in one respect I fear they have us beat, for
Eugene tells us, with absolute conviction, that 'every member
of the council had one wife, and among them, as among the
very old baboons of the troop, there was unbroken conjugal
fidelity'. Not long ago Beverley Baxter, that stormy petrel of

politics and journalism, happened to be spending a week-end with us, and he asked for something light to read. We offered him Marais' 'My Friends the Baboons'. Bax shook his head somewhat wearily. 'No, thanks,' he said. 'I am a member of the House of Commons.'

If Eugene shared with the baboons a total indifference to money, I shared with them an almighty fear of the dark. Baboons and primitive people can't endure the dark. Nor could I. Every evening about sundown a sense of depression descended upon me, cold as sea fog, and when the moment came for lights out I would play up frenziedly to postpone it. Any excuse was good enough, and I must have seemed very naughty. But Mother was sympathetic to my night terrors and did all in her power to combat them. Light suppers, night-lights, soothing bedtime stories, and, as a last resort, Jockie was allowed to bring his fleas into the house and harbour them under my bed. But nothing really helped. A hooded dressing-gown hanging at the end of my bed remained a wicked witch, a pair of shoes were rats, a belt was a snake, and there was a Chinaman lurking in my wardrobe. As to nightmares, they were legion. The worst was brought on by a Punch and Judy show I saw at a children's party, and it lasted for years. The quarrelling reduced me to tears, and the sight of Punch beating his wife to death and then swinging from the gibbet made me hysterical with fear. If these things are funny and fair entertainment for children, then my sense of humour is sadly at fault. My slumbers were also beset by Norman's caterpillars and Fred's anecdote about the squeamish medical student who didn't care about the dissecting-room. This miserable young man was found one night by his fellow-students sitting up in bed, stark, staring mad, devouring a partially dissected leg. I dreamed frequently that he was eating my knees. This, Daddy said, was because of my growing-pains.

Daddy was a saint about my nightmares. Many a night that poor weary man, who had been attending patients from dawn to dusk, and probably long after with an anxious case or a confinement, roused himself from an exhausted sleep to come to my little pink bedroom in answer to my terrified whimpers. 'There, there, Joytje, it was only a dream.' And he'd carry me to the big bed he shared with Mother and dump me down beside her. Oh, the comfort of her warmth and softness, of her arms and breasts! How could fear linger here in her embrace?

CHAPTER FOUR

THE EYES OF GRANDPA MARAIS

THERE were often Transvaal Marais uncles and aunts staying at Tees Lodge, especially in the summer holidays, when they brought their wives and families down to the Cape for the annual Christmas family gathering at Wheatfield. South African families of French and Dutch extraction are intensely clannish. They say, 'Blood is thicker than water,' and really mean it. A well-tried friend comes second to a tiresome relative. I suppose it is the result of the pioneering years when families had to hang together or perish. They were large, and they had to be able to survive the dangerous new country and the endless Kaffir Wars. The descendants of the first colonists are simple people who still live on patriarchal lines.

My grandfather Marais was a colossus in my eyes, and not alone in mine. 'Long Piet' he was called, and he was a considerable figure, both in the Transvaal and at the Cape. He was one of those early gamblers who witnessed the mushroom growth of Johannesburg when the Witwatersrand was found to be rich in gold for the fabulous length of eighty miles and the incredible depth of two. He lived in Pretoria in those days, and he used often to sit on the narrow presidential stoep drinking coffee with 'Oom Paul' Kruger, who shook his leonine head and said bitterly in Dutch: 'This gold is going to cause our country to be soaked in blood.' Later, when that blood flowed for three years, 'Long Piet' was living in Wheatfield, at the Cape, but two of his sons were Transvaal burghers who fought against the English, as did Louis Botha, 'Jannie' Smuts, James Barrie Hertzog, Deneys Reitz, and the other Boer generals whose names are known not only in South Africa, but throughout the world. Commando. Guerilla. Those words were put on the map by the Boers, and they stand for courage today.

My grandfather stood six foot five in his socks, and his magnificent silver head towered above those of his sons, mere minnows of six foot two. His shoulders were wide and free, and he was possessed of a splendid corpulence to which my uncles referred respectfully as 'the Dad's corporation'. They always spoke of him as 'the Dad', much as one speaks of 'the Garbo'.

But his eyes!

His eyes were terribly disfigured, and in that arrogant, handsome head they were somehow doubly piteous. They gave him the look of an old hunting dog that had been cruelly mauled.

'Grandpa's eyes, Mommie! Why are Grandpa's eyes like that?'

And Mother would answer me: 'Hush, darling; it's a long story. Some day I'll tell you about it.' Her tone was very sad.

The tale that was written in those ruined eyes was dreadful indeed – the tale of a woman's vengeance. The full story has no place here, with its load of passion, jealousy, avarice and hatred, but a brief outline of what happened is necessary, if only for the sake of my mother's final comment, which made a profound impression upon me.

Somewhere about the turn of the century 'Long Piet's' favourite son, Belfield, fell in love with a wicked, notorious widow named Marie.

'If you marry her,' said my grandfather, brandishing the time-worn threat of a rich man over his son, 'I'll cut you off without a brass farthing.'

But Belfield took the bit between his teeth and married his woman, who straightway made his life hell. Knives and crockery flew when Marie was in a rage. After some years Belfield could stand it no longer. He cracked – bolted, and fled the country. No one knew where he had gone, least of all his own father, but Marie chose to believe that 'Long Piet' had engineered his son's desertion. She made up her mind to be even with him. Cheated, first of a fortune and now (as she thought) of a husband, her hatred of her father-in-law assumed demoniac dimensions. She laid her plans for revenge with cold-blooded deliberation, and the agent of her destruction she chose ruthlessly – her own fourteen-year-old daughter by her first husband. She had a nice sense of the theatre, and the time she selected for the ghastly deed was the night of a fashionable dinner-dance at the Mount Nelson Hotel. She made sure that her victim would be there.

Yes, he had booked a table for three – for himself, his wife and his young daughter Girlie.

Marie decked herself in full décolleté, and her voluptuous beauty was enhanced by a lavish display of jewels. The instrument of her vengeance was clad, as became a schoolgirl, in white. The girl sat beside her mother in the crowded dining-room, clasping in her hand a little phial. There was to be some silly practical joke presently. She wished her mother were not so set on it. She would feel a fool, but she had been coached in her little act for weeks and she dared not fail. She feared this dark, sullen woman whose violent tempers beat upon their home like thunderstorms. Ah, there in the doorway was old P. J. Marais, an arrogant giant with his handsome wife and golden-haired daughter Girlie, and the head waiter fawning upon them obsequiously, and that little hush over the room that was an instinctive tribute to this king among men. He liked it, too, and expected it. 'Long Piet' was vain – and with good reason.

Marie bit her lip, a moist, red lip, and her black eyes blazed. Soon that silver head would be in the dust. Her moment was at hand. The dinner was at its height when she made a little sign to her daugher.

'*Now!*'

The girl rose, shy and coltish, a trifle gauche as she crossed the room to old P. J.'s table, ashamed at having to play this stupid trick on him in front of all these people. She leaned over his shoulder and addressed him. He raised his head, the silver hair, the silver beard, and looked at her inquiringly.

'What is it, my girl?' He felt no animosity towards this daughter of Marie's. He was only thankful that Marie had born no children to his son.

'*This!*' said the girl, and made a swift gesture. The mother's training had been good and the contents of the little phial splashed accurately into the wide, grey eyes.

Girlie Marais uttered a terrible cry as the burning fluid seared her father's face and spilt over the tablecloth, eating its way through everything it touched. And so did Marie's coltish daughter.

'It's water!' she screamed. 'It's water, only water!'

But it was vitriol.

My father and mother were sitting on their front stoep in the

35

warm summer twilight. They had not gone to the dinner at the Mount Nelson because their baby girl Valerie was ill. Suddenly they saw a cab drive wildly down Hope Street and stop outside the house. Young Girlie sprang out and ran, weeping, up the path.

'She's blinded him – she's *blinded* him!'

She did not need to tell them more. This storm had been gathering over 'Long Piet's' head for many weeks. Now it had come. The lightning had struck the splendid tree.

The days that followed were grim for all concerned, but for my mother there was an added burden. Pneumonia had taken her little Valerie. Every afternoon she went to see her father, who lay in a torment of pain and darkness. He groped for her hand and said: 'My child, how is your baby? Is she better?' Mother answered him steadily. 'She is better, Dad.' But even as she spoke a kneeling angel marked a small new grave in the family plot.

Six thousand miles away, in London, Belfield Marais opened a famous Sunday paper and saw the streamer headlines: 'SOUTH AFRICAN MILLIONAIRE BLINDED BY GRANDCHILD.'

My grandfather was not a millionaire, it was not yet certain whether or not he was blinded, and Marie's daughter was not his grandchild. But Belfield knew only too well that, for the rest, the story must be true. He caught the next boat back to South Africa and, crazed with grief and shock, fell ill with brain fever. When the liner berthed at Cape Town he was carried home to Wheatfield delirious, and for weeks his life hung in the balance.

When the vitriol case was heard my grandfather was led into the witness-box with bandaged eyes and the indomitable head held as high as ever. No one knew then whether he would ever see again. I wonder whether Marie found any sweetness in the musk and amber of revenge.

She went to prison for two years. It was a light sentence.

When Mother told me the story she said, with her fine eyes flashing: 'She didn't do it herself. *She made her child do it!*'

I realized then that those who have sins to commit stand a better chance of forgiveness if they do their dastardly work themselves.

The innocent girl, who had never even guessed at the terrible contents of the phial, was given into the care of some Roman

Catholic nuns, and I have no idea what eventually became of her.

All these things happened in 1904, the year before I was born. But there is a postscript to the story. One of my earliest recollections is of a brilliant pageant in Cape Town. My brothers Fred and Norman, who were aged about thirteen and fourteen, acted as pages to the Beauty Queen. I envied them their satin tunics edged with gold braid, and their yellow tights. And the Queen! Her name was Blanca, and she was one of the most beautiful women I have ever seen, 'divinely tall and most divinely fair', with a mass of amber-gold hair, finely chiselled features and Wedgwood blue eyes under narrow brows. Her 'divine' height was accentuated still further by a medieval head-dress and a sweeping high-waisted gown. Ever afterwards the word 'pageant' has conjured up for me a golden lady with two slim pages to carry her train. The next time I saw my golden lady was at Wheatfield when we were all assembled at my grandfather's table for the annual family reunion on Christmas Day. We must have sat down forty strong to our roast turkeys and plum pudding. The grown-ups, 'Long Piet's' sons and daughters and their wives, husbands and the older grand-children, sat at the main table in the long dining hall, while the little ones had their own table tee-shaped across its foot. There was a glittering Christmas tree in the corner with tinsel and candles and presents for old and young, and Uncle George, who could be a wonderful buffoon when occasion demanded, was a rollicking Father Christmas. There were toys, crackers, bon-bons, lemonade and ginger beer for us kids, and champagne for our elders. The coloured servants waited smilingly at table. They had a feast for themselves behind the scenes, and they, too, had enjoyed the bounty of the tree.

When at last dessert was brought in and the table cleared, the glasses were charged and my grandfather rose to propose a toast. I can see him now, that white-haired patriarch, lord of all he surveyed, standing at the head of his table while his children and his grandchildren gazed at him silent and expectant. He raised his glass, and those tragic, ruined, but not quite sightless eyes sought those of his son Belfield and the golden lady at Belfield's side.

'I give you a toast', he said. 'We will drink to Belfield's bride.'

For lovely Blanca was Belfield's new wife, and she gave him a son and a daughter in the fullness of time, and enduring devotion till the day he died.

CHAPTER FIVE

SCHOOLDAYS. GENERAL SMUTS AND THE WAR

MY schooldays started somewhat inauspiciously at the age of not quite five. What an unforgettable day!

When I ran in to say good-bye to Mother she was, as usual, reading the Afrikaans paper to Daddy in his dressing-room while he shaved. (My parents read the *Cape Times* at breakfast and *Die Burgher* afterwards while my father was attiring himself in morning coat and pin-stripe trousers. This they called 'getting both sides of the situation'.) Daddy put down his cut-throat razor and said: 'Hullo-'ullo-'ullo, Joytje; off to school for the first time? Give your old Dad a big kiss for luck!'

His face was covered in soap-suds, and he chuckled as I pecked at the top of his nose, which seemed a fairly safe island in the foam.

'Well, darling,' said Mother, putting down the paper and holding out her long, ringed hand, 'try and be a good girl, and don't forget what Mommie told you. If you want to ling-a-ling, put up your hand and flap it. And what will you say when the teacher asks what you want?'

'I'll say: "May I leave the room?" '

'That's right. Now run along with Nannie.'

I had a fine new satchel on my back, which got entangled with my tow-coloured pigtails, and I felt highly excited and important. Nannie and I walked sedately up Hope Street. We were rather early. Jock trotted at our heels.

'Will Jockie be allowed to stay with me in school?' I asked.

'What for an idea!' snorted Nannie. 'Dogs in school!'

We stopped at the Greek shop on the corner to buy me some cherries. 'Jerries' Nannie called them as she pinned a brace on to my dress. (Her German accent had been fortified by her

38

recent visit to her home in Dresden.) All the children in the Peninsula wore cherries pinned to their tunics during the season. I expressed a wish for chewing-gum as well, but Nannie was firm. 'Jewing-gum in school! What for an idea!'

'School?' The Greek lifted a swarthy interrogative brow.

'Just starting,' I announced offhandedly.

He gave me a bull's-eye for luck.

We stopped also at Mekelburg's. Mr. Mekelburg was the German newsagent and barber who supplied us with our papers and came to Tees Lodge every Sunday morning to cut my father's hair. When I informed him that I was on my way to school, he shook his square, clipped head and his little pale eyes gleamed.

'*Also!* Going to der schüle. Vell, you are getting a pig girl!'

My excitement remained at high pressure until we reached Orange Street, where we turned the corner and confronted an iron gate bearing the legend ST. CYPRIAN'S SCHOOL KINDER-GARTEN. Then suddenly I didn't feel so good and clung to Nannie's skirts, suggesting feebly that we go home again.

'Home indeed! What for an idea!' said Nannie. 'I know lots of little girls who would give deir ears to go dis kindergarten.' But she was strangely red in the face as she turned me over to Miss Potts, a gaunt female in a starched white cap, known to her pupils as 'Potty'. This good soul placed me next to a cher-ubic boy who immediately pulled my pigtails. But worse fol-lowed. My hand-flapping, about which Mother had taken such pains to warn me, was in the true British tradition – too little and too late – and presently the cherubic boy guffawed rau-cously and announced in an audible undertone: 'Holly-holly-ha! It's raining round here!'

In fact, when Nannie came to collect me at noon I was in a sorry state. Quite illogically that loyal woman decided that Miss Potts was to blame, and told her so in no measured terms, thereby opening up hostilities that endured unremittingly until I was promoted to the Big School.

When I was nine various things happened to change my life.

Nannie married an Englishman and left Tees Lodge. War was declared between England and Kaiser Germany, in consequence of which my friend Mr. Mekelburg put up his shutters and disappeared into an internment camp. And somebody else bought the newsagent-barber shop. My elder brother Fred (still a student in London) joined the Navy as a probationer surgeon, and Mother paled at the sight of a telegraph boy.

The war. South Africa was as remote from the origin of the conflict as is an estuary from the source of the river, but it was torn to pieces by the war, lashed into fury by those distant storms, and flooded with a torrent of racial strife. The turmoil and the bitterness was a nightmare back-drop to the peaceful setting of my childish life. It was all epitomized by my father's voice at breakfast, reading the news aloud between mouthfuls of egg and bacon. Battles in France and campaigns at home – German South-West Africa, German East Africa – Communist insurrections on the Rand and Boer rebellions against the erstwhile enemy, England.

There were terrible breaches between friends and relatives at that time, and Mother often sighed and said: 'Remember, darling, keep off politics and religion if you don't want to lose your friends.' Yet she herself could not keep off politics. Whenever there was a 'hot' debate coming off, one of her political acquaintances would ring her up to offer her a seat in the Ladies' Gallery and tea afterwards, and she would come home and give my father an account of the debate, which made him rock with laughter and fume with fury alternately. Mother was an incomparable mimic and could 'take off' anyone from John X. Merriman to James Barrie Hertzog, so that Daddy, who was too busy to attend the House, got the cream of the debate in his own home. No South African can 'keep off politics' any more than he can keep off the share market. Both are there at his door in their most elemental form and will not be denied.

Of all the Boer Generals who had fought against England for three bitter years in the Boer War, only two now took up cudgels for the Empire. These were Botha and Smuts, who as long ago as 1902, at the Peace of Vereenigen, had seen the necessity to stop and start again. I was ten when I saw them for the first time. The German South-West African campaign had been successfully concluded, and its leader, Louis Botha, was to be presented with the freedom of the city and an honorary degree by the University of Cape Town. Daddy was on the University Council, and he arranged that Mother should take me to the ceremony. It was not merely a presentation, but a recruiting meeting as well. I remember the packed City Hall, the palms and laurels on the platform, and the impressive rows of civic and university authorities, and my own father, unfamiliar in his mortar-board and gown. And, centre-stage, Botha and Smuts in their khaki uniforms. – Botha, thick-set, bearded, dark and florid, a veritable battle-axe; and Smuts, a little behind him, spare and flexible – the rapier.

Botha spoke in his halting English, telling us of the difficulties of the campaign, the long treks over desert lands, thirst and heat, and the courage of the men who combated these things, but even as he spoke someone leaned across me to whisper to Mother: 'Watch Jannie Smuts! *He* is the brains of the campaign!' Presently Smuts, too, made a speech, and because his heart was in it it was good. There was light in his soft, suave, foreign-sounding voice, like the silver and gold in his little pointed imperial, and the ice-blue gleam in his eyes, the eyes of a thinker and a fighter. Smuts could recruit. He could get men for the fields of Flanders and for the German East campaign. He knew the game. Had he not in 1901 ranged into the Cape with his guerillas to get more men to carry on the war against England – a war already lost? Had he not then, with his ragged, war-weary commando, ridden seven hundred miles in five weeks to find new soldiers and horses, guns, food and clothing for men who, starved and unequipped, were still prepared to fight on? Yes, Jannie Smuts knew how to get men. And I, child as I was, felt my heart lift at the words he said in that pale Dutch voice, the sentiments he evoked, and the tales he told. 'Slim Jannie' he was called by the Boers, his own people, who were also his bitterest enemies. The Boers saw in Botha and Smuts men who had 'gone over to the invader'. They could not see beyond the narrow confines of the vanquished Transvaal and Free State Republics into the broad conception of Empire – not a colonial empire ruled from London, but a sisterhood of vigorous self-governing young nations with a great destiny in world affairs. 'South Africa for the South Africans' was their slogan, and it never seemed to occur to them that, then as now, the means which they employed to gain that end might well finish up with South Africa for Germany. Beyers, the Minister for Defence in 1914, played into Germany's hands. Certain people in high places in 1939 did the

41

same thing with far less excuse. Beyers was still raw from defeat. These others had seen the federation of South Africa, the acquisition of Dominion Status, and they knew the still prouder place she could hold if she would cease to be what Smuts calls 'a cramped, puny country gnawing at its own entrails'.

Once in a century a man is born with world vision – a great statesman. The Boer Jannie Smuts is such a one, and so is the Englishman Winston Churchill. But however meteoric his career or great his international fame, for years neither was entirely trusted by his own people – and for the same reason. Both men refused to be fettered by party politics, and changed their political loyalties fearlessly to suit the necessity of the hour if their reason and their 'flair' dictated such a course. Both Smuts and Churchill were too clever, too forceful and too 'slim' for the man in the streets. Men fear what they do not understand, and whosoever sees further than his fellows cannot hope to be understood until, perhaps, it is too late. The trouble with England is that she has too many statesmen and few leaders, and the trouble with South Africa is precisely the opposite. If there were only two South Africans left in an empty world, both would insist on being leaders. Moreover, the statesmen of England make little effort to acquire the qualities of leadership, and the leaders of South Africa make even less to learn statesmenship.

Only two other incidents of the war, as it affected Cape Town, stand out in my recollection. One was the next time I was in the City Hall with my parents. There was no rejoicing then. The galleries and boxes were draped in black, and above the singing of the Requiem could be heard the aching sobs of women mourning their dead, their many thousand Springboks who had died defending a wood somewhere in France. Years later my husband and I went over those battlefields of 1914-1918, and we walked in Delville Wood among the naked, blighted trees. The soft rain of autumn fell upon the dust of France that is also the dust of my own country, and I could not see for tears.

The other occasion was a lurid and terrible night when the jingo rowdies got out of control and, with bestial howls and lighted torches, committed murder and arson in the town. From our house we heard the yells and the muttering and saw the flames as anyone with a German name was dragged from his property and that property destroyed. The injustice of mob fury came home to me when the warehouses of old Mr. Spilhaus were burned and looted. His granddaughter Freda was a friend and schoolmate of mine, and while the jingoes dealt with his business his grandson Jack, Freda's brother, a a lad in the Royal Flying Corps, was flying to his death somewhere in France giving his life for England and freedom, regardless of his German name.

'It isn't fair!' I cried when Mother told me what had happened.

'No,' she said sadly, 'but it is war.'

I never really enjoyed my schooldays, although there were a few bright spots in the general gloom – tennis and netball matches and the pet chameleons we kept on the morning glory that covered the playground wall.

In recess we often diverted ourselves by stroking our chameleons under their tails with fountain-pen fillers, a caress which caused the creatures to turn pale – an interesting metamorphosis to witness. Incidentally, Professor Lancelot Hogben has found the same thing and remarked upon it in 'Science for the Citizen'. We did not know about 'Science for the Citizen', but we did know about chameleons. (Professor Hogben has also discovered that frogs feel thirst in their toes, a piece of information I am unable to verify.)

Among ourselves we spoke a language as exclusive as that of the Etonian or the Wykehamist, I have forgotten most of it, but certain vital expressions remain fixed in my mind. If one girl saw another sitting in what Mother would call an unladylike attitude, the first girl would, with a wealth of facial contortion, make the simple observation: 'Sights!' A warning that a pair of pants or a petticoat was falling down was conveyed by the announcement that 'Sunday is longer than Monday', and derision could be beautifully implied with a mere 'So wah!' Translated into English, 'So wah!' or 'So waer!' means 'So there!' But if you try it you will see that 'wah' or 'waer' allows for much more malevolent grimacing. The nose can be brought more effectively into play.

Talking of languages, I have one personal grudge against General Smuts. When the Union of South Africa took place in

1910 and General Botha, as the first Prime Minister of a feder-
ated South Africa, made General Smuts his Minister of Education (among other offices), Smuts, anxious to foster the policy
of the fusion of Boer and British, brought in a ruling that English should be the official language of the schools and Afrikaans
optional. When the Nationalists came into power under Hertzog in 1926, English remained the official language, but Afrikaans was made compulsory.

Unfortunately for me, my education took place in the
interim – at least, that portion of it which might have taught me
Afrikaans – and, through my ignorance, I have missed a great
deal of entertainment. My Marais uncles were amusing fellows
with a gift for telling a good yarn, but the points of nearly all
their best stories were in Afrikaans, perhaps because these were
largely concerned with the naïvetés of country bumpkins. Afrikaans is a simple tongue full of diminutives and homely turns of
phrase and rich with rustic humour. My uncles told their tales
in English with gusto, and I listened enthralled until the end –
the gloriously comical climax – '. . . then the old Boer said to the
judge: "Skuus Meneer" . . .' And there they were, splitting their
sides, Daddy with his shoulders heaving in silent merriment,
Mother with her head flung back and tears of laughter running
down her cheeks, the uncles guffawing lustily, and me with a
stonily disappointed countenance, high and dry. 'What did the
old Boer say, Mom? Tell me in English.' And Mother, still
choking with mirth: 'It wouldn't be funny in English, darling,
only vulgar! Ha! ha! ha!' I have often wondered bitterly
whether it was not vulgar in Afrikaans!

In any case, I owe this particular frustration to none other
than Jannie Smuts.

When I was about thirteen I began to make myself con-
spicuous at school. Not, I regret to say, by proficiency in my
work, but by an unfortunate tendency to faint at prayers, in
chapel, in church, or upon any other occasion which required
me to do homage to my Maker. This foible the worthy nun
who was our headmistress regarded as an irreverent form of
exhibitionism. She was a masterful woman with prominent
features and a nautical roll, who rocked down the dark and
dingy corridors on creaking shoes, and the gust of her full-sail
passage chilled even the spider contemplative in his cobweb.

One day she sailed into the gymnasium to give us a lecture on self-control. She stood like a great blackbird behind her wooden lectern, and suddenly I was aware of her fishy eye, enormously magnified by the convex lenses of her spectacles, fixed upon me.

'In this very hall,' she said, 'there are Some People who should make a special effort to cultivate Self-Control. Those People see fit to faint at all religious observances, hoping, perhaps, to be exempted from prayers. . . .' She paused to let these words sink in, and while I tingled with mortification my companions nudged one another and giggled. 'There is no *need* for Those People to faint,' she continued. 'They could say to themselves, "I feel perfectly all right; I will *not* faint!" at the same time sitting forward on the pew and putting their heads between their knees. In this way they would *be* all right.' She impaled me upon an icy stare and concluded: 'I suggest that Those People try exerting Self-Control. Furthermore, I would like them to bear in mind that nobody is ever in any way the worse for prayer.'

Next morning there happened to be a service in chapel, and I determined to call upon my self-control to the uttermost. But half-way through the awful familiar weakness assailed me. Priest and altar wavered, the Madonna in the wall niche turned a lurid red, a black wave rolled down the aisle, and cold sweat broke out upon my forehead. I managed to get my behind on to the pew and dropped my head between my pointed black-stockinged kees. 'I do *not* feel ill. I am perfectly all right. Dear God, please don't let me faint . . . Oooh!' The mists unexpectedly cleared as I was sick as a poisoned pup all over my square-toed shoes. The chapel came back into focus, the Virgin resumed her alabaster pallor, and the chill dews evaporated. But Sister called me into her study afterwards.

'Joy Petersen, you will be excused from chapel in future.' She made it sound like a punishment.

'I'm sorry, Sister. Honestly, I tried self-control – like mad! and I *didn't* faint.'

She looked me over critically, and her stern features relaxed into a rare smile.

'You are getting a lanky girl,' she said. 'We'll have to put a weight on your head.'

The most popular 'pash' in the school was Sister Mary, a

rosy-faced novice with wistful eyes the colour of lapis-lazuli. She didn't look at all as if her healthy bloom ought to be sequestered by vows of chastity. She was the sturdy Aryan type Hitler's eugenists would have seized upon for the honour of bearing innumerable children to noble Nazi warriors, and even the youngsters at St. Cyprian's were aware of the incongruity of that glowing, girlish countenance austerely framed by the white wimple, and sought a romantic reason for it. One of the older girls went so far as to invent and spread the delicious rumour that Sister Mary had been in love with the young war poet Rupert Brooke, and that her grief at his untimely end in 1915 had driven her to take the veil. We instantly began to read his poems avidly, searching for traces of Sister Mary. Our pulses quickened as we came to the lines: 'When Beauty and Beauty meet All naked, fair to fair, The earth is crying sweet, And scattering bright the air. . . .'

'That's love,' sighed Freda, who the rest of us acknowledged to be an authority on the subject. But we were not entirely convinced. 'All naked, fair to fair' might indeed be love, but it didn't sound much like Sister Mary. Perhaps our imaginations were muffled in the voluminous robes. Perhaps, indeed, that was their purpose.

Sister Mary was never my 'pash', for I was under the dominion of a more tempestuous personality, one whirling in the high winds that blow outside the cloister's calm. Mina Freund, our elocution teacher, was one of those who trod the stars or plumbed the bottomless pit. Anything might happen when she took a class. Shakespeare might go whizzing across the room, or all might be undisturbed peace while the girls intoned 'The air down here is very bad for fair hair' – a phrase calculated to correct our clipped South African accents. Mina Freund was one of those rare blondes, a genuine platinum, with a trick of pushing back that straight, light hair of hers with a distraught white hand. Her nostrils quivered and dilated when she was angry, and her flexible, nervous body was charged with dynamic energy. Her mouth was wide and mobile, and she had a lovely laugh. I think her pupils drove her crazy, especially when there was a love passage in process of being mangled.

' "Romeo, Romeo, wherefore art thou Romeo?" Can't you see what Juliet is getting at, Doris, you miserable little turnip? The way you said that line you might have been asking for a telephone number. Can't you get it into your head that Juliet loves the one man she cannot, dare not, love? Can't you imagine what it means to a girl – and an Italian girl at that – to find she has given her heart to the boy who is, of all her suitors, forbidden? ... No, I suppose you can't! What should a very young turnip know of love?' and then the gesture, the nervous, generous finger-tips pressing back the mane of hair, pale as winter sunshine. A sigh, a smile. 'Go on, child. Try again. And remember Romeo is a Montague, and a Capulet must not love a Montague. Put some feeling into your voice, yearning, despair ...'

Mina Freund's outbursts affected me profoundly. They were storms and lightnings in the dark. There, in the dusty classroom, I heard an echo of life, the real thing that awaited all of us when we should be old enough to venture forth. She was the sea-shell that murmurs with the voice of the waves. Her very presence thrilled and enchanted me. I think she knew of her effect upon me, was touched by it. She gave me some good parts in her school plays, our yearly mutilation of poor William Shakespeare. But always comedy. And when I begged for tragic rôles she only laughed and tousled my fair head.

'You are a born comedian, child. Don't ever forget it!'

There are on the West End stage today two South African actresses who owe their first flame of inspiration to Mina Freund's teaching. One is Jeanne de Cassalis and the other is 'Scrappy' Van Hulsteyn.

Scrappy Van Hulsteyn? All right, let me give her stage name. She is a great actress, and she calls herself Marda Vanne.

CHAPTER SIX

HOLIDAYS. THE SEA AND THE VELD

If my schooldays were not to my liking, my holidays were the best any child could have had. They were all inextricably linked up with my best friend, Marjorie Morris. Marjorie was the daughter of my father's partner, Dr. Frank Morris, an Englishman from Gloucestershire, in manner quiet and reserved. Mrs. Morris was very pretty, with an attractive French accent. She came from Mauritius, and the Morris children chattered to their parents as freely in French as in English.

Every summer, just after Christmas, I went away to Onrust with Marjorie, her sister Phillis, and their governess, known to us as Tot. Sometimes Marjorie's elder brother Lawrence came too, with one or another of his school friends. Tot, worn down by years of caring for other people's children, remains in my recollection as a woman without age or substance, a voice to which we paid little heed, a two-dimensional personality with neither breadth nor volume, just the opposite to my German Nannie, who possessed both these attributes in abundance. There was a good deal of 'don't' about Tot, but she had a fine repertoire of schoolgirl howlers on a par with 'Eli was an old man, Eli was a sick man, and he brought up Samuel', which appealed to our simple sense of humour.

Onrust, which we dearly loved, was an out-of-the-way dorp between the mountains and the sea, a tiny hamlet on a dark, peaty lagoon. A little farther along the coast was Cape Aghullus, the southernmost extremity of Africa, and from our hotel we could see the beam of Danger Point lighthouse on the rocky headland. Our hotel was a primitive affair, and the amenities of the village were confined to a post office, a wheelwright's and Ma Kuys' store. From the wheelwright we hired rough, ill-mannered horses and bounced about the countryside on two animals named Jaapie and Pawpie (we discovered afterwards that Pawpie was the local distortion of Poppy). At Ma Kuys' we bought sweets, cookies, lemonade and other necessities of life. Ma Kuys was a brawny Boer widow with a sun-bonnet, and features that must have frightened Pa Kuys into an early grave. She boasted that she had built her shop herself, laying brick upon brick with her own large, raw-boned hands. She had also papered it with an advertisement for Springbok tobacco which Marjorie and I greatly admired, a polypicture of an old Boer smoking his pipe in a rocking-chair beside the fire and his wife sitting opposite him. Her knitting lies unheeded on her ample lap, and her raised nostrils are distended in delight. 'What a beautiful aroma!' is written over her head, and over his: 'Yes, wife, it is Springbok.' Two walls told this little tale in

48

English, and the other two in Afrikaans, for, since South Africa is a bilingual country, such valuable information must be imparted in both languages.

Even the drawbacks of Onrust added to our pleasure in the place. They smacked of adventure. For instance, every evening at dusk a suicide squad of bats zoomed through the open windows into our bedroom, attracted by the flickering light of our candle. Marjorie discovered that if we left our basins full of water while we went to supper the creatures never failed to drown themselves, but blowing out the candle and running from the room with that grey beat of frantic wings still whirling round in the half-dark was a creepy experience full of shrieks and giggles. And when, after supper, we returned to find the drowned bats, there inevitably ensued a heated argument as to who ought to empty them out. In the end this task was usually performed by William, a broad, beige menial with a vast flat face like a cardboard harvest moon. Then sometimes Tot, in combing our hair, would come upon a knot that was not a knot, but a tick. In this case the only thing to do was to put butter on its tail and wait. A tick is a tiny bush parasite which cattle, dogs and humans brush off the branches on to themselves in passing. The insect is a true vampire. He embeds himself firmly in the skin of his victim and blood-sucks until he is swollen to fabulous proportions. It is inadvisable to pull the bloated body away, as the head remains and sets up an infection, but an application of butter will make him release his hold. There were other dangers, too, that beset the narrow, winding bush-path to the beach, for snakes liked to sun themselves there in the soft sand, and anyone who treads bare-legged on a cobra or a puff-adder is unlikely to have the opportunity of doing so a second time.

Every morning we swam in the tepid, golden-brown waters of the lagoon and then dashed helter-skelter down the steeply shelving beach into the surf for a final bracing dip. At low tide we roamed along the succession of beaches in search of shells, for that turbulent, deep-voiced ocean, whose waves knocked the breath out of a man's body, cast up delicate mother-of-pearl Venus-ears and multi-coloured fans, flawless in their diminutive perfection. There was usually a Scout camp pitched in the hotel field, and we girls played rounders with the Scouts in the evenings, went to their camp-fire sing-songs and attended their Sunday morning outdoor church service. Once we went on an ox-wagon picnic with some of them over the Onrust mountains to Hemel-aan-Aarde (Heaven-on-Earth). We imagined ourselves voortrekkers, blazing the trail to the north, over the Dragon Mountains and the Blood River into the unknown land of hostile warrior tribes. The wheels creaked and groaned, our half-caste driver cracked his long whip on to the straining backs of the oxen on either side of the disselboom, the beasts bowed their patient heads still lower, and the dust rose in a fine cloud behind us. Occasionally a few brown children cheered our leisurely progress from their roadside huts. We outspanned in a shady kloof on the bank of a fast-flowing river, and the boys cooked chops and tea over the embers. We savoured there the very essence of South Africa, the languid noonday sun, the smell of dust and grass, the soft sound of the oxen cropping, the music of the river on its stony bed, the thin singing of insects, and the rustle of leaves in the breeze.

Onrust derives its name, which means 'Unrest', from the wild and restless sea which beats upon its shore. At Onrust I first came to feel the sea to be a vital force in my life. At high tide Marjorie and I loved to sit and watch the fifteen-and twenty-foot breakers crash upon the rocks, putting up showers of spray hundreds of feet into the glistening air, or spend themselves upon the beach with a thunderous roar. The voice of the sea on that coast was tremendous, and its power was of life and death. We heard it always – that great voice – and we went to sleep with it in our ears. Sometimes at the ebb tide on still summer days and moonlit nights its sonorous utterances sank to gentle murmurs, but that was only a pretence. That sea got into me. Its beat and rhythm thrilled me to the core, and one day I told Marjorie how I felt about it.

'I belong to it. I love it and I'm afraid of it. Somehow I know it is going to do wonderful and terrible things to me.'

I was a schoolgirl then, and I did not guess that one day I would marry a man of the sea.

My Uncle Wilfred, on whose Transvaal farm Mother, Marjorie and I often stayed in the June holidays, looked less like a farmer than anyone it would be possible to imagine. He was tall and lean in the Gary Cooper tradition, with spiritual grey eyes and a tongue that could, upon occasion, be scathing. His humour was swift and spontaneous, and his Marais 'damns' and 'blasts' were so gently spoken that they embellished rather than disfigured his brilliant and somewhat academic line of conversation. He was the most progressive and influential farmer in the Eastern Transvaal, and had often been urged to stand for Parliament, but this he refused to do. Wilfred, like his cousin Eugene, the naturalist, was a recluse by nature and eschewed the limelight. In any case, he considered politics 'a dirty game' and preferred to back his farming community in other ways. His ear, his time and his extremely effective pen were always at their disposal. Wilfred Marais, who today is South Africa's greatest authority on beans, was a graduate of Cambridge and a barrister by profession, yet he could not live in towns, and his educational advantages were used mostly to serve Strehla, his farm seventy miles from Johannesburg, his love, his child and his abiding joy. Strehla was about the size of an English county, and my uncle was a sort of lord-lieutenant of the district. The homestead, which stood upon a rise in the middle of the flowing golden grainlands, was a single-storied house, substantial, modern and comfortable, built and designed by my uncle. There was a billiard-room, a magnificent ant-heap tennis-court, and an outdoor swimming-pool. The view was immense, a rolling, empty landscape sweeping to far horizons. Only thus could my uncle live. The development and expansion of his spirit craved the immensity of the veld. Not so his wife Edyth, who was the most sociable and gregarious of women. She loved people, companionship, gaiety, the seaside, the races, a cinema and a gossip with her own kind. But more than all these she loved Wilfred. So for ten months and two weeks of the year she buried herself alive for his sake, and for six weeks he submitted himself to the rigours of a holiday at the Cape for hers. The races in Johannesburg they both attended, and the farm itself offered many diversions.

I was twelve when first Mother took Marjorie and me to Strehla. We were wildly excited at the prospect of the thirty-six-hour railway journey. I think that was the first time the beauty of South Africa really hit at me to hurt. Ever since then I have been hopelessly vulnerable to it. June is midwinter in South Africa, and the Worcester Valley was dazzling green under the soft Cape Province rains. Then came the dramatic Hex River Pass. Night had fallen. Mother and Marjorie were asleep, and I crept along my upper bunk till my face was pressed against the frosty window-pane. The blind was up and I was able to gaze out at the mountains, bathed in moonlight and blue-white with snow. We twisted through them, hugging them, cringing in their gigantic shadow and scaling their mighty flanks. I found myself clasping my hand to my flat little chest to still the anguish of all this grandeur and loveliness, absorbing it as a lover searches the face of his beloved, striving to engrave every feature and expression upon his memory, fearing to forget so much as a hair of her eyebrow or a lift of her smile. Next day there was the loneliness of the Karroo, studded with kopjes, round as maidens' breasts, some sheep, some natives, a dorp or two, an ox-wagon, and at length an interminable blood-red sunset slashed with purple and jade. There was an ostrich, too, sprinting hell-for-leather along a fence parallel with the railroad, and Mother told us how her friend Mrs. North had visited an ostrich farm and had her artificial eye plucked neatly out of her head by a bold bird.

'He meant no harm,' said Mother. 'It was the glitter that attracted him. Ostriches like glass and nails and bits of stone as a diet. If he had meant harm he could have done plenty. An ostrich has a very powerful claw and could rip you open with one blow.' We shuddered and decided to keep all ostriches at claw's length – one of the few good resolutions I have found no difficulty in keeping.

Next morning there was the Rand – mile upon mile of white mine dumps with little trucks crawling up and down them like beetles on sand-castles. Eighty miles of gold two miles deep! All round the glittering reef sordid native locations, made of old petrol tins, bits of cardboard, sacking and galvanized iron, glared balefully up from the bare brown veld into the bright winter sun. The natives who lived in those makeshift locations or in the up-to-date native compounds attached to the mines were all exiles from their kraals and their tribes, serving a profitable term in the city or deep down in the underground labyrinths, before they could go home to their people – enviable men, with bicycles.

In Johannesburg Uncle Wilfred met us and drove us out to Strehla, three hours across the veld; and dear, hospitable Edyth greeted us as if we were the only people in the world she really wanted to see.

Early next morning Marjorie and I ran down the avenue of blue gums to the barn, and watched the native women doing the final grading of the white and yellow mealies that had already been peeled and sifted by the threshing machine. They squatted on their haunches in the lee of the sunny wall, clothed only in bright homespun blankets, chanting softly to themselves as they worked. Some young mothers had piccaninnies slung on their backs. These natives were as different from the Cape coloured as is a tiger from the household cat. The Cape coloured is a mixture of many brown and yellow races, whereas the native is of warrior stock. There was a purple bloom upon the rich chocolate of the women's bare shoulders, their features were wide, their hair peppercorn, their teeth large and dazzling, and their eyes shy and smiling. Their voices were deep and rumbling and their smell so pungent that the sheer animal whiff of a houseboy or girl lingered in our bedrooms long after these had been swept. The piccaninnies ran naked on the veld, merry youngsters with taut, distended, mealie-fed bellies, who swung on the cattle-gates and cheered madly at the rare spectacle of a passing car. On Friday nights, after the farm workers had been paid, we could hear them singing and dancing in their location a mile away from the homestead and getting a little drunk on native beer. We were not allowed out on pay nights.

We were all tennis mad at Strehla, and the highlight of the holidays was the Strehla *versus* Witbank tennis match. Witbank, somewhat ironically named, was a coal-mining township about three hours' drive over incredibly bad veld roads. Marjorie and I, despite our callow youth, were included in the team and were given two local jongs (boys) as partners; Wilfred and Edyth paired up, and Mother and Smithy. Smithy was John Smith, the neighbouring farmer. His wife was perpetually in the family way, and they had a lively brood of brats with running noses. Smithy was an ardent player. He gave all he had and tore about the court, hair on end, shirt flowing in the breeze. From time to time there was a hiatus in the game while he rushed into a corner, turned his back on the other players, and thrust the recalcitrant shirt back into his trousers with frenzied gestures that seemed to stop at nothing. Marjorie and I were constrained to giggle, in the manner of young girls, and whisper: 'Now for it! Smithy is getting his rat out!' This because, in moments of stress when the score for Strehla looked precarious, Smithy would mutter to my mother, with a wild glint in his eye: 'It's all right, pard, I've got my rat out now!' When Smithy got his rat out a tornado on the court could hardly have expended more elemental energy, but, alas! he did not always get it out soon enough to retrieve a lost situation. Smithy's enthusiasm was no greater than that of the rest of the team. We all played with clenched teeth and outthrust jaws as if our lives depended on it, and the jongs, who were powerful as bulls, hit the ball with vigour magnificent to behold. This was tennis in the raw. A match in the heart of the high veld, played under a grey slag-heap.

Seven miles from Strehla there lived Edyth's sister Kathleen with her husband Towzer. Towzer had been a mining engineer and had contracted a spinal malady in the mines, and he was a very sick man. I was afraid of the mines when I saw poor Towzer walk – uncertain, stepping too high, even falling sometimes. At other times he lay groaning in dreadful agony. So that was what the mines could do to a man! Quite a young man at that. And Towzer was poor. The gold that he had brought out of the earth for the millionaires of the Rand had given him only this grim legacy, a sentence from which there was no reprieve. But his wife Kathleen was a brave and placid woman, and we loved riding over to see her. She had a magnolia skin, glossy dark hair and velvet eyes. Gazing upon Kathleen, Marjorie and I felt something new stirring within us, and presently we looked at one another with speculative eyes. I saw that my friend's retroussé nose was pink and peeling, and she observed that my features were obliterated by a camouflage of freckles. We had become skin-conscious. We urged Kathleen to tell us how to beautify ourselves, and, inspired by her words of wisdom, we galloped home across the newly cut grainfields and demanded that Edyth give us sour milk. We went to bed thereafter smeared with sour milk and smelling repulsive, and we slept the deep, contented sleep of the very young, who believe that beauty will fall upon them overnight like a benediction from on high. It didn't. But no matter.

Two evenings a week the merchants came to Strehla from the nearest dorp fourteen miles distant. They came after supper, for this was more a business than a social occasion. The matter in hand was poker, and the game had the same quality as the Strehla v. Witbank tennis match. It was a fight to the death

54

and no quarter given. The stakes were high, and even in this sharp company it was generally my sedate and gracious parent or eager little Edyth – a gambler to her finger-tips – who scooped the pool. Marjorie and I were bundled off to bed early on these occasions. 'Steer clear of politics, shares and poker,' Mother warned us as she refused to kiss us good night (owing to the sour cream). 'I only play when I am here, as I don't like to be a wet blanket, you understand. Poker is a very foolish game.' And she went out of the room with the light of battle in her starry eyes and her ringed, tapering fingers itching to get at the cards.

At breakfast we would make her 'take off' the merchants and, dying of laughter, would feel that, after all, we had probably had the best of the game.

CHAPTER SEVEN

SPANISH FLU AND FREE STATE FARM

In the following June of 1918 Mother took me to Pretoria to stay with Uncle Charlie and Auntie May for the wedding of their daughter Maisie to Charles te Water.

Pretoria was very homely, I thought, a pretty place, cupped with rounded hills and dominated by the great horseshoe of the Union Buildings. It was, with Cape Town, the dual administrative capital of South Africa, and my cousin Cicely and I spent a good deal of time arguing on the relative virtues of Pretoria and Cape Town. Uncle Charlie's house was in Sunnyside, high above the city, a pleasant place with an orange grove, well-equipped stables, a tennis-court and a croquet-lawn, and it had at that time the special atmosphere of a house where a wedding is about to take place, a mixture of hustle and romance, with everybody extra busy, extra emotional and extra impatient with the children.

Two of my cousins, Cicely (who was Maisie's twelve-year-old sister) and Peggy, were to be flower-girls, and I was sharply disappointed at having no such part to play in the proceedings.

Mother and Uncle Charlie were inclined to bemoan the fact that Grandpa could not be present at the wedding of his eldest grandchild (poor 'Long Piet' was in his big house at the Cape, already a very ill man, and his days were numbered). And there was a mild undercurrent of controversy about the bridegroom's politics. Charles te Water was a Nationalist and a pacifist, one of Hertzog's most ardent supporters, and most of the Marais were Smuts men. However, everybody graciously conceded that he was very handsome with his air of a nervous thorough-bred pawing the ground at the starting-post; moreover, he had been educated at Bedford School and Cambridge, and was ac-knowledged to be a fine barrister. I could not guess then that years later he would be South African High Commissioner in London and that I would go through the Munich crisis in his house in Princes Gate, with my ear very nearly at the keyhole of No. 10, Downing Street; or that he was destined to be the President of the League of Nations when the fate of Europe was in the melting-pot. All I cared about was that Cicely fell ill of a mysterious malady on the eve of the marriage, and I was much gratified when I was told to wear her dress and deputize for her.

But, alas! according to my custom, an awful wave of nausea engulfed me in the middle of the ceremony, and I whispered to Peggy, my co-flower-girl: 'I'm going to faint!' Peggy caught her lower lip between her teeth and said: 'You *can't!*' But even as she said it her father, Uncle Rupert, scooped me into his arms and carried me out of the church. Afterwards, in the vestry, deeply humiliated, I apologized to Maisie for 'spoiling the wedding'. But she laughed and kissed me and said: 'Nothing could spoil it, darling.' She was very pretty, with amber eyes, and her voice that day was brittle as glass.

Soon after this Cicely saw fit to tell me the facts of life, no doubt influenced by an atmosphere highly conducive to such a confidence. I was frankly shocked.

'It's a joke. You invented it.'

'I didn't. How could I?' She had a husky Tallulah Bankhead voice.

I replied darkly that I wouldn't put it past her.

'Well, then, ask your mother,' she suggested, in a fit of pique, but added hastily: 'You'd better not say who told you.'

I did ask Mother, and was dumbfounded when she

confirmed my cousin's information. It was in keeping with a certain fearlessness in Mother's nature that she did not try any evasions or prevarications, and I have always been grateful to her for her honesty. Of course, *au fond* she was probably enormously relieved at being spared the embarrassment of breaking the ice herself.

I was thirteen then, but I felt immeasurably old and wise – a crone among my fellows. One by one my illusions were slipping away. Father Christmas was Uncle George. The Mouse was my father. And Cicely's preposterous joke was God's design. It was all rather sad.

A few days later Mother, Auntie May and I all contracted Cicely's mysterious malady. We had high temperatures, a rash upon our chests, and sore throats. That was the beginning of Spanish flu in South Africa. When we got back to the Cape it was rampant in a hundred different forms.

At first the flu was a joke, and we children hip-hip-hurrahed when the schools were shut and our holidays indefinitely prolonged, but we were less well pleased that the cinemas, bathing pavilions and other places of amusement were also closed. And then the joke took a grim turn, and thousands who had heavy heads and hot eyes today were dead within the week.

My father worked from early morn to late at night, only rushing home to snatch a hasty meal or an hour's much-needed rest. All night long the telephone shrilled and there were frantic calls for him. 'Please ask the doctor to come *at once*! My husband is *dying*!' The Jewish patients forced their way into our house, wringing their hands and wailing, and literally dragged him from his bed to attend their sick. At last he himself fell victim to the plague from sheer exhaustion, but they still pushed into the hall, crying out that the doctor must come! I can see my mother standing with her hands on some distraught Jewish woman's shoulders and her tired eyes blazing. 'Listen to me, Mrs. Bernstein! I tell you the doctor is ill himself. He is very ill. You must find someone else. You shall *not* disturb him!' She had to use physical force and get Cookie to help eject them.

The flu took a terrible toll of the coloured population. They died like flies, and District Six was a place of tears and mourning. Old and young, healthy and sickly, were stricken alike.

Then on 11th November, 1918, the midday gun that fires from the Fort every day on the stoke of noon fired at 11 a.m. instead. Sirens screamed, hooters blasted, and bells pealed the message of peace on earth, and the rugged purple mountain flung the echoes of good cheer back and forth across Table Bay. The great killing of men by men was over for a spell. But not so the mounting death-roll of the flu. Cape Town was one of the world's severest sufferers from the Spanish scourge. The repatriated troops passing through brought wave after wave of the fatal epidemic with them. After a while there were scarcely any doctors left to tend the dying, or priests to administer the Last Sacrament, or coffins in which to lay the dead, or hearses to carry them to the graveyard. One profiteering vulture of an undertaker made a pretty fortune out of coffins with false bottoms. A generous tip to the grave-diggers and the corpse went to its last resting-place upon a plank, while the mahogany case and brass fittings for which the relatives had paid was drawn up again to be resold for the next flu victim.

The epidemic was at its height when my grandfather died, and that patriarchal old gentleman who had lived so much of his life in magnificence went to his grave without pomp or ceremony. One of his own sons, Rupert, had to say the burial service over 'Long Piet' Marais, while wagons, piled high with native, poor white and coloured dead, trundled by to communal graves.

When old P. J. Marais' estate was settled up and the many dependants had received their share, his sons and daughters found themselves very comfortably off. Mother invested her portion in a sensible, if humdrum, way, but the reaction of the Transvaal uncles was automatic and unanimous. 'Now we will buy ourselves farms.' Some of those uncles were business men, others had professions, but with inevitable certainty they turned towards the land. Piet, at the Cape, already had a beautiful farm in Constantia, and Wilfred had Strehla. Now the others would follow suit. The shrill protests and bitter tears of their town-bred wives echoed through my girlhood all the way to the Cape. My father himself somewhat absurdly hankered after a farm, but Mother managed to head him off, even when he made the brilliant move of urging that sentimental woman to buy Grandpa's old home, Nectar, back into the family. 'What can a doctor do with a farm?' she said sensibly. 'He has troubles enough as it is. Why, Julie, you can't even get your fees out of your patients! How do you hope to make money out of a farm?' She was quite right. With his unbusiness-like head and his kind, trusting heart my father would have been easy meat for any unscrupulous manager. The land was never really strong in him as it was in the Marais, those descendents of Huguenot husbandmen and Boer farmers. If it had been, Mother could never have fought it. If the land or the sea is really in a man, no woman can beat them.

During this time, when my Uncles Charlie, Belfield, Rupert and George were buying farms and subduing infuriated wives, the flu continued to rage with unabated fury. Every hospital and nursing-home was full to overflowing, and Daddy, who had been down twice with the dread disease, was in the forefront of the battle against it. Thus it was that when one of his patients, the Nationalist leader Charlie Fichardt, was suddenly taken ill it was impossible to find a bed for him, and my mother received an urgent telephone call from my father's consulting-rooms.

'Is that you, Ellen? Listen. I have Charlie Fichardt here in my rooms and he is very ill. I hope to get him into a nursing-home this afternoon, but in the meantime I am sending him up to Tees Lodge. You must put him to bed and give him an enema.'

Mother gasped. 'But, Julie, I don't know the man!'

'Ach! Ellen! What on earth has that to do with it? The man is sick, and you must do as I say. And prepare the dining-room as an emergency operating theatre. If I can't get him in anywhere else it will be necessary to operate at home.' And he rang off.

Ten minutes later Charlie Fichardt staggered out of a taxi and up to the front door. Mother, who had only seen this handsome fellow from her seat in the Ladies' Gallery, was filled with dismay. Charlie was dashing, with curly iron-grey hair, burning blue eyes, and a flow of eloquence that never failed to electrify his hearers. Educated in England, he was one of the most cultured and subversive speakers in the House. He groaned now as Mother opened the door to him.

'Mr. Fichardt?' she said. 'Please come in at once. My husband's instructions are that I am to put you to bed, and' – she swallowed hard – 'give you an enema.'

59

Charlie groaned again. 'Good God! I've never had one of those. It's out of the question, Mrs. Petersen.'

But it wasn't.

Luckily my father was able to find a room and a theatre in a nursing-home, and that afternoon he whipped out Charlie's appendix in the nick of time. This incident was the beginning of a firm friendship between the two families. Mrs. Fichardt was a lovable, gentle character of English descent, and I have often wondered how much she really subscribed to her hot-headed husband's political views. They had two sons, Gustav and Louis, and a daughter, Valerie. (Valerie was the name of the baby girl Mother had lost before I was born, and I think that was one reason why she felt drawn towards Val before she knew her.)

Charlie Fichardt was an Orange Free State man, and he had a lovely farm just outside Bloemfontein and a business in the town. His wife and daughter always accompanied him to the Cape during the Session, and for the rest of the year they lived up-country on the farm.

When I was fifteen they asked me to go and stay with them for the summer holidays. I was crazy to go. Val was eighteen and lovely to look at, with a sweet, spontaneous nature, and I adored her with that headlong, unquestioning devotion of which only the very young are capable. But there was a palaver before I was allowed to go. Daddy said: 'It will do the child a world of good. She is as thin as a rail and white as a ghost, and needs farm air and farm feeding.' Mother said: 'She'll come back a rebel. Mark my words.' My aunts shook their heads and said they didn't know what Ellen and Julie were thinking about to even contemplate sending the child into that hotbed of republicanism, and I believe it was their opposition that settled Mother.

'We'll risk it,' she said. 'There's too much high feeling about politics in this country. Joy can take her chance. If she comes back a rebel she does, and dommit boster!' Which means 'damn the consequences'.

So I went to stay at Brandkop in the summer of 1920, and those days of learning to be a rebel were among the best of my life, which is saying a good deal.

Charlie Fichardt, like Uncle Wilfred, was a powerful and

progressive farmer. He it was who had insisted upon the importation of Friesland cattle from Holland, and his beautiful black and white milch cows and a horrific bull were the pride and delight of his heart. He loved them nearly as much as Val loved her alsatians, Karl and Greta.

Brandkop had one advantage in common with the Constantia wine farms – it was near the town. Really it might almost have been a country estate. During the Session Gustav and Louis looked after their father's interests between them. Big, fair Gustav managed Fichardt's store in Bloemfontein, while rugged little Louis had his roots deep in Brandkop. He had veterinary and agricultural degrees, and he was both a scientific and a practical farm manager. His nails were always broken, his hands rough and his face deeply sun-tanned, and there were streaks of sun-bleach across his vigorous brown hair. When Louis made a special effort to polish himself up for a dance in the town, he looked a thorough fish out of water, but in khaki shorts and open-throated shirt, shouting at his labourers in authoritative Afrikaans, he was in character, and – I found – not unattractive. Mrs. Fichardt was a darling with her soft English voice and chestnut hair. Everything in that gracious homestead held enchantment under her hand. The silver glittered, the stinkwood shone, the roses filled the house with fragrance, the table groaned with good things, and after supper, if we did not go in to Bloemfontein to an outdoor cinema or dance, we youngsters gathered round the piano and sang to her accompaniment. Val had a clear, sweet soprano, Gustav a rich baritone, and Louis a fine tenor, while I chirped like a happy sparrow.

Val. What a strange mixture she was, in my eyes, of glamour and comfortable, homely kindness! Perhaps she was too plump for sophisticated standards, but her head and skin were incomparable. There was Saxon blood in Charlie, which probably accounted for his daughter's silver-gold hair and porcelain blue eyes, and perhaps even for her placid temperament, so unlike his own. The young hausfrau was latent in Val, the contented wife, the mother of many children. We shared a room and a four-poster, a little blue room with forget-me-not chintzes and stinkwood furniture of Jacobean design. That room was like its owner, a satisfying combination of the solid and the delicate.

Early in the mornings we rose and galloped over the

dew-spangled veld on our sure-footed, trippling Basuto ponies. The dogs followed us, the great danes, Frey and Freya, lolloping easily over the hard stubble, the alsatians, Karl and Greta, sinewy and tireless, and the spaniel, Rover, who went home on his own when he was tired.

'Frey and Freya are all right at this hour of the morning,' called Val as we pounded along towards the kopje, 'but they don't stand the heat too well, not like Karl and Greta, who are the best dogs I've ever had. Specially Greta – she's a one-man dog.'

Is there any human being who can resist a one-man dog – if they are that 'man'?

Before lunch we used to stroll down to the dam for a swim. It was a big dam and there was an island in it. Now there was too much of the island above water.

'We must have rain soon,' said Val and Louis. 'If we don't it's going to be a bad business for the farmers.'

I was fifteen and impressionable. From this brother and sister I learned something of the implacable needs of the soil. What did it really matter to the townspeople if the rains were late? We might go short of water for our gardens and have two or three hours a day when it was turned off at the main, but the word 'drought' was just a word. Here in the veld it was a threat to a man's whole existence.

Every afternoon the clouds banked up mockingly, dry lightning flashed along the horizon, distant thunder rolled like gunfire, and the air was so electric that a comb hissed through one's hair and scattered a shower of little sparks. But there was no rain.

Regularly at noonday the dogs lined up outside the rose-garden for their daily visit to the monkey. The monkey was chained to a mast with a little round platform way up in the branches of a green-gold pepper tree. He was an energetic little fellow who skimmed up and down his pole indefatigably and swung about in the pepper-tree boughs, where he found juicy black caterpillars. These he wrenched in two with a brisk gesture, ate the bodies, and flung aside the heads and tails. This was not nice if one was under the tree and allergic to caterpillars! The monkey was inordinately vain, and his favourite occupation was to hold a little mirror close to his face, stare at himself, kiss himself, chatter to himself and generally make a fuss of himself. But he had a proper appreciation of his duty to the estate, and from noon till two o'clock his services were at the disposal of the Brandkop dogs. He took them in order of size – the great danes first, the alsatians next, and finally humble Rover – and systematically de-fleaed and de-ticked them. Whoever was receiving his attentions stood patiently while the little monkey straddled him, diligently searching every inch of hair, parting it with nimble fingers, clicking some insects between his finger-nails and eating others that took his fancy.

Karl, the male alsatian, was the most arrogant of the dogs, the dangerous one, a serious bone of contention between Val and Louis. He had begun to worry sheep.

'He must be shot,' rasped Louis at last. 'He's been at it again.'

'You can't shoot him! I couldn't bear Karl to be shot!' That was Val.

Louis sighed. 'I'll give him one last chance. I'll tie him to the big ram. It's the only thing that may cure him.'

Karl was tied to the fierce old ram. He came out of the experience torn, bleeding and filled with such a mad hatred of all white woolly things that he went straight after the very next sheep into which he could get his strong wolf's fangs.

'Nou ja,' said Louis, 'that is the end.' And got his gun. But strong little man as he was, his sister's tears weakened him again. 'All right,' he said gruffly. 'I'll tell you what we'll do, jong. We'll give him to the police. He'll make a fine police dog. But I warn you, if he bolts home he's done for. They can have him, but they'll damn well have to keep him.'

'They'll keep him,' said Val. She walked away alone, down to the little family cemetery where she took her griefs and joys, and there she fought a small private battle.

'If he bolts home he's done for,' Louis had said. It didn't take a Solomon to find the answer to that, but it took courage for Val to face it. That afternoon Louis said: 'I'm taking Karl in to Bloemfontein now. Sorry, jong.' He patted Val's shoulder awkwardly. She said in a low voice: 'Take Greta too.'

'Greta?' He looked closely at his sister, and then, without a word, turned on his heel, whistled the dogs and slipped collars and leads over the necks of the two alsatians – Karl, the killer, and Greta, the one-man dog.

The monkey chattered at him as he walked towards the garage, his back defiant. The other three dogs sprawled in the sun, their noses on their paws. The great danes were magnificent. But they were weary again. They couldn't stand the heat.

Karl and Greta made good police dogs, and the Brandkop sheep relaxed.

Often in the afternoons people came out for tennis and a swim in the dam and stayed to supper. Boys and girls. There was one young man who told me that I walked like an Egyptian water-carrier (he had never seen one), but I was pleased with this, my first, compliment.

Best of all I liked the evenings when Val and I sat on the cemetery wall and watched the sunset. The heavy clouds, withholding their promise of rain, were pink and gold, the limitless veld was bathed in rosy light, and the mighty pageantry of the heavens was reflected in the dam. Little birds twittered in the trees, the lowing of cattle was a melancholy voice in the infinite, and we were filled with poetry and intangible hungers.

The cemetery was a peaceful place, a family burial-ground under tall pines and approached by an avenue of firs where the doves cooed all day. Generations of Fichardts lay there. There was nothing gruesome about it, no ghosts walked. The dead had returned to the earth of their fathers and lay at rest in their own land. The living visited them daily, and their favourite flowers bloomed upon their graves, and they were united in death as never in life, for the Fichardts were a high-tempered, quarrelsome lot and politics had driven deep wedges between different branches of the family. But when death struck they came home to Brandkop and all wounds were healed.

CHAPTER EIGHT

ON TOUR WITH THE REBEL LEADERS

SOMETIMES Val and I went to dances or parties in Bloemfontein without Gustav and Louis, and then we were escorted by a very old native called Pens. This gentleman, whose name means Paunch, crouched in the back of the car like an ancient ape, scrambling in and out to open the various cattle-gates. Pens was very proud of having charge of the two 'klein missies'. He had been with the Fichardt family since his childhood and had known and loved the 'oubaas', Charlie's father. When we came home we raided the larder for glasses of creamy milk, cake and konfyt (home-made preserve), and then, when we were in bed in the Jacobean four-poster, we whispered far into the night.

Val was in love. She was eighteen. It was summer, with hot languorous nights and moons that made the dogs howl and the cattle restive. And in this love of hers there was the essence of a star-crossed Romeo and Juliet romance.

If racial conflict and political antagonism were the background of my young life at the Cape, here in the Free State these things were right in the foreground of the picture. For years – ever since 1912, when General J. B. M. Hertzog* and a handful of followers had broken away from the Botha and Smuts Government (which was striving for co-operation with the British) and formed the Nationalist Party, whose slogan was 'South Africa for the South Africans' – that little group of republicans had carried their lives in their hands. During the war they had been tarred and feathered, pelted with rotten eggs and shot at, literally and figuratively. Yet they had prospered. In large parts of the country these men were regarded as heroes, but in the towns they were feared and hated for their growing power. In that summer of 1920 feeling was running high; in fact, a general election was pending, and the Nationalists had great hopes of it. Val and I were wildly elated because we were to be allowed to accompany the three leaders of the party, Hertzog, Tielman Roos and Charlie Fichardt himself, on their electioneering tour of the Ladybrand district, Charlie's constituency. But in the meantime there were many people in Bloemfontein, that garden city in the veld, who cut the Fichardt family in the street, and chief among these was the father of Val's Romeo. This elderly South African Montague, born of English parentage, would have no truck with the Free State Capulet. That rebel!

'Bill and I can't feel that politics matter if you really love each other,' whispered Val. A shaft of moonlight fell across the

* Father of Dr. the Hon. Albert Hertzog, Minister of Posts, Telegraph and Health from 1956 to 1968

sheet and over her white arm. 'Daddy and Bill's father aren't on speaking terms, and our mothers daren't greet each other, but *we* can't see why everyone shouldn't hold their own opinions and agree to differ. You understand, Joyful?'

I understood all right. Bill was attractive and full of fun, with a gnomish face and great humanity, and if his blood ran hot those summer nights it was not about politics. And Val, who had been brought up in a tumult of racial friction and cold shoulder, wanted her own life to be quiet and friendly and peaceful.

'I understand,' I said. 'Daddy and Mom have friends in every camp. Take, for instance, your father and Sir John Hewat. A Nationalist leader and a Unionist Whip. You couldn't get a greater political contrast! But Daddy thinks everybody is entitled to their views. . . .'

'Joyful.'

'Umn?'

'I've got to see him soon again. We'll be away a whole ten days on the tour. I must see him before we go.'

'Umn.'

'How'm I going to fix it?'

I recognized the role. I was to be the Old Nurse, the schemer, the plotter, the aider and abetter of this Juliet of the veld and her Romeo. Their vendetta was Dutch *versus* British; the Montagues were Unionists, the Capulets Nationalists; the balcony was a stoep, and the Old Nurse a schoolgirl of fifteen; but the sentiments were eternal. *All right, dear Val; we will find an excuse to go in to Bloemfontein tomorrow. Strange, but methinks I have a toothache! Sweet friend, I prithee bear me company unto the dentist. But if perchance, upon a sudden, capricious molars cease to plague me, hey presto! we will hie us to the telephone and there hold converse with your love.* After which I make myself scarce.

So it was that, while the rain refused to fall and the parched land lashed itself to fever heat about the forthcoming election, those two who were young and in love found brief respite in the heart of the cyclone – still, silent moments alone together at the core of a whirling universe. Val was radiant and benign in those hectic days, and I wondered if love made everybody like this – gay, beautiful and magnanimous.

*

We set off on the electioneering tour in the big seven-seater Nash. Val and Charlie took turns with the driving, and General Hertzog, Tielman Roos and I were the passengers. Val was a trained mechanic. Her father had given her a car on her eighteenth birthday, but a condition went with it that she must learn to service it, so she had worked for six months in a garage in Bloemfontein – a flaxen-haired girl mechanic in blue oil-stained dungarees. Any girl who lives on a farm and drives her own car must know how to mend punctures and do minor engine repairs. It is useless for her to sit hopefully on the dusty veld roadside waiting for Prince Charming to come and do her dirty work for her. She must turn to and do it herself. If Prince Charming does materialize at all he will be black as the ace of spades and totally ignorant of the foibles of modern motor-cars.

That journey with the Nationalist leaders was a strange eye-opener to a girl from the Cape – the peaceful, contented Cape that for a hundred years had been under British dominion, the fruitful vine-bearing Cape that had been sold to the British Government by the bankrupt Dutch East India Company for six million pounds. Six million pounds for the fertile vineyards, peach, pear and apple orchards and wheatfields of the Cape Province, to say nothing of a potential springboard to the north, to the diamonds of Kimberley, the gold of the Rand, the tin and copper of Rhodesia and the minerals of Namaqualand! Not a bad bargain.

But here in this wide granary of South Africa was a country that only twenty years ago had been vanquished in battle by Great Britain. For three years the Free State and the Transvaal had held out against the inevitable, and the men and women of this land – proud, ignorant, stubborn people – remembered those three years and what had gone before, not in the hazy mists of history long gone by, but in the bitter terms of yesterday's defeat. Kitchener's Blockhouse System was no mere tactical phrase to them. It signified the systematic burning of their farms and the herding of their women and children into concentration camps, where twenty thousand of those women and children died of typhoid. It signified utter ruination and the end of a long struggle for freedom. These Boers of the veld were the children of the Voortrekkers (those who went before). They were men with a heritage of hatred for British rule. Their forbears had hated it so bitterly that they had abandoned the homes they had built in the Cape Province, and the lands they had tilled, to inspan their oxen and trek away into the unknown. They had piled their women, their children, their chattels, their livestock and their bibles into the great covered wagons, and the wheels had begun to roll north. It was the exodus of a people who asked nothing of life but a farm, a pipe, a family, a bible, and the right to make and break their own laws. The ox-wagons of the Boer pioneers creaked and groaned over the Drakensberg Mountains, they forded fast-flowing rivers and crossed wide plains. When night fell the Boers outspanned and formed their wagons into laagers to protect them from wild beasts and hostile native tribes. Babies were born in the ox-wagons, old people died in them, young men and girls were married in their shadow, battles were fought from their shelter, and often enough whole parties were massacred within the burning laagers. There is a river called Blood and a town called Weeping (Weenen) that marks the passing of the Voortrekkers, but in the end they settled north of the Vaal and the two republics were formed. It is typical of the Boers that there were two. For a time there was even a third in Natal. But at last they had their land and their independence and they were content. Then in the Transvaal gold was found, and old Paul Kruger shook his head as he saw the foreigners flow on to the Ridge of White Waters, outnumbering his own people and claiming the rights of Transvaal citizenship while retaining their own nationality. The franchise. They clamoured for the franchise. But the old President stood at bay and said to the English Lord Milner: 'It is not the franchise you want. It is my country.'

Now, for the first time, I was jerked out of the dreaming, set-apart atmosphere of the Cape into this other. It was frightening and stimulating. At first, while we were still near Bloemfontein, the meetings were stormy, and we two girls had to keep hidden in the back of the hall, ready to make a bolt for it if the brick-bats flew. Charlie was often badly heckled in these South African Party strongholds, but he had a brain and a tongue like lightning, so it didn't worry him. Roos actually liked it. He invited heckling deliberately for the sake of showing up his adversary. Roos was a smooth dark barrister, inclined to be stout, with the soft white hands of a townsman, and, like Charlie Fichardt, he spoke equally well in English or Afrikaans. Hertzog spoke only in Dutch. How different those three speakers

were! Tielman Roos was suave and plausible, the perfect antidote to Charlie, who was an emotional orator. When Charlie
stood up on the platform his blue eyes blazed and even his
hands declaimed. Tielman was calm as the aftermath of a
storm, smiling, unruffled and then suddenly – like a cobra striking – vicious and relentless, his words venomous, his tone
deadly quiet. I got to know when Tielman meant to strike –
even though he might be speaking in Afrikaans. I got to know
exactly when that misleading smile was going to turn into a
sneer. He was sinister then, a dangerous man. Charlie was never
dangerous. He had too much heart.

Hertzog, the Hitler of our trio, seemed curiously innocuous
after the other two. He spoke in high Dutch, which was not the
everyday language of the ordinary Boer. Perhaps for that
reason it was impressive. He spoke not so much like a man
recruiting for a cause as like a dry professor expounding a case.
The people listened to him respectfully. In the foxy little General, meagre, bespectacled, wary and inclined to be muddle-
headed, they recognized a brave and sincere man. It was his
sincerity that got his audiences. He had none of Charlie's histrionic ability, none of Tielman's tricks, but he had a genuine
faith in the future of a South African republic, and he had
risked his life and sacrificed a lucrative post in Botha's Government to prove it. Moreover, he understood the minds of simple
men as his brilliant opponent Smuts did not. The people knew
where they were with James Barrie Hertzog, and that was what
they wanted, to know what a man was driving at. They were
never quite sure with Jan Christian Smuts. That was why Hertzog's party was growing steadily and Smuts' declining. The
Nationalist leader inspired trust in the backvelders, and 'Slim
Jannie' confused them.

For ten days Val and I journeyed with these three. On the
flat, dusty, golden track politics were in abeyance. Hertzog was
charming and rather mischievous, Tielman amusing and witty,
and Charles boisterous. We picnicked, sitting on camp stools
or on the running-board of the car. There was seldom shade or
a stream. The talk was always of the farmers, the need for rain,
the crops and the cattle. Sometimes Charlie tweaked my ear
and laughed. 'Don't you get bored, Joybells? What should a
little Cape Town rooinek care about the backvelders and their
problems?'

'But I do care! I'm terribly interested.' It was true.

One evening, as we approached an outlying township, I saw my first Boer commando. A cloud of dust on the horizon, and Charlie, suddenly excited as a schoolboy. 'A commando, fellows! A commando to welcome us!'

There was something very moving about that little commando, something that made Charlie's blue eyes moist. This was a tribute to him from his constituents – his people. Thus they must have ridden in the days of the Voortrekkers – the old and the young side by side, every Boer between fourteen and seventy a man. There they came on their trippling horses – smart Basuto ponies, bony old farm nags – riding loose-limbed and negligent, with a long rein and a long stirrup, khaki shirts open, wide-brimmed hats shading their faces, broad leather belts low about their khaki trousers and brown suede veld-schoene on their feet. There were bearded veterans, smooth-faced lads and vigorous hirsute young men. Val stopped the car and we watched them approach riding two abreast. Struggling behind came a separate little commando of small boys and girls – the under twelves. They rode anything they could muster. Mules, donkeys and weird old cart-horses shambled along with two or three youngsters on the back of one animal. These immature camp-followers kept themselves to themselves and from a respectful distance stared fascinated at our car as the spokesman of the men's commando dismounted to greet the three Nationalist leaders. Presently the commando set off back to the town, and we drove slowly behind them with the children's mounted brigade bringing up the rear.

Every day we bumped long hours over the veld roads and in the afternoons reached the town or dorp where the men were to speak. The meetings were held out of doors in the shady square, and afterwards there was always a supper and a dance at the local inn where we were staying. The jongs from the surrounding farms were there in full strength, wearing their blue Sunday suits, their tanned faces well scrubbed and aglow with a sort of heavy pleasure. They danced like Smithy played tennis – to the death – and lancers was their favourite. We had our feet ground into the floor by these well-meaning yokels, who were a little in awe of us and very much on their best behaviour. Most of them could talk English, but Afrikaans was the language of their homes.

Sometimes in the late afternoons the dry thunderstorms were so terrifying that I cowered in the back of the car, trying not to whimper with fright. But General Hertzog told me that the rubber tyres would act as lightning conductors and I must not be afraid. A dry thunderstorm was less dangerous than a wet one, he explained, as the wet tyres make contact with the earth. Yet if you leave your car and go into the open you may be beaten to death by hailstones as big as pigeons' eggs. Many sheep are killed by hail every year up-country, and often cattle too. Once I saw a girl who had been struck by lightning. She was twisted and partially paralysed. Since then I have always feared storms.

The last township we visited was Tweespruit, which had the distinction of having bought a champion Friesland bull for £2,000. What a bull! it was housed in a reinforced stall and heavy chains tethered the magnificent monster therein. It glowered at us with a wild red glare, and we glowered back. After which we went to see the cheese factory, where Zulus lay prone beside a swimming-bath of liquid cheese, which they stirred with their bare black arms. It was midsummer and the exertion made the Zulus sweat. When my son was small it was his habit to cast his socks at me with an airy gesture, saying: 'Time these went to the wash, Mom. Cheese!' But cheese to me does not conjure up soiled socks so much as a little Free State town, a ferocious bull and amiable black men with their muscular arms plunged shoulder-high into a thick yellow bath.

Maybe Tweespruit has found a substitute for the Zulus now – and even for that £2,000 bull.

CHAPTER NINE

GENERAL ELECTION. FAREWELL
VAL AND CHARLIE

As far as Charlie Fichardt was concerned, the tour through his very considerable constituency was a tremendous success. And Hertzog and Tielman Roos, the Transvaaler, were satisfied that the republican movement was gaining ground rapidly. Val was happy to be back at Brandkop because the shining thought of Bill was ever with her, and I alone was left with a confusion of mind and emotion.

Now, for the first time, I had become really forcibly aware of the internal political situation in my country. And I had seen and been deeply impressed by the methods of the Nationalists – the sure-fire reopening of old wounds. There was no ancient grievance against the English that was not revived and turned to account, and no lever for attacking Smuts that was not pulled. Up to this time politics had meant no more to me than a high wind blowing through the tree-tops; now I was swept by the hurricane. The impact of capitalism and agriculture – the mines *versus* the land – was stamped most vividly upon my receptive mind.

'My friends,' Charlie had said to his constituents, 'you are a farming community. What does Smuts care about your problems? He is sold to the English and the English are sold, body and soul, to the mines. Did the English want the Transvaal for grain-growing and cattle-farming? No, they wanted gold! Well, they have got their gold, and in the process they have taken your hard-won land. Nou ja, my friends, what should they know of your difficulties and struggles, you who are the backbone of South Africa? When the mines are worked out and the Rand is a long white ridge of barren earth and the English and the Jews have gone from Johannesburg, there will still be the land. Maize and cattle and farms for the children of Afrikaaners to inherit. Protect your farms and the future of your children! Put us into power! We, the Nationalists, will look after your interests. We, too, are men of the soil. We understand.'

Somewhere, deep down in me, there stirs this love of the land. I had known it quicken in Strehla when I had said to Edyth, 'Where is Uncle Wilfred?' and she had answered: 'He is down in the lands.' Down in the lands. To me the words had beauty and significance. I could guess how these backveld Boers felt, unworldly men who rode in ragged commandos and worked 'down in the lands'. The feeling for land is elemental, a primary sentiment, and it was easy for Hertzog and his lieutenants to play upon it and fan it into the sort of nationalism that might, in the end, prove a destroyer. Smuts had taken the more difficult path, the path of conciliation. To tear open a wound is easy. To heal it is difficult. Botha and Smuts had set out to be healers. But their own people could not see them in that light. Smuts was never 'Ons Jannie' or 'Oom Jannie'. He was 'Slim Jannie'. And it is only now, after forty years in the wilderness, that he is creeping deep into the hearts of his own folk and that they are beginning to call him 'the oubaas'. Hertzog, on the other hand, lost his hold towards the end of his life. He became too moderate for his own fire-eaters. He was left behind by the wave that carried him forward, but the old racial hatred has gone on with it and injures South Africa to this day.

The 'rebel' poison which entered my system in that tour of 1920 has long since worked itself out. I know the English now, their curious practical idealism, their obtuse generosity, their insularity so paradoxically combined with breadth of vision stretching to the uttermost corners of the earth. I believe that their influence in the world is for good and that it is from Great Britain that South Africa will one day receive her total independence. But in 1920 I saw the English in no such benevolent light. I saw them through the blazing eyes of Charlie Fichardt. In fact – let's say it and have done with it – I had become a rebel.

Charlie was amused and delighted with his convert, and he used to ruffle my hair and say: 'When you get home, Joybells, the fat will be in the fire!'

Val and I were spanned in to help at the Town Hall on the day of the election. We had to show people where to record their votes, and I was told that, if I got into difficulties owing to my ignorance of Afrikaans, I must answer all questions by saying: 'Vra vir Meneer Van Reenen' ('Ask Mr. Reenen'). One old farmer, who apparently liked the look of me, patted my head and asked me in Dutch where I came from and who my father was. He was mildly surprised when I answered brightly: 'Vra vir Meneer Van Reenen.'

That night as the results came through we stood, with the whole town and half the surrounding countryside, in Bloemfontein Square watching a big screen on which the results were flashed. Bloemfontein North and South had gone to the South African Party, and everybody went crazy with excitement. I found myself cheering wildly as Colin Steyn and Deneys Reitz (he who wrote 'Commando') were shouldered and carried round the town in triumphal procession. Steyn was rather fat and flabby, but Reitz's blue eyes glittered and he laughed and shouted as the boys lifted him on to their broad shoulders. He had a magnetic, powerful personality. Here, one thought, is a man! But Val tugged at the thin sleeve of my white voile blouse and said: 'Shut up, Joyful! He's a S.A.P.!'

'Oh,' I gasped. 'I'm sorry.' I wanted to laugh and cry and do mad things. I'd have cheered anyone, so great was the surge of emotion within me. I was under the same 'crowd stimulus' that gives Hitler his chance, and he knows how to exploit mass feeling if ever a man did!

Charlie Fichardt, of course, got in hands down for Lady-brand, and Hertzog and Roos also came in with flying colours. So did Nationalist candidates all over the country. The Smuts Government hadn't even a workable majority, and to correct this state of affairs the S.A.P.s and Unionists fused and Labour regulated the see-saw.

All that was important. But it was less important than the coming of the long-deferred rains. They came soon afterwards. The heavens opened, the parched veld was watered, and over-night there was a miracle. The lands flowered, the young em-erald grain pushed through the drenched earth, and the farmers gave praise to the Lord.

But their joy was short-lived. There came a day when Val and I returned to Brandkop from Bloemfontein, and in the west we saw a dense grey cloud obscure the sun. Nearer it came and nearer. 'It can't be a dust-storm after the rains,' puzzled Val. And then she cried out: 'Oh, God, it's locusts! We must put up the side flaps and the hood. Quick!'

She stopped the open tourer and we closed it in as best we could, but even then the great swarm drummed upon the car with the rattle of machine-gun fire. There were thousands of the big grasshoppers impaled upon our radiator and crushed against the windscreen, and hundreds were on the seats in the back of the car, stunned or dead. We had locusts down our necks and up our sleeves, and we screamed and laughed as they swept by, leaving their casualties on and in our car. But it was no laughing matter. Behind the swarm lay decimated crops and hundreds of farmers faced with a famine.

It was the first problem of the new Government, and only by

74

spraying the swarms from aeroplanes was it possible to prevent the entire country from being ravaged.

At the end of that year Val and her mother sailed for Europe, where the lovely light soprano voice was to be trained in Germany – and Juliet, incidentally, was to be weaned from her Romeo.

I saw her again at the Cape on her return two years later. She was more beautiful than ever, more vital.

'I am so happy to be going home, Joyful,' she said. 'I can hardly believe that I will really see my beloved Brandkop again. And Gustav and Lou and all my friends!' We did not mention Bill, but we looked at one another and smiled secretly.

The House was in Session and Val was to stay a fortnight at the Cape with her parents before returning to the Free State. And then suddenly we heard that she was ill. A few days later, in the grey of the dawn, my father was standing in my little pink bedroom, telling me very gently that it was no use my kneeling there all night praying my heart out for my friend. 'It's no good, little Joytje, no good.' His hand was on my shoulder, his face was drawn and weary, and his sad eyes were sunken. This was the second well-loved Valerie he had lost.

So they took her home to Brandkop – her beloved Brandkop. And only six weeks later fiery, handsome Charlie followed her. It was all over for those two – the loving and the fighting – and they lay side by side under the fir trees in the silence broken only by the lowing of cattle, the tinkle of the sheep-bell, the soft cooing of doves and the sunset twitter of birds.

CHAPTER TEN

OVERSEAS

IN 1921 I did what every South African craves to do, and went overseas.

My medical student brothers had both qualified, my father

75

wanted to brush up his surgery, my mother always made the most of an excuse for 'a trip to Europe', and after some discussion it was decided to take me from school that I might accompany them upon a European Odyssey.

'It will broaden her mind,' said Mother. Father grunted. I was enthralled.

So Nannie and her husband came to stay in Tees Lodge as caretakers. Daddy made arrangements with his partner, Dr. Morris, to take six months' leave. Moses, the gardener, who had contracted an unfortunate disease, was sacked, and Arend laid up the car and stayed on to tend the carnations. Cookie repaired to the bosom of her 'respeckerbul fambly' at Maitland, where the honest 'General' was bewildered to find himself at last in a position to enjoy his marital rights, and Teena took a temporary job as maid-of-all-work to Daddy's eldest sister, who was known to us as 'the Senior Aunt'.

We set sail in a Blue Funnel liner, crossed the Equator, called at Las Palmas, tossed into the Bay of Biscay and discovered that I was mercifully impervious to the horrors of sea-sickness.

At Tilbury my brothers met us. It was some years since we had seen them, and Mother was distressed to find that Fred looked 'dissipated' and Norman 'half-starved'. They both looked fine to me. Fred said to me: 'Good Lord! Old Fireworks has grown into quite a toothsome morsel!'

In London my parents immediately established a headquarters, and in the innocence of their hearts selected a hotel in Jermyn Street for that purpose. We had a pleasant suite of rooms with a piano in the sitting-room, at Mother's special request; and a charming Swiss waiter called Fatty ministered to our needs in the dining-room. The males of the family were frequently accosted in the environs of the hotel, but were very properly deaf to the blandishments of the 'Hello, ducky' brigade. Mother found the hotel 'so central' for shopping and theatres. We were keen theatre-goers, and I fell madly in love with Matheson Lang, no matter whether he was masquerading as a Jew or a Chinaman.

My brothers and I played in a number of tennis tournaments. Fred was partnered either by a fair-haired girl called Snib, or by Snib's mother, and Norman by an auburn-haired girl called Doreen. I played in the handicap singles. Fred was in love with

Snib and Snib's mother, and Norman was in love with Doreen, while I sighed that I could not play in the handicap doubles with Matheson Lang. We were all beaten without exception, but once Norman, who could upon occasion rise to remarkable heights, took a set off a Japanese Davis Cup champion – the same who subsequently committed suicide when beaten by an inferior opponent. Unfortunately, Norman was not that opponent. Norman's friend Doreen was very kind to me and I loved her dearly. She came to our hotel quite often, and we used to sing to Mother's accompaniment. When Mother and Doreen sang Daddy liked it, but when Norman and I joined in he called it caterwauling and left the room, and, crestfallen, we reminded one another that 'poor Daddy' was tone-deaf.

A number of my Transvaal cousins were living in a maisonette behind Harrods with an English lady of aristocratic connections. They had just been 'finished' at incredibly expensive schools and were now being bear-led about London and the Continent by the English lady, who cherished them tenderly. Never, hitherto, even in her wildest dreams, had she pictured such a windfall as that presented by these pretty young savages. I went to see them often. Cicely, who had once initiated me into the mysteries of life, had grown into a dancing sort of girl with luminous green eyes, precocious ideas and a rangy rhythm in all her movements. There was a photograph of a naval officer in full dress on her bedside table. She told me his unusual name, and years later, when he was no longer in the Navy but flying for Imperial Airways, I was to remember that name in tragic circumstances. I have never forgotten his face, bold, determined and frank. Cicely informed me that she was wildly in love with him.

'What's it like – being in love?' (Val had been inarticulate on the subject.)

Cicely pondered. Then she told me. 'It's to be so crazy about a man that you'd willingly roll in the gutter for his sake.'

I referred this hypothesis to my mother, who clicked her tongue impatiently and said: 'Ach, what! No decent person rolls in gutters – in or out of love.' Mother has always been a very literal person. She and I were at intermittent loggerheads during that period owing to an unfortunate difference of opinion over the question of lipstick. I desired to use it, and my parents forbade me to do so. 'A little powder, if you must, but not *paint*.'

77

Daddy pointed out the ladies of Jermyn Street and asked me if I wished to look as they did.

About now I began to lead a double life.

This came about during the ten days that my parents were stricken with anxiety about my brother Fred. Fred had gone into a nursing-home to have his tonsils removed, but his recovery was impeded by severe haemorrhages and he nearly died. While they haunted the nursing-home I secretly frequented a dingy 'studio' in Bloomsbury and strove to become a film star.

My experience with the X Studio came about through an advertisement in a magazine. 'PROMISING YOUNG ACTORS AND ACTRESSES, 18 TO 24, URGENTLY REQUIRED FOR FILM WORK. EXPERIENCE UNNECESSARY. Apply X Studio, —— Street, Bloomsbury.'

If there is a sixteen-year-old girl who isn't stage-struck, she is the exception rather than the rule. I read the advertisement and rose to the bait. So one afternoon, while my parents were at my brother's bedside, I cut out the address and set about following it up. To begin with, I must look eighteen. I was tall but very slight; however, four pairs of silk stockings in my blouse corrected that defect. Then I put up my hair in an amateurish bun, which I fondly believed lent me a year or more, but my face was a problem. There was something very juvenile about the freckles. I hoped the lavish use of the forbidden lipstick and a spotted veil from Mother's drawer might add sophistication; and, with my heart plunging about like a startled horse, I set out.

The London police are so wonderful. They directed me unerringly to the X Studio. ('Come into my parlour,' said the spider to the fly.) A Bloomsbury alley, some musty stairs, and, lo and behold! a notice on the door: 'X STUDIO'. A waiting-room, and the suckers sitting round in droves. One by one these were ushered into the manager's office to be interviewed. Even at that tender age I was staggered to observe the types who fancied their chances on the screen. Some were actually misshapen, others had squints, and all appeared slightly simple. There were ten girls to every man. There was a long time for me to wait, and I got into conversation with other 'promising young actors and actresses' and learned that the alluring advertisement had appeared in papers all over the country and that girls had come to London on the strength of it all the way from places like Little-Puddle-on-the-Green in search of fame and fortune. 'Experience unnecessary' had been the master-stroke.

'Next,' said the manager's secretary, an untidy girl who smelt.

Having seen the poor dupes waiting to be fleeced, I ought to have taken heed, but, on the contrary, I was puffed up with confidence (to say nothing of the silk stockings). If I couldn't put up a better show than these boobs, I'd eat my hat, veil and all!

The manager sat behind a large desk in a light room reeking of stale cigars. He was a Jew and he spoke American in the true Hollywood tradition.

'Wul,' he said. 'Keen on the stage? Let's have a look at you, baby. Off hat, up skirt. Legs pretty dandy. And how about the eyes? Important things, eyes.'

I removed my headgear, grieving that the sophisticated veil must go. The manager pounced upon me and drew me to the window with a clammy hand. 'Hair down,' he ordered.

Blushing hotly, I let my fair hair fall about my shoulders. The manager purred. 'Just what we want. Vurry sweet.' He stroked it absent-mindedly for a few seconds and then abruptly sat down behind his desk, and I once more battled nervously with hairpins, hat and veil.

'Now, then, to business. Tell me all about yourself. Have you any experience of acting?'

'Oh yes, quite a lot, especially comedy.' (Shades of Mina Freund and William Shakespeare!) 'But I prefer tragedy.'

He smiled queerly. 'Uha! That oughtn't to be so difficult. Now, how about screen? Have you done any screen work—'

I had to confess that I had not. 'But the advertisement said "Experience unnecessary." '

He waved that aside. 'Got to have a bit of coaching, you know. You can't put yourself over without a few lessons. But you are just the type we can use. Why, I've hundreds of letters here wanting girls like you. I'll tell you what, honey, you take a course of lessons in our studio right here and then we'll give you a screen test, and if it's good we'll find you a job. It's dead easy, and a sound investment for both of us. All you do is pay us three guineas and we give you six lessons. Every afternoon from three to four. After that it's all plain sailing.'

'But . . . I haven't got three guineas! I'm looking for a job.'

'Not got three guineas? Come now, honey, think again! However, you're such a promising kid I can see I'll have to reduce the fee for you. We'll make it two ten – and that's dirt cheap. Take it or leave it.'

'Maybe I could get the money.'

'Maybe. You'd be crazy to miss a chance like this. Reduced fee, a few lessons, a test and a part in the next production.'

'All right. I'll do it somehow. I'll be back.'

'Sure you will.'

Sure I would. Fatty, the waiter, lent me the money. I paid it to the manager and attended my course of lessons.

There was a man with an imitation camera, who shrieked at the deluded simpletons who were his pupils. There was a partition to represent a shack, a bundle of letters and a bundle of rags. We hid the letters, fondled the rags, defied the villain and fell into the arms of the hero, at which the man with the sham camera yelled: 'Cut!'

One of the rare male suckers was good-looking, and we rode back to Piccadilly Circus on the bus together and parted sedately, with mutual hopes that we would have the pleasure of acting 'opposite' one another again the following day. We agreed smugly that the rest of the class were congenital idiots.

During this week my parents found me a veritable angel of light, and Mother said: 'You see, darling, how much happier it is for everybody when you make a real effort to be good and sweet. You are a sensible little girl to go to the British Museum every day while Daddy and I are with poor Fred. Improving one's mind isn't necessarily dull, is it?'

I agreed that it was not. There is no doubt about it, the satisfaction of leading a successful double life is not to be missed. There is a stimulus about that 'you little know' attitude towards one's fellows which transcends all others. I dare say accomplished murderers experience it too. There can be no doubt that when the manager of X Studio strolled into our classroom, as he did from time to time, he must have enjoyed an ecstasy of just such gratification.

At the end of the course I asked for my screen test. The man with the sham camera took some sham photographs on sham plates, and the manager informed me that he had seen these and found them promising. But a little more coaching was required. The advanced course now – and another £2 10s., if you please!

By now Fred was recovered, my parents had bought a motor-car and we were to go to Devon for Fred's convalescence. Fatty was agitating for a refund of his money, and threatened to tell my parents that I had borrowed it from him. There was nothing for it but to tell them the whole truth myself. My double life popped like a toy balloon. My parents were upset. They blamed themselves for neglecting me, and me for deceiving them. They trembled at 'the risks the child had run', and Daddy went so far as to instigate inquiries into the activities of X Studio. These brought interesting facts to light. The studio made a steady income out of the suckers, and it did better (or worse) than that. The poor half-witted fools who came to London were fobbed off with 'lessons' and 'tests' till their money was all gone. Then when they hadn't so much as the price of a railway ticket home to Little-Puddle-on-the-Green, they were lambs for the slaughter. Well, perhaps after all they were not quite up to the standard required for stage or screen, but there were alternatives. Glamour and luxury could be found in other circumstances, and if X Studio couldn't place these 'promising young actresses' in Hollywood there were always openings in South America.

The whole racket was subsequently exposed by *Truth.*

Soon after this we all went to the Continent, where my father and brothers wanted to see the latest methods of surgery. Mother and I accompanied them to Paris, Brussels, The Hague and Berne, and then we stayed at a little hamlet on Lake Thün while they went on to Berlin and Vienna.

Our peregrinations were punctuated by our menfolk's account of their surgical riots. In Paris they were amazed to find major operations performed under local anaesthetics.

'Do the patients suffer?' asked Mother, who was always more interested in the human angle than in the triumph of science.

Fred chuckled. 'The surgeons swear their cases don't feel a thing. But they chain them to the table, and the poor devils yell like hyenas throughout.'

In Brussels they witnessed an 'ectomy' of some sort or another, a description of which made our hair stand on end.

'Never seen a finer operation,' they said. 'Wonderful!'

'How is the poor patient?' asked Mother.

'The patient?' they said vaguely. 'Oh, he's dead.'

For the rest, Mother trailed me dutifully round picture galleries, where my one idea was to find somewhere to sit down, which was very irritating for Mother, whose corns were giving her hell, but who felt that she must show an intelligent interest in canvases that bored us both stiff. We ate some strange fishes in Amsterdam, went over the Minerva works in Antwerp, saw naked women in Paris and returned to London glutted with sightseeing of all sorts. Soon afterwards we said farewell to my brothers, who had taken up house-surgeons' appointments, and sailed for home.

On the ship I shared a cabin with an elderly Hollander and a merry Rhodesian girl called Margie. Margie had been at school in England and was returning to Bulawayo with her parents. She and I struck up an immediate and lasting friendship, giggled a great deal, and probably made the whole voyage a martyrdom for our cabin-mate.

CHAPTER ELEVEN

ELEPHANT TUSK, LION SKIN, AND MEER-KAT

THE following Christmas I went to Bulawayo to stay with Margie.

I travelled north with a bishop, more by accident than by design. When Mother, with many misgivings, came to see me off at the station she looked along the name-cards of the Rhodesian mail and found, to her relief and delight, that the compartment next to mine was allotted to a bishop. Mother has unlimited confidence in the reliability of the Church, and she instantly introduced herself to the unknown and unsuspecting divine and implored him to keep an eye on me. This he very kindly did.

Alas! the influence of the Church soon wore off, and before very long I was in the toils of my first love-affair.

Falling in love for the first time is an adventure. There had, of course, been one or two clumsy passages with callow youths on the boat and the remote control sentiment inspired by Matheson Lang, but here in Rhodesia I felt that at last I had come upon the Real Thing. The moonlight and some Hawaiian gramophone records had a lot to do with it.

They say 'Love is blind', and 'they' are, as usual, right. James and I were blind as bats to everything except each other.

The other day my husband's messenger, Able Seaman White, was given a day's leave. He went to the Zoo. He had never been to London or the Zoo before, and this simple sailor described himself as 'flammergasted' by all that he beheld. He marvelled particularly at the crocodiles. I inquired whether he had also admired the hippopotamus which inhabits the same vicinity.

' 'Ippopotamus?' said White, with a harassed look. 'If there was an 'ippopotamus I didn't notice it.'

It was the same with me. If there was a Bulawayo I didn't notice it. There must have been. There was scrub and thorn trees, a dusty town, bungalows with wide wooden verandahs where we danced, lightning on the horizon every evening, deluging storms and fearsome claps of thunder, enormous insects that hurtled round outside our mosquito nets and sometimes inside them, and masses of white blinding moonlight. The Rhodesians were very proud of their moonlight and declared that you could read by it. I was otherwise employed.

James was the boy next door, and Margie and I made his acquaintance when her parents drove us to the Matoppo Hills to see Rhodes' grave and James came with us. We went in the late afternoon, and it was already nearly dusk when we climbed the winding mountain path to the heights that overlook the wild and lonely land Rhodes loved and desired for England, the land he took from the Matabele. Here in these hills Cecil John Rhodes once met the hostile chiefs and palavered with them for three days, winning their confidence and then betraying it. Yet here, in the end, they lowered his body into the mighty rocks, *'the black men he had charmed and robbed and charmed again gave him the royal salute; they saluted him alone among white men, as they salute their kings'* (S. G. Millin, 'The South Africans').

On the way home James held my hand under the rug, and when I confided this piece of audacity to Margie she flung back her head merrily and roared with laughter. 'He held mine too.' But poor Margie fell ill with bronchitis, and I made great headway, and thereafter, while I was in Bulawayo, James held nobody's hand but mine.

James lived in a rambling old bungalow. He had his own quarters there and a workshop rich with weapons wherewith he bowed the tusks of elephants to his will. There, while on a wheezy gramophone I played Hawaiian records sobbing plaintively of love, James wrought necklaces and bangles to my desire. Sometimes in the polished ivory he introduced harsh streaks of black, and these streaks were hairs plucked from the tails of pacyderms; thus from the two extremities of the King of the Primeval Forest did James fashion trifles for the delectation of his lady.

A few years later in the arid isle of Malta my baby son, profusely dribbling, cut his first teeth on a smooth ivory bangle tied about his neck with a gay blue ribbon.

'Just the thing for his poor little gums,' said Nannie with satisfaction.

'Yes,' I agreed, a thought wistfully. 'It seems a good omen to teethe on a tusk – and a fine tusk too. I saw it in the raw.'

When I returned to the Cape it was with the purpose of entering the University of Cape Town, where I was to be enrolled as a miscellaneous student for one year, attending what lectures I desired and aspiring to no degrees.

The University now stands on a magnificent site on the Rondebosch flank of Devil's Peak, overlooking the Cape Flats, the sea and the blue mountains beyond. But in 1922 it was just a friendly sort of mess at the top of Government Avenue. The Avenue was always full of undergraduates coming and going from the library to the Hiddingh Hall, their arms heavily laden with the wisdom of the ages compressed into the pages of closely printed textbooks. But on Saturday mornings the girl and boy students strolled down-town two by two under the oaks for eleven o'clock tea and a mild flirtation at Markham's or the Waldorf.

An old slave-bell in the quad summoned us to lectures in the various whitewashed blocks, dappled with the shifting shadows of the oak leaves, and there was, of course, a stoep where we had tea and buns at ten-fifty every morning.

There were men's and women's hostels to house the up-country students, but my friend Marjorie Morris and I, naturally enough, lived in our own homes. Marjorie was no dilettante like me. She was a fine scholar and enjoyed her work. She was already in her second year when I appeared as a fresher, and because she was a young woman of loyalty, determination and considerable character, she succeeded in getting me accepted by her 'crowd'. A fine crowd they were.

There was an initiation ceremony at which the new students were required to make clowns of themselves, and after it one of the professors told us the aims and objects of university life. The professor in question was one of the few who was not a Scotsman. He was a tall, lean Englishman with a lock of iron-grey hair tossed back from an intellectual brow. He had long, sensitive hands and tigerish, cruelly humorous eyes. He spoke well and amusingly, and I whispered to Marjorie: 'Do you know what he teaches? Whatever it is I'm going to register for it. I'm crazy about him.' She grinned and whispered back: 'Social Anthropology.'

That is how it came about that I became a student of social anthropology. My other subjects were English, French, literature and history. I worked hard at English because I liked the subject, and at social anthropology because I hoped to please the professor. So buoyant is human nature that already the Bulawayo interlude had set itself apart and was no longer a constant gnawing at my vitals, but a moonstone to be taken from its indigo cushion, sighed over a little and locked away again.

At social anthropology I learned about the habits, morals, laws and religions of primitive men, and in particular the African Bantu and the Andaman Islander, who were pets of the professor's. Much of his information was astonishing and some of it embarrassing; all of it proved the aborigine to be a more highly moral person than his betters. I wrote articles deploring the interference of the missionary with so many excellent primitive customs and suggesting that charity begins at home. The papers to which I sent such effusions immediately returned them. After every lecture the professor tossed back that truant steel-grey lock, cast a cynical feline glance round his class and said: 'Anyone wishing to ask any questions please stay behind.' I was full of questions. Once he lent me a weighty French tome on suicide. Perhaps it was a hint. It bristled with statistics from which I learned that more French people fling themselves into the Seine during the winter than during the summer. (Later, when my husband and I spent part of a winter with a French family in Paris, I was not surprised.) But one sad day the professor, toothless, lisped his lecture, the scales fell from my eyes and I was emptied of my questions. Social anthropology had lost its savour.

April brought the short vacation, and our crowd went camping to Gordon's Bay, chaperoned by two of the women professors. We climbed the mountains, swam, played games barefoot on the beach at dusk, and after supper huddled round a camp-fire and told ghost stories. Sometimes on these occasions I shared his lion-skin kaross with a sinewy dark young man with golden eyes. And once, when it rained, we ran arm in arm for shelter, with the heavy skin a savage, tawny umbrella over our heads.

In the winter there was rugger. Oh, that rugger! On Saturday afternoons Marjorie and I went to Rondebosch and watched breathlessly as thirty enormous huskies tore each other limb from limb, and then another thirty, and yet another. Tattered shirts and trousers strewed the bloody field of battle, the heavy panting of the players came to our attendant ears like the puffing of giant locomotives, there was the surging of the scrum, the easy doubling race of hare and hounds, and the timely passing of the ball until he who held it last made that final furious dash which flung him, hotly pursued and gasping, into touch. Then there was a great roaring of the crowd, followed by deathly silence for the kick, and after that the yell, 'A goal! A goal!' and a wild stampede of triumph, bellows and savage war-cries. The pinnacle of the season's glorious slaughter was the inter-varsity match when U.C.T. (University of Cape Town) played Stellenbosch, and the students filled the stands with their college songs and cheers that echoed up the mighty shoulder of the mountain and down through the pine-woods to the sea.

In summer we were more civilized. Marjorie and I were partners in the U.C.T. tennis team – third pair, but nevertheless a pair. And at Christmas time the Open South African

Championships were played at Rondebosch. We entered optimistically for everything, were swiftly beaten and then settled down to watch the more proficient players.

In the December-January of 1922-23 there was a naval pair who reached the semi-finals and drew a crowd. The one partner was the flag-lieutenant, half-brother of the famous Wimbledon champion Algy Kingscote, who had taught him to hit the ball early with forceful brilliance. The other was a steady powerful player, the gunnery officer of H.M.S. *Dublin,* who was never rattled no matter what the state of the score. We gasped appreciatively at the deadly volleys and hurricane service of the flag-lieutenant and applauded his partner's accurate backhand down the line, a speedy passing shot. They were beaten, but it was a lovely game to watch.

Romance wears strange guises sometimes, and it was through the bad offices of a loathsome meer-kat – a wild ferret of the veld – that I first got to know my future husband.

Now, it so happened that the Commander-in-Chief, Admiral Sir Rudolph and Lady Bentinck, were fond of wild animals, and someone had presented them with a jackal and a meer-kat. The jackal ranged up and down a wire run in the lovely rambling garden of Admiralty House like a wild unhappy dog, but the meet-kat had few restrictions placed upon his liberty. In fact, he saw fit to invite himself to tea in the drawing-room on the very day that Mother first took me to call on Lady Bentinck at Simonstown.

I was sitting beside my hostess, dealing politely with a sandwich and a cup of tea, when in came a steward bearing a plate of cakes, and at his heels, with a quick scrabble of claws on the parquet, tailed the ferrety savage-eyed Riki. Riki squatted on his narrow haunches just inside the door and surveyed the domestic scene wickedly. I could see his nasty little mind plotting evil. *'Sredni Vashtar went forth. His thoughts were red thoughts, his teeth were white . . .'* I recalled the terrible ferret in Saki's tale, 'Sredni', who eventually devoured Conradin's hateful guardian. Sredni Vashtar lived in a tool-shed and the boy Conradin worshipped him as a god of vengeance.

'Hullo, Riki,' called the Admiral's daughter. 'Come over here! Tsk, tsk, tsk! He usually likes running up Flag's trouser-leg,' she added brightly.

'Only *faut de mieux*,' remarked the flag-lieutenant, with a darkly significant glance at my silk-stockinged legs.

I trembled.

The detestable Riki, grinning all over his mean little wedge of a face, licked his lips and, in a flash, was across the room. The next moment my tea was all over the carpet and I was standing on my chair screaming lustily while Riki skimmed rapidly up my calf, regardless of the conventions. A dark-haired young man, quick of eye and action as becomes a tennis player, caught the brute by the tail just as he was disappearing under my already indelicately elevated skirt.

'A most uncalled-for and unprovoked attack,' he remarked, with a smile at Lady Bentinck. A crooked smile, somehow re-assuring.

That was my introduction to the man I was destined to marry, and to the Royal Navy, which was to be the framework of my future life.

CHAPTER TWELVE

PACK AND FOLLOW

THE Royal Navy.

I know the Navy now and love, admire, fear and respect it. And since the war I think the whole world has begun to realize something of its task and of the courage and endurance of those who keep the sea-routes open, convoying those wonderfully brave merchantmen who bring us the necessities of life without which our island would perish.

Before Noel Coward made that fine film 'In Which We Serve' he was staying with us, and we talked a great deal about the Navy. Noel had been to sea under war-time conditions in every class of ship. He had made himself conversant with every aspect of a sailor's life – his unremitting vigilance, his deathless fortitude in battle, his simple humour in the face of disaster, his persistent combat against the menace from the air, from the sea and from beneath the sea, and his deep enduring love of his ship. Noel discovered for all to see what every sailor knows – that ships have souls. That night at dinner, as we discussed this Service so dear to all of us, I tried to tell Noel something else – the other side – a lesson I have learned in all these years of being a naval wife. We who are the women of men who go down to the sea in ships must recognize one thing. The Grey Rival – the ship – will always come first, and if we fight her we will break our hearts. We, too, must try and love her. And, strangely, we do. There is a Christmas scene in the film in which the captain's wife says a few words to the girl who is going to marry one of her husband's officers. In that little speech Noel has clothed that thought in moving and human words, wise and kind.

Yes; now, after many years, I am beginning to understand ships. But when first I met the Navy I realized nothing of its purpose. I suppose most young girls are foolish and insensitive in their egotism. I don't know. I certainly was. To me in those days the Navy at Simonstown was there to give the girls of the Peninsula a good time.

And this it certainly did.

Marjorie and I were inclined to compare the midshipmen of the *Lowestoft* and *Dublin* with our college friends. The midshipmen seemed callow in comparison. The college lads, though of the same age, were more mature and more audacious. Both had their own absurdities. If you asked an undergraduate a simple question, he replied with such elaborations as 'Oh yes, he said, and wildly waved his wooden leg,' or 'Oh no, he said, as the elephant skipped from twig to twig.' A midshipman answered simply 'Yes' or 'No', followed by a nervous burst of giggling.

If you 'sat out' with an undergraduate, as like as not he made rough love to you, but if with a midshipman he spoke in shy little rushes of many things – sometimes even poetry. The South African boys were deeply tanned and hard as nails, honest in their thinking and of the earth, earthy. The English boys were tough too, but in a different way. Their toughness was the result of many years of discipline, often shut down for weeks in their iron box – and it was skin-deep. Underneath they were naïve, romantic, eager, and filled with a diffident endearing chivalry.

Marjorie said: 'They're awf'ly sweet, if only they didn't giggle quite so much.'

I agreed, and added: 'They have lovely manners, and Mother says it's nice the way they call Daddy "sir".'

Once we tried mixing undergraduates and midshipmen. It didn't work. They had nothing to say to one another.

'Men of the world and men of Mars,' we said, and laughed a bit ruefully.

My favourite midshipman was a blond young Viking of six foot five. His shipmates called him Tiny. He was often in our house, and we all loved him. He was a pugilist of repute in the Navy, and he came to Tees Lodge sometimes with swollen ears, purple eyes and sheepish mien. His nose was boneless, flexible as india-rubber. 'Perfect for a boxer,' he explained. At heart he was a poet – a Sir Galahad – gentle and lovable, with a kind, generous temperament, shot here and there with young flaming angers at this or that injustice, but always the injustice suffered by another. When he was going to fight he had to lash himself into a belligerent mood to counteract the natural diffidence of his disposition. In time he became the heavyweight champion of the three Services, and was only beaten in the finals of the Amateur Championships of England by a brawny policeman after a terriffic contest. On one occasion he fought against Carnera in the Albert Hall. Carnera, the great growling Italian gorilla with matted chest and inky hair, took on the amateur heavyweight champions one after another and knocked them out like ninepins. Tiny he treated with no more respect than the others; in fact, with a blow delivered with the force of a battering-ram, he sent his Nordic adversary spinning through the ropes into the front row of the audience.

At dawn on a fateful day of May 1941, my friend Tiny went into the ring for his last great fight. This time it was not in the crowded Albert Hall, but in the bitter, lonely North Sea; and in the brave moment of defeat – a moment of epic tragedy and drama – no applause broke the vast silence save the mutter of the waves, the thunder of the guns and the desolate cries of seabirds. He was one of the brave company of the twenty-one-year-old battle-cruiser *Hood*. Snow and storm lashed the dark sea off the coast of Greenland, and then a rift in the dawn mists revealed the German capital ship *Bismarck* and the cruiser *Prince Eugen*. The next moment the world's mightiest warships prepared to engage in battle. There was no turning away on either side as the old and noble *Hood* rode the storm into the teeth of annihilation. The modern *Bismarck* forged to meet her. The guns of H.M.S. *Hood* thundered as the range closed, and their orange flame was a brief brilliance against the sombre sea and lowering sky. The *Bismarck* replied and her shells found their target. The shuddering but indomitable *Hood* surged on towards the enemy with flames bursting amidships and her guns roaring again and yet again. But even as they bellowed defiance a deafening explosion shattered the giant battle-cruiser and a towering sheet of smoke and fire rose hundreds of feet into the air, together with the remains of the proud British warship and fifteen hundred men who served in her.

All but two of those boys who giggled and danced with us in the lovely Cape Peninsula have been lost at sea this war, and among them a South African, called Lindsay de Villiers, fell in the Battle of Narvik when the destroyer flotilla under Captain Warburton-Lea went into a snowy Norwegian fjord to almost certain death. And too many of the men who were once our 'college crowd' have died or been taken prisoner in the wastes of Libya.

After the Riki episode everything seemed to happen very quickly.

I woke one morning to find myself engaged to be married. The next instant my parents were whisking me off to Switzerland for winter sports because, I gathered, they believed in the efficacy of 'out of sight, our of mind', and they had a notion that 'young girls of eighteen can't know their own minds'. 'But they *can!*' I protested.

'You'll have to prove it to our satisfaction,' said Mother.

So there I was, once again, hanging over the rail of a liner, waving good-bye to Cape Town. But I soon cheered up, and before we were many days out a sombre fellow with aquiline features and the air of a disillusioned hawk was teaching me to play the dangerous game of bridge.

I say 'dangerous' advisedly, because bridge brings out the worst in the best. Even my parents, the most devoted of mates, ate a cantankerous breakfast every Thursday morning after their weekly Wednesday evening bridge contest against their neighbours, the Dilwaters. On Thursday mornings a brooding silence curdled the coffee and turned the eggs. Then Daddy would open hostilities with a broadside.

'Do you realize, Ellen, that if you hadn't put up your king in that spade hand we would have made a grand slam?'

A discussion ensued, at the end of which my father was wont to sigh: 'Last night, old chap, I was playing against *three* people, and' – the parthian shot – 'the Dilwaters were laughing up their sleeves.' Daddy came triumphant out of most of the early contests – until Culbertson joined the family. Culbertson was the Other Man. Mother welcomed him with open arms. She spent her spare time in his company, she learned to know him intimately, she understood his idiosyncrasies, modelled herself according to his advice, ignored my father's counsel in favour of Culbertson's – and went so far as to bring him to breakfast with her on Thursday mornings. When my father said, 'Now, Ellen, if you had supported my heart call over their clubs . . .' Mother merely answered good-temperedly, drawing Culbertson towards her with an affectionate hand: 'Quite impossible, my dear. I hadn't a trick and a half. Culbertson will tell you that . . .'

'Ach, Culbertson!' cried my father, riled. 'Why worry about the fellow? I play by common sense.'

'That's only because you won't take the trouble to learn your Culbertson.'

'*My* Culbertson! *Your* Culbertson!'

It is lucky Daddy's contact with the Other Man was indirect, or I fear he might have torn that eminent authority limb from limb.

It was very kind of Duggie Stuart to teach me bridge – or at least the elements thereof. He was, in his saturnine way, a very kind man. Few people on board recognized the world's foremost bookmaker. He travelled incognito, like a king, and the name by which he was known on the passenger list was not Stuart. He told me that his daughter was at an exclusive finishing school, where few people were aware of her father's identity. When she 'came out' he gave her a dance at a fashionable West End hotel which cost him a thousand pounds. Duggie never wanted to be a 'bookie', yet bookmaking was in his blood and bone, a career he could not have escaped. He was born in the Western Province, and as a little child he knew the meaning of want and poverty. As a nipper he washed bottles in a jam factory to earn a few coppers a day, and in his spare time he ran a book on the Saturday afternoon's children's sports on Green

Point Common. He was a kid himself, but he knew about book-making. It was there in him, that freakish, fortunate, sporting-commercial instinct that had to find an outlet. There was never a sports meeting anywhere where this thin, dark little lad with sad, precocious, hooded eyes and a flat, predatory nose was not taking bets and laying odds.

Today, in his own line, he is at the top.

'Sometimes,' said Duggie, whose face seemed scarred with the sorrows of ten thousand past lives, 'old ladies send me all their savings and beg me to put these modest sums on a horse – any horse. They say: "Put it on whatever animal you think best, Mr. Stuart. We trust you." '

This certainly struck me as taking the 'Duggie Always Pays' slogan too literally.

'What do you do?' I asked.

He sighed. 'What can I do? My business is not a charitable institution. It is my living. I send back their savings with a nice fatherly letter advising them to leave the wicked horses alone.'

Nobody had ever taught Duggie to smile.

In Switzerland we found that I had no aptitude for winter sports, and we soon moved on to Monte Carlo, where Mother derived much enjoyment from the tables at comparatively small expense.

Then one morning early in February I went to the sunny little station to meet a friend. Ah, there he was! The crooked smile, the reassuring voice, a suit-case and a tennis-bag. When we went on to Paris, oddly enough, he chanced to be there too. For my nineteenth birthday he gave me a little ring, a circlet of diamonds, and I wore it on the small finger of my right hand. Mother raised her eyebrows, smiled indulgently and shrugged. Presently my parents took me back to South Africa, demanding still more proof of the sincerity of my intentions, and my prospective husband, now promoted to Lieutenant-Commander, was appointed to the staff of H.M.S. *Excellent*, the Naval Gunnery School at Portsmouth.

After six months of somewhat hectic repining at the Cape, my parents allowed our engagement to be announced, and I transferred the circlet of diamonds to the fourth finger of my left hand and sent a cable to Portsmouth.

Lady Bentinck smiled the next time she met me. 'You don't know about life in the Navy,' she said. 'I do. From now on it'll be pack and follow for you!'

She never spoke a truer word.

Mother said, with lightly veiled pleasure: 'This'll mean another trip to Europe to see the child married. She must have someone of her own to stand by her.' Daddy agreed. There followed some rather absurd talk of my taking Teena to Portsmouth as my cook-general. The thought of Teena gave me confidence, and Teena herself was not averse to seeing the world. But Mother stamped upon such foolish dreams.

'Listen, my child,' she said gently. 'You must know that people need their own kind about them. You and Teena are looking no further than your noses. What do you picture that poor brown woman doing in Portsmouth on her days out, with neither kith nor kin to visit? Colour bar or no colour bar, the thing isn't feasible. No, darling, you'll have to buckle to and muddle through some other way. This is *your* picnic.'

So it was that one sunny day, early in the new year of 1925, trunks were piled high on the front stoep, and Daddy prowled back and forth, glancing ever and again at his watch.

'The taxis should be here soon. We ordered them for two-thirty.'

Jockie, poor animal, was slinking about with the dismal air of a dog who knows only too well the meaning of luggage. Mother said: 'I hope Fred gets to the boat in time to see us off.' (Norman was still in England gaining surgical experience.)

I added: 'And Nannie and Marjorie.'

'There'll be some of the relations, for sure,' put in Mother. 'I know Aunt Ethel and Ivo and Fay mean to give you a good send-off.'

'Ah, the cars are here!'

'Joy,' said Mother, 'have you said good-bye to Cook and Teena?'

I went to the kitchen. Cookie was washing up the lunch things and Teena was drying. The two little coloured women wiped their wet, brown hands as I came in, and I saw that they had been crying. Cookie dabbed at her eyes with her apron.

'Good luck, Miss Yoy, darling. God bless Miss Yoy . . .' Her voice broke and she could say no more.

I kissed them and, infected with their emotion, wept also.

Over Cookie's meagre shoulder, through the wide kitchen window, I saw, in a mist of tears, the fig orchard and the mountain behind it. A shred of cloud hovered in the cobalt sky; by this evening that wisp would be a Niagara pouring over the gaunt ledges of Saddle Face and the turbulent breath of the South-Easter would be singing in the leaves, tearing them from the swaying boughs and rustling them along the paths with a dry papery sound. But by then I would be gone – far out at sea. The bougainvillea was vivid purple on the garden wall; in the hot sun Arend pottered about among Daddy's carnations; a pigeon settled on the window-sill – a grey homer – and, of a sudden, some understanding of the finality of this farewell overwhelmed me.

Farewell, Tees Lodge, and all that is dear and familiar. Farewell, my home, where kindness and affection dwell side by side with laughter, to cooing doves and faithful servants, to freedom from care and responsibility, to a girlhood a-dazzle with gaiety and folly. Here in sun and storm I have been safe and sheltered and, good or bad, I have been loved.

At that moment, with Cookie's wet, brown cheek against mine and salt tears warm and heavy in my throat, that other call of the heart, so insistent before, seemed thin and far away. And then, at the last, Mother's cool ringed hand was on my shoulder, strong and tender, and her quiet voice was in my ears.

'Come, my child. It is time for us to go.'

I followed her blindly down the passage.

Part Two

VARIETY SHOW

CHAPTER THIRTEEN

EXOTICS IN A HOME PORT

BERTIE and I were married in Portsmouth on a silvery day in February, 1925, and we held our wedding reception on Whale Island, the Naval Gunnery School. A team of bluejackets towed our bridal car from St. Mark's Church down a dingy street, at the end of which, beautifully and incredibly, there flowed a broad strip of water spanned by a footbridge. As we crossed the bridge and went on board H.M.S. *Excellent* I felt like Joy in Wonderland. His Majesty's ship in this case was not a ship at all, but an island within an island. Portsea was the greater and Whaley the smaller island. Once Whaley had been a mud flat, now it was a flowering mosaic lightly and incongruously attached to the slums of North End. A rose garden, a Japanese garden and a miniature zoo and aviary were poised above the wide parade-ground, and in front of the stately naval establishment spread lawns and playing-fields, where the sea-gulls wheeled – the souls of gunners' mates. A swan who had sullied her wintry beauty with an inadvertent immersion in oil fuel brooded upon the greensward bank of the creek while a sailor conscientiously polished her bedraggled plumage.

'Sailors polish everything,' said my bridegroom, 'even swans.'

There were three hundred wedding guests waiting for us in the mess and I knew only four of them. My parents and my brother Norman, too, were strangers. They must have felt very lonely that day.

Our cake had been made on board. It was adorned with fierce little sugar cannons and flew the White Ensign. I cut it in the true bellicose tradition with my bridegroom's sword. Afterwards we were photographed on the steps outside the mess between two sinister projectiles.

We went to Monte Carlo for our honeymoon, and it was cold and wet as only the South of France can be in February. My fur coat (a wedding present from Daddy) was stolen, and, as it was not insured, I had to do without its warmth and comfort for the rest of the winter. Soon after our return to Portsmouth my parents sailed for South Africa, and, at parting, Mother gave me a valuable piece of advice.

'When you are homesick, darling, learn not to show it.'

At first it was not always easy to follow this wise counsel. Portsmouth, fanning out in interminable terraces of little semi-detached brick houses and undistinguished buildings between Cosham Bridge and the dignified purlieus of the Dockyard, seemed infinitely dreary to me. Several thousand bicycles, ridden to and from the Dockyard by 'mateys' in threadbare overcoats, dominated the traffic four times a day, the sky was grey and lowering and the air raw. The women, with their string shopping bags, were far from picturesque, and outside the grocer's and the butcher's stood shabby prams in which apoplectic infants strove like bulls to burst their harnesses, rocking their vehicles furiously and yelling lustily till their mothers appeared and shook them impatiently. 'Put a sock in it, Alfy, or I'll dot you one!' Only the sailors were engaging, with their square collars, taut behinds and bell-bottoms. How expressive are the backs of sailors – jaunty or dejected in the manner of small boys'!

I saw little beauty in Portsmouth in 1925, but now, in 1943, there is in this battered port a quality greater than beauty. There is grandeur. Nelson once said: 'The strength of a fleet is not in its ships, but in its men.' In this war of Hitler's there is more to it than that. The strength of a fleet is in its women too, and the wives of England's sailors have proved themselves strong indeed. 'Pompey' the bluejackets call their port, but it might be Pompeii now, so bitter is the ruin of the city, so cruel the devastation. The historic High Street, where Nelson walked and his men said to one another, 'There goes our Nel, brave as a lion and gentle as a lamb,' and the Blue Post, where he stayed before Trafalgar, are razed to the ground, the Guildhall is burned out, so are barracks, schools, churches, hospitals, cinemas and music-halls, and so also are homes where once the worst menace was the mother-in-law and the lodger. The children are gone from Portsmouth now, but the women have stayed on in the mean streets with the sinister gaps and windows boarded up. They are the wives and mothers and sweethearts of sailors, and when *he* comes home, 'unexpected-like', he will find them there – if home is still standing.

But I did not see the grandeur and the great heart in those early days, and I understood little of what England's biggest naval arsenal really meant. The foolishness of living by comparison obstructed my view like blinkers. I missed the golden light of the Cape, the bright, modern houses in gay gardens, Table Mountain with its cloth of cloud, the sparkling sea and its thunder, the cooing doves, the easy-going South Africans, and friends dropping in for a cup of morning tea. Against these things Porstmouth seemed gloomy and the people drab and reticent. But the mental attitude which judges everything by comparing it with something else is as foolish as that of the wife who reproaches her husband with the chivalry of his courtship: 'You wouldn't have said *that* to me when we were engaged'; or, if she be a widow, with the qualities of his predecessor: 'James never treated me in *this* way.' Perhaps not, but circumstances are altered and so is behaviour. Now, after years of wandering, I am able to accept new places and people on their own merits, perhaps because my standards of comparison have become confused. Just so the courtesan, no doubt, gives up comparing one lover with another. She has known too many men as I have known too many lands.

Till quite recently there were no modern flats in Southsea, and naval people lived in rooms or old-fashioned houses curiously partitioned and converted. My husband had taken a 'maisonette' for us in Eastern Villas Road, and when first I was confronted with the dark, narrow stairs and an intimidating brown wallpaper blazoned with loathsome birds my heart sank. I tried not to show it.

'Darling, how clever of you to find this place!' I cried brightly. 'We'll brighten it up in no time. We can distemper the walls and put new chintzes on the chairs for a start.'

'You can't paint other people's walls. The landlord . . .'

'But he couldn't *want* to keep those awful birds!'

'Presumably he chose them. Anyway, we can't afford to improve someone else's property at considerable expense.'

That, of course, is the crux of naval life.

But if the wallpaper was dreadful and the chintzes worn and faded, the view from our sitting-room was superbly out to sea – across the grey-green water to Spithead and the Isle of Wight. I loved this outlook, and when spring came a lilac tree blossomed underneath our window.

My inexperience led me into many pitfalls, and I hired a cook-general whose references a wiser housewife would have recognized as faked. Her name was Mary, she had black finger-nails and in due course she helped herself to items from my trousseau. My trousseau was, like most things about me at that time, rather ridiculous. Mother and I had not understood the needs of the English climate. There wasn't a tweed, a tailor-made, a vest or a pair of woollen stockings in it, and the bitter winds that whistled off the sea along the front cut mockingly through my flimsy lingerie. I was about as out of place in Portsmouth as the animals in Whaley Zoo. These, too, had been brought from remote parts of the world by gunnery officers, but they were more fortunate in that they had not lost their fur coats. When we went on board to church service on Sunday mornings we strolled round the island afterwards, and I hung nostalgically about my fellow-exotics.

There was Zimba, the pride of the zoo, a handsome lion who had been presented by a certain very lovely lady, the wife of a distinguished naval officer. One morning Zimba escaped from his cage and strolled down to the parade-ground. On board H.M.S. *Excellent* everything is always done at the double, and as they go about their work the sailors never walk; they run. One of them, seeing Zimba at large, doubled off to the commander of the island in more than usual haste.

'Sir,' he gasped, 'there's a lion walking across the parade-ground. What shall I do?'

'Tell him to double,' said the commander curtly.

Another time the tale of Albert and the lion was retold on Whaley with slight modifications. Albert was a naughty little cadet and twice a week he and his fellows drilled on the island. After drill it was their custom to go and see the birds and beasts. For a while they watched the antics of the ducks, and then Albert, bored, cried boastfully:

'Ducks! 'Oo cares about – ducks! Let's go bait the lion!'

He found a stick and, aided by two other urchins, scrambled on to the top of Zimba's cage, where he sat prodding the noble animal and yelling at him abusively. Zimba retaliated with a deep-throated curse, a leap and the sweep of a revengeful claw. Albert screamed and slid to the ground. But the seat of his trousers fluttered from the top of the cage like a captured flag, and tatters of his flesh remained there too. Thereafter Albert's father sued the successive captains of Whaley for the value of his son's posterior, which many years later was finally assessed at £70.

There came a grievous day when poor Zimba fell ill and died. He was duly buried, and his erstwhile owner was informed by telephone of her lion's demise. To everybody's dismay, she announced her intention of coming immediately to fetch the dead animal home. 'I'll be there in two hours,' she said. A party of sailors was promptly mustered and armed with clothes brushes. Zimba was exhumed and the sailors brushed him madly from stem to stern to remove all traces of his recent interment. And when the lovely lady arrived she found her Zimba immaculate in death.

There were also some kangaroos in the zoo. They were very small owing to overmuch intermarriage, and they eventually died out when the last pair of vitiated parents decided that such vest-pocket progeny were no longer worth putting into production.

Of the other big animals, all that now remains is a tombstone marking a communal grave on the windy bluff beyond the West Battery.

A.R.P.

Shot on 27th May 1940

In Memory of

Lionesses	Lorna and Topsy
Polar Bears . . .	Nicholas and Barbara
Sun Bears . . .	Henry and Alice

These animals were put down on 27th May 1940 in preparation for German Air Raids. Their loss was keenly felt by the whole Whale Island community.

A sub-lieutenant performed the hateful task of putting them down, and by way of compensation for the pale misery of that murky dawn he can now boast that he once shot two lionesses and four bears before breakfast.

I liked the aviary nearly as much as the zoo, and was fascinated by the golden pheasants – birds the like of which I had never seen before – as they strutted before their dusty mates, tossing shining blond Tutankhamen wigs. There was a silver pheasant, too, posturing in a gown of black and white with scarlet hat and stock – a Parisian *poule-de-luxe*; and scores of shrill canaries, blue budgerigars, white cockatoos with lime-green linings, and macaws clad in flamboyant sapphire and emerald plumage who floundered about on bandy legs with toes turned in and squawked grotesque orders to one another. The macaws were admirable creatures with a keen sense of discipline, proof even against the time when, for three months, fifty sub-lieutenants filed past the parrot-house on their way to the parade-ground and said, each in turn and with great emphasis, 'Bother the commander!' a subversive sentiment which the birds very rightly refused to echo.

In the Japanese garden there dwelt an indefatigable hen who had hatched out more than sixty ducklings.

'She's a good old soul,' said the gnarled, square-faced septuagenarian in charge of the aviary. 'But she falls down on teachin' 'em the way about this 'ere Serpentine of ours. They's always drowndin' theirselves, poor mites. Or they gets tangled up in the rushes.'

The ducklings, in true seaman-like style, took to the water with inadequate swimming instructions, so the square-faced man kept ever at hand a butterfly net with which he scooped exhausted fledglings from the miniature Serpentine.

The only other aspect of H.M.S. *Excellent* that concerned me was the windswept rifle range at Tipner, where I lay at the firing-point on many a Saturday or Sunday afternoon and spotted for my husband. It was part of his job to train the rifle and revolver teams, and he shot for them himself. Most week-ends there was a shooting match somewhere or other, and we went in our little two-seater Clyno, and I waited in mess, hotels, or just the car until the match was over. It was not a very lively programme for a young bride perhaps, but I was quite content. What pleased me less was returning calls. It was an ordeal and an anguish. Nearly every afternoon I trudged the streets of Southsea searching for improbable numbers like 14A or 7C, which concealed their whereabouts by many a strange device. When at last I ran them to earth there followed that wretched fifteen minutes during which I sat in the dim shadow of the aspidistra and talked politely to baffled English naval wives across a gulf six thousand miles wide.

CHAPTER FOURTEEN

JELLICOE AND BEATTY. GAS FIRES AND PETER

SPRING came and I saw my first English wood carpeted with bluebells and furtive primroses, green-yellow incarnations of evasive woodland sunshine. And presently it was summer and my husband was encamped at Bisley for three weeks in charge of the naval competitors in the National Rifle Association Meeting. In the last week-end of the meeting I drove to Bisley in 'Tommy' Clyno. There were competitors from all the Services and from every part of the Empire, and I had tea in the South African hut and heard again, with homesick ears, the clipped intonation of my countrymen.

There were several redoubtable women shots, and one of them actually got into the King's Hundred. She had a little husband who followed her faithfully to the shooting-point, carrying her gun and ammunition. It was also his privilege to spread her ground-sheet, pull her skirt down as she lay prone and arrange a rug over her spread-eagled nether limbs, after which he took out his field-glasses and spotted for her.

The prizes were presented by Lord Jellicoe. I was thrilled. Jellicoe of Jutland – the hero of the mightiest naval clash in history.

He was a stocky little mariner with a big nose and merry eyes. The gold braid of an Admiral of the Fleet covered his short arm from wrist to elbow, and a phalanx of medal ribbons sat well upon his sturdy chest.

'What was he like?' I whispered. 'Did he ever come on board the *Warspite*?' (My husband was serving in the Grand Fleet in H.M.S. *Warspite* at the time of the Battle of Jutland.)

'Certainly he did. Everybody from the captain to the ship's boy got a tremendous kick out of seeing him. He was always cheerful and very much head of the firm. He had a reputation for never losing his temper, and his personal staff adored him.'

Jellicoe came of a family of seamen. His father was a captain in the mercantile marine, and an ancestor of his was sailing-master in one of Nelson's ships of the line at Trafalgar. When he married he strengthened the bonds. Miss Cayzer, his bride, was the daughter of a shipping magnate. He was a good all-round sportsman, but not in the huntin', shootin' and fishin' manner of Beatty. Rugger was his game.

Jellicoe and Beatty. Ever since Jutland these two have been the subject of a bitter naval controversy. Jellicoe-ites and Beatty-ites frequently came to blows and proved the fact that a naval discussion consists of a statement and flat contradiction, followed by personal abuse. The only two officers who could not be drawn on the matter were the two most vitally concerned. They never stooped to recriminations, but set an example of admirable restraint and dignity.

The Germans claimed Jutland as a victory because von Scheer's High Seas Fleet had made what amounted to a successful guerilla raid on the Grand Fleet, nipping out of the Heligoland Bight, inflicting severe losses and getting back again. We claimed it because we retained our undisputed mastery of the seas, and the High Seas Fleet remained bottled up for the rest of the war. But could it have been cut off and annihilated? That is a matter for the strategists. The rights and wrongs of Jellicoe's and Beatty's judgment do not concern the average person, but what does fire every imagination is the almost incredible magnitude of the conflict. Sixty-four dread-noughts alone were arraigned against each other on that summer afternoon of May 31st, 1916, to say nothing of some forty-four cruisers and light cruisers and a hundred and fifty-one destroyers harrying the heavy forces with the suicidal courage of dogs attacking grizzlies. Altogether about two hundred and sixty warships were blazing at one another on the cold North Sea, sinking and being sunk, and great battleships were exploding in sheets of flame and showers of flying debris. Such a contest can never come again. In the combined navies of the whole world today there do not exist as many capital ships as fought at Jutland.

Less than two years after meeting Lord Jellicoe at Bisley I made the acquaintance of Lord Beatty, who came to church on board Sir Roger Keyes's flagship in Malta. His yacht lay in the Grand Harbour, for he was cruising in the Mediterranean, faithful still to the sea.

The morning light was dazzling on the pastel battlements of Valetta, the sea was brilliant, a-glitter with sun-diamonds, the breeze in the canvas awning over the quarter-deck sang a mutinous song as Admiral Sir Roger Keyes waited for his distinguished guest to come on board. Presently we heard the chug of the motor-boat and then Admiral of the Fleet Lord Beatty was piped over the side. Then, eleven years after Jutland, he was a man of fifty-seven, spruce and athletic. He had been a captain before he was thirty and an admiral at thirty-nine. At the present time our youngest and most spectacular promotion to admiral was that of Philip Vian, of the *Cossack*. He was forty-seven.

Beatty's was an arresting face with the power and personality of the born leader in the alert eyes and stern mouth. I could well imagine him as he must have stood on the bridge of the *Lion*, seeing with horrified amazement the dreadful spectacle of the *Indefatigable*, *Queen Mary* and *Invincible* blow up sky-high one after the other, and turning to his flag-captain in a burst of anger. 'What's the matter with our bloody ships today, Chatfield? Alter course towards the enemy!'

He was not very tall, but strong and spare with the hands of a horseman and the gait of a sailor. A little thin woman walked proudly beside him, beautifully dressed, sophisticated and assured – his American wife, the millionairess who had never been present at Court. Lady Beatty had previously known the misfortune of an unhappy marriage and divorce, and, though her husband was elevated to the peerage in recognition of his war service, she was not received by the King and Queen, for King George V and Queen Mary set their faces against divorce, no matter where the blame might be apportioned.

Beatty was an Irishman from County Wexford, and he had all those attributes which comprise glamour – courage, dash and a fiery temper. He rode to hounds and played polo, he was a yachtsman and a fine shot, a sporting gentleman. Wherever he went he created a sense of elation and excitement. But the most spontaneous tribute he could ever have received was in Flotta in 1917. My husband was in Scapa Flow at the time, and he told me about the incident. America had entered the war and her ships lay in the Flow. A year had elapsed since Jutland. Jellicoe had gone to the Admiralty as First Sea Lord, and Beatty had succeeded him as Commander-in-Chief of the Grand Fleet. Flotta, which is an island with a magnificent natural arena, was the scene of great trials of strength between the men of the British and U.S. Navies. The boxing contests were particularly hard-fought. All round the ring the men were stepped up on the slopes which formed a rough stand. The lightweight championship final was in progress; it was a first-class fight, and the audience was tense, at fever-heat. Then in the middle of the second round Beatty arrived unostentatiously, accompanied only by his flag-lieutenant. But somebody spotted him and instantly the life-and-death Anglo-American final was forgotten, cheer upon cheer echoed over Flotta, and the referee had to stop the fight until the crowd's noisy enthusiasm was spent.

After the show Beatty addressed the men. English and American they listened intently as he worked up to a rousing crescendo. The German Fleet was still skulking in the Heligoland Bight, but the day would come when the tortoise would put out its head again, and then, by Heaven, the Grand Fleet would be standing by to smash it!

'It won't be long now – and when that day comes let us bear in mind the ever-to-be-remembered, unforgettable words of Henry the Fifth at Agincourt . . . Damn it all, Flags, what were they?'

Was David Beatty, like most leaders of men, a bit of an actor? Or had he really forgotten the unforgettable?

The next time the German High Seas Fleet came out was in November 1918. It sailed into the Flow to surrender.

Both Beatty and Jellicoe were men of Mr. Churchill's choice, given their commands when he was First Lord of the Admiralty. It is interesting that while in 1914 he put an extremely young vice-admiral like Beatty afloat in command of the Battle-Cruiser Squadron, he recalled as his First Sea-Lord the famous Admiral 'Jackie' Fisher, then aged seventy-four.

Autumn changed the little English scene that was gradually creeping into my heart, and leaves fell in the Hampshire lanes in scurries of golden rain.

We had made a number of friends and we were often at the home of the Longstaffs. 'Cuddy' Longstaff was a retired naval officer, and he and his pretty wife Hillie had a lovely house in Southsea, with several dogs, some white Persian cats and a greenhouse full of rare plants and love-birds. They lived with great gusto and in considerable luxury. We played bridge with them at 2s. 6d. a hundred, which we couldn't afford, and I learned more about the game by paying dear for my lessons than I had ever done from the assiduous teachings of Duggie Stuart. But in spite of many years' expensive experience my partners still express displeasure at my play.

Our other close friends were the 'Macs', a naval surgeon from New Zealand and his Australian wife Wyn. Their little daughter had been my flower-girl. When I was in trouble I usually asked Wyn's advice.

'It's funny,' I said one day, 'but these gas fires get me down. We don't have them in South Africa and the smell upsets me.'

'They are an English institution,' said Wyn. 'I detest them too, but they save a lot of trouble.'

'Well, they make me sick,' I grumbled.

My husband, who, when confronted with a situation that requires action, always deals with it promptly, had the gas fires removed, and Mary of the black nails was much disgruntled at finding herself cleaning grates and laying coal fires. On the same evening that they were taken out of the maisonette we happened to be dining with the Longstaffs. On the way home I said very suddenly in a suffocated voice: 'I'm going to be sick.'

The Macs' house was close at hand, and with great dispatch Bertie turned 'Tommy' Clyno's nose straight for it. We rang madly at the night bell, and Wyn in a dressing-gown, with hair dishevelled and anxious face, dashed downstairs and let us in. I fled past her for the only room in the house that was any use to me, and dimly I heard: 'I'm sorry, Wyn, but Joy felt ill.'

'Well, this is a doctor's house. Have a drink.'

I explained presently, somewhat abashed, that I had been playing bridge with my back to the fire.

Wyn said: 'Was it a gas fire?'

'Well, no. Electric.'

She smiled. 'I suppose you can't think of any other reason for feeling peculiar?'

I thought hard. 'But isn't *that* mornings only?' I asked at length. 'Not necessarily.'

On the way home we were both very quiet. The little maisonette was cold when we got in and there were no gas fires we could light.

'Darling,' I said after a while, 'perhaps it's not gas fires after all. Maybe it's Peter.'

CHAPTER FIFTEEN

HOMEWARD BOUND AND OUTWARD BOUND

QUITE nonsensically, we went to Paris for Christmas, and Peter (for it was he) came too. Even then the boy evinced an impish humour, and it was his habit to assert himself at all manner of inconvenient moments. 'I'm going to be sick,' was the leit-motif of my existence. We went to see the Guitrys at the Comédie Française, and just as charming Yvonne Printemps appeared on the stage I had to make a hasty dash for the *dames*. When I returned to my seat Bertie whispered: 'I expect that's the first time the sight of Yvonne has made one of her audience sick!'

After Paris we finished our fortnight's leave with a few days in Shropshire. The ramparts and bridges with which the English had defended their land against the Welsh were under snow, the Wrekin was chastely white, the Severn sullenly grey and Wenlock Edge a lovely winding menace to our little car. We stopped at the village of Cressage, where my husband was born, and had lunch with the doctor who had bought the home of his childhood. It was a spacious and pleasant house perfectly situated on a hill. The grounds were lovely. But the luncheon was a gruesome fantasy. The French windows were wide open and the raw January day invaded the unwarmed room. Strange figures with burning eyes wandered into the dining-room and struggled painfully with monstrous helpings of bloody beef, and afterwards they disappeared like wraiths. I feared that I might be growing fanciful.

'They live in wooden huts in the garden,' said the doctor's wife. 'It's very healthy for them here.'

'They' were consumptives.

My mother-in-law lived at Grinshill, not far from Cressage. She was a little old lady whose misleadingly gentle exterior housed a spartan spirit. I was demented with chilblains and complained about them. My mother-in-law offered restrained sympathy and certain country remedies. I climbed the snowy hill in tennis shoes because my swollen toes refused to accommodate themselves to sterner footgear, and observed enviously that my mother-in-law always wore moccasins.

'No wonder Mother doesn't get chilblains,' I said. 'She keeps her feet nice and warm all day in those lovely soft moccasins.'

Her son smiled crookedly. He knew his mother well. 'You have cause and effect confused.'

'You mean . . .?'

'Yes, only she doesn't make a song about them.'

In February, a few days after my twenty-first birthday, my husband came home with news. He looked worried and sad, yet in a way excited, and his voice had a sharp edge to it.

'I've been appointed to the *Warspite* as gunnery officer. It's the Mediterranean Fleet, darling, and we sail about April. She's in Portsmouth now for refit.'

It was as if I had come down in a lift, very fast, from a great height.

'Not Malta, Bertie! Not *now* – with Peter coming in July!'

He turned away and stared out of the window. It was raining, and he could see only the mist and the sea and the splashing of raindrops on the pane.

'The worst of it is, we won't even be in Malta in July. God knows where we'll be. The ship'll be away on the long summer cruise.'

It was a trap, this thing that was happening to us. My heart stood quite still. To have my baby alone with no one of my own at hand. Not pleasant.

'Are the Maltese doctors good?' I asked shakily.

He shook his head.

'I don't know. But, my sweet, midsummer in Malta is no time to be having babies. It's hot as hell and all the wives who can afford it go home from June to September. . . . I know . . . I've been asking . . .'

So the trap was sprung. I said from the gathering misery in my throat: 'Must you take this job?'

He answered, after a pause: 'I have no option. The Navy is my profession.'

Presently he came and took my cold hands. 'There's your home, Joy-Joy. It's not too late yet. Mother and Daddy, your brothers, Cookie and Teena to spoil you. Go back to Tees Lodge till the little sportsman has made his debut, and then you can both come to me in Malta in the autumn. . . .'

I laid my head against his shoulder.

'It isn't fair . . . it isn't fair . . .'

But it was fair enough. It was only part of the game – the inescapable problem of naval people, the recurrent sickness of the heart that is parting. Home, husband, child. The sailor's wife must learn to say good-bye. That is all. We were learning early.

Before I sailed for South Africa he took me on board the *Warspite*. The huge battleship was in dry dock. She was gashed with red lead, and wire hawsers and ropes lay in tangled masses on the decks. It seemed as if she could never be ready to sail in a few weeks' time. I clambered up into A turret and stared at the astounding complexity of a fifteen-inch gun-turret and a breach heavy as a fireproof safe in the strong-room of the Bank of England. Here, in the Battle of Jutland, my husband, as a young sub-lieutenant, had been the officer in charge of the guns' crew. The three other turrets had been put out of action and the great ship had circled crazily out of the line towards the enemy with jammed steering gear, a helpless target for the High Seas Fleet. She had been the worst-mauled dreadnought to withstand the action, but she had survived and my husband had been one of her company. Now as he looked at that ship of his there was something in his eyes that made me catch my breath. It was the sharp stab of pain a woman experiences when she knows that she does not come first.

'Your grey mistress,' I said bitterly. 'Well, she's beaten me this time!'

I was too young then to know that she would always beat me – the grey mistress – or that I, too, would come to love her.

Peter was born at Tees Lodge at eight o'clock on a winter's

morning to the accompaniment of the tinkle of schoolgirls' pianos at the Good Hope Seminary opposite.

All my relations came to see him and discovered in the small india-rubber face likenesses that I was quite unable to see. German Nannie said in her decisive way: 'He's the dead spit of his father.' Cookie came in, wiping her hands on her apron, her black eyes soft with pleasure, while Teena trailed behind her. They peeped into the blue-and-white cradle, giggled a little and murmured 'Ach, foei tog! How sweet he is, Miss Yoy!' He blew them a raspberry, but I only turned my face to the wall and wept. Mother said, gently stroking my hair with her cool fingers, 'That's always the way after a baby. You can't help being tearful.'

It was my brother Norman, now living at Tees Lodge, who restored my sense of the ridiculous. A week before my son's birth I had come in to breakfast pale and wan, and Norman had required to know the reason for my haggard mien. I confessed to a terrible nightmare. All night long a Chinaman had been chasing me round the house. Now it happened that my new-born child elected to get an attack of jaundice. Norman, gazing at the bright yellow infant, sighed deeply.

'It's too bad, old girl,' he said, 'but I can't help thinking that Chinaman must have caught you!'

Peter was a month old when we set out on our long and complicated journey to Malta. We had to go to England first and from there overland via Paris, Rome and Syracuse, where we could get the boat to Malta.

Nannie came with us. 'What do you know about babies?' she asked very reasonably. 'I'll come with you for the first year. My hubby won't mind. He'll stay with his married daughter.'

Mother advised us to take patent food to last Peter six months. 'I hear there are no cows in Malta and the goats' milk isn't safe.' She also, in the kindness of her heart, burdened me with a large crate containing a Japanese tea-set and a charming dessert service. Daddy gave me a new fur coat for presenting him with his first grandchild.

In retrospect that Odyssey strikes me as a farcical example of incompetency. We started well enough. Mother had cleverly arranged for us to travel on the same ship as my cousin Maisie and her husband, Charles te Water, who had just been appointed High Commissioner for South Africa in London by the new Hertzog Government, and they were going to London to take up the post.

The liner was a slow intermediate which had come down the east coast from Mombasa, and there was a lady from Kenya on board with her lion cub. By the time we neared England the cub had grown alarmingly, and when she took him for his daily constitutional on the end of a chain he showed a marked tendency to stalk the toddlers on the children's deck and smack his lips at the varied assortment of young babies in their prams.

'I don't like the way that cub eyes Peter,' said Nannie indignantly. 'What for a silly pet to have!'

There was also an Irish Roman Catholic bishop on board on his way to Rome to receive the blessing of the Pope.

We arrived at Tilbury in the dawn of a grey September morning. No one who has not travelled with a young baby can imagine the impedimenta involved — the cots, prams, baths, patent foods and utensils for cooking them, and above all, napkins. As we went ashore I saw, to my mortification, Nannie pressing a frightful string bag bulging with unconcealed harrington squares upon the new High Commissioner.

'Here, Mr. te Water. You take these. I can't manage Peter and the nappies down the gangway.' Charles's face at that moment will remain with me for ever.

In London the te Waters went to stay with friends, and I took Nannie and Peter to the hotel which had once been my parents' headquarters. Fatty, the waiter, had gone, which disappointed me. The bishop, in evident trepidation, promised to telephone me at that so secular address. Next day I went to the travel agency which I hoped had booked our sleepers across Europe. Yes, these had been reserved by cable.

'The journey takes four days, and your train leaves from Victoria at ten-forty. Have you much luggage?'

I thought of Peter's paraphernalia and the crate containing crockery and my trunks and Nannie's. 'Yes, a good deal.'

'Then get to the station an hour early.'

I cashed a cheque at the bank for an entirely insufficient sum and returned to the hotel in high spirits. The bishop telephoned and very kindly arranged to travel to Rome by the same train as we were taking, on the strength of which I sent Mother a cable calculated to dispel any misgivings she might be entertaining on our account: 'Safe and well jermyn street going as far as rome with a bishop love joy.'

But alas! even bishops are vulnerable to the evils which beset men of baser clay, and mine caught influenza and remained in London while we three set out on our ill-considered journey.

We arrived at Victoria in two taxis, the drivers of which expressed themselves displeased with the size, shape and amount of our gear. The porter said, with a bleak glance at it: 'Want all this 'ere stuff registered?'

'I don't know. Should it be registered?'

'Course it should. What train?'

'The ten-forty for Dover.'

'Not an 'ope. Lucky if you get the ten-fifty. Best register what you can and do the rest at Dover.'

The train steamed out without us.

'Fifteen quid to take all this stuff by rail,' said the official who weighed our baggage. I felt rather faint.

'But I can't pay that much. I've only got twenty pounds with me to last the whole journey. Will you take a cheque?'

'Sorry.'

'Last train goes in eight minutes' time,' interposed the porter. 'You oughter've sent this pile by goods.'

'But I didn't know, and it's too late now. What shall I do? If we miss this train we are done, we'll miss our reservations all the way to Syracuse, and we'll not get more for weeks! And we've come all the way from South Africa. Please take a cheque!'

Nannie added her entreaties to mine. 'Think of it,' she said. 'This poor baby's father has never even seen his own son!'

'That's often the way of it,' remarked the official dryly. But he relented and took a cheque, much against his better judgment. 'A cheque it is, then, and, mind you, I'm the mug.'

We caught the train with nothing to spare, and the last we saw of Victoria were porters rushing madly down the platform, slinging trunks and crates into the van and hurling small luggage at us through the window. At Dover a railway official met me with a telegram demanding their tips, which in my panic I had omitted to discharge.

Somehow we got on board the Channel steamer and off it again at Calais and on to the train. We had to change in Paris and Turin, and by the time we reached Rome I had run out of money and so had Nannie. We looked at one another. What now?

'There's nothing for it,' said Nannie. 'You must borrow. Go down the train and look in every compartment till you see somebody with a kind face. I noticed a dear old lady in the coach next to the dining-car. Try her first.'

The dear old lady, however, took umbrage and muttered something about 'confidence tricksters'. I went to the toilet and had a good cry before setting out again in quest of a kind face. I found it, like the blue bird of happiness, nearest home. In the compartment adjoining ours there was a tin case on the rack, which gave me confidence. An iron-grey head was bent over a book, the features were powerful and generous. I confided our woeful predicament.

'We haven't a bean left. You see, I've never travelled with a baby, and I didn't guess . . .'

'That's all right. I'll lend you what you need and collect from your husband. I'm going to Malta too.' His smile was friendly. 'I know all about babies. I have four at home. All ages.'

His name was Burroughs. Today he has received a knighthood for taking vital convoys safely through to Malta and Murmansk, not once, but many times.

A train-ferry took us across the Straits of Messina into Sicily and soon we were skirting Mount Etna.

'That's the first volcano I've ever seen!' exclaimed Nannie, who had slept past Vesuvius. 'That smoke on top is the dead spit of an ostrich-feather!'

It was dusk when we drew into Syracuse, and on the platform I caught sight of a familiar but totally unexpected figure. It couldn't be! How could it? But the Commander-in-Chief's yacht had brought some notables to Syracuse and had given my husband a passage.

It was almost dark as we went on board the old *Maltana*, a little worn-out ship that made the bi-weekly eight-hour crossing to Malta. Nannie put Peter to bed in a dingy cabin with a gaslight hissing overhead and two interested cockroaches watching her.

'Come and see your son,' I said to Peter's father.

He had never seen a young baby, and Peter was only two months old, a travel-stained infant, hardly at his best.

'A fine little monkey.' He took the tiny hand, and a doll-like finger closed firmly over his thumb. 'Strong as a bull!' he added admiringly. His son favoured him with a wide toothless grin. I felt so happy and so tired that I wept.

CHAPTER SIXTEEN

MALTA AND SAILORS ON HORSEBACK

MALTA, the Island of the George Cross, has suffered greatly this war. Much of the historic town of Valetta lies in ruins, but the happy-go-lucky Maltese went stubbornly about their daily tasks, as undefeated as the indomitable people of the blitzed areas of England.

When we were there it was one of the gayest stations of the Navy. We arrived in the dawn, and the pink glow on the mighty fortifications of one of the world's most magnificent harbours was something not easily to be forgotten. Great grey warships lay in the Grand Harbour and dghaisas (sort of gondolas) swayed alongside waiting to ferry the ships' complements to and from the shore. Only when the gregale blew was it impossible for the dghaisas to withstand the turbulent waters. Then the warships, too, strained at their moorings, sky and sea were black, and there was no communication with the shore. The life of the ships was very close to us all in Malta. From our houses we could hear the orders shouted on deck, the clank of anchor cables, the charging of submarines, the bugle-calls, and every night at nine o'clock the sad notes of the Last Post.

We lived on Piéta Hill, up a steep, narrow alley known as Snob Street because various illustrious folk, far grander than ourselves, had taken the big Maltese mansions there. Our own villa was unpretentious and poorly furnished, with a glorious view across a narrow stony garden, blue with larkspur, to the bluer waters of Scaramanga Creek. The island is serrated with creeks forming innumerable excellent anchorages. Our house was typical Maltese, with stone floors, high bare rooms and a flat roof, where Peter often lay on a mattress in the bright autumn sunshine. Twice a day an odorous company of goats was driven past our front door, and every afternoon Nannie, who was soon queening it over the Nannies of the high and mighty, set sail with a flotilla of other prams for the daily baby airing. A gang of dark-skinned urchins awaited their return and were paid a copper apiece to push the prams up the hill again. Two handsome and amiable maidens, selected by my husband before our arrival, ministered to our creature comforts. Carrie cooked and her sister Angela, whose name suited her disposition, did everything else. These talented creatures spoke very fair English, and, no matter what Angela was asked to do, she replied with her enchanting smile: 'Very well.' A good-looking fellow, with a rose behind his ear, tended our garden twice a week and cast languishing glances at Angela. He was the only member of our household to whom she did not say 'Very well'.

'I do not wish to get married and make twelve babies,' she explained sensibly.

'But must you make babies if you get married?'

'Yes,' said Angela. 'The priest, he say we must.'

The Roman Catholic priests, Italian or Italian trained, were the virtual rulers of the island. Their round black hats, flowing robes and black umbrellas were the emblems of authority. In the churches rich treasure was stored, but the people remained poor and they multiplied exceedingly. The form of Roman Catholicism practised in Malta was mediaeval and primitively superstitious. In the churches there were always two clocks, one right and one wrong, so as to confuse the devil, who, taken in by this simple expedient, would never know at what hour to intrude his evil presence upon the performance of Mass; and when an islander thought himself to be dying he willingly impoverished his family in order to make sure of heaven by buying masses for his soul. All day long the church bells pealed, the angelus was the voice of Malta – the chimes of the carillon echoing in the clear air.

The city of Valetta, soaring above the harbour, had a queer half-Moorish beauty like that of the people. Women in shapeless black, wearing the faldetta like a giant cowl to keep the white sunlight off their faces, walked in the narrow streets that rose in stairways from the sea. More often than not they were jostled by dusty goats munching cigarette stumps and scraps of paper and wearing bust-bodices in conformity with the law. The honest goats, however, unaccustomed to their brassières, frequently wore these dangling uselessly and foolishly round their tails, just as Japanese ladies, striving after the fashions of the Occident, wear cotton stockings in loose folds about their ankles. Ever and anon the goatherd paused with his flock and called: 'Halib! Halib!' ('Milk! Milk!') A dark face would appear at an upper window and a tobacco tin or a bottle would be lowered over the sill on a string. The goatherd milked an animal into it, a coin was flung down and the fresh milk was drawn up again.

Carrozzin rattled gaily up and down Strada Reale and out under the old Porto Reale towards Florian. These were spidery conveyances with hoods and very narrow seats. The drivers liked, if possible, to have a squint-eyed boy sitting beside them to ward off the Evil Eye, but if the condition of the horses was any criterion, even the squint was not efficacious. The animals were, as a rule, emaciated and ill cared for, and English Service wives were in the habit of haranguing bored carrozzin men for neglect and cruelty. Everywhere in the world there are English-women scolding foreigners about horses.

There were dances in the ships and in the Governor's villa at San Antonio, and at night the scent of orange-blossom was sweet in our nostrils. Operatic companies came from Italy and grand opera was a feature of our social life. And, to go from the sublime to the ridiculous, there was the Malta Amateur Dramatic Club, which entertained us greatly. It was the M.A.D.C. which first produced a revue written by Anthony Kimmins, then a young lieutenant in the Fleet Air Arm, now playwright, producer and the B.B.C.'s finest naval feature broadcaster.

The island, only ninety miles in circumference, is arid and bare, but carefully terraced with innumerable little stone parapets. The soil, thus protected, had been imported in shiploads over a period of several hundred years. Under the ground are catacombs, and these when the need arose, formed natural air-raid shelters for the population.

The language of the country is Maltese, which is Italian in structure but mostly Arab in vocabulary, but the official language of the courts was Italian and the majority of the periodicals on sale in Valetta were in that tongue. A strong pro-Italian party aimed to break away from the Crown and become absorbed in Mussolini's new Fascist order, contending that Malta, by virtue of her geographical position, was almost entirely dependent upon Italy for her trade. This party did everything in its power to foster the Duce's dream of Mare Nostrum. In opposition to it was the pro-British faction, which recognized that the economic life of the island depended upon the Fleet and the garrison. Between the two was the Malta-for-the-Maltese group. The British Governor was usually a General, and he governed with an Executive Council of ten and a Legislative Council of six.

To the British Malta is, and always has been, of paramount importance. But for Malta, Egypt must have fallen into Axis hands. Aircraft and submarines, operating from there, denied Rommel his supplies; moreover, Malta, the springboard to North Africa, was a vital base for the invasion of Sicily and Italy.

In 1927 Mussolini must have realized its importance, since even the porters who handled one's luggage in Rome grumbled: 'Malta should be ours!' It is the key to the Central Mediterranean, just as Crete is the key to the Eastern Mediterranean. But later, dazzled perhaps by the dark glory of his new African empire, he must have lost sight of it. In any case, our continued presence there was evidence of his most asinine folly.

When on June 10th, 1940, he entered the war against us, as we had known for months it was his intention to do at the most propitious moment, he failed to strike at the one vital hostile fortress in the very heart of his precious Mare Nostrum. His fifth column had been firmly established there for some fifteen years, and he must have known the dispositions of every ship and gun that could be used for her defence. He must have been aware also of her pitiful weakness in the air. Malta then was destitute of fighters – in fact, of any aircraft whatever – and months later all she had to depend upon were four Hurricanes and a few old Gladiators. She was naked against the might of his entire Air Force. We hardly dared hope that we might hold her. Only fifty-eight miles separated her from Sicily – eight hours in the old *Maltana*, but less than half an hour in a modern bomber. If Mussolini had been as bold as the Germans or as astute as the Japanese he would, within one hour of declaring war, have brought off on Malta a combination of Pearl Harbour and the attack on Crete. It was too easy. He did nothing. What madness paralysed him? Did he think the Navy, utterly unsupported from the air, could stop him? Was he simply what Roosevelt described as 'the jackal waiting for the pickings from the kill made by the bigger beast'? Was he drunk with the lure of Athens, waiting only for October 28th to cross the Albanian frontier into Greece? Or did the two dictators, hatching their foul plot on the Brenner, forget that in her last resort England's life-blood is of the oceans, and while she retains so much as one sea base in the world the long tentacles of her might will reach forth and avenge her defeats?

Or was he just a coward and a fool?

Whatever considerations held him back, the mistake was irreparable, and when at last the Germans made up the minds of the Italians that a merciless and concerted effort must be launched to obliterate the island altogether it was too late. The fighters were there! The mobile aerodromes were in operation, and as one was put out of action the brave machines flew from another in defence of unbowed Malta.

Malta has endured greatly, and the humblest of her people are as worthy of that well-earned George Cross as is the dauntless island herself. And perhaps in her hour of suffering and heroism stupid barriers that once existed between the British and the Maltese have been broken down forever. When we were there no Maltese were allowed to become members of the Union Club in Valetta, or even the Marsa Sports Club. The Maltese aristocracy had their own club, the Casino Maltese, and once a year each institution entertained the members of the other. We Service wives and relations drank our morning coffee or our evening cocktail in the 'Snake Pit' (the Ladies' Lounge) and listened to the silly scandals that hissed venomously round the little tables. We seldom, if ever, came in contact with the fine old families who belonged to the island – a regrettable state of affairs which, I believe, began to improve before the war and is now, no doubt, a thing of the past.

The Commander-in-Chief in 1926 was Admiral Sir Roger Keyes, a brave and distinguished naval officer and a fine polo player. Such was his enthusiasm for the game that anyone with any aspirations talked, thought and bought horses, while the hoi-polloi, who could not afford such extravagance, cocked snooks and said, with a touch of sour grapes behind the libel: 'Ha! More polo promotions coming up!'

At that time in the Mediterranean polo was a joke, the climax of which was reached when an officer joined the flagship carrying a polo stick in one hand and a copy of Debrett in the other. Even the naval wives tried to emulate Lady Keyes and her three daughters, who formed a family polo team known as 'the bunch of keys'. But though polo in Malta may have been taken to extremes, there must be some special virtue in its practice, since famous sailors like Beatty, Keyes, Mountbatten and Warburton-Lee of Narvik were among its chief exponents – to say nothing of Winston Churchill.

Sir Roger Keyes was an officer who shared many qualities with Nelson. He was a fighting man, intrepid, highly emotional, and in feature he resembled portraits of England's First Sailor. Nelson frequently wept when he was moved; so did Sir Roger. In fact, it was an agony for him to speak on any subject close to his heart. The Navy knew and accepted this, as men who live much together recognize and allow for one another's eccentricities. When the Commander-in-Chief stood on the quarter deck with his ship's company gathered round to hear him address them and he remained completely mute, afraid to speak lest his voice break and his feelings master him, and then gave up without uttering a word, they understood. That was what happened when Roger Keyes felt strongly. That was all right. But to civilians it was often disconcerting. Once, as an Admiral of the Fleet, Sir Roger was asked to represent the Royal Navy at the Academy banquet. When the time came for him to speak on behalf of the Navy, he rose, said a few halting words and then, overcome with emotion, he stood helplessly tongue-tied.

'That's one speech quickly over,' murmured someone to another naval officer.

'You wait! He'll quite likely pull himself together.'

'I doubt it.'

So did Admiral Keyes. He was about to sit down, defeated, when he heard an audible undertone referring to 'the Nelson profile'. That did it. The Admiral braced himself against the Nelson temperament and words poured forth.

We neither played polo nor could we afford to keep horses, so while the white dust flew on the Marsa and hooves drummed we played tennis on the burning concrete courts.

My husband was often partnered in men's doubles by a tall fair young man called 'Wash'. This was Lieutenant-Commander Warburton-Lee, who was an all-round sportsman as useful on the tennis-court as on the polo-field. He and my husband, whenever they both happened to be in England, played together for the Navy side in the inter-Services matches at Wimbledon. 'Wash' was a fine equable player with bursts of brilliant smashing and serving. He won or lost with the same good humour, and when he was confronted with opponents of superior calibre he did not allow himself to be upset, but put up the best form he could show in the circumstances – just as he did in April, 1940, when a certain Admiralty signal relegated to him the sole responsibility for that hazardous operation in Narvik Fjord. He won the V.C. for the form he put up there. But the decoration was posthumous.

During that sunny and carefree winter we came to know two other naval officers who were destined to leave their mark upon the history of our time. One was Rear-Admiral Pound and the other was Captain Somerville. '(Sir Dudley Pound has been First Sea Lord throughout these strenuous war years, and Sir James Somerville has proved himself one of the finest fighting admirals of the war.)

Admiral Pound was then Chief of Staff to the Commander-in-Chief. He was lean, fit and fine-featured, a man of immense energy and vitality, whether he was working, shooting or dancing. When he asked me for a dance I knew that I needed to be as much on the top line as when playing a mixed doubles tennis match with Bertie at the Marsa! He was always first on the floor and last off it, and he usually danced double time and enjoyed every moment of it. His partners were left gasping and exhilarated under the amused glance of his shrewd, twinkling brown eyes. His wife was the most charitable and natural little lady in the world, and we all loved her. Many years later, when the war came, we recognized that her heart was as brave as it was kind. I saw her for the last time at Noel Coward's first night of the film 'In Which We Serve'. She knew, even then, that for her the sands were running out fast. 'But I'm going to see us win the war!' she said. But this was not to be.

Sir Dudley Pound was a determined and forthright character, and he and Winston Churchill have always understood one another admirably. Theirs has been a great partnership on the rocky road to victory.

James Somerville, then Captain of the *Barham*, was quicksilver. His bright green eyes always saw a move ahead of the game, his gift for brilliant and amusing repartee was famous, and naval officers repeated his latest retorts then as they repeat his signals now – with mirth and enjoyment. As for the wives – well, we always found it exciting to meet Captain Somerville or to sit next to him at dinner. He could make us laugh and think at the same time with that swift, stinging wit which had the effect of stimulating rather than intimidating others. His views on life were wide and his interests varied, and it was this universality of outlook which in due course endeared him to Jannie Smuts. As Commander-in-Chief of the Eastern Fleet in 1942–3, Sir James Somerville and the 'Oubaas' had many meetings and conferences. With him Smuts was never hampered by the knowledge that he was striving with a limited mentality and viewpoint. These two – the English admiral and the venerable South African statesman – were both men of flexible and far-reaching thought, and they liked and respected one another. It sometimes happens that a visionary like Smuts is able to extend the mind of his hearer temporarily beyond its normal capacity, but almost invariably it will spring back upon itself like elastic when the masterhand is withdrawn. Somerville's mind was not one to recoil; it could explore even further, outstripping the impulse which prompted it, and for that reason and many others he won the confidence of the 'Oubaas'.

The Mediterranean winter was cold and bright, but when spring came the bathing was wonderful and there were picnics to St. Paul's Bay and Delamara by day and by night. The island swarmed with pretty girls, known as 'the fishing fleet' – young friends and relatives of people on the station, who seldom returned to England unattached after a Malta season.

The ships went on various cruises and the wives who could afford to follow did so. I had struck up a friendship with Joy Borrett, the wife of another officer in my husband's ship, and we two Joys made some hilarious voyages. She was a pretty girl whose limpid green eyes saw life in terms of Greek tragedy or rich Shakespearean comedy.

'It's to be Gib for the spring cruise, and then Villefranche,' said Joy. 'We must follow!'

'I can't. No cash.'

'I've none either. We'll go on the cheap.'

It was her resourceful way to commit great extravagances with rare economy, and she afterwards forgot the extravagance and remembered only, and with pardonable pride, the thrift with which it had been conducted.

Nannie and Peter joined forces with another Nannie and baby who were being temporarily deserted, and Joy and I set sail for Gibraltar in a small German tramp carrying onions and a noble collection of livestock from the Hamburg Zoo. The odours were such as I have never known anywhere except in China, which stands alone when it comes to smells.

'I say,' said Joy, 'the lion-tamer gives me the creeps. He mesmerized me at lunch today. But I adore the lions!'

It seems my lot to be flung constantly into the company of carnivorae, but these were harmless-seeming creatures who allowed Joy to stroke them. There were a number of flying foxes too, who were very miserable, and a giraffe who died because Nature had never intended his neck design for ocean travel and mal de mer. The pelicans thrived and a skein of snakes, who did not bother to unravel themselves, slept the whole way to Gib, where we left them without regret.

Gibraltar was teeming with naval appendages, as the Atlantic and Mediterranean Fleets were both there for the spring manoeuvres. Several of my midshipmen friends from South Africa arrived in their ships, including 'Tiny', the boxer. That is the pleasant thing about the Navy. If the partings tear one to bits, there are always meetings, often unexpected and usually in new, exciting surroundings.

We went to Africa by boat and to Spain by car. We bought silk stockings and perfume duty free in the bazaars in the shadow of the Rock, and our windows in the hotel often rattled to the thunder of warships out firing. The *Royal Oak* court-martial was in progress, and we were embarrassed whenever we met pepperly little Admiral 'On-the Knee' Collard or Captain Dewar or Commander Daniel. Bandmasters at ships' dances were inclined to be sensitive, and admirals were self-conscious about addressing them.

'We must get to Villefranche somehow,' said Joy when the ship sailed.

'How?' I asked. 'Cash practically gone.'

'Steerage to Toulon and train third class from there.'

So we travelled on an Orient liner taking emigrants to Australia. There was an enormous Negro in the cabin opposite ours, and our other companions in the steerage were the toughest products of Limehouse and Liverpool. At meals we were left contemplating empty plates, as it was grab or do without, and we were poor grabbers.

'I'm worried about that black man,' said Joy, who could not resist dramatizing so striking and melancholy a figure. 'He spends half his time crooning in his cabin, and I don't think he's quite all there.'

'We might try and get a key to our cabin,' I suggested.

We asked the chief steward, a large and greasy individual with a tendency to be familiar, if we could have a key. He laughed uproariously.

'What do you want with a key? Ha ha ha! This ain't the first class. We got respectable people here!

Joy did the Negro an injustice. He was a well-behaved and courtly man, and every time I went past his open cabin door, while he crooned within, I caught a pungent whiff of Africa that took me straight back to Strehla.

On the deck we thought it best to display aloof dignity, especially during the after-lunch siesta hour, when the 'respectable people', carried away by the Mediterranean warmth and sun, paired off and spread rugs unnecessarily and significantly over their well-fed bodies and recumbent limbs, after which they apparently imagined themselves back on Hampstead Heath on a hot Sunday afternoon with the rest of the world stone blind. Between embraces they munched oranges and cracked peanuts and flung the skins into the scuppers, whence every hour or so a diligent sailor swept them overboard. Our aloof dignity, however, was unfortunately counteracted by my unhappy choice of a deck-chair. As we sat down, attempting to ignore the amorous proclivities of our fellow-passengers, the canvas gave way beneath me and I landed heavily on the deck with my feet in the air. Lovers ceased whisperings and caresses to fling back their heads and abandon themselves to an access of merriment. Even Joy, evidently regarding my mishap in the nature of Puckish comedy rather than Hellenic tragedy, joined discreetly but whole-heartedly in the general mirth and saw fit to quote Shakespeare:

'The wisest aunt, telling the saddest tale,
Sometimes for three-foot stool mistaketh me:
Then slip I from her bum, down topples she
And 'tailor' cries and falls into a cough:
And then the whole quire hold their hips and laugh:
And waxen in their mirth, and neeze, and swear
A merrier hour was never wasted there. . . .'

The steerage passengers were simple souls, easily amused, and they waxened in their mirth, and it seemed to me that they neezed also, but I, no doubt in common with the wisest aunt, found the jest a poor one.

At Toulon, which we were highly delighted to see, we observed French warships with the 'smalls' of French sailors flapping in the breeze as the housewife's knickers billow on the line in the grimy backyards of slums looking interminably upon railways tracks entering great cities.

We had decided to stay in Monte Carlo, the better to make a fortune at the tables. But we failed in our enterprise and returned to Malta by way of Syracuse, third class and no sleepers. We shared our compartment with two Italian Army officers, who wore hair-nets during the night.

CHAPTER SEVENTEEN

MR. CHURCHILL AT A DANCE. PLYMOUTH

THERE was a dance at Admiralty House in Valetta. It was in honour of Mr. Winston Churchill, who was staying in Malta as the guest of the Commander-in-Chief. He was then Chancellor of the Exchequer in Mr. Baldwin's Conservative Government, and he was on holiday in the Mediterranean.

Nannie pressed my best evening dress, a diaphanous affair that took much of her time.

'That was hard work,' she said, 'so mind you do me credit when you wear it tonight.'

I was excited at the prospect of seeing and probably shaking hands with Mr. Churchill. Two things I knew about him and held greatly to his credit. One, he understood the Navy; and, two, he understood the Boer. Anyone who has read his biography by Philip Guedalla will remember that his survey of the problems of national defence in 1901 is quoted, in which he said: '. . . the honour and security of the British Empire do not depend, and can never depend, upon the British Army. The Admiralty is the only office strong enough to ensure the British Empire. . . .'

Winston Churchill, a soldier by profession, has always loved the Navy and been loved by it. In 1940, when he relinquished the office of First Lord of the Admiralty to become the Prime Minister of the Nation, the Navy grieved at losing him. But he still found time to go on board warships, and the cigar under the yachting cap, the sturdy figure, feet planted firmly on the heaving deck, and the bulldog jaw out-thrust to face the weather, storm or shine, is an inspiration yet.

It is natural for an Englishman to love the Navy. Without it 'this precious stone set in the silver sea' would perish. But it is not at all usual for an Englishmen to understand the mentality of the Boer. Milner failed to do so, and Cecil John Rhodes, while comprehending, lacked patience with it. Churchill not only respected his country's enemy of the South African War, but went so far as to say so in Parliament. The Boer, he said, was 'a curious combination of the squire and the peasant, and under the rough coat of the farmer there are very often to be found the instincts of the squire'. It is a shrewd summing-up.

When Sir Roger Keyes introduced us to Mr. Churchill he made what, from his point of view as a host, turned out to be an unfortunate remark.

'Mrs. Packer comes from South Africa,' he said.

Winston stood beside the Commander-in-Chief with his hands behind his back and his powerful head aggressively forward. His eye brightened.

I don't dance much,' he said. 'But we might have some supper.' He spoke quickly with a slight lisp. As we made our way to the buffet he added: 'Are you keen on polo?'

My heart sank. I was no good at polo patter.

126

'I'm afraid not.'

'That's splendid. I've talked and seen quite enough polo these last two days.'

We found a corner in the palm court and presently we were engrossed in conversation about South Africa. One dance followed another and Winston took no notice. He was deep in the story of his Boer War adventures – his capture when he was covering the news as a war correspondent, and his escape from the prison camp in Pretoria wearing a Dutch clergyman's hat (he has always taken kindly to fancy costume), his experiences as a stowaway in freight trains and a coalmine, and his thrilling arrival in Durban, where he promptly joined the fighting forces as a lieutenant in the South African Light Horse. I listened enthralled. I had ceased to notice the lisp. The blue eyes of the Chancellor of the Exchequer twinkled and his narrative was rich with drama, comedy and excitement. Pictures of my own country took vivid form before my eyes; I saw the veld, the kopjes and the ragged Boer Commandos riding their gaunt half-starved horses, and my heart warmed to his appreciation of my countrymen.

'You had a wise man in Louis Botha,' he said. 'But you have a genius in Jannie Smuts.'

He asked me questions about Hertzog, who had just come into power, and the evening slipped away. It was a happy and a thrilling one for me, but Admiral Keyes was far from pleased. When we bade him goodnight he said sourly: 'I suppose you think you've had a succès fou.'

It has often struck me as odd that it is easy to talk to the mighty without shyness, whereas lesser lights can make one feel so 'out of it'. The truly great do not have to force the conversation on to their particular subject. The breadth of their experience and knowledge is too great for that. I expect Mr. Churchill talked polo with Lady Keyes, but he talked South Africa with me.

Next morning Nannie brought me my breakfast in bed.

'Well,' she said, 'did you enjoy yourself?'

'Tremendously!'

'Oho! Did Mr. Churchill dance with you?'

'No, but he sat out with me. He said my dress was lovely and that it must have taken hours to iron.'

Nannie beamed.

'Fancy that! What for an intelligent man he must be!'

Presently we found ourselves in Plymouth.

Sir Rudolph Bentinck was Commander-in-Chief, and we renewed our acquaintance with the abominable Riki. Lady Bentinck was ill, suffering from a poisoned arm which Riki had bitten. The meer-kat was not happy in England, although he had the run of a nice warm greenhouse, and more than ever he reminded me of Sredni Vashtar, whose thoughts were red and whose teeth were white. Fortunately, Lady Bentinck recovered from the creature's ravages and he was dispatched to a better world before he could do further harm. The jackal had been left in South Africa.

We took the usual rooms in the usual converted house that smelt perpetually of cabbage. We had no maid, and Nannie cooked for us, and we lived sumptuously on Teutonic dishes with names like coughs and sneezes – schnitzels, noodles and sauerkraut. Peter was crawling about by then, and it was no hardship to me to have an active hand in caring for my cheerful chortling little son. Occasionally we left him to his father for a few moments, but with unfortunate results.

'Please look after Piet while I get his bath and Nannie cooks our supper.'

'All right. Leave the sportsman here while I change.'

I came back to find Peter clinging, with blue knuckles, to an open drawer well above floor-level.

'Look at that! He skimmed up the tall-boy like a squirrel, and now he's hanging on to that drawer with the strength of a lion. A great lad!'

'And when he falls, what then?' I enquired coldly, prising my son's paws from the drawer and bearing him away.

Another time my husband brought the navigator of his ship back to supper. It was the same story. Nannie cooked, I prepared the child's bath, and 'the sportsman' was left in the sitting-room with the men while these operations were going on. When I fetched him I found him on hands and knees licking the navigator's shoes.

'How *can* you let him!' I cried furious.

'I say, I'm frightfully sorry. We didn't notice,' apologized the contrite navigator. 'We were discussing a new golf grip.'

My husband said, beaming at the child: 'He's a smart boy –

knows there's alcohol in boot polish. A pink gin, pilot?'

We were in Plymouth only for three months and we loved it. The little Clyno explored the moors, and those rolling expanses of lonely open country satisfied my craving for wide outlooks. We played golf at Thurlestone sometimes, where the sea beat upon tall cliffs and the gulls eddied above them like scraps of paper in a high wind. Our flat was on the Hoe and the view was out to sea.

My husband took this opportunity to write and pass the preliminary examinations for naval interpreter in French and German, and then obtained permission to go to Germany for three months to study for the German final.

We arranged to send Nannie and Peter to Shropshire to my mother-in-law and we made plans to go to Munich in the Clyno. We chose Munich because one of my father's relations had long ago married a German Army officer, and this officer, now an old gentleman rising seventy, wrote to us offering to instruct Bertie in the technical part of his work, while 'Cousin Olga', my erudite and cultured relative, promised to teach him grammar and conversation herself.

It was the summer of 1927. Old Hindenburg was still the President of the German Reich, though the name of Hitler was not unknown in Munich, where the Austrian Rat, gnawing under the floor-boards, had emerged for a moment on November 8th, 1923, to launch his unsuccessful anti-Marxist Ludendorf Putsch. He was brought to trial in April, 1924, and sentenced to five years' imprisonment, though his dupe, the old soldier Ludendorf, was exonerated. Hitler, however, spent only five months in gaol, a period of gestation resulting in 'Mein Kampf'.

CHAPTER EIGHTEEN

BAVARIAN SUMMER

WE crossed from Harwich to Hook of Holland one summer night, and at daybreak our little Clyno, bulging with luggage, was rattling over the cobbled roads of Holland.

We saw canals, vast legions of bicycles, lush meadows, apple-cheeked children in clogs, women in wide skirts with 'kappies' on their heads and market baskets over their arms, tall oaks casting their speckled shade on the pavé, and place-names such as Uitenhage and Doorn that had counterparts in my own country. Uitenhage, in Holland, was a clean leafy town on a fine canal, whereas in the Cape Province it was a rich farming district. Doorn, in Holland, was a forested place of exile, where the ex-Kaiser beguiled his interminable leisure chopping wood. In South Africa there was de Doorns, a little town in a fold in the gaunt Hex River mountains. Here, too, there were Dutch names on the shop fronts – Van Zyl, Zoutendyk, Van der Heever – and no doubt inside the gaily shuttered houses there were heavy carved kists such as Mother had in the study – chests, camphor-lined, in which the young Dutch girls were wont to collect their house linen against the day when they should find suitable husbands.

'Strange,' I said, 'to think that Grandpa Marais' ancestors set sail from this little country on such a long, hazardous voyage to a land they had never seen, probably never even heard of before! What headstrong, adventurous people they must have been, these emigrant colonists—'

He smiled. 'Accounts for a good deal. There's only one thing more obstinate than a Boer, and that's a mule.'

But it was not the distant historic association of Holland with my own people that took my heart home. It was the oaks, the familiar play and pattern of their shadow on white walls, their strength and height and air of permanence.

I was a schoolgirl again at my scarred desk. Doves in the branches outside, the shoulder of Devil's Peak framed in the window, the voices and laughter of the other girls at play in the sunshine while I sat there with my Cape history open in front of me – kept in because I had omitted to learn my homework. The names of the Dutch governors. There were only two I could ever remember – Van Riebeeck and Simon Van der Stel. Van Riebeeck because he was the first of them all, and – even more important – a mineral water was called after him, with which my father, the most abstemious of men, diluted his mild sundowner.

'Teena! A whisky and Van Riebeeck water for the doctor!'

Daddy, sinking into a chair on the side stoep. The evening

light very gold on my mother's brown hair as she sat beside him.

'Well, old chap, what have you been doing today?' That, oddly enough, was his query, not hers.

'I was at the House this afternoon. Hertzog was speaking. I can't follow the man when he talks that highfalutin Dutch of his.'

'Remember, Ellen, he was at university in Holland. He speaks more like a Dutchman than an Afrikaner.'

Teena galumphing through the French windows, bearing a little silver tray with a tiny one-tot decanter, a cut-glass tumbler and a narrow bottle of Van Riebeeck – the sun making prisms of all these.

Simon Van der Stel I could remember easily too, because Simonstown was called after him and so was Stellenbosch, the little Dutch town in the blue Drakenstein Mountains, where my grandfather, Long Piet, had been educated. There also Jannie Smuts and his wife Sybella had been collegiates. And Van der Stel had planted the Cape Colony with oaks – the cool, eternal oaks of Holland.

'You've gone into one of your dreams,' said my husband, slowing the Clyno down. 'Come back to earth and we'll stop on the bank of this canal and have a sandwich.'

We spent the night at Cologne, and all next day the lovely Rhineland was ours. Grey old schlosses brooding on wooden knolls, and, on the wide river, barges that had come hundreds of miles from other countries, islands here and there, and the Rock of the Lorelei. Bertie taught me the song:

'Ish weiss nicht was soll es bedeuten,
Das Ich so traurig bin . . .'

As a little boy he had once spent several months in a village on the Rhine with the family of his sisters' governess. (My mother-in-law had very definite ideas about the wisdom of teaching children foreign languages, and her own brood always had German or Swiss governesses.) As a child Bertie had his first swimming lessons in the Severn and his next in the Rhine. He went to school with the little German boys and quarrelled and played with them, and discovered that the way in which they were wont to insult one another was to call out: 'Ver-dammte Jude!' ('Damned Jew!)

Vineyards flowed down the slopes of the hills, cool summer

green with the sun on them, evoking a nostalgia that till yesterday had lain dormant.

Vineyards. Constantia – 'Les Marais' and 'Bel Ombre' – where my relations had their farms. There was Uncle Piet, from whose high stoep, banked with blue hydrangeas, you could look up the long valley of the grapes into the glittering cleft of Constantia Nek, forested with silver-trees.

I slipped my hand under that of my husband's on the wheel.

'When we have a house of our own I want it to be on the slopes – of a mountain, looking across a vineyard to the sea.'

His crooked smile revealed his insight into my thought.

'Constantia?'

I nodded.

A house of our own? It is still only a dream – a dream of blue hills and spreading vines and the far-off voice of the sea.

Next evening we were in the broad bright streets of Munich, a city of stately buildings, parks and gardens, where the cheerful earthy Bavarians drink their beer and eat their meals out of doors. The waitress flicks a cloth across the table – 'Helles oder dunkeles?' – and presently it is there, the foaming tankard of amber or dark brown Münchener beer on its little round cardboard platter.

We drove straight to the Pension Abbazzia in the Maximilliansplatz, where Cousin Olga had booked us a bed-sitting-room and bath. The Von Hagen family lived outside Munich, and we had written expressing a wish to stay in the city independently. But here was Cousin Olga to meet us.

I had last seen her seven years ago when, as a lanky fifteen-year-old, I had trailed round Europe with my parents and brothers. She and Renate, the younger of her two daughters, had met us in Switzerland on Lake Thün and stayed with us as Daddy's guests. Renate had been eleven then, a pale little undersized thing with immense blue eyes and amazingly light silken hair.

'Poor child!' Mother had said. 'Half-starved. That's what comes of wars.'

Cousin Olga, too, had been terribly thin, with the drawn aspect of one who has suffered greatly. For over four years she had been entirely cut off from her own people in South Africa, and the struggle to feed and clothe her two children, and to care for her little Prussian officer, broken by the defeat of his country, had not been an easy one.

Mother had remarked to Daddy: 'Olga is wonderful – as amusing and resilient as ever – but isn't it curious, Julie, how the German influence can stamp itself on a woman's appearance? She has a sort of learned dowdiness these days. She looks a real German matron, a frau, yet when she talks and laughs one forgets it. She has such charm!'

Mother loved Cousin Olga, although I believe she stood a little in awe of her academic brain, and when I used to try and show off with a pert remark she often said: 'Take a leaf out of Olga's book, my child, and remember that *really* clever people are smart enough to conceal their cleverness.'

Now, after the passage of years, Olga Von Hagen was almost unchanged. A little thinner, if possible, a few more lines on the kind, intellectual face, ashen hair rather whiter, but her voice was the same as ever, warm, emotional and very South African.

'Joy, child! How good it is to see you! ... Little Joy, grown up, married and a mother. ...'

A lump gathered in my throat. She was wearing one of Mother's discarded dresses. I knew it too well. Her tone held the same tender quality as my mother's, and she was putting out her arms to me. I had become unused to the spontaneous family affection that had once been an integral part of my life, and now it weakened me.

'What news can you give me of my Uncle Julie? And your sweet mother? You recognize this dress I dare say? I don't know what we should do without the clothes Ellen sends us. ... And this is Bertie?' She smiled and gave him her thin strong hands. 'I am so happy to meet you, my dear.'

She did not stay long, just long enough to see that we had all we needed, and then she said: 'You must be tired after your long journey. Tomorrow you will come to our cottage – it is only twenty minutes out of Munich in the electric train – and Bertie shall meet the General and Rēni. Erica will not be there. She is at Warsaw, where she has a post in the Embassy; but I have a hostage, her little boy Uli.'

I remembered Erica, whom I had met for a brief period once; sharp, domineering, a brilliant linguist, highly cultivated like her mother, but with her Prussian father's total lack of tact, and only recently divorced from her airman husband. As Cousin Olga spoke of her grandson Uli her eyes softened, and suddenly I knew that he was the most important thing in the world to her – more precious even than her two daughters Erica and Renate. As if she divined my thoughts, she said: 'We grandmothers are foolish about the grandchildren, perhaps; but it is understandable. When people are young, like Bertie and you, there is so much for you to do that there is very little time left over for your children, but as you grow older you have the leisure in which to enjoy them. But by then they are grown up and it is too late, so we give our quiet hearts to our grand-children instead.'

She kissed me and left us alone together. 'Bless you, child. I hope you will be happy here.' I found that I was crying. There was no need to explain to my husband that, like the oaks and the vineyards, she had brought another world too close.

Long before we reached the cottage with the honeysuckle creeper on the porch and the little wooden balcony, and the orchard where bees buzzed all day long and the boy Uli played, with swoops of his small hand and those zooming aeroplane noises that are the same in every child's language, we heard through an open window the Voice – rich, full, rippling in high, flexible coloratura.

Renate's voice was the very core of the Von Hagen family. In each member it evoked a profound emotion. To her sister Erica it was corrosive, a cause of friction and jealousy. To her mother it was a source of overwhelming pride and deep anxiety. A girl craving a career as a singer was a girl in moral peril. The life of the stage – ah, must it be that for this younger daughter of hers, a mere child of eighteen, with a small seductive figure, delicate limbs, milky skin and spun-gold hair? Rēni was too pretty. No director would let her get away with a decent contract without exacting his price. Yet the voice was there demanding recognition – magnificent in volume, range and quality – an asset hardly to be scorned by a family existing precariously on the depleted remains of Olga Von Hagen's capital, supplemented by the General's meagre pension.

To the old General his daughter's voice was one thing only, a joy and a solace. Its implications meant nothing to him. Only to be allowed to hear it was the ultimate delight. And to its owner it was many things – a Pandora's casket, exquisite but dangerous. There was dear Leo, who loved her, handsome, impecunious, well-bred Leo. They had danced together throughout the carnival season; they had gone on skiing week-ends together, up into the snows of Garmisch and Partenkirschen, in the free and easy manner of the new generation; they had gone on walking tours in the wooded hills of Bavaria; they were happy when they were together and they were in love. But what was the good? There was the voice to consider. 'I must go on working till I get into grand opera,' she said, refusing for the hundredth time to become engaged to him. 'I must build up my career. Marriage and babies are not for me. I must go on alone, Leo – free to sing!'

Baron Burmeister loved her too. He was influential, unhappily married, a thin-lipped weasel with a cruel smile that dragged the corners of his mouth downwards. Rēni laughed with him, flirted a little, enchanted and tantalized him, dangling him as a possible minister to the exactions of the voice which must one day soar across the footlights into the heart of the multitude.

She sang to us that first morning 'Softly Awakes My Heart', and we listened to her competent rendering of Delilah's love-song – the song of seduction – and we marvelled at the power and purity of the beautiful notes.

'But *her* heart isn't awake,' I said to Bertie. 'It's shut up in her music. It's quite numb. When Mother sings her ballads she makes one *feel* as well as enjoy and admire. Rēni doesn't do that.'

'Not yet. She is too young for tenderness. It may come.'

It did come. What emotion thawed the ice-bound heart I do not know. But two years later we tuned our wireless in to Munich, and there it was, true as a bell, but with a new sweetness and sympathy – the Voice. We stared at one another. 'Rēni!' Soon afterwards we heard that she was playing the lead in 'Cavalleria Rusticana' in the Munich Opera House.

CHAPTER NINETEEN

PAGAN YOUTH. BIRTH OF THE LUFTWAFFE

EVERY day we came to the cottage, and I sat in the garden by myself or played with Uli or talked to Rēni when she wasn't practising, while from the little wooden balcony I heard the drone of Cousin Olga's voice reading dictation or explaining the complexities of German grammar, or the sharp authoritative bark of the little General. 'How can I correct your essays if you refuse to dot your i's and cross your t's? *You* may not consider it necessary, BUT *I say it is!*' (ABER *Ich* sage es ist!')

AHBERR! How he rolled out the word, making of the hesitant 'but' a challenge and an ultimatum.

General Von Hagen was a Prussian to his irritable finger-tips, a choleric little dictator in his own home, humourless, musical, overbearing and blind to any point of view other than his own. He spoke no English, so, to be sure that we should understand him, he bellowed at us at meals and thumped on the table. When he spoke of the British he became highly irate, but when the French were mentioned he appeared liable to have a stroke.

'Don't let Erich get on to the subject of France,' implored Cousin Olga. 'It's bad for his health.'

We found it impossible to like the little man, but we were often sorry for him. He made me think of the jackal in Admiralty House garden, ranging up and down its wire run, wretched and bewildered – a creature born to hunt after its own fashion, used to the roar of the lion and the snarl of the beast at the kill, used to the stealthy prowl in search of food and the soft-footed path to the water-hole, suddenly confined in a space where neither scent nor sound gratifies the hungry cravings of instinct.

Von Hagen belonged to a lost caste in a lost world, and he had in his pale near-sighted eyes a haunted look of spiritual bereavement, as if he sought continually for some sign of van-ished but remembered glories. Only when he sat in the little music-room and listened to the songs of his daughter Renate did his nerves release him. His restless hand conducted automatically, but his features relaxed and were at peace.

Once he had moved in the pomp and glitter of Court functions with Olga regally at his side. He had been a member of the ruling Class – the military caste. In his day there/had been no more glorious calling than that of an officer in the Kaiser's Army. The military were the top – higher than the Navy, the Diplomatic, the Church or the politicians. Their allegiance to the Kaiser was personal and absolute. From the time of Frederick the Great onwards this sense of personal loyalty had been the mainspring of the German Army. It was the root of its iron discipline, its rigid outlook and its overweening arrogance. Even the woman fortunate enough to arouse the affections of so magnificent a personage as a Prussian officer was required to meet a high standard of all-round excellence before she was permitted to become his wife. She must be of impeccable character and social standing and possessed of adequate worldly goods. And at the close of his career the successful military officer knew his proudest and most memorable moment. No officer of the rank of General or above was ever retired from the Kaiser's Army without the formality of an invitation to luncheon with his august master, when he was presented with an elegant vellum testimonial thanking him for his honourable, devoted and inestimable services to his Emperor and his country, and signed in the Kaiser's own handwriting with his personal signature. To Von Hagen, bitterer even than the defeat of his country, was the way in which it disposed of his services after the war. The Kaiser was an exile in Doorn, there was no luncheon with his Emperor, no handsome script on a vellum scroll to prize and treasure, no dignity, grace or talk of honour, only a badly typewritten chit on an unheaded scrap of paper informing him curtly that he was to consider himself as retired from a certain date. To him that untidy, ignoble slip was the symbol of the disintegration of all that he held dear. It was the death certificate of an era, of the military caste to which it had been his greatest pride to belong, and it was the birth certificate of a new order devoid of tradition or sensibility, a régime which he despised and did not wish to understand. It was the deadly wound.

Cousin Olga grieved for him. 'He was not always like this, so irascible and – difficult. You must remember, Joy, that it is not easy for us older ones to adapt ourselves to this country as it is now. Or for the youngsters either, perhaps. We are all so terribly poor – our sort – and there is no hope of regaining any form of prosperity. Our lives and their work – even this child's – are forfeit to the war debt.' She laid her thin hand on Uli's shaven head, and he looked up at her and laughed. Her face was gentle as she smiled back at him. She found in the presence of her grandson, unscarred as yet by what might lie in store for him, the sort of respite that her husband found in music.

Several times we went with the Von Hagens to the opera. There was nothing chic about it like the opera in Paris, Monte Carlo or even Valetta, but the singing was wonderful and the Opera House was always packed. The audience was miserably dressed and took its brötchens to eat between the acts, but it was a good audience. There was no coughing or fidgeting with programmes or lifted lorgnettes to spy out the latest scandal and the newest fashions. It was there for the music and it enjoyed itself.

I wondered then what dreams were flitting through Rēni's mind as she sat motionless beside her ugly father, lips parted, wide blue eyes aglow and a little pulse throbbing in her too white throat. The General, as usual, was relaxed for a space – almost happy. And Cousin Olga? Was she really seeing the stout prima donna behind the footlights, or was she looking beyond her at her own Renate, a nightingale among vultures?

'Leo,' said Rēni, fluttering her thick golden lashes at him. 'these British relations of mine are mad about tennis. I don't play, so I am helpless. You are so good at the game, perhaps you can arrange something for them?'

Leo clicked his heels. Here was a chance of pleasing and impressing his beloved. Did he not belong to the most exclusive club in Munich?

'I will arrange immediately that they shall become honorary members of the University Students' Tennis Club.'

'Aren't we rather old for that?' I inquired, oppressed by the awful maturity of my twenty-two years and the sear and yellow of Bertie's thirty-two.

Leo laughed. 'But no! The members are not only students, but ex-students and their friends. I assure you!'

Thus reassured, we followed handsome Leo into the secretary's office of the club.

The secretary, a dark young man with formal manners, bowed and shook hands with Bertie and, as was becoming a matron, kissed mine.

'Before you can become members, will you kindly sign this form?'

He passed us a form, and I saw my husband's eyebrows go up a fraction as he read it. We signed it, and in so doing untruthfully averred that we had anti-Semitisch tendenz (anti-Semitic tendencies). People are inclined to think of the persecution of the Jews as being a particular fetish of Hitler and his Nazis. Actually it is nothing of the sort, although he has succeeded in carrying it to the final conclusion of barbarism. The Jew has been hated in Germany for centuries because it was thought that he profited by the misfortunes of others. Be that as it may, Hitler's bestial inhumanity in torturing this afflicted race is without parallel – the ultimate degradation of both oppressed and oppressor.

'Now,' said Leo, 'we will have a game. I will find Frau Weissgar. She is the lady champion of our club.'

He deposited us on the edge of a court where two young men were playing singles, and left us, returning presently with a swarthy dame entirely innocent of aids to beauty. The singles players finished their set, shook hands with one another across the net and went their way. We took their place and played a hard-fought match, and when Leo and Frau Weissgar had beaten us conclusively we went through the hand-shaking and hand-kissing ceremony that follows every game, even if it should be only one short set.

Frau Weissgar wiped her dripping face and said, 'Jetzt bin Ich nass mit Schweiss' (Now I am wet with sweat'), an unsavoury truth which was only too self-evident.

We met a naval officer called Francke at the club, who was thrilled to discover that he and my husband had been in the South Seas at the outbreak of war. Francke had been in command of a corvette, and Bertie had been in the battle-cruiser *Australia*, patrolling near Rabaul.

'Just imagine!' said Francke. 'There we were, hiding in a little bay off the coast of New Guinea, and we sighted you one day just before dawn. You could have blown our little ship to smithereens with one broadside! I did not even dare to sound off "Actions Stations", but went round myself shaking up the men who were asleep in their hammocks. All orders had to be given in whispers. It was a near speak for us!'

He insisted upon entertaining us to dinner. He and his wife had a tiny flat and she cooked the meal herself. They were, like all their class, very poor. The two naval men talked till near midnight of their war experiences, and the inevitable subject of Jutland came up – the Skagerak Schlacht as it is called by the Germans – but each, mellowed no doubt by a delicious Rhine wine, conceded that the other had done well at that Armageddon of the seas.

In a picture shop near our favourite restaurant there was, curiously enough, a huge canvas in oils of the Skagerak Schlacht. Great ships heeling on sunset waters, flaming wreckage, bursts of fire and a fine sense of majesty and awe. Bertie could never bear to drag himself past it. 'It's amazing – it was just like that!' We wanted to buy it, but the price was far beyond our means. When my husband asked Lieutenant Francke if he had seen this picture, he said: 'Ah, yes! It is so good, so alive and realistic. But then the artist was a naval officer. He was there.'

'I wondered,' said Bertie. 'You see, I recognized my ship in the foreground – the *Warspite*.'

Bertie often played singles with Leo or one of his friends as early as seven o'clock in the morning. These young men all worked very hard for long arduous hours. They were always in their offices by 8 a.m. Yet economically they stood to gain very little. There were at that time no prospects in Germany for the young German.

That, of course, was why Hitler concentrated his efforts upon the youth of the country. It was fertile soil, a vigorous post-war generation working out the punishment for the crimes of its pre-war fathers. It was a great force of latent energy awaiting his direction. As Frederick the Great had established a personal relationship between himself and his Imperial Army, so Hitler grappled German Jugend to himself for his purpose. He offered it the future as Satan on the mountain-top offered Christ the world. He infused the physical culture and athletic societies, already in being all over the country, with the spirit of regeneration, dedicating them to Greater Germany, He lashed the youth of the land into a fanaticism as great as his own, using theatrical and half-mystic means to amplify his power. Torchlight parades in the ancient city of Nuremberg, banners, music, dramatic effects of searchlights in a dark sky, till his audience was part of his black magic, absorbed into himself. Young men and girls ceased to be Leo and Renate and became instead mere particles of a body heading for disaster. They lost their identity in this swollen Frankenstein of mass youth animated by the mad Austrian corporal, and, as they assumed the dreadful mute obedience of a robot monster, they lost also their souls.

Hitler never concerned himself with General Von Hagen's class and generation unless, like Ludendorf or Hindenburg, they possessed famous names, honoured and respected as his own was not, and then he ingratiated himself that he might use the name to increase confidence in himself. But, for the most part, old Erich Von Hagen and his like wandered on blindly in the fog that had gathered about them after the defeat of their country. Only now the fog was thicker. It swirled about the ankles of their children. Strange forms were looming up and taking shape, and somewhere in the dark there was the muffled beat of war-drums, and somewhere else, as yet far distant, there swelled the low moaning of women whose men were doomed to die on the field of battle far from home.

In 1927, however, the post-war youth of Germany was still young and individual. It was mobilized into its athletic groups, but these were not then political; and, bereft of more expensive recreations, it had reverted to a mild form of paganism. The health-through-joy movement had developed, and on the shores of the Starnberger Sea young men and maidens frolicked like nymphs and fauns, naked as the day they were born.

'But surely it's all wrong,' I said to Rēni. 'Bit animalish, don't you think?' I was looking through the pages of one of the lavishly illustrated Nacht Kultur magazines on sale at every bookstall in the country. The photographs of nude men and girls ski-ing in the mountains of Partenkirschen or dancing in sylvan glades had a certain lively grace and artistry, but they were also aggressively crude.

She shook her head. 'Frankly, I see no harm in it. The English look at such things differently. They try to ignore their bodies. We accept them just as they are. We don't use make-up like you do, or any other artificial aids to nature. We are as we are, and our men prefer us that way.'

'That's just it. Your men like you that way. So is it wise to go jumping round with them without wearing so much as a fig-leaf – like these lads and lasses?' I flicked over the leaves of the pamphlet.

Her wide blue eyes kindled. 'Of course it's all right! By bringing our bodies into the sun and air we are being simple and clean. You wouldn't understand. British hypocrisy makes everything that is natural seem shameful. We understand comradeship and innocence.'

Some of you, I thought, but not all. Good-looking Leo might be a faun leaping in the sun, but what about your tight-lipped friend Burmeister? A satyr if ever there was one!

'Perhaps you are right,' I said. 'But it seems to me that the whole pagan creed is built upon sex. Look at the old Greek gods. They were terrific chaps for having their bit of fun, and carried on with all and sundry, regardless. The only way a goddess or a nymph could evade her lusty pursuer was by transforming herself into something as frail and inaccessible as a flower. Transformation into an animal was useless. If she turned herself into a hind or a heifer, the mischievous god promptly assumed the appearance and potentialities of a stag or a bull.'

'Nacht Kultur is not paganism,' said Rēni, 'and we are not Greeks, but Germans.'

One week-end we drove into the Austrian Tyrol and back to Munich by way of the little hamlet of Oberammergau, where once in every five years the Passion Play is performed. St. John the Baptist was working in his smithy, Joseph was at his cobbler's bench, hammering outworn shoe leather, and the Virgin was suckling a new baby. They gave us the Bavarian greeting, 'Grüss Gott', and their swarthy peasants' faces were kind and cheerful. All round the pretty pink village the grasses and wild flowers bloomed on the slopes of the mountain. We picknicked in a fragrant meadow, the air was crisp and brilliant, and the nodding heads of a myriad flowers and the darting wings of butterflies were indistinguishable from one another. I gathered a nosegay.

'All different! Hundreds of lovely little wild flowers, and no two alike.' I held them up to Bertie.

'Alpen blumen. They're beautiful.'

'It's queer,' I said. 'I thought Oberammergau with all its associations would be bound to increase my sense of religion, but now I'm here I feel just the opposite. Up in these heights there seems to be a lot to be said for paganism.'

He drew on his pipe for a while and then he said: 'There was an old sea captain once, the master of a tramp, who had trundled round the ocean most of his life. One day someone asked him if he ever doubted the existence of God. He answered: "Of course not. Sailors have time to think." '

I looked down at my bunch of delicate little Alpine flowers – so many and various, yet each with its own distinctive beauty – and I answered my husband with another story.

'There was a man who said that he didn't believe in God. His friend said: "Go into your garden and look at a flower." '

It is not very difficult to see why Hitler, the Austrian, chose Bavaria as his headquarters. Both geographically and historically it was the ideal place to ferment an underground movement.

Firstly, it was on the Austrian border. Secondly, it was in thought and behaviour curiously apart from the rest of Germany. It was Napoleon who first made it a kingdom, and until 1813 Bavaria supported him, though after that she was compelled to join the other German States against France. Even after 1870, when she became an integral part of the new German Empire, she retained her own kings – the mad Wittelsbachs, who gave Austria and old Franz Joseph the beautiful Empress Elizabeth, and Hollywood (so goes the story) Elissa Landi. In Bavaria Hitler felt himself to be outside both the Prussian and the French grip. From there he could conduct his war against Communism (which was spreading rapidly in Germany), and he could also combat the activities of the French, who saw in the partition of Germany their only hope of future security. They had already started the Spartacist (Separatist) Movement in the Rhineland, the Ruhr and the Saar, and they aimed also at a restoration of the monarchy in Bavaria. Hitler made it his business to be the deliberate counter to these intentions. The Communists might attempt to control Germany and the French to divide it, but he would do the opposite. He would weld it into Greater Germany – with what results the tortured world is only too well aware.

It was while we were in Munich that we were given the opportunity of seeing the first shaping of the weapon with which, in the fullness of time, he put his horrible plans for Europe into effect and laid waste our own English cities – the Luftwaffe.

There was no Luftwaffe in 1927. But there was the Luft Hansa, and the director of this far-reaching enterprise happened to be no less a person than Renate's admirer, Baron Burmeister.

Burmeister invited the Von Hagens and ourselves to lunch with him at the airport. He did it chiefly to impress Rēni. He was no fool, and he knew very well that a successful man is at his most imposing in his place of business. In his home a word or a look from his wife can, at one blow, deflate his ego and reduce him to nothing; but in his place of business he is the master. A woman who sees him thus, in command of his ship, so to speak, glimpses great realms of power and activity where she is negligible and he is king. She is impressed.

The Baron's ego had it all its own way that day. He was the head of a faultless organization far in advance of anything we had ever seen before.

The world in general was not air-minded in those days, and we were startled and aghast when Burmeister showed us a map of Europe with hundreds of lines raying out from Munich in every conceivable direction. On the landing-ground the liners came and went with the regularity of trains, and as soon as a machine arrived from a long distance it was immediately flown over to the workshops at Weilheim for overhaul in readiness for the next trip. There was never a hitch. The wheels were perfectly oiled.

I could see the effect upon Renate, the little pulse fluttering in her throat, the excitement in her eyes. Here was a man with authority. He might help the Voice on that steep path to success. He was fully aware of her reaction and he played up to it.

'We operate all over the Continent,' he said, 'as far north as the Arctic Circle and as far south as the Mediterranean. We have not yet got a line through to Turkey – the Turks will not allow a foreigner to fly over their territory. But you wait! When the time is ripe we will be the ones to open up an air service to Istanbul.' (Prophetic words. The first foreign air service permitted to operate to Istanbul was in 1938 – eleven years later – and it was the Luft Hansa which received the concession.) 'We have thousands of first-class pilots,' continued the Baron.'They never fly the same trip for long. By changing them constantly they learn to know every route. They need some knowledge of languages too. In fact, we demand a high standard of efficiency from them.'

He introduced us to several pilots, lean, hardy young men kept in fine physical condition by their athletic clubs.

'You realize, of course, that the whole of this enterprise is purely commercial,' said Burmeister, with his narrow smile and what appeared to us rather unnecessary insistence. 'Our country is not allowed to train or possess an army, a navy or an air force. She is crippled by the army of occupation and the war debt, and she exists only to be exploited by foreigners who come here to take advantage of the currency. . . .' His voice was acid, but now a new note crept into it, one of defiance, almost of warning. 'This Luft Hansa – this commercial enterprise – is our one great effort to keep alive! Our circumstances may be lamentable, but we still have our value, we can still give the lead in something. We are giving Europe the means for eliminating time and space; when it comes to modern travel the sky is ours, and we are proving that we can keep abreast – perhaps even ahead – of the times, in spite of everything that has been done to push us out of the picture!'

Yes, the Luft Hansa was a remarkable achievement in the circumstances, and my husband did not fail to observe that most of the machines appeared easily convertible into bombers, fighters or troop-carriers.

'Would you like to go up?' asked Burmeister. 'You could fly over to Weilheim and I will arrange for a car to meet you there and take you home.'

Renate and I were thrilled. It would be our first flight. Cousin Olga looked a trifle pale, and the General obviously did not fancy the notion of taking the air at his age – ABHERR he mastered his nervousness with iron determination and a timely visit to the Herren.

'I hope you don't mind taking out life insurances,' said the

Baron, getting these out of a slot machine. 'A mere formality, but compulsory.'

We climbed into the plane that had just come from Warsaw. As we took off I felt my heart pounding, and the tremendous roar of the engine seemed to be right inside me, part of me. But, once in the air, all sensation of speed disappeared and one had the impression of labouring slowly through space with great effort.

We said good-bye to the Von Hagens one evening in late August. The summer was almost over and so was our German interlude.

Cousin Olga held me tightly. 'Good-bye, child. God grant we meet again before too long.'

'If it weren't for seeing Peter soon I'd be sorry to go,' I said.

It had been an interesting and a happy time, and the people had been kind to us. Even the tennis club, poor as it was, had presented us with a plated salver on our departure. I think it was intended as consolation prize for my husband, who had played a five-set exhibition match against Dr. Reuter, the club champion, who beat him seventeen-fifteen in the fifth set on a grilling hot day. They had inscribed it to 'unsere lieben Gästen . . .' ('to our dear guests . . .').

We left Munich in 'Tommy' Clyno very early in the morning, in the greyness that precedes the dawn. The trees were tall ghosts fringing the auto-strada; the sky was blanched; the last stars still flickered.

'I have never seen a star go out,' I said.

There is mystery in that hour before daybreak, vast loneliness and a sense of stealing a march on the rest of humanity asleep in its bed. I looked up at the high empty heavens. A flight of birds, V-shaped, winged into view. Birds? No, these were too big for birds, too solid and steady in their unwavering formation.

'Planes!' I cried. 'Where can they be going to so early in the morning?'

My husband stopped the car and followed my gaze in silence. At last he said slowly: 'The Luft Hansa! Commercial machines practising formation flying at this hour, before anyone is awake . . .'

And so, while the world slept, we saw in the dawn sky the birth of the Luftwaffe.

146

What has happened to Cousin Olga or the old General or Renate and her Leo or even the child Uli we have no means of knowing. We never saw them again. But sometimes when playing with my wireless, tuning in to one station or another, I hold the needle steady on Germany for an instant, caught by an echo of that Bavarian summer – a flexible thrilling phase of song – the Voice.

CHAPTER TWENTY

END OF A PARTNERSHIP

WHILE we were in Germany Hillie Longstaff had taken the Clock Tower for us in Southsea, where we were to be stationed for the next few months.

It was an enchanting and incredibly noisy place – an oc-tagonal flat with a large bright attic in the squat little tower above an automobile showroom. Mullioned casements opened over the constant flow of traffic that swirled round the foot of our fastness.

The Clock Tower is still there, but the clock no longer goes, and the squat little tower is islanded in a silent sea of devas-tation, the work of the Luftwaffe.

Peter, nose flattened against the window-pane, gazed down at the scene of perpetual motion on the street corner below and uttered his first word. 'Car!' he said, and pointed a stubby finger to show that he knew what he was talking about. Tipsily he learned to walk, fell heavily in a sitting position and made his second contribution to the conversation: 'Bum!' His third word was more personal. It was the refrain of the nursery – 'Nan-na-nan'. Nannie spoilt Peter outrageously, and when she most wished to be angry with him she failed ignominiously because he made her laugh.

'You didn't spoil me like that,' I complained.

'You were naughtier than our child.'

That may well have been the case, but it was not the reason. The truth was that she regarded 'our child' as a grandchild and

147

indulged him accordingly. He was appreciative, and as his vocabulary increased he paid her his first compliment. 'Nice BIG Nannie', he said with such evident pleasure and simple sincerity that her heart melted in her breast and she clasped him to her and murmured: 'Engelchen! Meine kleine liebling!'

One day I climbed the short staircase to the bright attic nursery with a heavy heart. Nannie was knitting contentedly in the low cane chair, and Peter was in his play-pen, absorbed in building a train with his bricks. He was sturdy and his cheeks were pink. Nannie looked up and smiled.

'Well, aren't you going to play tennis this afternoon? I thought I heard Peter's daddy come in. Or is he coming up here to call on his son?'

'Nan,' I said, 'you were right. He has come in. But he has news for us. Nan . . . it's to be Malta again. . . .'

She drew a quick breath and knitted a little faster.

'Just when Peter's doing so well on cow's milk,' she said, baulking the main issue.

A pause. Then: 'I daren't ask you to come with us. Your hubby . . .'

She turned her head away and the needles stopped clicking. Presently she said in a muffled voice: 'How can I leave him to somebody else – who wouldn't understand him, perhaps? He's naughty sometimes, but he doesn't mean it. It's only his iron will. At heart he is so loving. . . .'

I realized that she was not alluding to her neglected spouse, a quiet and reserved man of outstanding worth. 'I'll come with you for the first year,' she had said at Tees Lodge, and here we were well on in the second. I left her sitting on the low nursery chair with tears glistening on her sandy eyelashes and a half-knitted jersey lying unheeded on her lap. She had a sore problem to solve. Next day she was pale but determined.

'I'm coming with you – for six months, anyway. Neither of you is fit to be left on your own, and I will write and ask my hubby to postpone his trip to England from Christmas to next June. It will be nicer for him to have the summer in Europe,' she added defiantly.

Nannie's 'hubby' was employed by an English shipping company, which granted its employees a free return trip to England once in every so many years, and the time was now ripe for him to take his leave. It had been their plan that he should meet her in England, and they would then visit his people in Liverpool and Wales and hers in Dresden.

So before very long we were back in Guarda Mangia with the white glare and the goats, and Angela and Carrie laughing and exclaiming: 'Peterr! How she has grown! What a big boy he is!'

This time, however, things went less well for us. The 'big boy' missed his cow's milk, the colour gradually drained from his cheeks and he grew sallow and peaky. A round little Maltese doctor came often to our house and shook his head and talked about chronic colitis. At length we cabled my parents suggesting that when the Fleet went on the long summer cruise I should take Peter home. They cabled back offering to pay half our fare. Nannie's 'hubby', that long-suffering and adaptable soul, arranged to meet his errant wife at Tilbury early in July.

'I will see you safely on board the ship for South Africa,' Nannie promised me, 'and then you will have your son to yourself for a change.'

Bertie's tin cases had gone to his ship already, and the villa on Piéta Hill had the stripped and dismal look of a house just about to be abandoned. Bertie was to sail that afternoon, and Nannie, Peter and I were to leave the following day.

'Good-bye, Sportsman!' Peter's father swung his son into his arms. 'What do the big guns say?'

'Boooom!' answered Peter fervently.

'And the little guns?'

'Bang!'

Years were to pass before these two would meet again.

I stood on the Barracca and watched my husband's ship weigh anchor in the Grand Harbour, then ran along the great rampart to the end of the Mole, where I knew he would pass so close that I would see him quite distinctly standing up for'ard. The sailors were lined up on deck as the huge warship got under way, a tug hooted, a destroyer barked like an angry dog, and then she was steaming out past the breakwater, with the bow-wave hissing and the band playing. We could have spoken, so near did the tall ship pass. I waved a white handkerchief till the churn of her wake was quiet by the Mole and she was only a shape on the horizon and a high tripod mast.

Nannie and I had a day to wait in Paris on our way back to England, so we decided to take a charabanc tour. It was very hot, we had come a long way, we were far from immaculate and must have looked rather odd. I wore a crumpled cotton frock and no hat, Nannie had on a printed creation and a curious Panama hat perched on top of her head, and Peter was armed with a toy dog of about his own size, from which, with guttural growls, he refused to be parted. The other passengers looked askance at us and we cast them ingratiating grins.

We took our places in the middle row. Peter and the dog sat on Nannie's capacious lap and I was squeezed up against a stout American matron whose headgear was as peculiar as Nannie's own.

'Car go!' demanded Our Child loudly and imperiously.

'It will go, darling. In a minute.'

'Car go *now*!' said the boy more urgently.

Nannie's face grew red. Fortunately, the charabanc, now filled to capacity, went. It went to Notre Dame, where it stopped and a man with a megaphone leapt to his feet and gave us a brief résumé of the cathedral's history. But not enough for Peter's liking. 'Car go!' he cried in exasperation. The American matron said 'Hush!' Our Child's face began to pucker and he let out a loud yell of rage, one of these deep stomach screams with which very small children are apt to assert themselves. The passengers looked at us and clucked, the man with the megaphone sat down, scowling, and our vehicle resumed its journey. Peter's suffused face cleared and he prepared to enjoy himself. The American matron, spurred on by her educational urge, said severely: 'You must keep that boy quiet. When I go on a sightseeing tour I like to know what I'm looking at. Thanks to this child, I could not hear one word the guide said at the Notre Dam.'

'He'll be asleep in a minute,' I assured her wildly. And indeed it seemed possible, for his cheeks had already expanded, inflated by the approach of slumber. But once more the charabanc paused and he of the megaphone rose and shouted his parrot-like discourse through the horn. Peter's eyes snapped open as if on springs, and he lifted up his voice and repeated the now familiar war-cry 'Car go!' on a rising note of fury. With one accord our fellow-passengers turned upon us balefully. Nannie, blushing hotly, said in desperation, 'Here Joy, you take this dog!' and thrust it upon me. In her agitation she spoke in German, which did not endear us further to the company. Peter opened his mouth wide and gathered himself together for a mighty bellow, but no sound came forth. Nannie had placed a horny hand over his mouth and was holding it firmly there till he of the megaphone should have said his say. Peter's astonished eyes, above the large hand, blazed.

'Can he breathe?' I whispered anxiously.

'His nostrils are free,' she whispered back.

The American matron, with pardonable irritation, strove to ignore our antics and give her full attention to the guide. As we continued our journey peace was restored in our row. But not for long. With the perversity of human nature, Our Child, who had hitherto demanded only that the wheels keep rolling, now voiced a new and imperative need. 'Peter want to get out,' he announced, and made it clear to our neighbours why. The American matron came to the rescue. 'We stop for tea at the Eiffel Tower. We are very nearly there. Can he wait?' We said he could and hoped that we were right.

'Well,' said Nannie, when we got back to our hotel, 'what for an afternoon! Our Child certainly gave us something to think about.' In retrospect we could laugh – we could hardly stop. That was the best of Nannie. Her sense of the ridiculous was irrepressible.

We arrived at Southampton early in the morning, dirty and exhausted. It was a silken summer's day as we went on board the ship by which Peter and I were to sail for Cape Town that afternoon. Hillie and Cuddie Longstaff had wired promising to come on board to lunch with me and to see us off.

Nannie said: 'I will stay and give Peter his dinner and then I will leave you with Commander and Mrs. Longstaff and catch the early afternoon train to London.' She was to meet her 'hubby' at Tilbury next day.

Her face was swollen and smudged with grief for suddenly at Le Havre she had been overcome by the imminence of parting, and from then on we had both been intermittently in despair.

A flat-footed old steward showed us to our cabin, and a woman with pasty cheeks, black hair and the mean eyes of a Borgia announced ungraciously that she was the stewardess.

'What for a horrible woman!' muttered Nannie audibly. She

began to unpack Peter's little garments and put them tidily away, giving me instructions the while with tears raining down her face. 'Never let him go without his Chilprufe binder, remember his poor tummy. . . . And keep on his vest, even in the tropics. . . . He can wear these linen smocks in the hot weather with his dark blue pants; that'll save you lot o' washing. . . .'

At noon we ordered some soup for Peter, and while Nannie fed him he touched her tear-stained face anxiously. 'No Nannie cry,' he said.

'I'll put him down for his sleep,' she gulped. 'Poor little man, he's that tired!'

It was the end of a precious and successful partnership. I don't know how she saw her way down the gangway. From the deck I saw her dimly stumbling along the quay, a stalwart, clumsy figure with her handkerchief to her eyes. I turned and went back to the cabin, where Our Child lay fast asleep.

Hillie and Cuddie brought a box of chocolates for me and a weird pink animal for Peter – a cross between a cat and a penguin, as significantly rounded as a Botticellian Venus.

'Put it where he will see it when he wakes up,' said Hillie.

And Cuddie said: 'We'll have champagne with our lunch. You look as if you need it!'

We were already passing the Needles when Peter awoke. His eyes fell upon the pink cat-penguin which smiled at him from the foot of his bunk.

'Amalun!' he said simply, and sat up and put out his hands for it. 'Nice amalun.'

Suddenly his face, flushed from sleep, grew pale.

'Where's Nannie?' he asked in his extremity, and was presently very seasick.

Where's Nannie? He could not believe that she was gone. I took him on deck next morning, a tiny figure in a scarlet sou'wester. The ship was tossing and the cold flavour of the wind was wet and briny. Showers of spray left dewdrops on his little red macintosh. A few people with pea-green faces lay about on long chairs, huddled in rugs and shawls, and several bolder folk walked unsteadily round and round the deck. Suddenly Peter caught sight of a pair of ankles disappearing round the corner – sturdy ankles in woollen stockings and a pair of wide, honest leather shoes.

'Nannie!' he cried joyously, and flung himself after them. He had clasped the substantial extremities before I could stop him. 'Nannie!'

Their owner turned and looked down curiously – a stranger's face with hard brown eyes. 'What's the matter, little boy?'

He stared back and wept aloud.

Table Mountain was in sight – azure and ethereal in the first rosy glow of the sunrise, and the flag flew from the mast on Signal's Hill to say our ship was in.

''Ullo, 'ullo, 'ullo, Joytje; welcome back!' Daddy's voice, and Peter being swung on to his grandfather's shoulder while Mother and I embraced. Now all my troubles were at an end. Now everything would be all right. Arend was waiting with the car at the end of the jetty.

'Welcome home, Miss Yoy. An' Master Peter! I doan' s'pose de klein ba'as ever seen a black person before. I t'ink perhaps he be scared.'

But he wasn't scared, and in that moment of meeting a life-long friendship was formed.

Mother said: 'Fred and Cecil are coming to lunch, and Norman will be there, of course.'

Fred was married and Cecil was my new sister-in-law. She was charming to look at, with the soft supple charm of a tortoise-shell Persian kitten. The friend of my schooldays, Marjorie Morris, had married Noel Gilfillan and gone to live in Johannesburg, and there was no longer the same pleasure for me in the tall house at the corner of Orange Street, where once we had exchanged so many confidences and voiced so many aspirations. One of the big Marais uncles had died and a Petersen aunt. There are always changes on homecoming, the faces and figures that come and go, but the essential pattern is always the same, and it is the pattern of the land itself – the shape of the mountains; the veiled blue of the hills; the long lines of surf and the perennial bearing of the vines; the feel of sun-warmed sand under bare feet; the scent of mimosa; the drifting mauve of jacarandas; the gathering roar of the South-Easter and the soft cooing of doves. And at the core of it all is the gabled house under the mountain, the carnations on the polished mahogany table, the serene presence of my mother, and the wide, kind smiles of the brown folk who serve her so faithfully.

Peter was everybody's grandchild in Tees Lodge. He was 'Klein Ba'as' to Arend, 'Sweetheart' to Cookie and 'My Love' to Teena, who was told off to look after him. As a nurse she was a farce, but as a loving and trusty caretaker she was incomparable. She galumphed everywhere in the wake of the masterful child and did his bidding and indulged his whims, with her enormous smile ever upon him like a benediction. To all of them he was Our Child, and imperceptibly his name changed from the English Peter to the South African Piet.

When the time drew near for me to return to Malta, Daddy said: 'Joy, old chap, your little boy is doing very well here. Is it right to drag him back across the world with you? We are gradually getting him strong again, and if you take him away now all our good work may be undone. Think it over well. Mother and I would love to keep him.'

It was my first experience of this particular decision that is a heart-tearing part of the lives of all Service people. Shall I take the child? Shall I leave him? Often circumstances compel the wife to make the decision alone without the help and counsel of her husband. In any case, it is a special anguish at which the woman with the settled home can only guess. Sleepless nights, heart and brain fighting one another in the small hours when trifling problems loom immense and great problems gnaw into the most Spartan vitals. What is best for the child? Will he miss me? Oh, he will, he *will*! But can he do without me? Yes, he can; there will be others to love him. . . . *Can I do without him?* . . . The sodden crumpled handkerchief, the tear-stained pillow, the exhausted doze at last with its painful dreams, and then the morning – the lovely spring morning heavy with this unsolved trouble, and every look and smile and word of the child a sword. But at last the decision is taken and the heart that was all turmoil and feeling is empty. The harrow has passed over it. After that there must be no looking back.

So the cold little cable was sent. 'Peter doing well suggest leaving him tees lodge will join you as arranged love joy.' And there came the brief reply: 'Quite agree wisest leave peter if dad advises it longing see you love bertie.'

There was a farewell visit to the senior aunt, and a remark to my mother that hit at me like a blow.

'Well Ellen, I can't congratulate you for encouraging Joy to shelve the responsibility of her child.'

154

And in a flash Mother was on her high – her very high – horse. Her pearls quivered a little on her throat, which had grown suddenly pink, and her grey eyes were dangerous.

'How can you in your lovely permanent home, which you never leave from year's end to year's end, *begin* to realize the circumstances of naval life? We won't even discuss the question!'

So there was packing again, and the dog – no longer Jockie, but a foolish airedale called Kismet – was wandering about as if his last hour had come, and little Peter was making up his mind whether he would take his Mickey Mouse or not (Amalun, of course, must go with him), and there was the bitter necessity of telling him that neither he nor Amalun would be leaving Tees Lodge. . . .

And then, at the last, it was the siesta hour and he was asleep in the nursery. Outside the half-closed venetians the fig-leaves danced formally in the light spring breeze and the mountain was violet and clear-cut. Teena was weeping quietly into her apron, and Mother was saying: 'Don't wake him, darling. Just slip away. . . .'

When I reached Rome I heard disconcerting news. Etna had been in eruption and the railway to Syracuse was cut by the lava flow. So I had to wait a few days in beautiful Taormina while it was cleared.

No white ostrich-plume of smoke rose delicate as the feather head-dress of a debutante from the virginal snows of Etna's summit. The mountain was debauched. A pall of grey, sulphurous vapour hung over the crater, and at night the sky above it burned with an evil red glow as if reflecting the great blast-furnace of hell itself. Her fair flanks were cicatrized with long black scars, farms and villages, olive groves and orange orchards had been devoured and thousands of peasants rendered destitute. I took a car to the point where the molten river of death had been halted. Nearly half a mile wide and forty feet high, it had been arrested like a gigantic roller, petrified at the very moment of breaking. Smoke rose from the great wave's crest and a stench of sulphur. In the face of the towering lava roller was embedded a little church like a fly in amber.

'De Virgin, she stop it,' said the guide simply.

My husband was promoted to Commander in July, and we

sold the Clyno in Malta and returned to England on leave. At the end of August we went to live with a French family for four months.

'When I have qualified in French as well as German I'll be eligible as an attaché,' said Bertie. 'That will be interesting one of these days.'

CHAPTER TWENTY-ONE

BOURGEOISIE AND BOHEMIAN

WE bought a Morris Six, an impersonal sort of car, which never really became one of the family like 'Tommy' Clyno, and we crossed the Channel once more to join the Bonnets at St. Aubin in Normandy, where they were spending the summer. During the winter months it was understood that we should live with them in Paris.

St. Aubin was a little seaside resort at which I instantly turned up my nose. The beach had length and breadth, but it was a sordid tangle of fly-ridden seaweed, with dead birds on the high-water mark, and the coarse sand was alive with jumping fleas like the young locusts of the veld, whose springing heralds disaster for the crops. Even the jaundiced sea despised this wretched strand and retired sulkily at the ebb, so that we had to pursue it for miles if we wanted a swim. But there were compensations. We had rented an adorable cottage from a certain Madame Emile, who was Bertie's technical instructress, and we had this doll's house to ourselves – a cockleshell in a sea of apple trees and rich meadow grass – two raftered rooms, one for living and one for sleeping, willow-pattern chintzes and a dresser with willow-pattern plates. A peasant girl, bovine as the heifer in the field, helped me keep it swept and tidy, and we ate our meals across the road with the Bonnets. Where Madame Emile lived we never discovered, but she gave Bertie his lessons at the cottage.

Madame Emile was not an attractive woman; her soul had long since been cremated in the fires of economy, and she was physically afflicted with a chronic catarrh. She ministered to its needs with alternate handkerchiefs. When one was too damp to serve its purpose she spread it carefully on her chair and sat on it to dry it while the other did duty in its place. Her daughter, Madame Claire, sometimes deputized for her. Madame Claire in her spare time carved sacred figures in wood and sold them to churches and convents. She had just completed a Negro Virgin when we met her. 'It is for a convent in Africa,' she explained. We did not care for it. She had a brittle little husband with a gollywog head, and a boy of four with the pert grown-up air of French children, who graduate straight from mother's milk to the vin ordinaire of the restaurant and who have never heard of nurseries. She possessed also a remarkable tuft of hair on her chest, and it was her eccentricity to wear her blouses cut low specially to reveal this unusual feature.

'Imagine to yourself such imbecility!' said Madame Bonnet, who did not like Madame Claire. 'She thinks it is attractive!'

Madame Bonnet's young daughter Yvonne uttered her little trill of laughter.

'Perhaps she fancies that her lock has EET.'

'Eet' ('It') was the only word of English Yvonne knew. The family spoke only French, for they considered, in common with most of their countrymen, that all well-bred people should know French.

'What is EET?' inquired Madame.

'Feminine magnetism for the male.'

Madame snorted. 'In the case of Hortense Claire her only magnetism was her dot.'

Madame Bonnet was a war widow with the pinched look of one who has been out in a cold wind for a long time; even her laugh was as chilly as the tinkle of ice in a cocktail shaker, but infinitely less gay. She was continually harassed, poor woman, by the responsibility of her son and daughter and her aged mother.

Renaud, the elder of her two children, was the pivot of her existence. He was a tall, dutiful medical student with melancholy red-rimmed eyes and dandruff on his collar. Whatever he did and wherever he went his mother called fond advice after him. 'Don't forget to put on your blazer after tennis!' 'Don't stay in the water too long and don't go out too deep!' Don't, don't, don't.

She nagged Yvonne too, but less solicitously. Yvonne was a lissom eighteen, with brown hair and eyes, insouciant and gay, with ready laughter that rippled like drifts of bird-song from an unseen garden. Perhaps she had inherited this gift of spontaneous merriment from her Corsican grandmother. La Grand'-Mère, as we called her, was crippled with arthritis, but brave as a lion and bubbling over with little jokes. Her shoulders were bowed under the black woollen shawl; her mittened fingers ever busy for the entire household, were gnarled and swollen and plied the needle painfully; she could not hobble from one room to another without her crutches; yet she never complained. She had the simple faith and philosophy of the truly good. She thanked the bon Dieu for her blessings and said 'Thy will be done' to the afflictions He saw fit to impose upon her. We all felt better for la Grand'-Mère's wise little grey presence. But we very soon discovered that the most important person in the house was Aline, the sour-tempered Breton bonne. When Aline rattled the dishes in the kitchen like sabres we knew we were in for a bad day. When she smiled the sun shone.

'She's impossible!' exclaimed Madame impatiently when Aline was in one of her tantrums. 'And why? That's what I want to know. She is, in fact, the luckiest person in this house. In her stocking, under her mattress, I assure you she has enough money to induce any man to marry her, in spite of her stodgy figure and her plain face. She is thirty-five years old, and ever since she came into the service of my husband's family twenty years ago she has been in a position to save every sou she earns, so that now she is a rich woman! Not like our poor little Yvonne, who hasn't a bean to bless herself with – no dot whatever.'

Here the entire family sighed, and Renaud looked even more than usually mournful. This lack of dot was such a sore point that even la Grand'-Mère's optimism was not equal to it.

'Who will marry the poor child?' she asked of fate in general.

Their misgivings were infectious, and even Yvonne herself was sometimes disturbed. She had no wish to live and die an old maid.

'Perhaps one day an American will fall in love with me – or an Englishman,' she would suggest, her large eyes half mocking, half serious. 'Maman says dot is of no importance to them because they are all rich.'

It was a strange thing, this tremendous preoccupation with money. One felt that it was at the very root and core of the French mentality. In the last resort everything seemed to resolve itself into a question of money.

Without dot Yvonne's young beauty would fade unwedded. Fantastic surmise! But no more fantastic than the crimes passionels that were the daily fare of the newspapers. When we studied these more closely we nearly always found that these 'passionate' murders, supposed to have their inception in the hot blood of love betrayed, were carefully premeditated and executed and somewhere in the background there was invariably the faint, crisp rustle of paper, not the billet doux, but the bank-note. Then again, after the Great War the French actually charged the British rent for the 'hire of the trenches' in which millions of Empire troops had suffered and died. It did not seem ludicrous to them to do this. Where there is money to be made the Frenchman makes it as a matter of course, whether out of love, vice, or death itself. He is essentially practical. Then, too, it was money that compelled the jangling, irritable association of Madame Bonnet and Madame Emile. These two loathed one another as only two women economically dependent on one another can do. Madame Bonnet housed students and Madame Emile taught them, so this team of two were forced to keep more or less together, even to the extent of taking holidays at the same time and in the same place. They had all the French individualism and aversion to team-work, and it was only with the utmost difficulty that they remained civil when they met. And later we were to see how money very nearly made human sacrifice of Yvonne.

When Madame Bonnet heard that we had lived in Munich for a short time she was greatly interested, but she quickly grew incensed when she spoke about the Germans, and we could not help remembering Cousin Olga imploring us not to let the General get on to the subject of France. 'It's bad for his health!' But although Madame Bonnet hated, feared and mistrusted Germany, there were times when we suspected her of feeling almost as strongly about Great Britain.

'Germany is arming against us,' she would state with her lips curling. 'And the British pretend not to see that this is so!'

'Germany is not allowed arms or an army' – mildly from Bertie. 'The biggest army in the world today is France's.'

'Zut! The German are building up their army *secretly*. And even the English cannot be such imbeciles as they make out. Even *they* must be capable of realizing that the German athletic clubs are in reality training centres for soldiers. But will they admit it? No, never in your life. British hypocrisy condones this German regeneration, and we in France will have to suffer and die when the armies march again!'

'Chérie, chérie,' murmured la Grand'-Mère to her explosive daughter, 'calm yourself! Do not fall upon our guests for the shortcomings of their statesmen.'

Yet when the Teutonic hosts advanced again it was Great Britain which led the field against them – and held on grimly after France had fallen. For it was not British hypocrisy but British blindness which had allowed Germany to rearm. So often this blindness, this failure to see the obvious, is misnamed hypocrisy. When Able Seaman White came back from his visit to the Zoo and said, after gazing long at the crocodiles next to the pond where the hippo loomed immense, 'If there *was* an 'ippopotamus I didn't notice 'im,' he spoke the simple truth. His attention had been concentrated on the crocodiles to the exclusion of the larger beast. So it was with our statesmen. Only Winston Churchill saw the monstrous shape of the German hippopotamus yawning from its mire, seeking to devour, and strove with might and main to bring it into the focus of his colleagues. But they were absorbed with the crocodiles snapping 'Disarm! Disarm!' and when at last the hippo lunged upon them, roaring with the voice of Adolf Hitler, they saw too late the horrid form.

Madame Bonnet found it impossible to credit the British with sincerity. To her they were double-faced – perfidious.

'It's no good,' I said to Bertie as we strolled back to our cottage through the moonlit orchard. 'Your well-meaning English race is just about as popular abroad as a well-meaning woman is at home.'

Every morning at dawn a heifer with a voice like a fog-horn came to our window and bellowed till we awoke. Bertie resented her serenade – first, because she banished sleep, and second, because every sailor hates a fog-horn.

'Perhaps someone has taken her calf from her,' I suggested, a fellow-feeling making me wondrous kind, even at 5 a.m. But Bertie complained to Madame Emile, who sniffed juicily and shrugged.

'Elle fait de réclame' ('She advertises herself.')

'The brute wants a husband,' explained Bertie.

'Has she any dot?' I asked. 'If she has I know the very person. Oh, how she'd love that two-thousand-pound Tweespruit bull!'

'You're an incorrigible match-maker.'

The heifer, however, was not to be indulged, and her lament in time lost its urgency and became a mere dirge which she trumpeted with less and less conviction. Everywhere and in everything there was the same sense of fin de saison, and eventually the day came for the exodus from St. Aubin. We had decided to go to Paris independently, making a détour to include the battlefields, an arrangement which suited the Bonnets admirably, as it would enable them to settle in before we rejoined them at their Paris apartment.

Autumn in the countryside of Normandy was laden with the melancholy beauty of the declining year. The roads ran long and straight between the ragged poplars, and on either side the rich plough swept grandly to the horizon; sometimes we saw the heavy farm horses labouring up the straight deep furrows, dragging the spidery harrow, and in the sight I found the same profound appeal that had stirred me long ago in the words 'down in the lands'. 'Where is Uncle Wilfred?' I had asked Edyth on Strehla, and she had replied: 'Down in the lands.' The phrase had haunted me. It held the same quality of eternity as there is in the sight of a well-ploughed field. Those who plough, the husbandmen and lovers of the land, abide their hour and are gone, but the yielding earth endures for ever.

The moment we entered the Bonnets' apartment in the Rue Rosa Bonheur we were absorbed into the intimate life of the family. It was impossible to hold aloof in such cramped quarters. It was like sharing a small cabin with a total stranger for the duration of a long voyage. One learns with surprise the sort of underclothes she wears, the shape of her body, the number of teeth she takes out at night, the books she reads, the photographs she carries with her, bits of her past, most of her present and a suggestion of her future. It is inevitable.

It was like that with the French family and ourselves.

They lived on the third floor of an Edwardian block of flats on the left bank of the Seine within a stone's throw of the broad Boulevard Montparnasse with its clattering trams, its art- and book-shops, its studios and boîtes and bars, and only a few minutes' walk from the dazzling Rue de la Gaité with its crazy little theatres, cinemas and music-halls – a world which we entered and explored at once, but of which the Bonnets seemed completely oblivious. They had the healthy bourgeoise dislike of the Quartier Latin. They didn't approve of it and they preferred to ignore it. It was Madame Bonnet's private hippopotamus. When I was foolish enough to ask her about the studios of Montparnasse, she said: 'I know nothing about them. Those places are for the benefit of the foreigner.' It was as if she had said: 'All right, there may be a hippo in the pool if you see it there, but it is not French!' We took the hint and the Latin Quarter was eliminated from the conversation.

We had a bedroom with a writing-desk in it for Bertie's homework, and the only bathroom in the apartment led out of it. Anyone wishing to use the bath had to pass through our bedroom. In the mornings Aline brought us delicious coffee and long, crisp torpedoes of bread, and if we had occasion to emerge from our room a scene of frenzied domestic activity greeted us. Madame in a red dressing-gown with her hair done up in steel curlers whisked round the flat with a duster; la Grand'-Mere in grey flannel déshabillé, her head similarly mechanized, hobbled about tidying up the stiff, formal little salon, separated from the salle-à-manger by folding glass doors; Yvonne, in a gay printed wrapper, pounced at the upright piano and practised scales reminiscent of the Good Hope Seminary; Aline grumbling audibly, helped fold away the camp stretcher on which unfortunate Renaud slept in the salon; and Renaud himself, with a final wild hunt for hat, scarf and gloves, banged out of the apartment, followed by a volley of maternal advice: 'Don't get your feet wet! Don't be back too late! Don't forget your muffler!' There was the echo of his footsteps pounding down the stairs. And presently, as the storm subsided, Aline, with a market basket over her arm and an umbrella beneath it, set out to do the day's shopping. Even in Paris she wore her voluminous Breton dress and her white coif, and on great occasions she flaunted her purple embroidered Sunday best and was Elizabethan in her splendour. Punctually at ten o'clock a nasty little girl with oily corkscrew curls came for her piano lesson from Yvonne, who contributed thus to the family purse, and soon afterwards Madame went out to take groups of English and American girls sightseeing. We knew not only how the family conducted itself, but how it felt and thought. We were, willy-nilly, part of it.

The Bonnets often told us about the naval couple who had preceded us in their ménage, and we gathered, with gratification, that Monsieur et Madame 'Jornstoan' had been très bien elevé and that their behaviour had always been comme il faut. They set great store by these two things. I think they found us sufficiently well brought up, but they made no secret of the fact that my incursions into la vie Bohème were not their idea of what was comme il faut.

Before we left England an artist friend had given me the name of a studio in Montparnasse only about twenty minutes' walk from the Rue Rosa Bonheur.

'La Grande Chaumière is marvellous value,' she said. 'You can take lessons there or just paint. It's dirt cheap and there are plenty of models.'

So I invested in pencils and sketch-books and occupied myself pleasantly and not unprofitably while Bertie was labouring over French grammar and naval terms with Madame Emile.

I had been to the School of Art in Cape Town as a girl, but we had spent most of our time drawing 'still life' – a piece of silk draped over a book or a vase of flowers. We copied innumerable plaster casts, and as a special concession we were sometimes given a Roman head as a model. But the closer and grosser contacts of 'drawing from life' were never vouchsafed us. We groused a little among ourselves, and Marjorie, who had recently read 'Trilby', said: 'In Paris – in the Latin Quarter – there are real people as models and they don't wear any clothes.'

'Nothing at all?'

'Not a stitch.'

'But surely they'd have a leaf or something, like these chaps?' We looked round at the Greek heroes all modestly clad in fig-leaves.

'Well, perhaps a moochie,' conceded Marjorie, thinking of the small buckskin loincloths of our own noble savages.

However, I soon discovered at La Grande Chaumière that the models, male or female, had no use for the cache-sex in any form. Nothing could have been more humdrum or prosaic than the nudity of the studio. It was a typical dusty, untidy studio of the Quarter, noisy with the brawls of the Italian models (they were mostly Italian) and the shrill voice of the concierge shrieking at them or admonishing her child Tutu. There was the come and go of hundreds of down-at-heel students of every age, sex and nationality who attended classes in the various at-eliers. In one there was the class for L'Art Publicatoire et pour la Mode, which I attended three mornings a week. In another the two-and-a-half-hour life pose. In yet another you would find the model for the week, usually attired in some colourful costume, inviting treatment in oils on a large canvas. And then downstairs there was the crowded popular Atelier Libre from five to six every evening, where there was no professor and the model changed his or her pose every five minutes. It was mar-vellous practice for the eye and pencil.

As a child I had always marvelled that the kopjes of the Karroo could be so ethereally amethyst at a distance and so honestly dun at close quarters. Montparnasse and its models were the same. In Cape Town I had thought of the Latin Quar-ter in terms of romance and glamour, and an artist's model was no less than Galatea with Pygmalion at her feet. But the life I now saw at first-hand was homely in the extreme. The models were ill-paid, often middle-aged and shapeless, with about as much glamour as Eugene Marais' baboons, but less shyness. They were hardly more beautiful than the apes, and certainly less picturesque, and their chatter was just as vociferous and, to me, only a little more comprehensible. They were, poor things, less hirsute so their sole concern was that the concierge should keep the stove well stoked, which she did with a good deal of lively backchat while the child Tutu trailed at her heels, her wide button eyes reflecting an awful sophistication. The models were models, not because they were divine to look upon, but because they were too lazy and stupid to be anything else.

Mimi was the nearest thing to glamour that ever came our way at La Grande Chaumière. She was French, fair and vol-uptuous, and could hold an exhausting pose for an indefinite period without the slackening of a single muscle. When I paid in my studio plaque (value thirty centimes) and the concierge said, 'Merci, ma'mselle. Mimi pose en haut ce soir,' I, like everybody else, made a bee-line for the two-and-a-half-hour pose. Mimi was alabaster pale and she was young. It amused me, during the ten minutes repos, when she touched her toes, yawned, slipped into her shabby coat and squatted by the stove to knit her numb fingers warm, to go around and look at the canvases and sketch-books of the other students. It occurred to me that a curious nostalgia informed their work. A Dutch girl had rendered Mimi's swelling contours innocuous, flat as Holland itself; a German girl had put in the crude photographic realism of a Nacht Kultur magazine; three giggling Japanese young gentlemen had discovered twin Fujiyamas in the pointed pallor of the model's breasts; and a big Negro from Martinique had represented her with barbaric savagery. As I stood behind his easel I saw in the bold brave lines and curves, not blonde Mimi, but the free, lithe body of a young native woman laughing by a wayside station in Rhodesia, unclothed except for a few coloured beads. Almost I could visualize the dusky bloom on the hot melting chocolate of her skin.

'You like it?' he asked in French, with his wide smile reminiscent of Teena's.

'Very much. It has great simplicity.'

'S'il vous plâit, ma'mselle.' It was the voice of the professor. Mimi cast aside her coat with a shiver and a smile and resumed her pose.

It was Bertie's habit to fetch me at the studio at six o'clock and then we went to one or another of the little bars in the Boulevard Montparnasse for a cocktail and a snack. The Coupole was our favourite. Olaf, the Swedish barman, knew everyone who came there. There was Kiki, who had been a model and had amazingly become a film star (she had the plebian charm of Gracie Fields – a sort of impudent challenge: 'I am what I am, a girl of the people, and if you don't like me that way you know what to do about it'), and Fernande, who had been the wife of a famous Japanese artist, and who brooded in her corner with her heavy black hair falling in a bang over her heavier eyes, while she alternately killed and revived his memory with 'snow' and Japanese lovers. 'Maintenant elle n'aime que les Japonais,' shrugged Olaf, 'a perverted taste – poor creature!' There was, too, a ghostly little artist with a frayed red beard, who came every evening for his long thin glass of absinthe, drank it with a vague smile, paid for it like one in a dream and disappeared through the swing doors into the rainy darkness, stepping high as if he walked on air.

'Snow,' said Olaf laconically. 'Tonight he is in the clouds. Tomorrow it will be another matter.'

Sometimes one of the habitués sketched Bertie or me and tried to sell us the likeness, but I quickly sketched them in return, and they laughed and gave us up, recognizing that though we were foreigners we were not sightseers.

We walked back afterwards, arm in arm, under my umbrella. It was always wet those winter evenings in Paris, with thin slivers of ice in the slanting rain and a rawness in the air more penetrating than the rawness of London. The Métros of the Boulevard Montparnasse yawned their invitation at intervals, and a black mass of tired, undernourished little men and women surged into the entrances and were absorbed into dark maws regurgitating with the rush and rumble of the trains. High heels clicked along the pavements and trams clanged, umbrellas dripped. Sometimes we were lured by the Rue de la Gaîté and the tawdry music-halls and variety shows. The humour was ever the same – the mayor caught out in the brothel, hiding ignominiously behind a plush sofa, or the lascivious professor in the library demanding a tome from the top shelf because the librarian is a pretty girl who climbs the ladder to get it, the while the old gentleman stands beneath and regales the audience with the excruciating double entendre of his impressions. All this was diversion – a side of life that had no more reality than the shadow play on the silver screen. But as we climbed the stairs to the little apartment on the third floor and put our key into the lock we knew that we were stepping right into the warm, solid, bourgeoise heart of France – la famille française – our family, any family.

CHAPTER TWENTY-TWO

A QUESTION OF DOT. TELEPHONE CONVERSATION

YVONNE wanted a husband and Renaud craved a bowler hat. I think, on the whole, Renaud's desire was the more urgent. It seemed an unaccountable passion to me who am allergic to bowlers. In South Africa they are seldom seen, for the sun-tanned face of the man from the wide open spaces, if hatted at all, is shaded by a wide-brimmed felt at a rakish angle, and when first I visited England I was unable to restrain my mirth at the sight of the London legions scurrying about their business under headgear round and black as the kitchen pot. But Renaud was offended when I put this light-hearted view to him.

'For a doctor', he said firmly, 'a bowler hat is essential. It is a mark of distinction.' (He called it 'un chapeau melon'.)

I remembered then that my father had been wont to wear one with his morning coat to go his rounds, and that I had implored him, with tears, to remove 'that po-po hat', just as years later Peter, seeing his grandfather in a topper, had wept aloud and commanded wildly between his sobs, 'Gramp take off dat funnel-hat!' which interference must have been irksome to my parent. However, Renaud's chapeau melon was a matter for neither laughter nor tears, since it was as yet but a figment of the imagination surmounting, with ineffable distinction, the melancholy features of our impecunious medical student.

It was through the good offices of Gilbert, his friend, that he was at last enabled to realize his ambition.

Gilbert was a shrill little bantam in his final year at medical college, sprightly, intelligent and over-voluble, with finger-nails chewed to the quick. He had, in fact, decided to assume the rôle of deus ex machina to both young Bonnets, but wisely he curried favour with Renaud before attacking the main objective.

Gilbert put the hat-earning proposition at dinner one night, talking very fast, with his mouth full of haricot verts. La Grand'-Mère flung up her mittened hands and cried, 'Impossible! C'est trop fort!' and Madame Bonnet and Renaud exchanged glances of alarm and despondency, while Yvonne laughed so much that she did the nose trick.

The suggested source of revenue was an elderly female American 'eccentric' living in a suite of rooms at an expensive hotel. It was this lady's main concern in life to be quit of it – but not sordidly – oh no. She was hastening pell-mell to a better world by way of the foaming rapids of unlimited champagne – the golden tributary of the River Styx – and while thus engaged she employed her private physician to watch over her. But there were times when this harassed individual felt impelled to take an evening off, and on these occasions it was his habit to hire a medical student to take his place for the night.

'Every Saturday night you remain in the lady's suite,' said Gilbert. 'It is quite simple. Several of our internes have done it. You help her catch lizards and then, if necessary, you give her an injection. In a month you will be able to buy the finest chapeau melon in Paris, and a scarf into the bargain!'

Renaud's dull eye brightened and Yvonne flung herself back in her chair in an access of merriment. 'Oh, la, la! Quelle fantaisie!'

So for the ensuing weeks there was no camp-bed in the salon on Saturday nights, and no Renaud, and at déjeuner on Sundays that estimable young man's heavy, red-rimmed eyes had the wild, haunted look of one who has witnessed witches, revels. But there came a day when he had passed safely through the ordeal and reaped the reward – the victor's crown – a bowler hat impeccable in rigid dignity, a sombre phoenix risen from the hot fumes of the dipsomaniac's Veuve Cliquot. The camp-bed returned to the salon seven nights a week and la Grand'-Mère expressed unqualified relief.

'Magnifique! Comme tu es chic, grace à moi!' crowed Gilbert, who was never a modest benefactor.

When Gilbert looked upon Yvonne his beady eyes grew hot with desire and his chewed acquisitive fingers twitched, while she, for her part, threw him tantalizing glances and trilled with laughter at his facile staccato witticisms. He and her serious brother were all that she knew of youth. She went to no dances and few cinemas, and she moved in no young crowd like an English girl of her own age. She gave her music lessons, made her hats and dresses with nimble fingers and did not repine. She recognized that where there was no money there could be little gaiety. But somewhere within her there was a secret garden, and its sunshine and its bird-song were free to all of us.

One day, when we came in, we found the ménage in a state of high excitement. Madame's face was radiant and she clasped my hands impulsively.

'We have wonderful news, Madame Joy! Yvonne is affianced – to Gilbert!'

Renaud, mellowed by his bowler, saw no objection to Gilbert as a brother-in-law. On the contrary it would relieve him of any future obligation to provide for his sister. Madame Bonnet was overjoyed that Yvonne was marrying into a well-to-do-family, and la Grand'-Mère said, removing her spectacles to wipe away a sentimental film: 'Comme je suis contente. C'est un brave garçon.' They were all acutely aware that a young man who was prepared to waive the prickly question of dot was proving both devotion and magnanimity of character.

Yvonne herself wore a little air of triumph, as if to say: 'Alone I did it!' But she was glad chiefly for her mother's sake.

'Maman has been responsible for all of us since my father was killed, and she worries so much. Now, at least, my future is assured.'

'But, *Gilbert!*' I said to Bertie afterwards in our room. 'She doesn't care the shake of a dog's tail about him.'

'This is France, my sweet. The French are a practical people.'

The fiançailles were celebrated in the Bonnet apartment. Madame and Yvonne indulged in the unheard-of extravagance of a new dress each, made by a dressmaker instead of at home; la Grand'-Mère unearthed a black taffeta gown of the Victorian era and a violet shawl; and Renaud hired a morning coat; but Aline put everybody in the shade with her purple embroidered Breton costume. There was a buffet in the salle-à-manger laden with hors d'oeuvres, cakes, jellies, pastries and sweet champagne.

The relations arrived in two detachments. First, the home team, apprehensive and very conscious of its material short-comings, and then the opposition, headed by Gilbert's widowed mother, heavily draped in mourning veils as if for a funeral and positively rustling with patronage. At first the game was heavy going and we noticed some dirty work in the scrum, but after half-time and the charging of the glasses the pace was faster and we were relieved when the afternoon ended with honours even. Two or three times Gilbert's mother permitted a wintry smile to escape her window's weeds – a triumph indeed for Yvonne – and even Madame Emile, sitting on the usual damp handkerchief, lace-trimmed for the occasion, seemed to enjoy herself as she watched her small grandson gorge himself on cakes. ·

'He will need no supper tonight,' she remarked to her daughter, savouring this infinitesimal economy.

'No, indeed,' agreed Madame Claire. 'More likely a dose of medicine.' Her low-cut afternoon gown revealed the proud plume on her chest specially pomaded.

At Yvonne's side there was always Gilbert, preening at her loveliness, and pecking at it with blunt fingers, but often she glanced down at his nails and evaded his touch with a swift, darting movement, and I wondered how soon she would begin to hate him.

The weeks passed and Christmas was at hand – a joyous season. Yet something had happened to Yvonne. The trills of mirth were rare now, the brown eyes often heavy, and at meals it sometimes happened that at a word or a look from her mother she rose hastily and left the table, and from her little bedroom we heard passionate muffled sobs.

'She's impossible!' exclaimed Madame. 'Quite unbearable these days.'

Even la Grand'-Mère deliberately closed her eyes to what was really amiss. 'C'est l'amour. Young girls in love are tem-peramental.' But her mittened hand shook a little and her eyes were troubled. In her heart she, more than the others, realized her grand-daughter's frame of mind. Perhaps she, too, had once suffered thus.

I had no illusions. I had seen lovers together often enough – the looks that dare scarcely meet lest they fail to break apart, the note in a voice sweet as the chime of a bell, a chance contact sending a wave of colour into pale cheeks, the little swing of a girl's hips that is an ancient rhythm and the lift of her head that is a new pride, and about their meeting a radiance that is a shaft of light in a dark room. I knew these things. But between Yvonne and Gilbert there was only the heat of his desire and the sharp discord of her recoil. When lovers are kept apart by lack of money it is sad indeed, but it is less sad than when a young girl barters herself body and soul for security.

One day when Yvonne ran weeping from the table I asked permission to follow her.

'Go, by all means,' snapped Madame, 'but you won't get any sense out of her. She's crazy.'

She was lying across her bed, her face buried in the pillow, her shoulders heaving convulsively. It was a dreary little room. All the stiff elegance of the Bonnet apartment was in the salon – in the shop window. A green felt hat, half-made, lay next to her work-basket, and her well-worn pantoffles peeped out from under a wooden chair. Her gay floral wrapper hung behind the door like a banner of youth. I sat down beside her and touched her soft brown hair.

'Yvonne, what is it? Can't you tell me? I, too, am young. I think I could understand.'

She calmed down and presently looked up with drenched eyes. There was hope in them. Perhaps I could help her. I was foreign, in effect a stranger and sometimes it is easier to open your heart to a stranger than to a friend. A stranger goes away, and there is no need afterwards to recall, with regret, what has been said.

'Is it Gilbert? Is it that you don't love him?'

She shivered. 'I hate him! He is so mean – and quick, like a little animal, a rat! He treats me as if he had bought me already. And his hands repel me – those nails! His eyes too, following me about, sharp and bright. . . . Madame Joy, I believe they glow in the dark!' She laughed tremulously through her tears and then clenched her fists. 'When he touches me I curl up and die!'

This, then, was the touch of frost that had nipped the summer garden of a young girl's heart.

'Does your mother know how you feel about him?'

She nodded. 'Maman says it is a phase which will pass. That when we are married I will accustom myself to these things. . . .

But is she right? I doubt it. Ah, how I doubt it! Do you think it can pass – this – revulsion?'

What answer could I give? This was France and Yvonne was a French girl, without dot, without opportunity, and Gilbert desired her enough to take her young loveliness unendowed – a fact which even in the maternal eyes of Madame appeared to be remarkable. With him she would find security, a home, and later, perhaps, children, who might compensate her for many things. The alternative seemed to be years of drudgery, only to wither at the last, unfulfilled.

I said at length: 'If you want the life Gilbert can give you badly enough you will learn to discipline yourself into accepting him as a necessary part of it. Or you can be courageous and break your engagement. You can wait for love – take a chance on finding it. It's worth so much, Yvonne . . . it's worth a long chance. . . .'

She stood up and bathed her eyes and brushed her hair in front of the mirror on her cheap dressing-table. Then she turned and said, with a curious mature mixture of resignation and defiance:

'I am eighteen years old, almost nineteen, and no man except Gilbert has asked me to marry him. A young girl without dot cannot afford to take chances. I will be sensible.'

She forced a smile. But I knew that Yvonne had walked out of her secret garden and locked the gate behind her.

There was a stir in the family on Christmas morning. La Grand'-Mère, who was permanently chained to the apartment by her arthritis, was going to Mass. It was an agonizing and heroic decision, but she insisted that she must go.

'Le bon Dieu has seen fit to send us a good husband for our little Yvonne, and I must thank Him. My grandchild need not fear for the future now; she will want for nothing, and I am very happy. I must tell Him in His own house that I am grateful. Is that not right, Yvonne?'

'Yes, chérie.' The grand-daughter's voice was low.

Madame Bonnet helped her mother into the Victorian black silk and wrapped her up well in a coat and shawl. Yvonne took the crutches and Renaud carried his little grandmother down the three flights of stairs to the waiting taxi. It was snowing lightly.

Bertie and I crossed the Seine to the Rive Droite to spend our Christmas much as we had spent it in the first year of our marriage. We had sentimental ground to cover – and comic too.

'Do you remember the fool little old Peter made of me here?'

'Do I!'

We did not return till the evening.

We knew that Aline was out and that Renaud and Yvonne were spending the evening with Gilbert's people. All the same, there was an ominous quiet in the apartment as we entered. La Grand'-Mère was in the salon, lying on the settee, and this in itself was unusual. She must be very tired after the effort of her church-going, I thought. Madame Bonnet sat near her, sewing. In the light of the lamp we saw that her features were swollen and her eyes suspiciously red. She rose as we came in and put her finger to her lips.

'Maman is asleep.'

'No,' said the old lady, 'I am not asleep.'

Her voice had changed. It was muted and thick. Slowly she turned her face towards us. I caught my breath and grasped tightly at Bertie's hand. 'Oh *no*!' The whisper broke from me before I could control it.

The lined, gentle little face, so kind and humorous, was tragically distorted. (I remembered that I had once seen a girl struck by lightning.) When she spoke only half her mouth moved. Her left eye and the whole left side of her face had sagged.

'It is a form of facial paralysis,' said Madame, dabbing at her swollen eyes. 'Renaud and the doctor think it is a chill. She ought not to have gone out this morning – in the snow. . . .' She sniffed miserably.

La Grand'-Mère, who for all her lion's heart, was only human, said slowly, said with difficulty: 'I cannot understand it. All my life I have been devout. When le bon Dieu saw fit to cripple me I did not complain. . . . I went today, in spite of my pain, to thank Him for His goodness to our child. And He has smitten me. I have never cared for worldly things or vanity, yet now, when I am old and weary and must soon be taken to Him, I must go into His presence disfigured – stricken thus in His own house. I do not understand.'

'Ah, Maman chérie,' cried her daughter. 'Do not ask of le bon Dieu that He shall be logical! Ask only that He be merciful.'

But for answer the old lady turned her disfigured face away, and tears trickled weakly over the seamed, twisted parchment of her skin.

In London, early in April, I received a letter from Yvonne, I kept it because it seemed to me even then to be part of a great design – the answer, perhaps, to la Grand'-Mère's cry, 'I do not understand!'

I opened the thin foreign envelope and read the contents eagerly. The neat angular writing slanted sharply across the page like the cold November rains of Paris, but between the lines the sun shone and the birds sang, and I knew that merry, brown-eyed Yvonne had returned to her secret garden and that there too it was spring.

'DEAR MADAM JOY (she wrote in her own language),

'You have always taken so kind and friendly an interest in our joys and sorrows that I feel I must tell you what has happened since you left us in the New Year. My engagement to Gilbert is broken. At first Maman was not at all content. She thought I was mad to throw away security, but now she has become resigned – but only because my grandmother has given me such wonderful support.

'It is strange that one of her upbringing and generation should have understood so well my emotions on this subject. She has put aside all the worldly considerations that are so important to us in this country, and it seems that she really believes with me now what you once tried to tell me – that Love is worth waiting for – worth a long chance!

'You will rejoice with us to hear that her facial paralysis has almost passed. There is scarcely any disfigurement now, and the doctor says the small suggestion of weakness that still lingers on the left side of her mouth will soon disappear. . . .'

When we left Paris and went to London early in 1931 I decided to find myself a job.

Bertie had been appointed to the Royal Naval Staff College at Greenwich and was away all day and three nights a week.

We were hard up at that time and London was expensive. For our semi-basement flat in Earl's Court, with its view of the area railings and other people's ankles, we paid more than four times as much as we had done for our big bright Maltese villa in Guarda Mangia. And I was lonely without Peter. That sort of loneliness, which is of the heart, is something to fear, and the best antidote to it is work – either work that exhausts the body or absorbs the mind, depending upon the ability and inclination of the person concerned.

But what work? I wanted to write, which is a very common urge in people with no qualifications for anything else, or even that. I also hoped that I had learned enough about l'Art Publicatoire et Pour la Mode to illustrate dress articles. Moreover, it pleased me to recall that in the few months preceding my marriage I had strolled down to the sunny *Cape Times* office every morning, groaned up to the fourth floor in an aged lift operated by Rip Van Winkle, and willowed into a room marked 'WOMEN'S PAGE', where, in the agreeable company of Anna Syfret, the editress, and a dark-haired girl called Pearl Aschman, I had been permitted and actually encouraged to write articles from 'Chromium in Your Bathroom' to 'Crocodile Shooting in Trinidad', for which effusions I was remunerated at the princely figure of 1s. an inch.

But how did one break into journalism in London? As I felt about Fleet Street, so must gangsters who have had their appetites whetted by minor hold-ups successfully accomplished regard the Bank of England. An ultimate but practically impregnable goal.

While I brooded over this knotty problem I wrote several short stories and sent them to various magazines, whence they returned with the beautiful fidelity of Tees Lodge homing pigeons. Usually they were accompanied only by a printed slip of polite rejection, but now and again a rash editor deigned to find them 'promising', but 'too daring'. I fear the gaudy influence of La Grande Chaumière and the Coupole was stronger in my pen than the admirably comme il faut outlook of the French family. I wrote of an artist's model who married a Negro (I had Mimi in mind and the big black man from Martinique) and of Fernande deserted by her Japanese lover in his hour of success, and even of an English chorus-girl who spent a week in Paris with an impecunious artist.

One editor, very properly preferring the manner to the matter of the chorus-girl tale, asked me to call on him. He was helpful and lectured me like a Dutch uncle. He explained that seductions in popular fiction may, at a pinch, be contemplated, but must never be consummated, that nobody posed for the altogether. (Trilby, he pointed out, was almost entirely for the foot.) Negroes must be kept in their own setting. . . .'

'But in real life—' I broke in.

He held up his hand and shook his head at me.

'Please! We only hold up the mirror to what we wish to see.'

I thought of Madame Bonnet and the Latin Quarter, and realized that here, too, there was a hippopotamus – many hippopotami from which we should avert our eyes. I uttered a final feeble protest, however: 'In books things happen like life – or they don't. Look at Zola and Michael Arlen. One is realist, the other isn't, but both are shocking.'

'Ah, *books*. That is different. And when a writer is well known he can be as outrageous as he pleases.

'Now, this little story has glamour,' continued the editor. 'But you can't go sending chorus-girls to Paris with their Bohemian boy friends. If they were university students hitch-hiking it would be all right. One could still give them the benefit of the doubt. But you have packed them off to Paris. . . . Well . . .'

So a hippo could not be sublimated either, endowed with enchantment and delicacy. To the right-minded that side of life which threatens conventional respectability has one aspect only. It is a coarse and evil monster, black as night, widemouthed, insatiable and best regulated to the muddy bottom of his pool.

Thus, laden with food for thought, I rode back from Ludgate Circus to Earl's Court on the top of a big red bus, and it came to me gradually that those who love beauty most be careful where they seek it, lest they find it in forbidden groves and follow it unheeding.

One night we went to dinner at the Vernays'.

The Vernays had a lovely house in Berkeley Square, which charming American Marian always referred to as 'our little house'. Arthur Vernay was an explorer in his spare time. His last expedition had been through the Kalahari Desert, and we had met him soon after his return from South Africa. Dinner at the Vernays' was always a keen delight to me. The 'little house' had its special grace, its atmosphere of breeding, its poise and intimacy. 'I am pedigree', it seemed to say, as the butler opened the black lacquer door, 'but I am not at all haughty or snobbish. If you appreciate me we will be friends. See for yourself the wisdom that is stored in my library, the silks and embroideries of the East that adorn my bedrooms, the pottery and china of lost eras that grace my shelves and alcoves, the silver that glitters on my board, the Venetian glass flowing with the red and gold of rare vintages, and the flowers my lady arranged herself with such incomparable taste.'

And there was Marian, slight and graceful by the Adam fireplace, gowned by Chanel, the soft light burnishing blades of silver in her dark hair and the silver flash of her nails as she extended her hand in greeting. Arthur, tall and spare, was talking to Sir Harcourt Butler about the possibilities of a certain Burmese expedition and another to Tibet.

At dinner I found myself seated next to the American-born son of the Hon. Mrs. Lionel Guest. 'Johnny' Dodge was his name. The sybarite in me blossomed in Marian's 'little house' and I fancied that the rare vintages lent our conversation the sparkle of 'beaded bubbles winking at the brim', and presently Johnny said: 'I haven't been so amused in years. Do you write?'

'I try.'

'Then I've a friend who'd be interested. Do you write like you talk?'

'Unfortunately, there isn't often champagne around when I'm writing.'

'Well, take my advice and go and see the Editor of the *Daily Express*, Beverley Baxter, and tell him Johnny Dodge sent you.'

'Beverley Baxter? I haven't heard of him.'

Johnny roared with laughter. 'That's the cream of it all! Bax'd never believe that!'

Bertie had gone to the Staff College as usual and would not be back till next evening. It was nine a.m. The 'little house' in Berkeley Square, Johnny Dodge, the dry sparkle of Arthur Vernay's Veuve Cliquot and the cloying sweetness of Constantia Van der Hum were part of last night's dream. So was the echo of an easily remembered name – Beverley Baxter.

It was cold and grey and the ankles in Cromwell Crescent bustled past the windows of our dining-room. Inside, our flat was attractive in a bare modern way. The cook-general came in to fetch the breakfast things. She had a slight squint, and I felt suddenly that this was lucky. If carrozzin drivers liked a cross-eyed boy beside them, perhaps a cross-eyed cook was a good omen. The number of our flat was eleven, and that too was reassuring. Eleven was my lucky number.

Now, I knew enough about editors to know that these great men are hemmed about by an impenetrable bodyguard of highly trained secretaries whose duty it is to protect them from marauding job-hunters with letters of introduction. If it came to that, I hadn't even a letter. I knew just what would happen if I tried to see this Beverley Baxter in his stronghold. First, there would be the commissionaire pushing a slip of paper at me. 'Party you want to see, your name an' business?' There would follow half an hour in the chastening twilight of the waiting-room and then a bland secretary: 'I'm so sorry, Mrs. Packer. Mr. Baxter can't possibly see you today. He's up to his eyes in work, but he asked me to tell you that it really is a complete waste of your time to come back because we haven't an opening *anywhere*. In fact, we are reducing staff every day. The depression, you know. . . .' And so down the stairs again with the smell of newsprint in my nostrils and the clatter of typewriters in my ears and a great hunger to be part of it all in my heart – and the bitter disappointment of a child who has seen the table set for the party and been sent home in disgrace.

No, *that* wasn't the way to throw away this ghost of a chance.

I teased the pages of the telephone directory. A to K. Ah, here it was, A. Beverley Baxter, and the number. With my heart pounding and my breath coming fast I dialled it. The thin little voice of the maid. 'What name shall I say?' 'Please say a friend of Colonel Dodge's.' A pause. My cheeks are burning. This is an act. I must be the Hepburn, the Garbo and Marlene Dietrich rolled into one.

'Yes? Who is it?' A soft, mellow Canadian voice with a rising inflection of cautious curiosity – slightly defensive.

'I'm Joy Packer. Johnny Dodge told me to get in touch with you. He said you'd want to snap me up for your paper. . . .' (Hepburn, self-confident.)

A groan. 'Johnny's kind heart is my burden. He's always doing things like this to me! I don't want to snap anybody up for any reason whatever. Journalists out of a job are howling round the doors of the *Express* like hungry wolves.'

'I'm a South African, just arrived from several months in Paris, bursting with new ideas and new angles on almost everything. Johnny said you'd want to see me because you like fresh minds.' (Greta, laying it on thick.)

A pause. Then kindly: 'There's not a paper in London that isn't reducing staff. It's really useless, you know.'

'Don't you think it's a pity not to see what you're missing?' (Marlene at her most out of focus.)

'Do you know, young lady, that I haven't one free moment to call my soul my own until I put the first edition to bed at ten-thirty tonight.'

'That'll suit me beautifully! I'm dining at the Savoy, and I'll come straight from there to the *Express* building at ten-thirty.' (Hepburn, on an inspiration.)

'You will?'

'Of course, Mr. Baxter. Au revoir, then.'

My knees, as I put the receiver down, were india-rubber.

CHAPTER TWENTY-THREE

BEVERLEY BAXTER. MODEL GIRL

I DON'T know what our staid and excellent cook-general thought when she beheld me at ten o'clock that evening in my best black velvet evening dress and white fur jacket ringing up for a taxi and evidently on my way to an assignation. Her squint increased a trifle and her eyebrows lifted.

The taxi disgorged me in Shoe Lane, and above the low murmur of the city the presses clamoured. A tremendous sense of excitement and elation filled me. Now for it!

The night porter seemed surprised when I said: 'Mr. Baxter is expecting me. I am Mrs. Joy Packer.'

The waiting-room, five minutes and then the porter was

back. 'Mr. Baxter's with the night editor. 'E says will you wait in 'is orfice?'

It was a fairly large room, insulated from the rest of the building by the secretary's sanctum. Aha! It wouldn't have been possible to storm *this* citadel in broad daylight! There was an easy-chair. I sank into it feeling suddenly weak.

A quick step in the passage and Beverley Baxter was in the doorway. Not tall, but very arresting, with narrow piercing eyes under thick winged brows.

'Did anyone ever tell you that you looked like Gladys Cooper?' And then he was entrenched behind his big desk and the narrow humorous eyes were summing me up.

'So Johnny Dodge sent you? Have you known him long?'

'I've met him once.' Bax showed no surprise. Like all editors, his capacity for astonishment had long since been exhausted.

'Ah, well, then I'll tell you about him. Johnny's the nicest, most charming fellow on earth. . . .' He gave me a quick word-sketch of his friend, penetrating, amusing, intensely human. It was, though I was not then aware of it, an example of the very essence of this man's success – his flair for people. People come first with Bax. They are life itself to him. He is as unconscious as a child of the Insignificance of Man. Show him the 'dreaming spires' of Oxford and he will reflect less upon their beauty than upon the influence of that beauty on the young minds expanding for generation after generation under their slender shadow. Show him a modern battleship, 'that mighty, intricate engine of destruction hurling forth thunderbolts', and he will wonder whether the ship's boy is afraid when the guns give tongue. Give him an idea and he will develop it swiftly and adroitly, but the idea must be infused with the breath of humanity, it must be a potential force for good in the lives of men and women. An abstraction, lacking human interest, is no use to him.

I did not know Bax then, but I know him now, and he is not changed. When he talks he can be mischievously provocative and inconsistent as a woman, but when he writes he is a knight wielding a supple rapier against fools and evil. As a politician he is often the naughty boy of the school, poking fun at his teachers and his betters, but give him a cause to fight and a pen in his hand and he will write with blood and tears and vitriol. In the Battle of London, when the guns were shaking the tortured earth and the bombs were tearing into the homes of the high and the humble alike and death was a sobbing of engines in the heavens and a human shriek in the flames below, Bax was flaying the foolscap pages in his study, writing messages of courage and determination that lifted millions of sick hearts and weary heads – writing as he had never done before, gathering strength and power for the devastation that grew nightly about the city he had come to love more dearly than his own Toronto. And then, in the small hours, while London still shuddered in its shelters at the whine and rumble of high explosive, he slept in his house in St. John's Wood peaceful as a child.

But this was not 1940–41. It was 1931, and the Editor of the *Daily Express* was asking me a question.

'How old are you?'

'Twenty-six next month.'

'Are you married?'

'Yes.'

'Do you love your husband?'

I laughed. 'That's my affair – and his.'

'Uhu. . . . Well, Joy Packer, what makes you think you could be a journalist?'

'I have a little experience and plenty of ideas. I can write and draw and I've lived in South Africa, Malta, Munich, Paris and England. I have audacity too, or we wouldn't be talking now.'

'That is so.' He thought for a few moments and presently played for time. 'We are running a cameo tale series in the paper – thousand-word short stories. Write one and send it to me personally. If it's good enough I'll talk to you again.'

The night editor came in with some copy, the presses thundered like the voice of the sea at high tide, and Bax began to talk of the paper, of its power for good and evil, and after a while he drew a sheaf of foolscap from a drawer and said: 'Listen, Joy Packer. How do you like this?' He read me a passage from his autobiography, 'Strange Street', which he was then writing. While he read his sensitive hands were conducting an imaginary orchestra.

'I like it. Read some more. What were your parents like?'

'My parents?' He turned back a few pages. 'Ah – here they are. ". . . My father was . . . a perfect Niagara of Philosophy, a lover of good conversation and as kindly as he was humorous. He loved to talk. On Sundays he played the organ and led the choir in Queen Street Methodist Church. ... my mother was the soprano soloist, and even allowing for the illusions of childhood I know her voice to have been of outstanding beauty." '

'Oh, but how strange! My mother has also sung solos in our cathedrals at home! She was a contralto.'

'Is that so? That's very interesting – but listen to this. . . .'

I listened. A glimpse of a child in Toronto, of a young man selling pianos in Cobalt, of the trenches and Max Beaverbrook, of a London house and lovely Edie Letson, who became Mrs. Beverley Baxter, of a brief incursion into grand opera. Here he sang a few phrases of 'Butterfly', and the Canadian voice was rich and warm as South African sunshine. The night editor appeared. He did not seem particularly surprised to see his chief giving way to song. Bax, I realized, was a law unto himself. The telephone shrilled.

'Hello! Oh yes?' The room was immediately filled with disembodied dynamics and the responses of the Editor were tinged with reluctant respect. As he put down the receiver his narrow eyes laughed across at me. 'D'you know who that was?'

'Donald Duck.'

'Max Beaverbrook.'

'Then you'll be busy – and I must go.'

Max and Bax. Much has been written of these two Canadians who work together and quarrel and work together again. And much will still be written.

My cameo tale, 'Nigger Baby,' was accepted and published, though its title was changed, and I was paid £10 for it. I went to see Bax again – this time in the broad light of mid-morning.

'Good morning, Joy Packer. How are you?' The narrow, searching eyes were vivid blue by day, attacking eyes.

'Fine, thanks. What about that job now? Women's page features, anything you like.'

'What ideas have you?'

'Well, here's one. They're bringing out the new fashions soon – *English* fashions made with English materials, because we don't want any foreign stuff dumped on us – not even clothes for women. I could go and get a line on it – the human angle on how the things are being designed and made – English firms,

English mannequins and all sorts of clients. Little shots from life—'

Sharp as a needle he saw his loophole of escape. 'Have you ever been a mannequin yourself?'

'No.'

'You've got the figure. Get the job. Write about it – behind the scenes stuff. If it's good I'll take some of it.'

'You're getting rid of me.'

He smiled.

'Only temporarily, I fancy. When you've proved that you can really write I may be able to fit you in somewhere. Go to it.'

I went into several exclusive dress shops and tried my luck without success; then I found my way into one which I shall call 'Collette's'. The head saleswoman looked me over.

'Any experience?'

'No, but I can learn.'

'As a matter of fact, we prefer to train our girls ourselves.' (It was cheaper.) 'You might do. Come this way.'

She led me through the lingerie department into the dove-grey French salon. There were mirrored panels and crystal chandeliers and gilt Louis Quinze chairs and, along one wall, a row of little mirrored fitting-rooms. She left me in one of these and returned presently with a brocaded evening gown.

'Just try this on.'

It might have been made for me. Miss Long – for this, I learned, was her name – called out: 'Mr. Gosling! Will you come here a moment. There's a girl here with Ivy's measurements who wants a job.'

Mr. Gosling, the director, was a tall, rather distinguished-looking Jew with a nervous twitch at the corner of his mouth and a cranium like an ostrich egg. He put me through a few paces.

'You'll do,' he snapped. 'The Gander' always snapped or hissed. 'But let me make one thing clear. I don't pay a beginner a living wage. If you have to keep yourself on your earnings you must look elsewhere for work. I won't take you on. But if you have a home with your parents—'

'With my husband. I'm married.'

'Good – with your husband, then – you can start tomorrow. You'll get thirty shillings a week, and in your case it's earn while you learn, so you're lucky.'

'What time must I be here?'

'Nine o'clock.'

'Very well. You can count on me.'

'Excellent. But first of all I must have a reference. Someone who'll guarantee your character.'

'Will the High Commissioner for South Africa do? His wife is my cousin.'

'Oh, er – yes. Just write the name and address here. Thank you. Tomorrow at nine, then. Ask for Miss Long when you arrive.'

When Bertie came home that evening and I told him what had happened he drew hard on his pipe.

'What's your mother going to say to this?'

'By the time she has reacted it will be too late to matter. I'll have the 'copy'. I *must* get it, darling! Do you mind terribly?'

'If you've taken on the job already I don't see what difference it makes whether I mind or not.'

'Let me try it – just till I've got the material I want. After that I'll chuck it. Promise.'

'All right. But it's your own affair.'

Collette's was 'copy' all right. The February morning was cold and damp and I felt like a fresher in a very odd college. Miss Long greeted me severely.

'The model-girls don't come in at the shop entrance. They clock in through the basement. Dawn! Take this new girl to the locker-room and give her Ivy's things. They came back from the laundry yesterday.'

Dawn had the sort of loveliness that would give anyone a pang. She was like a very tall child with soft pale gold curls, clear slate-blue eyes and a fair skin transparent as Lalique glass illumined from within. She led me down some steps from the French salon into the chilly locker-room. A deal trestle table, with a bench on either side of it, ran down the middle of the basement, which was lined with the lockers of the staff. There was a double-sided looking-glass on the table and some make-up boxes open in front of it.

'We do our faces down here. There are six of us,' said Dawn, who had a strong Southsea accent. 'This is Ivy's locker. She left last week – got the sack for catching a fellow's eye in the showroom. We aren't allowed to do that here. Goosey Gander says any man who comes into Collette's with a lady does so to look at dresses for *her* and not at girls for himself – and that suits the Gander, who likes husbands and boy friends to spend money here. So mind you dim your headlights, my girl. What's your name?'

'Joy Packer.'

'Well, Joy, you'll soon get to know the other girls. I expect you'll be with Dixie, Cornelia and me, modelling the inexpensives – little rags up to about fifteen guineas. Marigold and Ann do the exclusive models – the thirty, forty and fifty touch. Now, here are your things. The firm supplies us with these – shoes, stockings, step-ins and a wrap.'

I slipped out of my clothes into the flesh-coloured step-ins, stockings and satin shoes. The flamboyant wrapper reminded me of French Yvonne – the banner of youth hanging behind the door in her bare little bedroom.

'Now you'll want a light showroom make-up,' said Dawn. 'You can use my grease-paint. I'll do it for you if you like.'

While she made me up she chattered about the other girls.

'Cornelia is Dutch. She comes from Java and she has a husband in business in the City. Dixie has been Miss England twice and she's the most photographed model-girl in London. Ann's marvellous for sports things, and Marigold can make anything look a million dollars. Where d'you come from?'

'Cape Town.'

'Married?'

'Yes.'

'What's your husband?'

'A naval officer.'

'Then you're hard up. I know about the Navy. I come from Southsea. Tell me, do they have model-girls in Cape Town? I'd like to go there and try my luck.'

'No, not real professionals like here.'

'*Dawn!* Are you going to be down there all day?' came a bleat from above.

'That's old Rum-tum-tum! She's our dresser. . . . Coming, Miss Rumble! We're just ready.'

Miss Rumble was waiting for us in the showroom, and the moment I saw her I thought of 'Tot'. This was Marjorie's erstwhile governess in a new guise. Here, too, was a meagre two-dimensional spinster with a strong tendency to nag.

To the few customers who come into a model-house like Collette's to buy a dress in February the place seems dead. It is out of season, the blank that comes between the sale of the winter stock and the birth of the new spring fashions. But to us it was anything but dead. That thirty shillings a week was hard-earned, but it was worth far more than that to me. It was a first-hand glimpse behind the scenes – a jolly good look, in fact.

First of all, there were the girls, my daily companions in the model-girls' changing screen. Shivering against the radiator in their gaudy kimonos, they reminded me of the carmine and white hibiscus flowers in Tees Lodge garden, quivering in the first breath of the South-Easter. We were seldom all there at once, which was as well because the cubicle was small, but while waiting to be called they twittered of their beaux, the latest gossip about other well-known mannequins, the films – Greta Garbo was the universal favourite – and travel. They all wanted to travel and most of them had already been about a bit. Dawn had spent her last summer holiday in Spain.

'My uncle took me,' she said, innocent as a tall child, and thoughtfully plucked a few silken hairs from the delicate arch above her left eye.

Marigold giggled. Mention of Dawn's uncle never failed to amuse the others.

Marigold was Collette's best paid mannequin. She received five pounds a week, a high wage in her profession. She had a Renaissance head, copper hair and a wonderful figure – tall, of course (the minimum height is 5 feet 7 inches), with the requisite 36-inch hip measurement; but for all her slenderness she had a voluptuous grace that glamourized every gown she wore. She was always chosen to model furs.

Ann's streaky head was bent over some darning. She was the quiet one and had the trim figure for sports suits and tailor-mades. She was 'growing her hair out' after a bleach, and this gave her an outdoor sun-gold look. Cornelia had a little trick of humming to herself snatches of sentimental song-hits. 'It's *you* again,' she sang softly. '. . . I'll be blue again. . . .' Her Dutch accent was so slight as to be attractive, and she spoke good French and German. She was the smallest of us, dark with the long liquid eyes of Java. She often told us about Sourabaiya, where she had been brought up, and the tropic jungle and

186

mountains where you were thrilled because it was cold enough to need a blanket.

'I could do with some "trorpic yongles" myself,' said Dawn. 'Whyever did you leave Java and come to this benighted town?'

'To be married.'

'Do you *have* to work?' I asked.

She shook her head. 'I do it not to get bored. Besides, I love clothes.'

She did indeed. Cornelia was in love with pretty clothes and with her pretty self in them. When Miss Rumble slipped a dress over her head the Dutch girl stroked it caressingly down over her breasts and hips, then stood for a moment savouring her own charm before going lightly into the grey and silver showroom where the mirrored panels gave her again and again her own reflection. This was Cornelia's way of paying homage to her own beauty. She was Narcissus leaning over the lip of the pool, and she would lean thus till the last petal was faded.

Dixie, who had been to Paris and South America to represent England in international beauty competitions, was no English rose. She was dark and intense, and whenever I saw her she put me in mind of the hard rushing flame of a blowlamp. Her photograph was in every illustrated paper advertising cosmetics, dresses, cigarettes, soaps, anything you like, but they lacked the quality of the original. Dixie had integrity of the spirit rare enough in her world. If a smutty joke got a laugh in the changing screen, she held herself aloof and her lip curled. She was in love with a poor man and she intended to wait for him. Her beauty had a queer bitterness sometimes. She was not, like Cornelia, a mannequin by inclination. Her appearance had thrust this futility upon her and she resented it. Dixie was a bird of paradise with the wild heart of an eagle, and she alone among her companions beat her wings against the silver bars of her cage.

Such were the girls who plagued Miss Rumble, the dresser.

'There, Marigold, you've left lipstick on this gown! You're always doing that!'

'Well, how can I help it if you jerk it over my head as if you were trying to strangle me!'

'I'd like to strangle the lot of you sometimes.'

Dawn said: 'What's eating you today, Rummy? Corns? Cheer up, there's a dear.'

Poor Miss Rumble! Every day she had to minister to glamour-girls, to see and touch and envy skin, faces and figures that quicken the hearts of men when her own life was barren. No wonder she hated the mannequins sometimes.

Miss Long put her head into the changing-room. 'Joy, come to screen two; you are wanted for a fitting.'

Hours of standing followed. I have never been good at standing. Now it was a lesson to be learned.

Collette's had their own designers, fitters and workrooms. When the drawings had been selected the name of a mannequin was written across them and the dress was made on her. Several evening gowns and a few cocktail dresses had been allotted to Ivy, and these were now made on me. I felt like a doll as I stood in the fitting-room, silent and inanimate, while the designer and fitter, with the picture stuck up in a corner of the mirror, decided exactly where every line and seam and gather should be placed on the stiff transparent gauze of the white 'shadow model'. When they were satisfied the Gander was called. He stood, with twitching lips, staring from the sketch to the tarleton. Miss Jennings, the fitter, and Max, the designer, trembled as his wrath struck them.

'Those gathers in the front seam are hideous!' (*Heejuss* was what he said, and it sounded sibilant and dangerous.) 'Pass them out, for mercy's sake, and remember, Max, this isn't a maternity gown!'

The offending folds were smoothed away, and I was a stone statue with the fitter's murmurs rustling at my feet – dry leaves in the high wind of the director's temperament.

Seven hours of standing, with brief periods of rest in the models' screen. It was a long day. I ate my lunch in the canteen. The mannequins, in their gaudy kimonos, sat at their own little table, apart from the hundreds of sewing-girls – hibiscus flowers in the cabbage patch. Rum-tum-tum was at the head of the table, a governess with an acid tongue.

'If you eat that suet pudding, Dixie, you'll be sorry. You can't afford a centimetre more on that waistline of yours.'

'Oh, shut up, Rummy! My girth's all right.'

Cornelia hummed between mouthfuls: 'You belong to *meee*, bordy and sol . . .'

When I clocked out and went home after the first day my feet ached and so did my back.

'Well,' said Bertie, 'how was it?'

'Interesting.'

'Tiring?'

'Not specially. Just a bit unfamiliar.'

'I see.

On Sunday night we went to supper with Charles and Maisie te Water in Wilton Crescent. The tall house was essentially London. It had the same assurance as the Vernays' 'little house' in Berkeley Square, the same lofty confidence in its own good breeding. Only this was a dowager among houses, a heavy-weight. It accepted the South Africans graciously and wore upon its high walls the pictures of South African artists as a dowager wears the diamonds of Kimberley.

It was extraordinary how many of my cousins were in London that year, and those Sunday evening parties were more informal family gatherings than anything else. To me it was the best evening of the week.

Charles, tall and fair with sensitive features and very blue eyes, was a charming host – informal, amusing and even able to exercise a certain amount of control over his wife's wild, if spectacular, relations. There was usually Maisie's brother, 'Mike' Marais, at the grand piano, and perhaps Cicely or Peggy leaning over it, crooning 'What is life without a song? . . .' Aunt Stella, slim and elegant, mixed cocktails; Maisie, pretty as the day she was married and I let her down by fainting in the church, was a warm-hearted hostess; and somewhere in the background, curled up on a chair, there was Mike's exquisite wife Midge, watching the capers of her husband's family out of immense cynical black velvet eyes.

'Dangerous damn clan,' she said, her voice soft as wavelets lapping a quiet strand at low tide. 'You have to watch out or you're absorbed into it. Marais means Marsh, and in this case it's a bog – you get sucked under. Charles is all right. He's the head man here, and Joy's Rooi-nek could never be absorbed into anything without his own volition. But I have to fight to keep my own individuality'

I smiled across at my Rooi-nek (Englishman – red-neck). We did not think it likely that Midge would 'be absorbed'. She was as different from the Marais as midnight from noonday. She was the glimmer of gardenias on a dark night, the song of a nightingale in a cypress grove, or the new moon caught tiptoe on the spire of an Eastern minaret.

Charles wore an emerald-green love-bird on his shoulder, and the little creature's liquid chirrupings rippled round the lobe of his ear. It made me heart-sore when the love-bird perched on my arm or whispered against my cheek, because it said, 'Peter-Peter-Peter', which is what they twitter in their little bubbling voices.

Charles said to Bertie: 'Look here, you Rooi-nek! What's your young woman been up to? I had a letter from Collette's yesterday wanting to know if she is respectable.'

'She's taken the bit between her teeth again. She's got a job there as a mannequin.'

Charles ran long nervous fingers through his fair hair. 'Well, what did I tell you? Marais women may be a damn nuisance, but they're never dull.'

Aunt Stella said: 'What will your mother say?'

I laughed. 'That's what Bertie wanted to know. But when the apron-strings are six thousand miles away they don't tug so hard.'

At supper we were offered South African wines, and for dessert there were peaches and pears from Groot Drakenstein and grapes from Constantia, and afterwards we talked about our own country and our own people. The Rooi-nek smoked his pipe and listened. At ten o'clock there was tea for those who wanted it – and the Rooi-nek hid a smile as he helped himself to whisky. Tea at that hour! But he loved those Sunday suppers almost as much as I did.

'Your folk make me feel that I'm one of them,' he said afterwards.

'Would that be the first step towards being absorbed?'

He shook his head. 'It's true South African hospitality. You offer not only the shelter of your roof, the food from your larder, the wine from your cellar – and tea – but also something of yourselves. It is hospitality of the heart.'

As the time drew near for the three-day dress parade that

was to launch Collette's spring collection, the atmosphere of the whole establishment became charged with temperament. We mannequins stood all day while the designers, fitters and colour experts squabbled over the models and the Gander rushed in and out of the screens shouting 'Heejuss!' We were driven about like sheep to newspaper offices and film studios to be photographed, with the result that one awful day my sins went all the way home to Cape Town to roost. Mother and the Senior Aunt went to the cinema and saw a Pathé's Gazette featuring Collette's latest evening gowns. The Senior Aunt wiped her spectacles and looked again.

'Ellen!' she gasped. 'Is it possible that that young woman half naked on the film is your child?'

Ellen, equally appalled, gulped. 'It's very like her. The young people these days—'

My salary had been raised to two pounds a week, and all the time I was standing like a doll I was observing, listening and taking mental notes so that afterwards I could go home and write.

It was March 10th. On the morrow the French salon would be a theatre and we the show-girls.

Dawn came running into the models' screen waving a copy of the *Daily Express*. 'Can you beat it! There's an article here on the centre page all about model-girls – and Collette's at that! We are all in it – though not by name – and even Goosey Gander saying 'Heejuss!' Who on earth could have written it?'

They crowded round her.

' "All This to Make her Chic",' Marigold read aloud. ' "To-morrow the fashion cat will be out of the bag . . ." '

'Give here! Let's see! Why, if this isn't Rum-tum-tum, who is? And Miss Jennings and Max! I say, Miss Long, come and read this!'

Even the director came in and looked sheepish as he read the article.

I lounged against the radiator in my bright wrapper – the spy in their midst – and my cheeks burned under the grease-paint and the powder. The long hours of standing in the fitter's screen, the shivering in film studios, the aching feet, meant nothing now. 'All This to Make her Chic' was on the feature page – splashed! The smell of newsprint and the mutter of the presses were in my nostrils and ears and my heart beat high. After this, Fleet Street!

The parade had its own little dramas off-stage. Even the most experienced mannequins were nervous. Only Dutch Cornelia was unconcerned, humming 'My dear leetle Oliss blue gown . . .', pirouetting in front of the mirror – Narcissus nodding in a summer breeze. The designers and fitters gnawed their nails. The favourable reception of a model would be their justification, indifferent glances their shame. Goosey Gander was the captain of a ship going into battle, no longer shouting 'Heejuss!' and twitching his lip, but suave and encouraging. There were half a dozen free-lance mannequins employed for the three days, and Rum-tum-tum had to allot them various models and help us all in and out of our clothes like an inspired maniac.

There was a stage rigged up at the far end of the showroom with a black velvet background, and a spotlight followed us as we crossed it slowly, turning this way and that to show off our models, removing a cloak or a fur, and then walking down between the rows of little gilt chairs, pausing ever and anon as someone stopped us to feel the texture of the material or to ask the number of the dress. The two most spectacular gowns were the gold lamé court dress worn by Marigold and the white peau d'ange bride's dress worn by Dawn. An ovation greeted them and a little gasp of pleasure. The burnished copper of Marigold's Renaissance head and the three Prince of Wales feathers rose more haughtily in response, while Dawn's spun-gold curls, veiled and wreathed in orange-blossom, inclined demurely.

Yet afterwards, when it was all over, I found Marigold slumped over the make-up table in the locker-room weeping as if her heart would break.

'Whatever is it? Are you ill? Has the boy friend let you down some way?'

She looked up at me. The mascara was grotesquely smeared on her high cheek-bones.

'It's that ruddy Rumble! What d'you think she d-did? G-gave my hand-painted négligé to one of the extra girls. Sh-she knew how I loved wearing it . . . it's the one model I mind about – m-much more than the stinking court dress. She did it to spite me. . . . The extra got a hand—'

'Oh, Marigold, don't be so miserable! Rum-tum-tum'll see you wear it tomorrow if you really want to all that much. I'll ask her. But don't accuse her of doing you dirt on purpose. That's all I beg of you.'

I knew how Marigold felt. Of the many models made on us, we each had a special favourite we really loved – one that we were happy in, one that was not just a dress to be shown, but a dress to be cherished and desired, one that we recognized as most intimately ours. It is a woman-thing. Any woman will understand. Miss Rumble had understood full well. I sought her out.

'Marigold's in tears. It's the hand-painted négligé. She's crazy about it and a free-lance wore it – by accident, of course – but it was tough luck. I told her I knew you'd have saved it for her if you'd realized.'

Rum-tum-tum sniffed. 'Where's Marigold?'

'In the locker-room.'

I heard her go in, and presently her voice. 'Don't grizzle, my dear. I'm sorry an extra wore your négligé. I'll be sure it doesn't happen tomorrow.'

For once the old dresser forbore to nag. She had avenged herself sufficiently on Marigold's beauty and she was content with her poor little triumph.

When the three-days' parade was over I gave Miss Long my week's notice. It was not letting her down. The fittings and the show were over. I knew that any girl could wear 'My' models – and Bax had offered me a chance on the *Express*.

CHAPTER TWENTY-FOUR

'DAILY EXPRESS'

BAX's Laughing Buddha eyes gleamed at me across his wide desk.

'Well, Joy Packer. You are on three weeks' trial, and you'll be paid like a free-lance – expenses and the stuff that goes into the paper. If you don't make the grade, out you go on your ear.'

'And if I do?'

'For a start you'll get six guineas a week and expenses.'

'What's the limit in journalism?'

He conducted an imaginary *Gloria* with his narrow hands. 'The sky's the limit.' (It is the only limit he has ever recognized.)

Bax was then at the peak of his spectacular career in Fleet Street. He was building up the circulation of the *Express* as if by magic. From 700,000 in 1925 it was well on its way to the two million mark, which it attained in 1933 – the highest circulation of any daily newspaper in the world. Behind those mocking eyes there was a white flame of genius. Beaverbrook had recognized and used it.

That year of 1931 was not only the year of the depression and economic crisis; it was a year of destiny. That year the fate of England and her Press were bound together irrevocably as always in any national emergency, such as the Abdication and the many sore moments of hardship and defeat we have suffered in this war. The British Press may be a tiresome (if healthy) goad to the politician, but when the nation is in danger it is also his stand-by – a friend and adviser to the people, bidding the man in the street – Strube's Little Man – be of good cheer, encouraging him to carry on though his meagre fortune may be swallowed by an economic earthquake, though his future may be forfeit to the past muddling of those in power, or his very life endangered by the years of unpreparedness. In the autumn of 1931 England went off the Gold Standard and there was a general election. Beaverbrook, who had used his Press to the uttermost to flog his Empire Free Trade policy, abandoned that well-loved crusade to give his full support to the National Government, for in every national crisis unity of the Press is a point of honour.

Of that mild Sunday morning in September when the crash came Bax wrote:

Lord Beaverbrook was at his town house overlooking the park.

'It's come at last,' he said. 'The public does not know it yet and I am telling you in strict confidence. We have been driven off the Gold Standard.'

'Is this a real crash?' I asked.

He stood silent for a moment, and I saw by the trembling of his lips that he was making a supreme effort to control himself. 'Tomorrow,' he cried, 'this proud nation must admit defeat at the hands of the bankers of New York and Paris. It may be a crash or a panic or anything, because we have let events control us instead of controlling them. The foreigners have won.'

A messenger came in. It was an official communication for me from Downing Street. I read it and passed it over to Beaverbrook.

'The Prime Minister wants to see me at seven o'clock,' I said.

'Ah, yes,' said Beaverbrook. 'It will be a general conference of editors.'

It was a typical specimen of what the staff called Max-Bax dialogue.

While I naturally suspected that the Prime Minister did not want to see me alone, it was the way of the Beaver to reduce things always to their lowest denominator.

Next morning we announced to the public that Britain's liberation from the Cross of Gold had been achieved. Now the compass was set for smoother waters. 'No longer,' thundered the British Press, 'is the pound backed by a metal, but by the character and resources of the British people.'

Next day the Englishman backed his fancy for the 2.30, bought and sold his merchandise and never gave the matter a further thought. Through the foresight of MacDonald the Press had been given time to prepare the case, and they had brought the nation through a financial revolution which carried evil germs in its blood-stream.

It still fills me with retrospective exultation to recall that I was in Fleet Street at that time, an insignificant particle of the great British Press which guided the nation through a moment of peril.

However, my business in March was not with world affairs, but with women's angles. Bax is a musician, and there is in every musician a strong streak of feminine intuition. Perhaps it was this streak that made him realize the vital importance of his women readers. He was building up the gigantic circulation of the paper mainly in recognizing the needs and interests of women. And here, as a feminist myself, I want to point out that such a policy does not mean a lowering of the quality of the material that goes into the paper. Women are eager, intelligent readers and they get as good value out of a live, interesting paper as men. Moreover, on an average they have more time in which to enjoy and assimilate its contents. Women have, of course, always had their own sphere in the popular dailies – the home page with its various feminine interests. But it was the *Express* which first put the woman's angle on to news in a big way.

When Bax offered me my chance on the paper I fully expected to be handed over to Gordon Beccles and Jean Burnup, who ran the home, fashions and beauty sections, or perhaps to the feature editor, or even to scrounge a paragraph here and there for gossip. Instead he flung me straight into the deep waters of news to gasp and struggle and drown at once. Or learn to swim.

'Now listen, Joy Packer,' he said. 'When J.B. sends you out on an assignment, write as you think and feel from your own point of view – it'll be every woman's angle. That's why I'm giving you an opportunity. The woman's slant on life is the human slant, and that's what makes a story.'

J. B. Wilson came in at that moment J.B. was the finest news editor in Fleet Street – a man of steel, tall and lean, silver-haired, with keen grey eyes and the intellectual features one might expect to see under the white wig of a famous criminal barrister. Perhaps a great defending K.C. like Marshall Hall and a news editor like J.B. have certain gifts in common – the ability to smell out the human story from a welter of dull evidence and to present it to the public with brevity and drama. J.B. lived for the paper, and, as news is the life of a paper, so it was the breath of his sensitive nostrils. He and his chief had a quick discussion on some topical story, and then Bax said: 'This is Joy Packer. I want you to try her as a reporter. Woman's angles, interviews, anything you like. She can have three weeks to learn the ropes and then she can come on the staff or go out on her ear.'

It struck me that this 'out on her ear' refrain from the singing Editor was being slightly overdone.

J.B. gave me a cold impersonal look. He never did look at me other than impersonally, but in time the ice thawed slightly. I followed him meekly through the Big Room, where the sub-editors sat at their desks hacking the reporters' copy to ribbons, and into his office, which was about the size of Collette's smallest cubicle. Miss Secker, his assistant, had her desk in profile to the door. She was the epitome of brusque, cheerful efficiency. An exceedingly attractive girl was talking to her, neat, perfectly groomed, with a retroussé nose and clear, cool blue eyes. This was Margaret Lane, who later married Edgar Wallace's son and wrote her father-in-law's biography before her marriage broke up. Margaret Lane was a brilliant journalist. She approached a news story as analytically as a surgeon examining a patient. In an instant she diagnosed its value, and when she came to write it she excised and exposed that precious human element cleanly and fearlessly.

J.B. scratched about under a mountain of paper slips and brought out one with a name and address scribbled on it.

'You might follow this up, Miss Lane. There's a story somewhere under this. You may need to be away a day or two, but it'll be worth it.'

She glanced at it. 'Umn – Cornwall. Yes, there's something here. I'll have to go home for a toothbrush.' She was gone, a business-like figure, slim and determined.

J.B. turned to me. 'I haven't an assignment for you yet. Something may turn up later.'

My knees were shaking. 'What do I do in the meantime?'

'Oh, just hang about in the reporters' room, where they write their stuff. Opposite the Big Room. You can find a desk there, I expect.'

I looked in at the reporters' room. There were two or three men sitting at desks writing busily. Then I wandered down the passage to the Ladies and locked a door on my misery. Here was a situation to be faced. I knew absolutely nothing about news reporting and not one soul on the *Daily Express* except the Editor, who had, very rightly, washed his hands of me. Journalists with real experience were being sacked daily, and their colleagues were hardly going to look kindly upon a total greenhorn who had slipped in through the back door at dead of night. Panic seized me, and I was sick. After that I felt better able to think. Was it possible to lay one's cards on the table, go to J.B. and say, 'I never reported a news story in my life, but I believe I can do it if you'll tell me how'? But with that glassy look still in my memory I thought: No! The only thing to do was wait for the assignment and trust to inspiration.

The morning dragged past, I ate an egg and drank a glass of milk at an A.B.C., the afternoon waned, it was six o'clock, and still no assignment. The hectic night life of the paper was tuning up, everybody was in a terrible hurry and very busy, and no one addressed me.

When I got back to the flat in Earl's Court, Bertie was already home.

I had to gather myself together with an effort before going into the living-room, where he was reading the evening paper. He put it down and began to fill his pipe from a miniature oak barrel, and he said, carefully not looking at me after the first glance: 'Well, how was it?'

'I've been handed over to the news editor.'

'What happened?'

'Nothing much. Just learning the ropes' – with an attempt at jauntiness.

'You'll learn them,' he said. 'It's starting a thing that's always the worst. After that you can do it on your head.'

I grinned feebly. 'If I can't do it on my head, it's out on my ear.'

Three days went by and still no assignment. But progress had been made. Two of the reporters, 'Tommy' Tomlinson and Stanley Bishop, had spoken to me.

'Bish' was the crime reporter. He had curly pepper-and-salt hair, glasses and a very kind heart, and perhaps because seeking out the truth behind the crime was his business, the wise eyes spotted at once that here in the office was a miscreant – a young woman trying to get away with something and not succeeding. It was three in the afternoon, a Wednesday, and I was sitting at a spare desk whiling away my depressing leisure by writing a mannequin article I hoped to sell to a certain woman's magazine. Bish came and sat on the desk.

'Very good paper this morning,' he volunteered. 'Did you have a story in it?'

'I haven't had an assignment yet.'

'Really! But you've decorated the office for three days.'

I laughed ruefully. 'It's awful.'

'Why don't you go up to the *Sunday Express* on the next floor and see Russell Stannard, the news editor? He may have something for you.'

'But what about J.B.?'

'Tell him where you'll be.'

I took his advice.

The offices of the *Sunday Express*, on the top floor of the building, were 'stiller than a deep well at noon, or lovers met; than sleep, or the heart after wrath' compared with the babel below. The news editor was unprotected by the usual phalanx of secretaries, and he actually said 'Come in' when I knocked at his door. Russell Stannard had a slight cast in a sympathetic brown eye, which I instantly took to be lucky for me. He had iron-grey hair, an easy manner and a ready smile. The moment I saw him the accumulated nervousness of the past three days fell away from me. A Sunday paper does not really get busy till Thursday afternoon, and Wednesday's atmosphere of time being no object was immeasurably restful.

Russell Stannard did not ask me my age or if I loved my husband, but he inquired mildly if the colour of my hair was the fashionable platinum, and was disappointed to hear that it was only ash.

'I can give you a country wedding to cover,' he said. 'It's a minor foreign royalty getting away with a wealthy Quaker. The agencies'll be looking after it, but we might as well send our own reporter.'

When I told J.B. I would be away next day for the *Sunday Express* he received the news calmly.

Russell Stannard read my copy on Friday morning while I sat quaking; then he looked up, tore at his hair and groaned.

'My dear girl, this isn't a news story! It's an *essay!*'

'Oh' — crestfallen. 'Could you explain how it ought to be?'

'It's this way. When you set out to cover a news story you are not trying to write an article. A paper buys articles from out-side writers — free-lances. It hires its reporters to bring in and present the *news*. I can see you know nothing about news, so I'll tell you the two oldest chestnuts in Fleet Street to give you an idea. When a dog bites a man it isn't news, but when a man bites a dog it is. And there was the cub reporter who was sent to cover a wedding. He came back empty-handed, and when the sub-editor asked him for his copy he said: 'There wasn't any story. The bridegroom didn't turn up.' That boy didn't know news when he had it on a plate! Get me? When you write a news story you've got to snap right into it and *dramatize the human interest*. What've you done here? You've given a leisurely description of the little town where the wedding took place and then you've wandered on to chat about the bride. Good heavens girl, no one cares about the place; they want to hear about the people! Now, *here's* your human interest buried under the frills. There were eight bridesmaids, and you noticed that none of them wore any make-up, not even a dab of lipstick. *That's* the point – a big society wedding, a Quaker community and no make-up. That's the woman's angle and that's what we want. Bang right into that and forget the little medieval town. Go and rewrite it.'

Russell Stannard showed me how to twist a news story so that its human content hit the reader like a torpedo. If I failed to do so it was my fault, not his. He gave me courage and a measure of confidence. His office was a friendly place. Sometimes a short, energetic man with cynical spectacled brown eyes came in. This was Christiansen, now the Editor of the *Daily Express*. It would be easy to be afraid of Christiansen. He had the ruthlessness essential to success. At other times the monstrous figure of Lord Castlerosse rolled into the office with the copy of the 'Londoner's Log'. His mischievous dark eyes in the vast expanse of his face were laughing piccaninnies in the immensity of the pale winter veld. I was introduced to Nathaniel Gubbins – for that is indeed his name – and he levered himself out of his chair and allowed his lugubrious features to relax in a melancholy smile.

In the library, where I used to pester Mr. Long, the librarian, for information about one thing and another, the slight shoulders of H. V. Morton were often to be seen bowed over his notes. He was writing his 'In Search of London' series for the *Daily Express*, and he wandered, wraith-like, in and out of the tall building in Shoe Lane, dreamy-eyed, gentle and apart. Sometimes in a corridor I ran into a short, square, thick-set man with a big nose, quick perceptive eyes and untidy hair. He carried a huge drawing-block under his arm. This was Strube, the famous cartoonist, bearing his 'little man' to the art department. Once, as I was leaving my typewriter with the commissionaire at the end of the day, a rather heavy dark man with a kind, clever Semitic face and a grizzled moustache stopped me and said: 'I haven't seen you about before. Who are you?'

I recognized the Editor-in-Chief, R. D. Blumenfeld, the best-loved and most respected editor in London.

'I'm Joy Packer, and I'm working on your paper. Three weeks' trial.'

'Come to my office.'

He led me down the corridor to a much more luxurious office than that of the Managing Editor.

'Sit down and tell me about yourself. How old are you? Are you married? Do you love your husband?'

'Blum' was a sick man then, near the end of his time on the *Express*. In Fleet Street he was renowned for his kindness – and kindness is a rare quality in the hard, quick, black-and-white newspaper world where yesterday is more dead than Tutankhamen. He asked how I was getting on and told me not to be disheartened when my stories were cut to a line by the sub-editors or thrown out altogether, and he gave me a few valuable hints.

Presently J. B. Wilson began to give me assignments with scope in them, and I was no longer terrified when he handed me a slip of paper with a name scrawled across it and some address, as like as not miles out of town. Necessity is a swift and brutal teacher, and I soon learned to ferret out news and to write my copy in a bus or tube, to telephone it from the country extempore, and to interview without taking notes, because I found that a notebook and a pencil worried most people and that they told their story best by talking all round it first – and, in any case, I remember conversations easily. I learned to spot when people were trying to get free publicity out of an interview and that newspapers do not give advertising 'puffs' in their news columns, and so my three weeks' probation slipped away and, shivering with fear, I went to Bax's office.

He looked at me with his half-smile and his twinkling, inscrutable Buddha eyes. 'Well, how are you doing?'

'That's for you to say. My three weeks' trial is up. Is it out on my ear or is it six guineas a week and expenses?'

'Come back this afternoon and I'll tell you. But I expect you're fired.'

When I went back he said: 'J.B. can use you in news. Go ahead.'

My heart sang. The smell of the newsprint was frankincense and myrrh, the clatter of the typewriters was the music of the spheres, and the big red bus that carried me back to Earl's Court was a chariot of fire.

'Out on your ear, I suppose?' said Bertie.

I fell on his neck in a whirlwind of ecstasy. 'I'm on the staff! I belong! Oh, darling, darling, you're married to a journalist!'

He was wonderfully patient about being married to a journalist. Sometimes we went together in the car to chase a country story, often I was late home, and once or twice I had to be away for a night following up some interview or another. But he was working very hard too, and I think that he was glad that I was so fully occupied, for he knew that otherwise the flat without Peter and Nannie would have been dark indeed.

Margaret Lane had gone to America, and Kitty Courlander (an experienced journalist) and I were the only two women reporters on the staff. We were hard-worked. My interviews covered a wide range, from a Whitechapel tenement where I talked to Kid Berg, the lightweight boxing champion – Mother Berg looking wildly incongruous in a mink coat – to a Mormon conference, where Brigham Young's elderly grand-daughter assured me nasally that her illustrious grandparent's nineteen wives had never had a quarrel!

But as autumn came with the gathering force of the economic hurricane that was about to strike England and drive her off gold I began to realize another side of journalism. More and more it was borne in upon me that a great newspaper has a responsibility towards the public – the Popular Press most of all. The woman's angle became subservient to the morale angle. Every story written at that time was calculated to reassure and encourage, so that, when the storm broke, the Press with its sanity and good judgment brought the ship of the 'Little man' safely into port.

On the night of the general re-election Bertie and I were at Gordon Selfridge's roof-garden party on the top floor of the huge Oxford Street store. Two bands played. Women in gorgeous evening gowns danced with men in tails and white ties. Champagne flowed. England might have been at the height of her prosperity. In a separate room a cinema showed the names of those elected to Parliament and loud-speakers shouted them. The Conservatives came in with an overwhelming majority, and we knew that the nation had weathered a crisis successfully. And I knew how much of that success was due to Beaverbrook himself. He had relegated his cherished vision of a British Empire economically united against the world to second place in order to give his undivided support to the Conservatives because he believed that their policy of foreign tariffs was a step on the way to his own wider conception.

Lord Beaverbrook. Many times I had heard him addressing political meetings when his Empire Free Trade candidates were standing for Parliament – frail and forceful, a fanatic hobgoblin rising superior to ill-health to back his beliefs and slash right and left at his adversaries As a boy in Canada Max Aitken had known the literal meaning of the word 'hunger'; now his mouthpiece, the *Express*, was a power in the land second to none. He interviewed me one day at his home in Leatherhead. He wanted a columnist, and Bax thought I might do. The Beaver's mansion was a huge bleak building on a hill-top overlooking a panorama of hill and dale, wood and meadow such as I had scarcely realized existed in England, where the next house is always just round the corner. The room in which we sat was spacious and lofty, furnished in a harsh, light modern way, and all one side consisted of french windows opening on to that wide vista.

The Beaver sat beside me on the sofa, a dynamic gnome with burning eyes.

'How old are you?' And presently he said: 'Do you love your husband?'

Strange that Bax, R. D. Blumenfeld and now Beaverbrook had all asked the same question. Is a happily married woman too smug to be a good journalist? Does the germ of domestic discord heighten her faculty for seeing and dramatizing that all-important human interest? Perhaps.

Beaverbrook is intensely personal, a quality which he shares with other great men. When he concerns himself with mere nobodies he does so with a vital interest which galvanizes them into something greater than themselves. He killed any shyness I might have felt at once, just as Winston Churchill had done in Malta. But he decided against me as a columnist.

'Stick to news,' he said. 'And try your hand at more short stories. This "Gallant Lie" is good.' (My cutting-book was open at 'Nigger Baby', renamed 'Gallant Lie'.)

It was nice of him to turn me down so gently, for gentleness was not his way.

A small child danced into the room. She was Jeanne Campbell, his grand-daughter. She interrupted his conversation and clambered on to his knee, regardless of his frown. She was followed presently by a distinguished statesman.

I returned to Earl's Court dazed and exhilarated. Meeting Beaverbrook had been like heading into a storm.

It is a curious thing that many of our friends who had not been at all shocked when I became a mannequin were sincerely outraged at my taking a job as a reporter. To most people newspaper reporters are scrofulous little creatures prying into other people's affairs, or they are the Hollywood version – drunks wearing their hats in the house, or sob-sisters without any decent scruples. They are, in fact, just ordinary individuals doing their work to the best of their ability like anyone else, and giving the public its news at breakfast-time. Some specialize, others get no further and become 'hack reporters', and a few move on and bestride the earth. These are the foreign correspondents, who sense where a story is going to break or a war break out while the Foreign Office is still dreaming in the rarefied atmosphere of its own creation – a sort of diplomatic fourth dimension. Unfortunately, most heads of British missions are too suspicious of the Press to use it. They are apt to regard all newspaper men as unreliable and subversive rogues who may get them into trouble. Ambassador Davis, the American Ambassador in Russia from 1936 to 1938, was wiser, but then he was not a diplomat de carrière, but a trained lawyer, and he was shrewd enough to use the experienced newspaper men on the spot to keep him informed of the trend of events, with the result that he was more than a step ahead of his colleagues in two particulars. Through his Press contacts, so carefully and generously fostered, he knew not only what was happening in the country, but the shape of things to come.

One evening Stanley Bishop, Tommy Tomlinson and Earle Spencer came into the reporters' room and invited me to go with them to the Cheshire Cheese for a drink. I stepped over the sawdust of that ancient and honourable public-house, which had known Ben Jonson and Samuel Pepys, more proudly than when I trod the rich carpets of Buckingham Palace to be presented at Court.

Elated with the honour and the gin, I went home and said to Bertie: 'The chaps took me to the "Cheese"!'

His smile was understanding. 'So you feel as if you'd just been elected to the Royal Yacht Squadron?'

One evening in December, when I came back late and tired, I saw at once that my husband had something to tell me. His eyes were shining and excited, yet somewhere behind them lay an obscure regret.

'You've heard about your next job?'

He nodded.

'Oh, my dear! Tell me quickly, where is it? Somewhere healthy where we can have Peter?'

Simonstown perhaps? A flame leapt within me, and was quenched with a word.

'CHINA.'

He had been appointed second-in-command of the cruiser *Kent*, refitting at Chatham.

'I'll have to sail with the ship from there,' he said. 'No chance even of seeing Peter. But you must go home and be with him for a while. Then you can join me in Hong Kong.'

So that was the excitement – and the regret.

On January 8th, 1932, I walked down Shoe Lane for the last time.

I collected my typewriter from the commissionaire and said my good-byes. 'Bish' and Tommy were in the reporters' room. They were smoking cigarettes and waiting for J.B. to give them their assignments.

Bish said: 'We'll miss the blonde decoration.' And Tommy said: 'Seen this?' He handed me the journalists' 'trade magazine', the *World's Press News*, and showed me a small paragraph that meant more to me than any social 'puff' in the *Tatler* or *Sketch* could ever have done.

'Miss Joy Packer, who has just left the *Daily Express* to travel to South Africa and then on to China to join her husband, is one of the prettiest women reporters in journalism. She is also one of the hardest working and can take her share in any story with the best of men. She will be greatly missed in Fleet Street.'

The Royal Yacht Squadron indeed! I looked at them, almost too thrilled to speak.

'Who put it in?' I asked at last.

'Ah!' said Bish, and studied his nails thoughtfully.

Part Three

THE DANGEROUS YEARS

CHAPTER TWENTY-FIVE

SOUTHWARD BOUND AND EASTWARD BOUND

'WE must hunt out some China birds,' said Bertie, 'and see how the land lies. Then we'll know whether we can uproot the sportsman from Tees Lodge or not.'

There are always 'China birds' about – naval people who have been on the Far Eastern Station. We asked their advice about having Piet with us and learned that it is not wise to take children over six out East. 'Anyway, you'll have no home. It's Hong Kong in the winter, Wei-Hai-Wei in the summer and anywhere from Java to Japan in between whiles – if you can afford to follow the ship.'

Bertie and I parted for several months in Chatham. The hotel where we spent our last night together was sordid. There were grimy lace curtains at the windows and blood on the bread at dinner. The waitress had cut her finger. But we weren't hungry, anyway.

The *Kent* was a three-funnelled cruiser and she was not dark like the ships of the Home Fleet, but light tropical grey, and she looked brave and rather fragile as she sailed away. To me she was always 'the pretty ship'. There were other wives and families to wave her farewell, mostly ratings' wives, and it was worse for them than for me. I would see my man again in China, while they would be alone for two and a half years or more. Some of them were crying.

A month later I was hanging over the rail of a liner docking in Cape Town. Mother and Daddy were down on the quay, and between them a little boy danced up and down in a state of wild excitement. It was an eternity before the ship was cleared. But at last I was running down the gangway, past the guard, and the thin, dancing little boy legs were flashing towards me. The small square hand clasped a carnation, and, half-suffocated by my embrace, Piet gasped, 'I picked it speshly for you, Mom!' and I answered, between laughter and tears: 'Such a beauty, darling! White with a frilly red border, my favourite sort!'

'I know. Gramp told me.'

' 'Ullo, 'ullo, old chap! It's good to see you back home.' That was Daddy. And Mother said: 'My child, you look half-starved. We must fatten you up.'

Arend was waiting at the car.

'Well, Arend certainly doesn't look half-starved!' I laughed.

The brown man grinned cheerfully. 'I get so fat, Miss Yoy, de baas give me a new uniform.'

Mother, with her light, ringed fingers on my arm, was saying: 'Arend's wife has just presented him with the tenth baby.'

At home Teena welcomed me with her enormous smile. 'Master Peter was so excited, he talk in his sleep all night.' And Cookie came out to greet me, giggling joyfully and wiping her hands on her apron just as I had known she would do. She announced happily that my brothers were coming to dinner, Fred with his wife and Norman with his fiancée Molly, who was still a stranger to me. 'An' we got roas' pigeons an' grana-illa cream and dere's sampain in de ice-box.' It was my regular home-coming menu. Cookie's husband, 'the General', was paying his bi-weekly visit to Tees Lodge, and with him was their young daughter Chrissie, that surprising blossom of Cookie's early middle age, a gentle-featured girl with enormous eyes and two pigtails. Cookie blushed in her own petunia fashion. 'What Miss Yoy t'ink of Chrissie? She getting a big girl now. Nex' year she come work for Madam.'

'Master Peter got a surprise for his Mommy,' said Teena. 'Have you tell your Mommy about it, my love?'

My love led us to his nursery and opened the door. Teena galumphed after us.

'Well, this is a funny surprise,' I said. 'It's pitch dark!'

Daddy chuckled, my love laughed delightedly and Teena turned on the light. The shutters were closed and the blinds drawn, shutting out the hot February sunshine. A miniature railway was laid out on the floor. Chrissie and 'the General' stood in the doorway, their eyes bulging with interest. 'It's 'lectric,' announced Piet. 'Gran and Gramp gave it to me for Christmas.'

The nimble little fingers operated a couple of switches and a tiny engine bustled round the room at high speed while the green eyes of the child shone with pride.

Nearly two years ago I had stood in this nursery looking down at a sleeping toddler, longing to take him in my arms, not daring to wake him, and here was a sprite of six with the baby look already gone from his mischievous face.

The wheels of the little train whirred, Piet gazed fascinated, absorbed, changing the points often so that the engine made sudden unexpected détours, and we watched in silence – my parents, the coloured servants and the prodigal mother.

'Teen! Turn off the light!'

'Yes, Master Piet.' Obediently the brown hand sought the switch.

'There, Mom, look!'

The little engine had its own headlight and a miniature searchlight played on the station. Tinkerbell weaved this way and that in the gloom as her owner shifted the points.

'Foei tog!' gasped Cookie. 'What you t'ink of dat, Chrissie?'

I felt Mother's hand slip into mine in the darkness. There was a salty taste in my mouth and my eyes smarted. What were the steps that had led from the simple comfort of 'amalun' to this complicated toy? What were the thoughts and childish hopes in this little stranger's mind? What made him laugh? What made him cry? When Teena put up the lights again it was too soon for me.

Gradually I learned to know 'our child' again. He had none of my fear of the dark, but he hated the sight of blood, and if he was upset or unhappy he turned very pale and his voice took a queer brittle pitch that pulled at my heart. He couldn't bear the sound of a fog-horn, but he roared with laughter at my father's abominable habit of sneezing full blast. It was difficult to prevent him from giving away his toys, and when he played draughts with his grandmother a ludicrous situation arose with both parties striving with might and main to lose, as neither could endure to win from the other. I found, with amusement, that he objected violently to his grandmother's liaison with the inexorable Culbertson, and when the Thursday morning post-mortem took place at breakfast after the weekly bridge battle with the Dilwaters, Peter cried aloud from his porridge: 'No bridge talk! No Culbertson!' He had what Nannie was pleased to term 'an iron will'. His best friend was Arend, and these two spent hours in the 'carpenter's shop' contriving and constructing a glorified soap-box on wheels, in which Piet and a kindergarten companion named Hans careered about the neighbourhood at breakneck speed. Sometimes, when Hans was not available, Piet and Teena trailed 'the cart' up the mountain-side to collect fir-cones, and Piet rode down Hope Street again seated in triumph on his cargo while Teena screeched at him, her voice incredibly high with anxiety: 'Go slow, my love!' But my love only laughed and waved and swerved wildly to a standstill at the gate. I discovered that he liked best to visit Nannie's cottage and eat her 'noodle-süppen' and chocolate blancmange; and that he had both gentleness and gusto, since it pleased him to stroke my hair; but when I kissed him good night and he appeared most angelic, as often as not he opened his mouth wide and bit my nose. Most of all it made me smile to see my mother appealing to his better nature and explaining painstakingly why good children were always happier than bad ones. Poor Piet, whose better nature was highly susceptible, fell for her line, hook, bait and sinker. He went whistling about the house on errands for his grandmother (he whistled on one side of his mouth only, drawing in his breath in a thin little sound that made us smile), and Mother said to me, for his benefit: 'You see how pleased everybody is to see Piet because he comes along skipping and whistling. Now, if he were a *sulky* boy, no one would want to have him around!'

'Oh yes,' I agreed. 'People love cheerful children.' I recognized the technique.

It was strange and lovely how quickly I slipped back into the ways of Tees Lodge. Here alone, in the transitory pattern of my life, was permanence, ways and habits and people unchanging as the blue hills and vineyards so dear to me.

When I woke that first morning at home there was Cookie flinging back the shutters.

'Did Miss Yoy sleep well?'

'Beautifully. Where's Piet?' (What warmth and contentment in the thought that he was here!)

'He's still very excite. He'll be coming to see his Mommy in a minute.'

Through the open french windows I could see the sun on the violet shoulder of Signal's Hill. There was the soft cooing of doves, the tinkle of scales from the Good Hope Seminary, the click of the gate and the automatic barking of the airedale Kismet as the postman's brisk step sounded on the flagged path and his double ring at the front door. And then there was the patter of my son's feet down the passage and his merry 'Mornin', Mom!'

Everything was as it had always been. Once a week the Malay washerwoman, Sabela, more mountainous than ever, swayed up to Tees Lodge to collect her money, resplendent in candy pink, gaudy purple or lime green, a fantastic combination of Gauguin and Epstein. On Saturday mornings Kismet was washed in the backyard, and on Sundays Daddy pottered among his carnations or carpentered with his grandson. When there was a breeze Piet and Hansie flew their kites from the garage roof. Nannie came to see us often, and every Friday morning Mother and I had tea with the Senior Aunt on her sunny stoep at Rondebosch. She had grown a little frailer and lost much of her acerbity. I saw, suddenly and with a pang, that she was old. Her skin was cold and light as I kissed her cheek, as if it might crumble into powder beneath my lips. As a little girl my grandmother Petersen's skin had felt like this to me.

'Well,' said my aunt, 'how do you find your child? Your mother spoils him, of course.' But her tone was less sharp than her words. She drew me close to look at me, for her bright, twinkling eyes were almost sightless. 'Too much lipstick,' she murmured from force of habit. 'You young people are all just façade. My generation was real. So was Ellen's.'

Almost I saw what she meant, even then. Now I understand. It has taken the grim years of war to rub the gilt off my generation and reveal it as sound. The old and the young of 1940 were sound as a bell. We were the doubtful quantity, the children of the last war and the matrons of this.

Most Sunday afternoons we called in at Les Marais to see one or another of my cousins. The vineyards were heavy with fruit and the purple haanepoort grapes were shadowy under the emerald leaves. The squirrels chattered in the fir trees.

We went for picnics to the haunts of my childhood, and

Daddy and Peter grilled chops together, and afterwards we gathered great bunches of wild flowers, and one day Arend drove us over the mountain passes to Onrust, where Marjorie and I had spent so many school holidays. We stayed there for a week and saw the baboons scampering over the rocks with the babies astride their mothers' backs, we had tea on Ma Kuys' stoep and I marvelled as of yore at the formidable features under the starched kappie, and every morning Piet fished for minnows in the dark amber lagoon while I idled in the sun and listened once more to the deep voice of the sea and thrilled at its power.

The arums grew along the cliffs and in the fields and gulleys, and the rock daisies dozed on the beaches with their white and yellow faces turned upwards to the sun.

We went often to Muizenberg, where my son clung to my shoulders like a limpet as we rode the long lines of surf together, lying flat on my board. Then it was April with rainbow moments of simultaneous sun and shower – 'monkey's wedding' we call that in South Africa – and soon it was May with a chill in the air. Now the roar of the South-Easter was silent in the fig orchard and the first soft rains of autumn were falling, and at last there came the painful day when a small Dutch cargo-boat, bound for Java, sailed from Cape Town with only one passenger on board.

A handful of people sped that small ship on her voyage – a little boy and his grandparents and his two broad-shouldered uncles. The coloured chauffeur stood behind them, sad for the sake of the child. The little boy ran to the end of the quay with his white handkerchief fluttering from his hand. I saw my mother follow him and lay a restraining touch on his shoulder, while Daddy stood beside her with his fists deep in the pockets of his overcoat. He looked old and bowed and dejected next to his two tall sons. When would I see them again, these folk of mine? There was the familiar ache in my throat and the familiar taste of tears and spray. The sea was choppy, white horses plunged in the bay and outside there was a heavy swell. I stood alone on deck till the last of the Twelve Apostles was a phantom in the sunset, and then suddenly I realized that it was bitterly cold and nearly nightfall.

The *Roggeveen* was very old and she suffered severely from

an advanced form of St. Vitus' dance. In fact, so violently did she vibrate as she dawdled across the Indian Ocean that it was impossible to write a letter on board. So I used my typewriter instead, and even then it sometimes cavorted away across the table in the little saloon which served as writing-room, bar, lounge and music-room. The music was produced by a wheezy old gramophone belonging to the chief engineer. We carried no purser, and the Chief did all the business with money and papers that pursers usually do. There was no stewardess either, but Javanese stewards with gay batik turbans looked after the ten cabins. Instead of a bathroom there was a cubby-hole with a tub and a ladle so that you could sluice yourself down with cold water. If you wanted hot, the steward brought a can to the cabin. Such was my home for four weeks.

As far as Durban I was the only passenger, but there we reaped an inconsiderable harvest of two, Mr. Roundel and Miss de Jonge. Mr. Roundel was a Falstaffian fellow of about sixty, who had decided to take a cruise to Batavia and back to reduce his weight. 'I'm told it's like living in a Turkish bath,' he said. 'Just what I need.' He sat in a deck-chair all day with his multiple chins and pendulous paunch quivering to the throb of the *Roggeveen*'s engines.

Miss de Jonge was a frenzied septuagenarian with her thin white hair screwed into a tight knot at the back of her head and her weak red-rimmed eyes ever straining for the sights and sounds of alien shores. For over half a century she had taught geography in a school in Amsterdam, 'and now I am going to see the world for myself,' she pronounced firmly. 'I have my pension and my savings, but so little time!'

She strode through the tropics, her lined old face dripping with perspiration, her camera clasped in her clammy hand, and her Panama hat shading the voracious expression magnified by her glasses. I trailed after her through the dank, clove-scented heat of Zanzibar and Mombassa, and together we absorbed an atmosphere of decay on the coast of Mauritius. We lounged against the rail and gazed at the dark outline of Madagascar, and my thoughts flew a long way down the years to a certain summer night in Bloemfontein and a general election – Val and I standing side by side in the square and the crowd cheering as Deneys Reitz, the successful South African Party candidate, was chaired through the town on stalwart shoulders. I had cheered too till Val had clutched my sleeve to remind me that I was a rebel and Reitz a Smuts man. It was here in Madagascar that Reitz himself had once been a young rebel in voluntary exile just after the Boer War, and here that he had written *Commando* between bouts of fever and convoying goods by ox-wagon from the swamps and forests of the interior to the coast 'across mountains sodden with eternal rain'.

I thought of the woman who had recalled this young hothead from his self-imposed exile to his own country. A very remarkable woman, and none other than Mrs. Jannie Smuts. She had written to say that if her husband could see fit to work for South Africa under British rule Deneys Reitz could do like-wise; and on his return she had nursed him back to health of mind and body for three years. Gradually the loyalty of the Boer lad to his defeated country had developed into the wider conception of the South African looking forward to a glowing future for his land. Mrs. Smuts, who has played an unobtrusive part in many such conversions, is a strange mixture of the ma-ternal and the blue stocking. She and her husband were fellow-students at Stellenbosch University, and through the years they have been bound together not only by common interests, joys and sufferings, but also by a rare mental affinity. Her husband's work and their children and grandchildren are the mainspring of her life. He says of her that his Sybella is a 'child of Nature', and indeed she is famous – even among the easy-going South Africans – for her complete indifference to the conventions. But although she may be oblivious of the dresses that hang in her wardrobe, she is always concerned lest the latest grandchild's 'nappies' that wave on the line be not sufficiently aired. Perhaps that is why she is known to the people of her own land and beyond as 'Ouma' ('Granny').

We acquired two more passengers at Mombassa, a young Australian coffee-planter who had lost all his money in Kenya, and the matron of a hospital in Tanganyika. The young man had a 'lean and hungry look', but I did not find him dangerous, and the matron was wrung dry by malaria. She wore a pith sun-helmet and the reflection of its green lining was corpse-like on her sallow skin.

The passengers took their meals with the officers at a long table always loaded with good things, and the captain, who had the face and figure of Winnie the Pooh, presided with a nursery air reminiscent of Nannie. In just such accents had Nannie urged my small friends to eat what was good for them at Tees Lodge children's parties. The first officer was heavily handsome and a bit of a wag, but, as his English was limited, he expressed himself chiefly by the able use of a pair of liquid black orbs. The Chief was squat and strong as a gorilla, with a huge nose and a passion for teasing the life out of everyone on board. His favourite target was the doctor, who was a sinister old scare-crow, wizened yet sprightly, like an African medicine-man. One felt that he should be wearing a necklace of teeth and toenails with the skull and cross-bones for a sporran. When he flicked his sharp, rheumy, jaundiced glance round the table my flesh crept. He seemed to be 'smelling out' a victim.

'He does his best,' remarked the Chief, with a twinkle, 'but ven it is important operation I make it. For example, I deliver de babies. I have exberience of my vife—'

Miss de Jonge begged him to desist. 'Do not explain further. I am sure we shall have no need of your attentions in that respect.'

'I hope not,' said the Chief, and favoured me with a broad wink. He was incorrigible.

There is a point in every voyage where one's attitude of mind effects a sort of change-over from harking back to looking forward. This happened to me at dawn one morning three weeks out when the amethyst peaks of Mahé rose from a dreaming sea.

'The Coral Islands of the Seychelles,'* murmured old Miss de Jonge rapturously, 'the islands of the double cocoanut, of turtle soup and tortoise-shell—'

'And some of the finest deep-sea fishing in the world,' added Mr. Roundel.

The matron from Tanganyika pointed out a verdant rock at the entrance of the harbour. 'The leper colony,' she remarked, and the soft sweet morning turned chill.

The Chief's eye gleamed roguishly. 'You can buy a wife here for the price of a few fish – a beautiful café-au-lait girl with frangipani flowers in her hair.' He sighed wistfully and de-parted to assemble the *Roggeveen*'s football team.

We chugged ashore in the ship's boat, and through the trans-parent water we could see shoals of bright fish swimming over

* *Now a fashionable international playground.*

the coral reefs. A little group of people in tired whites stood on the jetty.

'Anyone collect stamps?' asked the local doctor as we stepped ashore.

'I do,' panted Mr. Roundel.

'Care to see my collection?' The doctor's voice was eager. 'You would? Fine. Then come along with me and we'll have a mug of beer at my house.'

The ship's officers and the soccer team, accompanied by the young man from Kenya, made their way to the football ground, where the islanders, playing barefoot, defeated the Dutch and Javanese *Roggeveen* players. But Miss de Jonge led the matron and me firmly to the Botanical Gardens in search of the double cocoanut, which grows nowhere else in the world. The moist heat dewed our foreheads, the scent of frangipani was heavy in the sun, and in the gardens we met an old French botanist, who took us to his wooden bungalow for a glass of lemonade. Behind it, among the palms and tropical trees, was a cool virginal grove of silver birches.

'I planted them to remind me of home,' he said. 'They are very young, delicate as aigrette's feathers, but they are doing well. They are my children – my French children.'

'But won't you go back to France?'

'I came here for two years' research and I have stayed for twenty-five. Now my blood is too thin for me to go back. I have left it too late.'

When he heard I was South African, he said: 'We have a countryman of yours here. He came to Mahé for six months' deep-sea fishing. He is a good friend of mine.'

'You will miss him when he goes back.'

The old botanist shook his grizzled head. 'He will never go back. He came here for his holiday seven years ago, and he is still here.'

Giant spider-webs festooned the trees and there was a drowsy silence over the place, broken only by the calls of strange, brilliant birds and the high songs of insects.

'Civilization has passed us by,' smiled the old gentleman wanly. 'We have no theatres and no cinemas here, no banks and very few shops. I dare say these – amenities – will catch us up. But not yet. General Gordon believed that this island was the Eden of the Bible – the cradle of humanity. Each to his own fancy. *I* know that it is the Island of the Lotophagi, and we who have stayed here too long have eaten of the fruit of oblivion.'

As I looked into his heavy eyes, the whites as yellow and lustreless as his withered skin, I knew that he was right. '*Now whosoever of them did eat the honeysweet fruit of the lotus had no more wish to bring tidings or to come back, but there he chose to abide with the lotus-eating men, ever feeding upon the lotus and forgetful of his homeward way.*'

It was with the utmost difficulty that we wrenched Mr. Roundel away from the stamp-collecting doctor's house and dragged him with us to the launch. The spell was upon him, and but for us he might have missed the ship and remained for ever with the Lotophagi.

When we returned on board we found the Chief looking even more than usually like a mischievous Caliban. He had a present for Miss de Jonge and he produced it with pride. A giant double cocoanut. The old school-ma'am gazed at the hairy black Siamese twin, aboriginal and monstrous as the missing link. 'Ach,' she said at length, 'all this time I have desired this fruit, and now I find it revolting.'

'C'est la vie,' remarked the Chief, with his prodigious wink, as he threw it overboard.

One night there was a weird red glow in the velvet sky.

'That's the volcano Krakatao,' said Winnie the Pooh, who always allowed his passengers on to the bridge when there was anything worth seeing from that vantage-point. 'When last Krakatao erupted there was an earthquake and the shock went twice round the world.'

Thus we came at last to the Java Sea and the spice islands of the Dutch East Indies.*

Batavia was modern and prosperous. Fine buildings kept the jungle at bay, and in the tidy canals of Holland dainty Javanese women in boldly painted sarongs did their washing.

My room at the Hotel des Indes opened on to a verandah, which in turn led into a courtyard, where spotted deer grazed indolently under a heavy blanket of heat.

Night fell with its bright display of stars and summer lightning, and Winnie the Pooh came to fetch me for a farewell dinner. Mr. Roundel had promised to join us, but we found him

* *Now Indonesia with Batavia (renamed Djakarta) the capital.*

on his verandah eating ice-cream and bathed in perspiration.

'It's no good,' he said. 'I've showered twice and changed my collar five times and I'm still dripping. You must go without me.'

'You'd bring your weight down still more if you'd come out and dance,' I suggested.

'Don't!' he groaned, his multiple chins sagging. 'It's too hot to talk or even think, much less dance.'

So I dined out of doors alone with Winnie the Pooh. Little lizards scuttled about the walls and ceilings of the wide verandah. They chirped like chickens and devoured the insects that collected round the lights. A Javanese coolie dragged his shrimp-net in the canal that flowed past the restaurant, and a Dutch band played, but it was, as Mr. Roundel had said, too hot to dance. I discovered afterwards that all the East listened in to Java dance bands, which were superb. Java was a happy colony, the richest in the East. The Dutch had colonized there as long ago they had colonized the Cape, with understanding of the country and the needs of its people. Most of the enormous wealth derived from the Indies went back into their development.

It was after midnight when we drove out of the town to the Old Cannon. There, among the banyan trees, the ghosts flutter, little ghosts with the crooning voices of doves – of contented babies rocking in their cradles. For the Old Cannon has a potency greater than that of the young husband, and the barren woman who sits astride the long nozzle will be endowed by its magic with the gift of fertility.

The Dutch mail sailed for Singapore next day in a shower of flowers, champagne and paper streamers, and Winnie the Pooh waved me good-bye before going back to his own little *Roggeveen*.

CHAPTER TWENTY-SIX

CHARLIE CHAPLIN AND CHINESE EDEN

IN Singapore I transferred to a Japanese ship, the *Terukuni Maru*, ironically one of the first liners to be sunk by a German submarine in this war.

There was a little man on board, jaunty and arrogant, with thick silver hair and flashing eyes. He spoke to nobody except his brother (an oafish fellow) and a girl with golden hair, caged in the state-room adjoining his. All day long the nimble digits of Goldilocks beat upon her typewriter till the keys were slippery in the heat. She was typing the little man's holiday experiences for an American woman's magazine.

In the heavens above the China Sea the crowded constellations blinked at the young moon riding our rocking mast. On deck there was a movie show. It was a very out-of-date Wild West performance, and presently I noticed the little man slip into the chair alongside mine.

'Lousy picture,' he murmured. His voice was unexpectedly pleasant. (Why always the silent medium? I wondered.)

'Rotten,' I agreed.

'Care to come and see the pictures I took in Bali? They were developed in Batavia, and I'm showing them privately to-morrow evening. Only a few of the ship's officers and my brother.'

'I'd love it.'

That was my introduction to Charles Chaplin.

It was five days from Singapore to Hong Kong, and several vignettes of the little tramp of the screen remain fixed in my mind. I can see him, dapper and cynical pacing briskly round and round the deck with his bucolic brother in attendance. One or two women smiled tentatively from their deck-chairs and wished him good-morning. He pretended to be deaf and blind. I taxed him with his rudeness.

'It's my defence,' he said. 'Being Charlie Chaplin makes me everybody's property, and belonging to everybody is an impossible situation. When strangers address me I look straight through them or walk away. I hate doing it, but one must have some privacy.'

I can see the animation and vitality which infused his conversation, the flash of his dark blue eyes and the almost fanatical fervour with which he spoke of the Balinese. He was bewitched with Bali, the Dutch East Indies island, where the natives understood the meaning of neither time nor money, where the name Charlie Chaplin had never been heard and where art and dancing were not graces imposed upon the pattern of life, but an integral part of it, as natural as eating, sleeping and mating. He talked to me about Bali far into the moonstruck nights. But if the influence of Bali was strong on Charlie Chaplin when I met him, the influence of Fleet Street was equally strong on me, and I found that I was interviewing him almost without either of us knowing it. (The interview bore fruit and was subsequently published in the *Cape Argus*.)

I asked Charlie why he still stuck to the silent picture. He had not then let himself go as he did years later in 'The Dictator', much to the disgust of many of his fans, who thoroughly disliked his propaganda speech at the end of the film.

'I expected you to have a bad speaking voice,' I admitted, 'and it's a most attractive one.'

'Because I aim for beauty and expression in my pictures, and to my mind music is more beautiful than the human voice and more expressive than words. I intend to make talkies, but when I do they will have more music in them and less words than other films. Rhythm, dancing, music, beauty, sentiment, humanity and the thin knife-edge between laughter and tears – those are the ingredients of my pictures. I think "The Circus" is the best thing I ever did. It had all that.'

Charlie was sincere about his films just as he was sincere about Bali. On every other subject he was cynical. His notions on love were puckish. 'Spare me the gusty sighs of a grand passion,' he groaned. 'I'm forty-three, too old to pant over young girls in scenes of renunciation and eternal remembrance – they love that sort of thing. I'd rather pinch a fat dowager's behind while she's pouring out the tea.' Yet renunciation seems to be Charlie's rôle in private life, if bidding farewell to successive wives in the divorce courts can be so described. What he does about fat dowagers we have no means of knowing.

Sometimes he would abruptly abandon his man-of-the-world attitude and enact the part of the little tramp. When he did that, clowning in his immaculate dinner-jacket with his glistening silver hair sleekly brushed, it was as if two personalities had merged – the lovable sentimental little vagabond and the brilliant satirist and psychologist who had created him. One had the queer feeling then that the little tramp was none other than Charlie Chaplin's better self.

One morning as I was doing my hair at the mirror directly opposite the port-hole a silent reflection told me that we were near the coast of China. A great wide-sailed junk with a high massive square stern was majestically framed by the port-hole, and then another and another. The eyes painted on the bows stared sightlessly out to sea, the sails, some square, some fan-shaped, all patched and corrugated, billowed in the breeze.

I hurried up into the warm windy sunshine. Soon now I would see Bertie again! The pain of leaving my home and my child had been tempered by the thought of this moment. We entered Lymoon Pass, the fleet of fishing junks, like brown moths, headed past us out to sea. Now we steamed by a clutch of clumsy trading junks crazily laden with cargoes of wood, baskets and saucepans and teeming with humanity. These seafaring folk of China have no abodes ashore. They are born, married, give birth and die in their sampans and junks. They are the water people, the men, women and children of the great rivers and the wild pirate-infested seas.

Now the Peak rose from the busy waters like a green and purple sugar-loaf, and we sailed quietly between Hong Kong and the mainland. The harbour was alive with craft. Liners hooted, destroyers barked, there was the roar of a seaplane, and the slim grey shapes of warships took form. I strained my eyes eagerly for a three-funnelled cruiser. Where was 'the pretty ship'?

We berthed alongside Kowloon wharf, and the hoarse shouts of the coolies came to our ears and the rasp of their hawking and spitting. I went to my cabin to see that my things were all ready. Any moment Bertie would be here to meet me. I sat on my bunk for a second, my knees jelly with excitement. There was a step in the corridor and a naval officer was standing in the open doorway, smiling rather sheepishly and very trim in tropical uniform. I knew him. But he was not my husband, and, as far as I was aware, he was not in my husband's ship. Bertie must have a day on, I thought, so he's asked Gerry to meet me.

'Wonderful to see you,' said Gerry, 'but I'm afraid I've disappointing news for you. The *Kent* isn't here. She's gone up to Wei-Hai-Wei. Bertie sent me a signal to meet you and put you on to the first steamer going north.'

I felt rather sick. 'Oh Gerry, it isn't fair – after all these weeks!'

It was after sunset when the mauve cardboard mountains of Wei-Hai-Wei mainland carved a cloudless pattern against the jade and lemon sky of evening, and the island – my new summer home – rose in wooded beauty from a burnished sea. Seven weeks had elapsed since a child's hand holding a white handkerchief on Cape Town docks had held also my heart, and five months had gone by since I had waved 'the pretty ship' good-bye at Chatham.

The pretty ship. There she was, riding at anchor in Wei-Hai-Wei Bay, somehow essentially feminine in her grace and pride, and presently a black dot was lowered over the side and a white V-shaped bow-wave was forging towards the *Shun-tien*.

Bertie was standing in the bows of the motor-boat, and I could see his welcoming smile. How often we two have met in strange far countries at the end of long odysseys! There is a rhythm in our lives – this meeting and parting – and the stern discipline of heart-hunger, hunger for the husband or for the child, but there have been rare, brief, blessed spells when womanhood was satisfied and there was a house here or there with husband and child in it at the same time. I can count those times on my fingers, and each is precious. There are many whose lot is similar – not necessarily in the Navy.

When there is everything to say one speaks, in little rushes, of nothing. It was so with us as we went ashore in the *Kent*'s motor-boat.

Rickshaw coolies with cheerful sun-tanned faces handled the baggage, and I noticed that they were a sturdier breed than the scanty men of the south. There was a little row of shops on the foreshore, and on the zinc roof of the largest was written in huge letters: 'SIN JELLY BELLY. NAVAL OUTFITTER.' The banks of naval officers were sometimes a little astonished when expected to cash cheques made to to Jelly Belly, but such was the appellation Jelly Belly junior had inherited from his father, the owner of a noble and prosperous paunch, which bespoke a life of ease and plenty and was the envy of every Chinaman on the island.

The Island Hotel, where we were to live, was a long rambling wooden building with all sorts of haphazard annexes dotted like summer-houses about the unkempt garden. We had the usual naval accommodation, a bedroom, sparsely furnished, and bathroom with primitive toilet accessories – a 'thunder-box' and a Soochow tub, the latter being an earthenware tub in which one bathed in about three inches of brackish water. But life was really lived on the verandah, which was furnished with cane chairs and a table and was partitioned off from the next verandah by a strip of cocoanut matting. There was no escaping from the next-door jokes and the next-door quarrels and the next-door gramophone.

The island was one mass of acacias, and the petals fell in a soft white rain and strewed the paths with confetti. The pomegranate trees were rich with cardinal blooms; in the evenings there was the monotonous metallic insect-concert of the cicadas, and sometimes a swarm of long typhoon flies blackened the air.

Across the garden from our verandah was the harbour. Bertie had engaged an amah for me – a little yellow woman with tiny triangular bound feet like hooves. She wore a crisp white tunic and cornflower blue trousers, her face was round and flat and merry, and her greeting was the high twittering of birds at sunset. She was efficient too, and I unlocked my valises and let her get on with the unpacking as best she might. Bertie had already organized a cocktail tray and 'small chow' on the cane table.

'I can mix you a gin and lime; or a bamboo – that's gin and sherry – but you can't have it shaken on ice. The water the ice is made of here isn't safe for drinking.'

'Gin and lime for me.'

When I put down the empty glass Bertie refilled it.

'What's on your mind? I can tell there's something the matter,' I said.

223

'Wise girl,' he said gently. 'I'm afraid it's going to shake you a bit. We sail tomorrow for Hankow. It's hell to land you a crack like this the moment you arrive – poor Joy-Joy. . . .'

I said out of a cold grey weariness: 'Will you be gone long?'

'About a month. The Communists are cutting up rough and we are going full speed.' He drew on his pipe for comfort. The *Shuntien* had sailed again and the bay was empty save for a destroyer, the *Kent*, the submarine depot-ship *Medway* with her submarines close against her flanks, and a few sampans, their sails rosy in the after-glow. Across the harbour the mountains were topaz.

'Can I go to Hankow?' The question was automatic. I knew the answer.

He shook his head. 'Back to Shanghai and then seven hundred miles up the Yangtse? No, my sweet; there are Communists and cholera in Hankow and we have no cash in the bank. You must settle down here. Just laze and rest and maybe write a bit.'

'So we have tonight – and then you go?'

'That's the shape of it.'

'I could have had another month at home.'

'It's no good jobbing backwards.'

So the next day 'the pretty ship' got up steam and I was alone again, friendless in a strange world.

But what a lovely world!

There is a certain enchantment which is special to islands. It is as if the sea had set them within a magic circle. When I think of Wei-Hai-Wei it is with a mingling of delight and melancholy, for it was Eden then and now the Nippon serpent has entered it. The Chinese who were happy there are slain or fled, British warships that lay in those bright waters are fathoms deep in the seven seas or ranging far and wide in search of the enemy, and many who manned them have been lost at sea.

Picture this dream island two and a half miles long by two miles wide, rising conically from the sea, aquiver with the delicate green of acacias, the dark polished green of pomegranates, and the sombre grey-green of firs. There were bathing beaches where the baby-amahs foregathered with their charges, and rocky cover where young men lay in the sun with young ladies who had followed the fleet north for a summer holiday. In the row of little shops on the water-front you could buy trinkets of jade and soapstone, necklaces of crystal, agate or turquoise and lapis earrings blue as a technicolor sea. There was silk from Shantung or Japan and exquisitely embroidered household linen stitched by the Chinese orphans in the convent on the mainland. Naval establishments ashore were housed in pagodas with winged eaves to which clung little gods and legendary creatures, and the sailors' canteen was in a most exotic temple. There was no traffic other than the rickshaw, no cinemas except those on board the warships on Sunday nights, and no hairdresser, so that every Friday morning at the Island Hotel the camp-followers of the fleet sat on their verandahs in the sun, their heads covered in strange contrivances calculated to beautify them for 'Black Friday', the weekly dance at the club. There was a handful of bungalows on the island, and anyone who managed to get one of them for the summer was considered extremely lucky. There were some tennis courts and a golf course in charge of a jovial old rogue called Ah Tam. He it was who summoned our caddies with raucous yells, rude boys with heads like dusty pen-wipers and running noses who bawled with equal gratification 'Owbow! or 'Onna gleen!' ('Out of bounds!' or 'On the green!') For me it was more often 'Owbow!'

The island had its indelible personalities. There was Tomato-Face, who was the acknowledged king of the sampan men, a corsair with a certain bold magnificence in every gesture. It was his chief business to ferry men back and forth from the ships to the shore, but he had many sidelines. He organized the barrels of fresh water that arrived at the Island Hotel from the ships twice a week so that we need not use the brackish well-water for washing our clothes and hair, and his sampans were on tap for picnics on sunny days or to sail batches of Shanghai young things over to the mainland bungalows of Half Moon Bay and Narcissus Bay on moonlight nights after ship's dances. Tomato-Face had tact. He knew when to lounge against the rudder facing his passengers and talking to them and when a young couple might prefer that he should keep a watchful eye to seaward. For a Chinaman he was rather larger than life, a sturdy northerner, powerful as a bull, with a huge sunburnt countenance glowing like a harvest moon. He had innumerable progeny, and, of all the Chinese, he alone permitted himself to refer to his wife. 'My wife have makee new cheese-eye' ('cheese-eyes' are children). He understood the British. The British thought nothing of mentioning wives, those humble creatures who should be kept for ever in the background, and Tomato-Face took his cue from the British.

He blustered and jested with the other sampan men, and he knew the moods of that typhoon- and fog-ridden stretch of water as he knew the back of his own horny copper-coloured hand. He knew many things. Ask him a question and his currant eyes snapped. 'Me savvy.' He savvied when ships were coming and where they were going long before we wives of the officers had any inkling of what was in the air. There is a sort of bush telegraph that operates among the Chinese, and Tomato-Face was master of its magic. His stooges were Tomorrow-Fish and Yesterday-Fish, the other two lesser sampan men, who were grateful for his leavings.

When the Japanese took Wei-Hai-Wei in 1937 they made these three kneel on the little jetty with their hands tied behind their backs. Then they struck off their heads – even the great round head of Tomato-Face, bland as an August moon.

A *Kent* wife lived in the Wooden Bungalow. Her name was Margery. She had a very small girl called Penelope Ann and a very large, fierce Nannie who ruled them both with a rod of iron. When any of us tried to take Margery on a moonlight picnic or any other nocturnal nonsense, she drew her fair brows together and her blue eyes clouded.

'Nannie won't let me leave her alone with Penelope Ann.' She was a wiry wisp of a thing and a bit off her words like candy.

We scoffed. 'Wei-Hai-Wei is the safest place on earth bar none!'

'Nannie says there's a man hanging round and he presses his face against her window.'

'Hope springs eternal—' murmured someone.

So instead of going out Margery often had parties in the bungalow, and after dinner we sat on the verandah and played the gramophone and the cloying scent of wistaria and orange-blossom floated up from the garden like a drug.

'There's your sinister figure lurking among the fig trees,' I said. 'No wonder Nannie's scared!'

But the others laughed at me. 'That's only old Ugly.'

'Ugly is the gardener,' explained Margery. 'He is afraid the boys will steal the figs and oranges, so he prowls about all night. Goodness knows when he goes to sleep.'

I came to know Ugly well in time. We all did. He was very old, a wizened little creature whose shrunken countenance bore out the theory of Eugene Marais that there is little to choose between a man and a baboon. Most mornings he came humbly round to my verandah with a bunch of flowers or an offering of fruit, taken, of course, from Margery's garden. 'Ugly gottee figs for Missie, gottee flowers . . .' He wore an ancient battered straw hat which cast a kindly shadow upon his dark, finely wrinkled skin, and when he smiled I thought of Teena, for his smile, like hers, was filled with gentleness and good-nature. When a ship was expected, Ugly went to the signal station on the summit of the hill and kept watch, and when she came in sight he informed the waiting wives at the Island Hotel. Sometimes he sent me a 'flen' with plants – a gawky coolie with baskets of flowering shrubs slung over his bare shoulders – or he persuaded the local policeman to let me have a blue hydrangea or a bunch of amber snapdragons from the police gardens, where the convicts worked leisurely in the sunshine, chanting contentedly and laughing, coughing and spitting sociably.

A very lanky coolie with black cotton gloves and a smiling apologetic mien came daily to our bathroom. This diffident fellow with exquisite manners was the sanitary system of the island, and we knew him as 'the foo-foo coolie'. He was the brother of Ugly's gawky 'flen', the flower coolie, and it seemed to us a nice social balance that had assigned to one brother a task so fragrant and to the other a walk in life odoriferous even for China. I had my own rickshaw coolie, who was somewhat disfigured by having no ears. He had been captured by bandits as a child and he carried many scars to tell the tale. He was the fastest runner in Wei-Hai-Wei, which, in the circumstances, was perhaps hardly surprising. He smelt pungently of garlic, but I was told that if I minded his odour he probably objected just as strongly to mine, because the Chinese say that Europeans smell like goats because they eat cheese. He always carried a pet hedgehog under the seat of his rickshaw, as did most of his fellow-runners, and when we went to the golf course the coolies beguiled the time of waiting with hedgehog races. Sometimes they tied two together on a short string and betted on the resultant tug-of-war. But these activities went on secretly in our absence, and as soon as we appeared hedgehogs were bundled back under the seats again.

If I wanted a length of silk made up I called for the hotel room attendant, who padded on to my verandah with a brisk swish of his long white gown.

'Catchee Wei Kong, wantchee he,' I commanded.

'Can do, Missie.'

He flapped away to 'catch' Wei Kong, the tailor, which individual presently appeared in his voluminous blue cotton gown, in the recesses of which were hidden tape-measure, pins, scissors and a notebook. Wei Kong was thin and narrow-chested with a long neck and sloping shoulders. His thumb-nail was large and spatulate and his index finger-nail exceedingly long. He tittered anxiously and frequently. Poor Wei Kong was a born sucker. When asked 'How much you wantchee I pay?' he would nervously and tentatively venture his modest fee, and always he mistook the spontaneous astonishment of his client for amazement at the enormity of his demands, which flung him into confusion and put him in the wrong. No matter what he was asked to do he answered, 'Can do, can do,' in his light husky voice. We spoke of him as 'the little tailor', and there were women who bullied Wei Kong, for even in the heaven of Wei-Hai-Wei there were bad angels.

Every morning Goo, my amah, tapped into my bedroom with the curious gait of one who walks on stilts. 'Missie gottee washee-washee, sew-sew?' So a swallow would have spoken had its twittering been translated into words. Goo, like most Chinese women, was already a trifle bald, and her parchment crown was visible under the lacquered strands of her hair drawn tightly across it into a neat coolie bun confined in a black silk net. Her hair was plucked well up on to her forehead to lend her piquant little face a misleading air of intellect. She had several gold teeth, a sign of affluence much coveted by all Chinese and Japanese, who would willingly have every tooth in their heads extracted if they could replace them with a glittering gold denture. She was a widow with two daughters. 'Amah master makee die,' she explained, crossing her little hands on her flat bosom, bound as were her feet, and rolling her narrow eyes to heaven. 'Amah gottee two girl bebbee, but two-piece girl no good. More better catchee one-piece boy.' And she pointed to Peter's photograph. I agreed fervently.

As she pottered about gathering up my odd bits and pieces of washing and mending I watched the stiff movements caused by the deformed feet. Thus must the Little Mermaid of Hans Andersen's story have walked, painfully and jerkily as if on knives and red-hot needles. Presently she went into the compound and filled her great hollow flat-iron with charcoal, ready to be lit and fanned to the right temperature. All the wash-amahs worked there, and the sound of their chatter took me back to the early days of my marriage and Sunday mornings at Whaley when Bertie and I strolled down to the aviary after church.

Later in the mornings the baby-amahs sauntered down to the beach with their little charges, passing under my verandah. The Chinese love children and spoil them as a matter of course. It was amusing to hear small tyrants of two and three bossing their nurses from their prams in a ready flow of pidgin interspersed with a few of the lurid expletives no Chinese can resist teaching children. To hear an infant scarcely out of its cradle let fly a filthy oath is to them the very quintessence of humour and convulses them with merriment. There were a number of naval offspring in Wei-Hai-Wei, but none of Peter's age, and for that I was grateful. When a woman has not got her own child with her it is painful to her to see another mother happy with a child of the same age – not because of jealousy, but because it is salt in a deep wound. There are too many phases of my son's childhood that I have missed, and I think of them always as 'the lost years'. There are legions of women who grieve thus in many walks of life, and there is a sort of freemasonry between us.

We naval people really meant little more to the island than the snipe alighting on the marshes of the mainland in their seasonal migration south – except that we brought money, whereas the snipe brought only the summer.

Across a blue haze of cornflowers in the garden of the Island Hotel was Sunny's verandah.

Sunny was a destroyer wife, the very young bride of a slightly less young sub-lieutenant. She squatted on the wooden steps of the verandah of a morning dressed in an abbreviated bathing-suit. Her bobbed brown hair shone in the sun as she bent over her mending or her knitting, or rewound her over-worked gramophone. She had not been long enough in the Navy to be infected with any dreary seniority complexes, and to her all human beings were alike. She judged them according to their humanity, regardless of their status.

On the morning after Bertie's departure she stepped through the sea of cornflowers and looked up at me as I stood rather forlornly on my verandah. The freckles on the bridge of her snub little nose, her wide smile and the flecks of gold in her brown eyes were homely and engaging.

'You are Mrs. Packer, aren't you? And the *Kent* has left just as you've arrived. Rotten luck! The same thing has happened to me, as a matter of fact. Richard's destroyer sailed for Hong Kong last week. Come over and gossip awhile.'

I found that Sunny was a born philosopher.

'That's the worst of the Navy,' she said comfortably. 'Never being sure about anything. But so long as you don't expect security you can put up with not getting it, I suppose.'

'The awful part is leaving one's children behind – in my case, child—'

Sometimes a good grumble is balm to the spirit, and most of us preferred grousing to each other rather than to our husbands, who could do but little to alleviate our lot, poor souls.

'And always keeping the ache for them bottled up can't be much fun,' she agreed. 'But it isn't fair to moan and groan to the unfortunate man who is responsible. It can only make him feel guilty and miserable.'

'How do you know so much about it? You haven't any babes. You are one yourself!'

She smiled. 'We mean to have children one of these days, so we've considered all the complications. We want a little house somewhere near Portsmouth – or perhaps Plymouth. I love Devon. Then I'll live there with our family while Richard goes to sea.'

'Won't you be a pack-and-follow wife like I am?'

'No, I'll be a bundle-of-trouble at home.' (When a sailor marries he acquires a 'bundle-of-trouble' and becomes known as a 'bundle-man'.) 'You see, we haven't a brass farthing between us, and I was only able to come out here on our wedding-present cheques – third class. This China adventure is our lucky break. Later on we'll just have to settle down. Luckily we are very domesticated. I like cooking and Richard wants a cabbage patch. We'll make our own intermittent heaven. ...' She laughed and put a record on the gramophone. 'I brought these out from home,' she said. 'They are good records.'

'But that's "Butterfly"!' I cried.

I don't know what memories it evoked for my companion, but for me it was grand opera in Monte Carlo on our honeymoon; it was Malta, where opera was part of our lives; and Munich with Reni's love-in-a-mist eyes hungry for fame; and it was night in the Street of Adventure with the presses thundering an accompaniment and the Editor of the *Daily Express* bursting into song for the benefit of a young woman who wanted 'a job on the paper'.

One day I found Sunny sitting on her steps painting her toenails red.

'Expecting Richard?' I asked.

She tossed back her hair, newly washed and shot with tortoise-shell lights.

'Tomato-Face, he savvy,' she smiled. 'By-an'-by Ugly talkee destroyer come!'

That evening at dinner, as I looked over the top of my book, propped against the cruet, I saw that Sunny was no longer alone at her table. She was flirting outrageously with a tall, very young sub-lieutenant with curly black hair. I was glad for her.

CHAPTER TWENTY-SEVEN

SHANGHAI SHIRLEY AND TSINGTAO
INTERLUDE

OVER a month went by before the clear summer day when Ugly came hurrying down from the signal station to my verandah. His shrivelled face beamed beneath the discoloured straw hat, and he carried neither figs nor flowers, but, better still, he was the bearer of good tidings.

'*Kent*-ship, jus' now come, Missie.'

Goo, my amah, began to twitter from the bedroom where she was putting away my things.

'Missie master come back! Ting hao! Ting hao!' ('Good, good!')

And soon, through the thin lacework of the acacias, I saw the slim grey ghost slide into her anchorage, and the long harsh rattle of the anchor cable rent the morning silence. There were four of us *Kent* wives, and as soon as we spied the liberty-boat and the motor-boat leaping across the water we strolled down to the jetty, hoping our men might be among the first ashore – a vain hope in my case, as the commander of a warship is always the first on board and the last ashore. He is the father of the family.

There followed a blissful three weeks which even the plague of caterpillars that beset the island could not mar, despite my inordinate horror of the creatures.

'They are really rather dramatic,' said Bertie, as we walked round the island. They fell down our necks from the fir trees and pomegranates and exploded under our feet as we trod on them. Other naval couples braved the caterpillars too. Walking round the island was their only method of talking confidentially. The hotel was a sounding-box.

'Look at that gorgeous fellow bustling across the path! He's like the Blue Train we caught on our honeymoon.'

'With the Golden Arrow hot on his heels. Ugh! They give me the shudders!'

'They'll be butterflies soon,' said Bertie. 'Think how beautiful the island will be then.'

But Wei-Hai-Wei did not need to await the convenience of the caterpillars for its butterflies. These had already come swift-winged from Shanghai and Hong Kong in the wake of the Fleet. Loveliest of them all was Shanghai Shirley.

My first glimpse of this speed-nymph was fleeting. It was the middle of a fresh blue-and-gold morning and I had just emerged from the silk-shop on the waterfront with a dress length of raw silk under my arm when a roar like that of an aero-engine gave me pause. A speed-boat surged into sight and swerved round the bows of the *Medway* trailing Shanghai Shirley like the tail of a comet. As she flashed past the submarine depot-ship on her water skis she laughed and waved her hand and her hair streamed away on the wind like sun-gilded spindrift.

The *Medway*, scandalized, drew her submarine chicks closer

under her wing, and the open mouths of the sailors on deck resumed more normal contours as they said to one another 'Corblimey!' or whatever it is that sailors say in such circumstances.

Shanghai Shirley and her widowed mother, Mrs. Cooper, were staying over on the mainland in their pleasant little bungalow Rockhaven, overlooking Narcissus Bay. It was Mrs. Cooper's custom to watch the doings of the Fleet through a telescope from her vantage-point, and she knew nearly as much about the movements of ships – and ships' officers – as Tomato-Face.

The moment we met Mrs. Cooper we liked her. All that she said and did reminded me of my own flamboyant relations. She was no longer young, but she thoroughly enjoyed her game of tennis, and her passing shots and donkey-drops were baffling to behold. In this and all her other sporting proclivities she resembled my mother. She too was fond of bridge, though less under the influence of the estimable Mr. Culbertson, and she played poker with the Chinese as Mother, Edyth and Uncle Wilfred had been wont to play it with the Leslie merchants at Strehla – to the death. Then her tales of China and her experiences there were as good as any of those told with such gusto about South Africa by the Marais uncles. They had a pleasing domestic flavour about them too. For instance, there was the story of 'The Ugly Nurse'.

'I always chose ugly nurses for my children,' she said, 'because the pretty ones were married off before you could look round, and children need a feeling of permanency in the nursery. Well, one day I engaged a hideous woman with a long, narrow, pointed nose – the sort of nose no man could possibly contemplate marrying. But – will you believe it? – on our way to Tsingtao in a coasting steamer that summer a rat bit the end off it while she was asleep! And that nip off the tip of her nose improved her appearance so much that the doctor who attended her fell in love with her and married her. I was furious. Ask anyone you like.'

I retaliated with the incident of the enterprising ostrich who had pecked out Mrs. North's glass eye, and described my Uncle George, who had been addicted to pulling snakes out of their holes by the tail and cracking them like whips. Mrs. Cooper laughed without a shadow of incredulity. She knew that nothing was impossible. When she spoke of Shanghai, I recalled my mother's accounts of the early days of Johannesburg. In both cities fortunes were made and lost overnight, men were wild and women were fair, the great financiers were famous Jews and the scandals were sharp with all the spices of East and West.

Only two things troubled Mrs. Cooper seriously. One was indigestion and the other was Shirley. The indigestion had no lighter side, but Shirley was an alternate source of mirth and despair.

'She has no sense,' groaned her mother. 'She is utterly irresponsible. But I always have to laugh at her!' With which she chuckled and sighed.

Shirley had the face and figure of Greta Garbo, but her behaviour was Harpo Marx at his most inconsequent. It was this bizarre and comic streak in her which endeared her to the Chinese. The Chinese love a spoilt child and a colourful character, someone who will make them laugh. Jay, Mrs. Cooper's Number One who was to her family what Cookie was to ours, would do anything for 'Young Missie'. His smooth, ageless Oriental face, with that strange pride in it which is so much a feature of the Chinese, would pucker with amusement at her antics or he would scold at her indulgently.

Of her admirers Shanghai Shirley demanded first and foremost that they be good-looking. But her standards had been set inordinately high by the Argyll and Sutherland Highlanders stationed in Shanghai – young men of exceptionally fine appearance and quality, too many of whom were doomed to lose their lives fighting that hopeless rearguard action down the Malay Peninsula in 1941–42.

But although Shirley loved the absent Argylls, she was not blind to the charm of the present Navy, and a certain young officer in the Fleet Air Arm was considered by most of us to be a likely starter. His name was John and he had all the attributes by which his lady set great store. He was tall and fair and handsome and he had a dash which matched her own.

One day the *Kent* wives heard through the Chinese bush telegraph that the ship was going south once more, to Tsingtao, so Margery and I hired Tomato-Face's sampan and crossed over to the mainland to inquire at the shipping office in the city whether there was any vessel touching at Wei-Hai-Wei on the way to Tsingtao.

'Tsingtao is supposed to be the Lido of North China,' said Margery, 'and I happen to know there's a Russian hairdresser there who could give us a decent perm. We both need it.'

Tomato-Face, with the sail set and running before the wind, offered us his advice.

'No can do English ship, but Maru boat can do all same day *Kent*-ship go.'

Margery said, brusquely biting off her words: 'I can't take Nannie and Penelope Ann in a coolie-ship. No b'long safe, Tomato-Face.'

The sampan man shrugged his wide shoulders. 'Missie want-chee go Tsingtao-sides.'

'Not all that much. I'm not prepared to put my young into a death-trap for twenty-four hours.'

'Can't you leave her here with Nannie?' I suggested. 'It's only a fortnight's jaunt.'

'You forget the burglar. Nannie would never allow it.'

'But there isn't a burglar.'

'I know. But Nannie has decided that there is.'

The shipping agents bore out Tomato-Face's statement. There was the *Burma Maru* of a few hundred tons or nothing. We told the other two wives what we had learnt, and the husbands went into a huddle. They were unanimous in their conclusion. 'Absolutely out of the question.'

The *Kent* sailed at noon, and it happened that I was lunching on board the *Suffolk* that day with Captain John Godfrey, a tall naval officer with a large wise head as full of weird odds and ends of information as an encyclopaedia. (When the war came he was made Director of Naval Intelligence.)

Captain Godfrey had the tastes of a sybarite and kept an excellent table. And presently, primed with delicate food and wine, I began to lament aloud that there was no ship other than the unthinkable *Burma Maru* to bear me to Tsingtao in the wake of my elusive husband.

The glacial eye of my host wandered to the open scuttle. 'Would that be the *Burma Maru*?'

A small one-funnelled black steamer, looking like a grubby old-fashioned toy, was anchoring in the bay. We went out on to the little after-gallery to see her better, and a curious noxious odour was wafted towards us over the water – the smell of a Chinese coolie-ship, which must be about as distinctive as that of an African slaver in the days of yore – and not much more savoury.

As I stared, fascinated, at this wretched craft, it suddenly dawned upon me that there, across the harbour, experience was opening wide her arms.

'John,' I said, 'will you arrange a ticket for me and send Bertie a signal after I've left? After all, it's only a day and a night one has to stand. I'm going to catch that thing. I'll get ashore right now and be packed up in half an hour.'

Tsingtao was worth the coolie-ship. It gave me only happiness on that occasion. The day was to come when that gay summer resort on the coast of North China was to see me brought low, but I had no inkling then of what fate held in store.

When we got to our hotel I was delighted to find that we had a large bedroom with real walls instead of a mere partition through which the naval couple next door could hear every word we had to say to one another. Better still, there was no naval couple next door.

Among other things, Tsingtao was my introduction to Chinese chow and the United States Navy.

At the Chinese banquet given by the Mayor in honour of the *Kent* I could not help thinking of my mother, who always liked to know exactly what she was putting into her mouth. 'Your mother is not an enterprising eater,' my father had been wont to say. He could hardly have levelled the same accusation at me that night!

The Mayor, who was also an admiral, had just annexed four warships from his rival admiral in charge of the Cantonese Navy, so he was feeling very pleased with himself, and the party was in the nature of a victory feast. Minions fanned us gently while we partook of bird's-nest soup, shark's fins, boiled sea-slugs and flaky rice, fillets of snake, Peking duck and bears' paws, supplemented by a score more courses and washed down with rice wine (which tasted like hot dry sherry), or, for those who wanted it, the local white wine maufactured by German experts from the Rhineland.

'You must dip each mouthful of food into your soya sauce,' explained my neighbour, a member of the Central Government, who was instructing me in the use of chopsticks.

He put a slug into my bowl.

'I have an uncle who is growing the soya bean in South Africa in a big way,' I volunteered, playing for time. 'He says that it is the most important and useful crop in the world. Oh, dear, there goes my slug on to the floor! No, not another, please. Really, I couldn't.'

Next day Bertie and I were not at our best. We agreed that it didn't do to be too enterprising an eater in China.

In the evenings, when Bertie came ashore, it was our habit to wander along to the Pavilion Café, a big barn-like shack on the beach, where the latest rumours of war, bandits, plagues and floods drifted through the air in many languages. We usually joined up with some American Navy acquaintances.

The thing that struck me about the United States Navy was its amazingly democratic atmosphere compared with our own. One had the feeling that there was really no reason why the ship's boy shouldn't marry the admiral's daughter.

But in this case the admiral had no such encumbrance. The only womenfolk to cherish this forthright friendly seaman, who had a most unnautical moustache and a magnificent record of service in the Far East, were the wives of his flag officers.

Admiral Tayler's Flag Captain and Chief of Staff, Captain Frank Jack Fletcher, was devastatingly downright, a bit of a dandy, quick as a whiplash, and complained that he had never been misunderstood by his wife. Martha, his understanding wife, was one of the strongest personalities I have ever met, with a charming intellectual face, a vigorous retentive brain and a stimulating line of talk. Like so many American women, she could translate her interests into a line of conversation. American women lay themselves out to be interesting, and either they succeed or they are crashing bores, but it is not their habit to sit back and depend upon their pedigree to pull them through a party, as so many of their English prototypes are apt to do.

Henry Goodwin Moore, the Admiral's Flag-Lieutenant, was attractive and very good company, while his wife Beatrice was a lovely Titian-haired young woman addicted to reading in her bath. I discovered this weakness later when I stayed with her in the Philippines and heard uncanny gurgles of laughter coming from the bathroom whenever Beatrice was taking a bath. Her taste in literature was cheerful.

These two couples looked after the Admiral as if he were their favourite uncle, and somehow we were drawn into the family circle. They encouraged me to air my views on the little I had seen of China.

'But you have to realize that Wei-Hai-Wei and Tsingtao are not China at all,' explained Martha. 'The island is an ivory tower where nothing ever happens, and Tsingtao is a cosmopolitan mess. It has been Chinese, German, Japanese and Chinese again, and now it is mostly Russian.'

She referred, of course, to the White Russians. The flood of refugees from the Revolution had poured through Harbin into China, and Tsingtao had become one of those pockets of the dispossessed that are to be found all over the East and in the Balkans. They fitted into the picture well enough, for the Russian is a man of two hemispheres and two ways of life. Both Orient and Occident do battle in his blood. Life is his enemy, fatalism his master and death his friend.

'Is Shanghai China?' I asked.

Martha shook her smooth dark head.

'Not really, not any more than a man's office is the core of his life. Shanghai is sacred to Gog and Magog. It is the shrine of international commerce.'

'Hong Kong, then?'

'A British colony.'

'Well, where is China?'

She leaned forward across the marble-topped table and her hazel eyes were intense.

'Go up the Yangtse River, fifteen hundred miles into the interior till you are as near Delhi as Shanghai and you'll find pastoral China. It is there, in the hills and valleys of Szechwan. Or come to Peking in the fall. Recreate the Cathay of Marco Polo and see the Forbidden City where the emperors lived sequestered in luxury and infamy.'

Martha's way of talking was exciting. She had the same effect upon my imagination that once long ago Mina Freund had had in the classroom at St. Cyprian's. Martha, too, was a shell with the voice of the waves, evoking pageantry beyond my ken. When she spoke of Peking in the fall I knew that we would meet again there.

I found the American naval wives refreshingly gregarious compared with ours. They seemed so much less oppressed by petty Service considerations. There was none of that pushing each other in and out of ships' boats in what they considered to be the correct order of importance. None of that '*You* go first, Mrs. Mugwump. Your husband is senior to mine.' A grey head or a wooden leg entitled one of their number to more solicitude than four stripes on her husband's arm.

It is rather pathetic to observe how the average British naval wife goes through life under the delusion that she is a sort of projection of her husband's rank. Especially when one considers that her importance in the eyes of their lordships is so microscopic as to be, to all intents and purposes, non-existent.

The American sailors were wilder than ours. The ships were dry, but ashore the reaction set in, and every night scores of 'outs' were collected by the naval patrols and taken back to their ships like statues. The American wives, unlike ours, had their passages paid from the United States to the station (Manila), and ratings sometimes took advantage of this fact to marry a girl 'for the commission', on the basis that the wedding-ring did not need to signify a life sentence.

When, after a fortnight, the time came for the *Kent* to return to Wei-Hai-Wei, I was confronted with the problem of how to get there too. Not even a coolie-ship was available this time. So I decided to take a coasting steamer to Cheefoo, the United States summer base north of Wei-Hai-Wei, and take a car across country from there to the old city of Wei-Hai-Wei on the mainland, where Tomato-Face could meet me in his sampan and ferry me across to the island.

'You are quite crazy,' sighed Beatrice Moore. 'Did no one ever tell you about bandits?'

Martha shook her head at me. 'Last year the whole of the Shantung Province was at war, and this year a lighthouse-keeper, only a few miles from Cheefoo, was kidnapped and his ear sent to his relatives with a demand for ten thousand dollars.'

'Did the relatives pay?'

'Of course not.'

'What happened to the lighthouse-keeper?'

'Lighthouse-keeper finishee, as the Chinaman says,' murmured Beatrice.

We were on board the English coasting steamer by then, as they, too, were bound for Cheefoo.

'Don't eat that melon!' Beatrice implored me, as I helped myself to a luscious slice. 'Nobody seems to have taught you anything. Don't you know that melons are sold by weight in China?'

'What's that got to do with it?'

'The merchant squirts them full of water with a hypodermic syringe to increase their weight – and unless water is chlorinated in this country you are asking for typhoid or cholera. Do try and be your age.'

We parted with many misgivings on their part and mutual assurances that we would meet in Peking in the autumn.

'Don't forget,' said Martha. 'Peking is the soul of historic China. You must see it even if you have to do so without Bertie. It's like nowhere else in the world. I'd give anything to be able to see it again for the first time – not with the knowledge of it – but for the first time. . . .'

Beatrice looked over the rickety open car in which I was to go to Wei-Hai-Wei city.

'Not much of a tumbril.'

The driver, who spoke no English, cleared his throat in a manner known to us as 'the Chinese national anthem' and spat an astonishingly long distance.

I got in.

The journey was only fifty miles, but it had its hazards, for it was wild country. There were no bridges over the gulleys which intersected the empty landscape, and we rattled over them on planks placed roughly the space of a car's wheel's apart. Often the road disappeared altogether and we took to the open country. There were wide stretches of kaoliang, the ten-foot grain which bandits are in the habit of using as cover, and here I quaked a little, knowing full well that bandits assess the ransom value of young foreign women inordinately high. But at last the walled city with its grey tiles and winged eaves came in sight above the sparkling sea. And there was the sampan of Tomato-Face waiting for me, and warships in the harbour, and on the island a community of British naval women – very safe and smug.

CHAPTER TWENTY-EIGHT

CITY OF EMPERORS

AUTUMN arrived rudely in Wei-Hai-Wei on the wings of a typhoon which piled up some junks and sampans on the rocks, drowned a number of Chinese and carried the rush-matting partitions of our verandahs wholesale out to sea.

The wrecked craft were salved and the drowned were philosophically written off as a sacrifice to the sea-god and nobody bothered to replace their rush matting.

The season was over.

Shirley, the speed-nymph, was seen no more in the bay. She had returned to the kilts in Shanghai. And the *Kent* had gone north to pay an official visit to Japan. Most of the ships' wives decided to go direct to Hong Kong, but I hankered after seeing Peking.*

'Why not?' Bertie had said. 'It's a chance that may not come your way again. If the Japs keep on as they're going they'll swallow Peking before so very long.'

So one afternoon in September I found myself in a dust-storm on Tangku Station waiting for the Peking train, which would convey me for six hours through lawless lands not unlike the South African high veld in outlook. There were Japanese soldiers on the station with white masks over their mouths and noses, white-muzzled apes coming and going through the grey wall of dust.

Martha and Beatrice met me at the Peking Hotel.

'What sort of a journey was it?' asked Martha.

'I hardly know. It was a tunnel of dust all the way.'

Beatrice laughed. 'It often is. They call Peking "the city of dust".'

Martha said: 'I've taken a room for you overlooking the

* *Occupied for a time by Japan. Now the capital of Communist China.*

Forbidden City. What about a drink to wash the dust out of your throat?'

'No, thanks. A bath is the only thing I crave for at the moment.'

When you want something very much, and when it is there at your elbow to be had for the taking, it is fun to put off the moment of enjoyment, savouring it in advance. There were french windows leading out of my room on to a little balcony, and the balcony faced straight out over the twenty-foot rose-coloured walls of the Forbidden City into the courts and pleasure gardens of the erstwhile Lords of Ten Thousand Years. Even more than the luxury of a bath I longed to go out on to that balcony. But I deliberately postponed that pleasure. Martha had said, in the voice of an acolyte: 'I'd give anything to see Peking again for the first time. . . .' Well, this was the first time for me, and I was going to get full value out of it.

A floor-service waiter in a long white gown brought me a pot of jasmine tea, and when I spoke to him in pidgin he answered in ordinary English. 'We do not speak pidgin in Peking,' he said, smiling.

I rested on a long divan and listened to the voices of the city floating upwards: the deep resonant street cries, the strident shouting of rickshaw coolies and the whirring Æolian music of pigeons in flight. The Chinese attach bamboo tubes to the tails of their pigeons, and the air rushing through the tubes produces the song of Ariel, spirit of wind and water.

'Sounds, and sweet airs, that give delight and hurt not,
Sometimes a thousand twangling instruments will hum about mine ears. . . .'

Presently, bathed and rested, I went out on to the balcony.

The September evening had powdered the western hills with blue, and beyond that ethereal-looking barrier lay the vast deserts and mountain ranges of Central Asia. Right under my window was the sanctuary of the Sons of Heaven, the Forbidden City itself. Like the outspread pinions of bright exotic birds, the yellow imperial roofs and the green tiles of the princes caught the evening light amid a lacy canopy of leaves. Down there, amid the lotus lakes and gardens, the occupants of the Dragon Throne had lost all touch with reality. Corrupted by eunuchs and luxury, they had turned blind eyes to the West, hungry for trade, and to the Islands of the Rising Sun, already avid for conquest. Nor did they deign to hear the ominous mutterings of the starving multitudes grovelling in the grey Peking dust on the other side of the rose-coloured walls. Down there had been hoarded priceless treasures from Europe and Asia, and always the coffers of the eunuchs had been heavy with bribes.

Now all that was over. The age of arrogance was as dead as the stone lions that drowsed in the deserted courts. The people of China, guided by the great revolutionary, Sun Yat Sen, had overthrown the Manchus and the days of the Middle Kingdom were done.

But from that playground of emperors there rose to my senses faint emanations of the past. Down there love, intrigue and murder had played their part, and I knew that there were nights when kings and concubines trod the terraces and paused upon the marble bridges; but their footsteps were soundless and the water returned no reflection of the ghost faces that gazed into its mirrored surface.

When I was a child my father had once told me the story of a man who cultivated strange tropical orchids in his hot house. He was obsessed by his passion for these creeping plants, and then, one day, they got him. They wound long tendrils about him and hugged him to death.

The tale made me nervous about going into our own innocuous conservatory and increased my tendency to nightmares, while Mother said: 'Julie, why do you frighten the child with such yarns?'

Maybe it was a true story and maybe it wasn't, but it might well have been applied to Peking. Peking was like those orchids. It got people. And it did not always let them go.

There was Jane.

Jane was the young wife of a military language student. They lived in a Chinese bunglow in the Legation Quarter, and everywhere that Jane went her Tibetan lion-dog went too. To the uninitiated that lion-dog might conceivably have been mistaken for a peke, but Jane explained, in her lofty way, that he was infinitely superior to any peke. The animal evidently thought so too, for his air was, if possible, even more disdainful than that of the lap-dog of emperors.

Jane had the lips of a Rossetti angel and she walked on the clouds. But in spite of her remoteness she had a strong social sense, and she took charge of me both kindly and competently and showed me the way I should go. She had been brought up in the Legation Quarter. It was her milieu, and I could have had no better guide to the existence of which Ann Bridge has written so authentically in her novel, 'Peking Picnic'.

Hand in hand with Jane I entered the conservatory where bloomed those homicidal orchids.

Beyond the outer fortifications of the city, which was the terminus of the great trade route from Central Asia, the trans-Siberian express was regularly derailed by bandits and the passengers kidnapped. The presence of the Legation Guard bore constant witness to the Boxer outrages of 1900, when some hundreds of thousands of Christian Chinese and foreigners had been massacred all over the country; and from the Great Wall came rumours of Japanese aggression and more Japanese aggression. The diplomats only sighed and sighed again, bemoaning the fact that soon the diplomatic centre would have to be shifted to Nanking, the capital of the Central Government. In the meantime they appeared to be suspended in time – each cultivating his own particular orchid.

Jane took me to dinner with Charles and Jack, the two young secretaries to the British Legation who shared a Chinese house furnished with lacquer and hung with Oriental embroideries. The guests each arrived bearing some treasure. One had a little musical box of exquisite workmanship, another had brought a small bronze horse. A good-looking Frenchman carried a jade Buddha, and Jane unwrapped a crystal ball on a black velvet hassock.

'Whose birthday is it?' I asked, as these objects were displayed. 'Jack's or Charles's?'

'Nobody's,' said Jane, with that rather surprised look of hers. 'These are just things we may decide to buy, and we like each other's opinions on them.'

Her husband added: 'That's a subtle Chinese trick. The merchant lends you anything you show a tendency to buy. He knows that if you keep it in your house you will get attached to it and give him his price.'

The Frenchman said: 'It's the only way. You cannot tell whether you really want to keep a thing or not until you have lived with it, whether it happens to be a jade Buddha or a pretty woman.'

Somebody else had found another quaint timepiece to add to a prodigious collection of fancy clocks. The emperors had been partial to clocks and many had been sent from Europe as presents to the Sons of Heaven, but since the sack of the Forbidden City these had come into circulation among the merchants who bought and sold in the shadow of the mighty walls and towers of Peking. So had much priceless tribute silk and pottery.

At dinner I listened, tongue-tied and baffled, to conversation that concerned the mythology and history of long-ago dynasties and their bearing upon the treasures to be picked up in the markets.

'Any crystal-gazers?' asked Jane later. She was fascinated by the globe. And so was I.

Now it burned like a fire opal; now it was colder than the heart of a glacier; now it was summer moonlight on the white gables of a Cape homestead. I lost myself in its changing depths. I saw the face of a sleeping child, and over him a bowed silver head. Beyond open french windows broad fig leaves stirred in a night breeze. The child moved. There were pin-points of perspiration on his upper lip and the little fingers, half-folded on the sheet, unfurled . . .

'Look out, young woman! That sort of thing is dangerous!'

I came back to my surroundings with a weird sensation of emptiness and momentary bewilderment.

Jane took my place and stared intently into the globe. As she lifted her head she pushed back her bright hair with nervous fingers and her eyes were clouded with disappointment.

'Nothing there,' she said. 'Not a darn thing. I'll give it back tomorrow.'

'Let us go and dance at the roof garden of the Peking Hotel,' suggested the Frenchman. 'I am told the Young Marshal may be there. If he is it should be amusing.'

He took me in his car. Most of the others went in rick-shaws.

'Do you care for Peking?' he asked. 'Me, I find it has great character.'

'I love it. Those monstrous walls and towers that surround it – and then the kernel of it – the Forbidden City. Why, the name alone is romantic and mysterious.'

He said: 'But can a city have any significance to a woman until she has had a lover in it?'

'Peking can stand on its own merits.'

He raised his eyebrows and laughed.

There were other Europeans dining in the roof garden, and several tables of Chinese, and over in a corner by herself sat the most notorious girl in Peking, a Chinese garçonne dressed in the dinner-jacket of a European man.

'She always wears foreign men's clothes,' said the Frenchman. 'There's no law against that sort of thing here.'

Suddenly we were aware of one of those queer moments of suspense which sometimes take control of a room full of people. Conversations were broken off, waiters sprang forward, couples involuntarily stopped dancing and even the band ceased playing in the middle of a foxtrot.

The Frenchman touched my arm. 'Look! In the doorway. The Young Marshal, Chang Hsu Liang.'

A youngish man in military uniform, with tragic haunted Mongolian eyes, strode across the floor to a table where a frail Chinese girl who seemed carved out of old ivory sat with an older woman. His personal bodyguard of thirteen followed him. Chang Hsu Liang smiled at the girl and she rose and went into his arms as the dove to its nest. The band began to play and tension snapped. But the thirteen guards were dispersed round the ballroom floor and they kept levelled revolvers on Chang's partner. One suspicious move and the thistledown body would have been ripped with bullet wounds. Her tubular dress was displayed by the slit skirt, and her tiny nimble feet were shod in high-heeled slippers. She was light and graceful as a reed in the wind. Chinese women, who for centuries have been crippled by foot-binding, love to dance.

'He daren't move without his thugs,' said Jack, with his tired brown eyes on the Young Marshal. 'He is terrified of assassination. Everybody blames him for the loss of Manchuria, and there's no denying that his troops put up a feeble resistance. The Japs had a walk-over.'

'His eyes look odd,' I said, 'sort of drugged.'

There was a pause. Then Jane said vaguely: 'Well, you never know. The Japs are making a business of spreading the drug habit in China. They have subtle methods and they fly high.

They'd like to make an addict of anyone who might be a leader. The Young Marshal *should* be a natural leader in North China. His father, the Old Marshal, was one of the bravest and best-loved generals China ever had.'

Charles said: 'The distribution of dope is part of the Japanese policy "to weaken" the enemy. They sell millions of heroin-doped cigarettes to the coolies of Manchuria – very cheap cigarettes. The coolies don't know what's in them, but they do know they get to want them so much they can't do without them.'

The Frenchman's eyebrows went up cynically. 'My friend, don't forget who forced dope on China in the first place. Your traders brought opium here in their ships from India, and when the Manchus tried to stop its importation you fought a war about it. The Japs are doing for patriotism what your own people did for money.'

'Please,' protested Jane, with the expression of a hurt angel. 'It's silly to discuss things that happened nearly a hundred years ago. Joy wants to know what's going on now. Take, for instance, the case of Pu Yi. You have to admit the Japanese knew how to make that little puppet dance.'

'Who was Pu Yi?' I asked. 'Remember, I'm starting from zero. I know nothing.'

'Pu Yi was the child-Emperor – the last of the Manchus. He abdicated in 1911 when the revolutionaries overthrew the dynasty and declared China a republic. The Japs immediately saw their chance and seized it. They offered the child sanctuary in their consulate at Tientsin, and he grew up under their influence and domination. He was the trump card up the sleeves of their kimonos. Then last year, when they had completed the military occupation of Manchuria* and established themselves there, they put Pu Yi on the throne of the new puppet State they had renamed Manchukuo. As the Manchus were the hereditary rulers of China, you can see that Pu Yi was the thin end of a very powerful and useful wedge.'

Perhaps Hitler learned his lesson from his Oriental Axis partner. There is no doubt but that Henry Pu Yi, ex-Emperor of China, was the first of our modern Quislings when he was placed on the Japanese-controlled throne of Manchukuo in the face of a moribund League of Nations.

But if the Japanese made a thorough job of Henry Pu Yi,

* *Manchuria is now once more Chinese.*

they were less successful with the Young Marshal. Chiang Hsu Liang went to Europe early in 1933 on a long visit. He was recalled by Generalissimo Chiang Kai Shek to help him put down the recurring Communist risings in the Yangtse Valley, and there he did much to reinstate himself in the confidence of his leader and of the people.

Next day I sought out Martha.

'It won't do,' I said. 'There was a dinner-party last night, and from A to Z I hadn't the faintest idea what anybody was talking about.'

She smiled. 'Peking, I expect.'

'Yes, Peking. How does one learn anything about it?'

'By seeing and reading.'

'How does one set about seeing and reading intelligently?'

'There's Juliet Bredon's book "Peking". And I could shepherd you round a bit.'

'That would be grand.'

I read Juliet Bredon as Mother read Culbertson and learned off the dynasties like bridge leads. Martha was amused. She was wonderful. Every fact and legend of interest was at her finger-tips. Under her guidance I enjoyed sightseeing for the first time in my life. She also found me a rickshaw-man called Wang who was no mean guide on his own account. Wang it was who described the scenes of the revolution and its results to me in graphic American.

'Peking is modern now,' he assured me, indicating the clanging trams with a lift of his chin as he loped steadily along. 'But when the first street-car came here the rickshaw coolies mobbed it. They were afraid it would ruin their living. Twenty of them were put to death at the Bridge of Heaven. Shot – modern style.'

Martha took me to the Bird Market in the Tartar City, where the rich and the poor flocked in search of caged songbirds. Men in long grey gowns took their birds for an airing as we take out our dogs. We went to the Thieves' Market in the early morning, where Mongol princes and Tartar camel-drivers rubbed shoulders; and to the Lung fu Ssŭ (the People's Fair), where children rode upon dragons in the merry-go-round, and a long queue collected philosophically to have their teeth drawn 'while you wait'. For encouragement the dentist displayed a bowl of decayed teeth recently extracted with his own hands. The physician had his booth too, with a huge diagram of the human anatomy drawn upon a piece of cardboard. The patient pointed on the diagram to the seat of his ailment and the doctor diagnosed accordingly and sold the poor sucker some patent pills and potions.

One evening we went to the Chinese theatre to see Mei Lan Fang in the classic play 'Beauty of Beauties'.

I had met Mei at a cocktail party at the Legation. The Minister, Sir Miles Lapson, had introduced him to me. They were a curious contrast – the Minister, six feet five, fresh-complexioned and genial, and the young actor graceful as a woman with a waxen skin and brooding eyes.

Mei Lan Fang was the idol of Peking, and the theatre was packed. 'The Beauty of Beauties' was the life-story of a king who had been sent a beautiful woman as tribute and whose kingdom was disintegrated from within by her wiles. For the benefit of the theatre this history was compressed into a mere five hours. The audience settled down to the performance much as one settles down to a long train journey. They brought peanuts, oranges, candy and cakes; they came and went as they pleased and laughed and talked among themselves, thus lending the spectacles on the stage some of the lighter attributes of cabaret, an atmosphere further enhanced by the scene-shifter, a ragged coolie, who went frankly about his business in full view of all and sundry, dragging away a throne here or planting a tree there. The prompter, whose voice was often heard, sat ostentatiously in a box facing the actors like an orchestra conductor, while a few musicians hammered out noises on and off with the aid of gongs, cymbals, pipes and various other instruments. The company meanwhile played their parts under much the same conditions as we, in my schooldays, had produced 'The Comedy of Errors' or 'The Merchant of Venice'. The gorgeous costumes seemed to have been taken from stock regardless of size or fit and appeared to be made of tinsel and paper; the fierce whiskers of the war-lords were palpably false, and many of the characters had made themselves more impressive by resorting to horrific masks. The action of the play was stylized and the dialogue intoned in a high wailing monotone, reminiscent of a feline ballad of love on the garden wall, but lacking its infinite variety.

Only when Mei Lan Fang appeared did the audience sit up and take notice. He came on wearing an elaborate headdress and gown with long narrow sleeves that flowed over his hands like paying-off pennants. He willowed about with ineffable grace and his caterwauling was several tones higher than anyone else's, for he was impersonating none other than the Beauty herself.

'But why is he playing a woman's part?' I whispered to Martha. 'Only the funny man in the pantomime does that.'

'He always plays the feminine lead. There are no women in any decent Chinese theatrical companies. There are a few companies composed entirely of women, but they are considered extremely second-rate. Watch his sleeve-work, how graceful he is and what glamour he has! The people are crazy about him.'

Mei Lan Fang and the king had one of those long romantic set-to's that are all wind and no action, and then, when they had exhausted one another with poesy, the ragged coolie strolled on to the stage towing a small flat-bottomed boat. The Beauty and her royal lover stepped graciously into it, and the coolie, labouring somewhat, towed them off stage while they tottered insecurely in the bows. Just so would we have competed with the situation at St. Cyprian's. I felt very much at home.

But wherever we went the beggars swarmed like maggots. Their trades union was the most powerful in China. If a merchant refused them 'squeeze' (protection money), they haunted the threshold of his shop so that no one would enter it; or, if a rich man scorned them, they waited till there was a wedding or a funeral in his family and then they gathered in strength to follow the cortège, a yowling throng parading deformity and disease, men without legs leaping along on hands and buttocks, and men without any limbs at all rolling down the road. Deliberate mutilation was freely practised by the mendicant fraternity, and the hands and feet of children brought up in this shocking tradition were lopped off so that they should be able to beg much more effectively. Thus too, less than half a century ago, men became eunuchs for monetary gain.

It was indirectly through Jane that I happened to go to tea with the palace eunuchs, who had been thrown out of a job by the Revolution of 1911.

'You like weird experiences,' said Jane. 'Why not ride out to the Eunuchs' Monastery? The American Naval Attaché knows the way and could take you. Then afterwards we could all meet at Jack's and Charles's temple in the Western Hills for dinner. I can't come with you. I've given up riding for the time being.'

'Out of consideration for the cherub?'

She laughed and nodded.

'It'll be here next spring, and I'm taking no chances.'

So the American Naval Attaché lent me a horse and we set off from the racecourse outside the city. It was a long ride, and then a bridle-path led us to the eunuchs' hide-out. A troop of camels lay at the side of the track and, as we passed, one of them craned his neck at us and spat.

'Good job he missed us,' said the Naval Attaché. 'Camel spit smells like nothing on earth, and you can't get rid of it once you've got it on you. Like spring onions, only worse.'

At last we dismounted at a lonely monastery in the foothills. A mafoo took our ponies from us in the courtyard and showed us into the building. He seemed about thirty years old, yet his yellow cheeks were smooth and soft as a girl's and his voice was that of a child.

We drank green tea with two old eunuch monks. They were as fat as our Malay washerwoman, Sabela, and their tone had the same high-pitched inflections. They pointed with pride to an altar tapestry depicting their patron the Warrior Eunuch, Kang Kung, who lived in the fifteenth century and who (strangely for one of his ilk) was always in the forefront of the battle. We saw also the burial-ground of the most infamous of all eunuchs – the hideous coolie Li Lien Ying, who held the Empress-Dowager in the palm of his grasping hand. He is supposed to have encouraged the Boxer riots, and he persuaded the Empress to build a pleasure-boat of marble in the lake of the Summer Palace with money intended for the Navy – thus losing Korea to Japan. Li Lien Ying began life as a rickshaw coolie, but the power-bug was under his skin. When he realized that the greatest wealth and influence of the Forbidden City was held by the Chief Eunuch, he made up his mind that one day that position should be his. He took the initial step towards such an end alone and unaided and endured his self-inflicted agony with superhuman fortitude. After many vicissitudes his determination was rewarded and he became the power behind the Empress-Dowager's throne. This woman, known as 'the Old Buddha', was a combination of the Red Queen in 'Alice in Wonderland', whose slogan was 'Off with their heads!' and of the women of the Borgias. Li was her evil genius, and there were those who whispered that his surgery had been incompetent and that he was also her paramour.

'Whew!' I gasped, as we cantered away from the monastery. 'That was a queer tea-party! I feel as if I'd looked into somebody's rubbish bin and found it crawling with caterpillars.'

He laughed. 'The poor wretches don't make a very attractive picture, do they? But there it is. They were the virtual rulers of the Middle Kingdom, believe it or not. They point to an aspect of life as it used to be in Peking. And you wanted to learn about Peking.'

'Peking is fascinating. It has a kind of spell.'

He frowned slightly. 'Call it a spell, if you like. It is certainly like no other city in the world, and I've seen a few. It has a certain violence. Whatever happens here happens suddenly and unexpectedly. This place is a hot house where everything grows too fast and usually out of all proportion to its beginnings. It may be an emotion, an intrigue or an illness. In Peking the most harmless of these are liable at any moment to develop a sinister character and become dangerous.'

Queerly my father's story floated to the surface of my mind. Given the necessary conditions, even a flower may become a killer.

Jane and the two young secretaries were waiting at the week-end temple.

Charles and Jack were not unusual in hiring a temple as a sort of shooting-box, since it was customary for residents in Peking to rent the ruined temples that abound in the Western Hills and use them as week-end dwellings. And some of the loveliest gardens in China were those old temple gardens that had fallen into alien but tender hands.

We had dinner under the baleful glare of three monstrous gold Buddhas and their attendant deities.

'It seems sacrilege,' I said.

Jack's pale Byronic features relaxed into a smile and his tired eyes cast a mild glance at the Buddhas.

'Oh no. Chinese temples are very homely. You'll often find them used as granaries and storehouses, with chickens and ducks and even pigs making free of them.'

All the same, I didn't fancy it. And said so.

'D'you think the gods will put a curse on us?' asked Jane, as she slipped a morsel of meat to the lion-dog at her feet. 'If so we can propitiate them with a little bowl of rice apiece. How about that?'

The gold Buddhas only smiled inscrutably.

A week later I left to join Bertie in Hong Kong.

Martha and Beatrice bade me good-bye at the hotel.

'Mind you come to Manila when the *Kent* pays her official visit,' they said. 'We'll look after you.'

Jane was at the station with her lion-dog under her arm, his glowering eyes inquisitive pin-points behind a ragged veil of blond fur. Jack and Charles were there too.

'We'll meet again somewhere soon,' they said. 'One always does in China.'

'Good luck with the cherub,' I called to Jane as the train steamed out.

Her lips curved upwards into their Rossetti angel smile and she nodded happily. The autumn wind caught at a strand of her coppery hair and tossed it across her eyes. She put up a hand and pushed it away. The movement brought back a picture, and I saw her raising her head from the crystal globe. 'Nothing there, not a darn thing,' she had said, her expression disappointed.

The cherub was born in the German hospital in the spring, and Jane made an excellent recovery. She took her new treasure back to the Chinese bungalow in the Legation Quarter. The poinsettias reflected the red lacquer of winged gateways and eaves. The young military language student was immensely proud of his tiny daughter, but the lion-dog sulked and took up an attitude as patronizingly mystified as an emperor dethroned.

Then, quite suddenly, on that evening of home-coming, Jane fainted. One of those brief inexplicable Peking infections had taken her in its jaws. Three days later a weeping baby-amah was rocking a motherless cherub in her arms.

I saw Charles again five years afterwards in Sofia when the

253

roses were in bloom. But an illness, the course of which might have been stayed in Europe, proved fatal to Jack. So he, too, never left Peking.

In 1937 the footsteps of the Japanese conquerors echoed in the paved courtyards of the Forbidden City, and their wide mouths opened still wider under the masks they wore against the fine grey dust as they looted what they desired from the mansions of the rich and from the little shops of Jade and Embroidery Streets. This city was surely a treasure-house!

But there lingers in my imagination the story my father told me as a child, and I think that if I could look into that crystal globe which for Jane had held no future I should see there strange blooms within the great walls of Peking and hungry tendrils seeking to clasp the invader.

CHAPTER TWENTY-NINE

THE FRAGRANT HARBOUR

HONG KONG means, in Chinese, 'Fragrant Harbour', and the name always reminded me of my mother wrinkling up her fine little nose at any mention of China. During that epic voyage round the world with her father, 'Long Piet' Marais, she had found herself one sunny day seated in a rickshaw in a Cantonese alley-way.

'Missie puttee hankee nose-sides,' advised the guide. 'This b'long Stleet of Lefleshing Bleezes.'

'Street of Refreshing Breezes!' exclaimed my mother when, in the fullness of time, she related the experience to her children. 'Why, even a camphor handkerchief couldn't keep out the stinks! The Chinese must be an exceptionally poetical race to think up a name like that for such an alley!'

The odours of the Fragrant Harbour were likewise somewhat mixed, and these were wafted out to sea to meet the new arrival half-way – strange whiffs of wood fires and incense, soya sauce, dried bats and primitive sanitation.

Hong Kong was the winter base of the Fleet, and Bertie and

I made our home in the Peninsula Hotel, a vast square building on the mainland of Kowloon, which, in due course, was to serve the Japanese well as their military headquarters. The European hotels in China were modern and comfortable, and we had a pleasant, if somewhat impersonal, bedroom and sitting-room on the fifth floor. Our windows commanded a superb view across the busy harbour to the Peak. Just under our lee the great liners berthed, and the sound of their coming and going was as the lowing of cattle at twilight.

Sometimes a round-the-world luxury liner lay out in the bay with floodlit stacks, and when this happened a number of young naval wives made a few dollars by working as 'extras' in Mrs. Gray's Yellow Lantern Shops. I did a day's work for Mrs. Gray on several occasions myself. She was good-tempered and easygoing and there was very little she didn't know about human nature. Her speciality was underwear. Nowhere in the world could you buy more glamorous lingerie than in the Yellow Lantern Shops, and it was as cheap as it was exquisite. Chinese silks, embroidered by diligent Chinese hands in dingy back rooms in Shanghai, were cut on the latest Parisian patterns, and the chiffon nighties and step-ins we sold by the hundredweight to rich American tourists were worthy of a film star's trousseau.

I did other jobs in Hong Kong. Journalism and broadcasting. Bertie washed his hands of these manifestations of energy. 'Hell's delight! I can't keep track of my bundle of trouble! She's always up to something new.'

Mrs. Cooper and Shanghai Shirley were also in the hotel for a few weeks, and there was always a cocktail party in somebody's sitting-room of an evening after golf or hunting. The golfers were more dangerous than the riders because they had that execrable habit of demonstrating shots to one another wherever they might be.

'I've adopted a new putting stance,' said my husband, helping himself to the lemon I was about to cut and squeeze for the martinis. He putted it neatly along the carpet. 'How about that?'

'Fine,' agreed Hong Kong's leading barrister and golfer. 'But your drive still needs a good deal of freeing up. Like this.' And before we could stop him he drove the lemon mightily. Fascinated we watched it explode like a bomb against the distempered wall.

'What will the management say?' I asked in some trepidation.

'Nothing,' he answered, surprised. He knew what I had yet to learn, that there were many things you could get away with in China, and that a lemon slathered all over a sitting-room wall was the least of them.

Our amusements were manifold and as varied as the scents of the Fragrant Harbour. We played tennis and sailed, and on week-ends we took sandwiches and were borne to Fanling in the 1.10 train in company with other golfers and riders. There were gamblers, too, on their way to the Casino just across the border between the Leased Territories and China proper. These were usually Chinese gentlemen in European clothes accompanied by young ladies in tubular high collared dresses slit thigh-high up the sides. But often as not we waved Mrs. Cooper au revoir at Fanling and she was carried over the border with her fellow-gamblers.

'I feel I'm in luck today,' she'd say.

She always felt she was in luck, and that was why the autumn of her life was as bright and colourful as a Hampshire beechwood in October. Even when she was doing a voluntary war job in London throughout the blitz, growing nightly younger in the atmosphere of menace and death that reduced most people to red-eyed exhaustion, she would say: 'See how fortunate I am – touching wood – not a window gone!' Fate respects courage and philosophy, and Mrs. Cooper and her windows rode the blitz on the crest of a wave just as she rode the crazy switchback of life in the Far East.

We now developed a habit peculiar to rich men and those who have lived much in the far East. We never carried money. There was no need, because one never paid cash for anything. One signed a chit, and at the end of the month there was a nasty moment when the chits were presented. After that bad or careless payers were dunned by a person in cotton gloves like those of the foofoo coolie, a trilby hat and a grey gown. This individual carried a black cotton umbrella to match his depressing gloves, and he wore an expression both ingratiating and stubborn. He was the shroff, or collector of bad debts.

The chit system, applied to sailors, drove commanders of warships demented, as the sailors spent what they hadn't got like children and hoped for a miracle at the end of the month. They were always hopelessly swindled in any case. Storekeepers were warned not to give credit, but few of them heeded the warning, with the result that the shroff, clambering up the long gangways of men-of-war, was only too common a sight.

In many ways our life in Hong Kong resembled a winter in Malta. There was the military garrison, the Navy and the Air Force, and there was Goverment House on the Peak, presiding, benevolent and aloof, over the activities of the colony. And, in general, the attitude of the British towards the Chinese was exactly similar to their attitude towards the Maltese – a combination of lofty disdain and aloof patronage.

It is a remarkable fact that wherever the British go they concern themselves almost exclusively with the highest and the lowest. In Hong Kong we met socially the rich and mighty among the Chinese (there was one, and his name was Sir Robert Ho Tung) or we observed with admiration the way in which the peasants of the Leased Territories flourished under British rule, and the fine battle which Hong Kong law was putting up against the evil of mui tsai – the adoption of little children, who were virtually sold into slavery to their 'adopters'. But we had little opportunity of meeting any of the many educated and thinking Chinese who shared the amenities of the Fragrant Harbour with us.

The upper-class Chinese, like the upper-class Maltese, resented this attitude, which discriminated against them in such a way as to make it clear that the British regarded themselves as the ruling class in Hong Kong, and they in their turn treated us warily.

If I had been determined to learn about China from a Chinese it would have meant taking infinite time and trouble to win his or her confidence and friendship first. Perhaps there is an instinctive mistrust of Europeans among other races because for centuries their countries have been exploited by white men. That is why even missionaries are so often looked upon askance by the lands they most desire to benefit. Missionaries have in the past been followed by the trader, and the trader has been followed by the flag. It was the natural sequence of progress, and it brought the benefits of civilization to many dark corners of the earth. But benefits thrust down the protesting throat of the beneficiary are inclined to be indigestible, and China was no exception to that rule. Then, too, there is in the educated Chinese a deep resentment of anything that suggests patronage, and this is easily understandable. Up to the present century foreigners in China have been regarded as barbarians with habits little better cultivated than those of wild beasts, and it must have come as a rude shock to the arrogant Chinese to find that there was really much to be learned from such uncouth savages. One of the best ties modern China has with the Occident is Madame Chiang Kai Shek. This highly cultured and enlightened Americanized woman has done, and will continue to do, invaluable work in bringing the West into perspective for her country and vice versa. She is the contact and link that will shape China's future relations with Europe and America. The Generalissimo could have found no finer partner in his life's work.

When I asked a certain Chinese acquaintance of ours whether Madame Chiang Kai Shek's marriage had been arranged in the traditional manner of her country, she laughed.

'Heavens no! They were crazy about each other. Why, the Generalissimo, who knows very little English, has been taught to say "darling" by his wife. It is the one word he really knows. As a matter of fact, her family are said to have been against the match just at first, because they have been Christians for generations and the Generalissimo was not. However, he has become a Christian now under the influence of his wife.'

It is triumphs such as this, I suppose, that compensate missionaries for the odium and opposition they incur both at home and abroad and even, perhaps, for the martyrdom that is so often their fate.

Later we got to know the Lo brothers and their families in the course of a tennis tournament in which Lo and Miss Lo beat us soundly. After that we went often to their fine foreign house on the road to Repulse Bay, where they had two beautiful grass courts. They all lived there together, the parents, the sons and their wives and children, in the manner of the Chinese throughout the centuries. The majority of Chinese have always adhered to this 'greater family' system, in which all property is shared by the family. There was one old patriarch in the time of the Tang dynasty who had members of nine generations living under his roof, and when someone asked this good man, whose name was Chang Kung-yi, how he managed it, he wrote down the Chinese character 'jen' a hundred times. 'Jen' means forbearance. It is a lesson many people in Great Britain learned in this war when the evacuation filled their homes with relatives from danger areas or even with strangers. The English are not a tribal race and they do not take kindly to a clannish way of life.

Sir Robert Ho Tung, who was in high favour in governmental circles, was less an individual than an institution. He was the traditional picture of an ancestor, and wherever he went he took two wives – Lady Number One, the wife of his bosom, and Lady Number Two, the mother of his children. He took also his lorgnettes, but these he invariably lost, and the two ladies spent much of their time searching for them down the sides of chairs and couches.

Christmas came with sun and storms, and we went on board the *Kent* for Christmas morning service.

There was a party in the wardroom afterwards, and we were all very cheerful on the surface and not a little homesick deep down. Then we went to the gunroom, where the midshipmen, with their charming manners and tendency to blush, took me back to my teens in South Africa with a pang; to gunroom dances and flirtations and the unconscious betrayal of shy idealism. After that we all trailed after the officers up and down hatches to see the gaily decorated mess-decks and to wish the ship's company the season's greetings. They had all vied with one another to have their particular mess in the brightest gala dress, and some of the men clowned for us in fancy costume. Sailors are children in many ways and simple things entertain them. The ship's cat had had kittens, and the men had made one big hammock and five little ones for the cat family, which they tucked in at nights. And the ship's mascot, Ordinary Dog Pluto, had been given a most magnificent Christmas bone. Many years of living in the close confinement of their iron box have taught men of the sea to make their own fun and to find pleasure in the little things of life. Most sailors are good sons and husbands and fathers, men who set great store by their own firesides. I have asked many of them what they liked best about Noel Coward's naval film, 'In Which We Serve', and their answer was invariably: 'Them 'ome bits, ma'am.'

Seeing them now, I could not help recalling the quay at Chatham one grey day early in this year and the little groups of women and children who stood to watch 'the pretty ship' sail away to the China Station, taking their men so far from home for two and a half years. I saw again the quiet weeping and the brave smiles, desperate above a weight of tears, and the hands that waved handkerchiefs to the last in the cold wind, and I felt a hard lump rise in my throat. Another Christmas must pass, and perhaps even a third, before these men could hold their dear ones in their arms once more. What doubts and fears and longings must fill their hearts? Babies they had never seen were lying in their mothers' laps even now; girls they loved were dancing with other men; perhaps (horrid thought) the lodger was taking the missus to the pictures, or mother-in-law was spitting a drop of poison into a young wife's ear. Hard to keep your home together when ten thousand miles of ocean separate you, hard to steer a steady course – whether it be man or woman who must follow it.

Most of the officers, too, had wives and families at home. Few could afford the long passage to China, or, if they could, the children were too old or too young to be left. For all of us that Christmas there was the same sharp deep pain of the divided heart.

In Tees Lodge it would be midsummer, a hot, still day. There would be a family party for midday dinner and a Christmas tree in the drawing-room. Fred would be opening the champagne and filling the glasses as Teena came in with the turkey, and Mother would say to Piet: 'Come, darling, you shall have a sip of mine.' Daddy would raise his glass to 'Absent friends', and Mother's grey eyes might fill with tears for an instant and the pearls on her throat quiver, but her grandson, mischievously making his sip into a gulp, would miss her moment of sentiment. After lunch she would go to the kitchen hand in hand with Peter.

'Well, Cookie, that was a beautifuly turkey. You've never given us a better.'

'I'm glad Madam t'ink it was good' – a giggle and a sigh. 'I wonder where Master Piet's Mommy and Daddy is now. . . .'

In fact, Peter's parents were eating their midday Christmas dinner at the Fredericks' lovely house built upon a spur of land five hundred feet above the sea. There was a fork-tiffin for a score or more guests, and my recollection of it is a warm, hazy picture of too much to eat and drink, a siesta after lunch, a highly dangerous shooting competition in the garden after tea, a tragic great dane infatuated with a dachshund ('A sort of futile Russian passion,' said Babs Frederick. 'He'd commit suicide if he knew how!') and then, to round off the day, we all went to see the Marx Brothers in 'A Night at the Opera', and, for the first time, I found them hilariously funny.

CHAPTER THIRTY

NORTHWARD TREK

THE northward trek began in April, and 'Daddy' Wallem, a robust Norwegian friend of ours who owned a shipping line, offered me a free passage as far as Shanghai in one of his ships.

'But you can't go alone,' he boomed. 'You must take another girl to keep you company. And it's no liner – only a little coaling ship, so if you are particular you must make other arrangements.' He eyed me fiercely. I recalled the coolie-ship and grinned. 'I'm not particular.'

Thus it was that I bethought myself of Sunny, who was also going to Wei-Hai-Wei and who jumped at the offer of a free passage, so she and I set out on a very small, very black vessel with an iron deck covered with a fine gritty coal-dust surface that stuck to the soles of our shoes.

Our coaler was in no great hurry. She was calling at Keelung on the way north, and to ships of her ilk time is not a matter of urgency. We were well satisfied with this leisurely attitude and we relaxed and made ourselves at home. We were pleased, moreover, that we would have an opportunity of seeing Formosa,* once a Chinese possession and now Japanese.

'The Japs are pretty cagey about Formosa,' said Sunny. 'We are lucky to be touching at Keelung.

* *Formosa is now Taiwan, for many years Chiang Kai-shek's last stronghold against Mao's Communism.*

We found that we were to occupy the captain's cabin, which was a small stuffy den heavily upholstered in red plush. We examined the photographs of his family with interest and decided that the good mariner had not wasted his time ashore, for there were six little steps, from the baby to the nine-year-old son, to his credit.

'But we can't turn you out!' we cried falsely, when he inquired if we were comfortable.

The Norwegian captain was a great shaggy grizzly bear with eyes set very close together. 'That's O.K.,' he said in his heavy accents. 'I turn out the first officer and he turns out the engineer. We don't care what happens to him.'

The engineer was a red-haired young man who blushed readily. Sunny flirted with him a little to put him at his ease. We had our meals with the officers in a tiny plush dining saloon. They were Norwegian, but all spoke English. Our days we spent on deck in the sun reading, talking and sewing.

Sunny looked a bit pale the first morning, and when she got out of bed she clung to the rail giddily.

'Seasick?' I asked.

She forced a grin. 'Well, sort of. It's young Richard. He's not been established very long and he unsettles me rather.'

Later, as we lounged in our deck-chairs, I said: 'Aren't you a trifle fussed about starting young Richard? I mean economically. Nurses are an expense and so is travelling with a babe.'

'No,' she said. 'We've gone into all that, and we've decided that its well worth the difficulties. When we get home I am to have that little house near Portsmouth or Plymouth with a garden. I don't want a nurse. I'd rather have young Richard to myself, and I don't even need a cook, because I cook rather well and so does big Richard. We want to be young with our children.'

'But when Richard goes to sea – abroad perhaps?'

'When he goes to sea I'll have the small one to keep me company. And if it's abroad – well, if there's enough money for me to follow there'll have to be enough for small Richard too. Or, if not, there are grannies. At a pinch we have parking places.'

'Yes,' I sighed. 'What would naval children do without

grannies?' Sunny smiled, and the light made tortoise-shell ripples in her hair as she bent over the tiny jacket she was knitting. There was a golden dusting of freckles across the bridge of her nose. She had a brave, happy little face. I remembered her words: 'We'll make our own intermittent heaven.' Intermittent heaven. That was life in the Navy.

We docked at Keelung at six a.m. and were to remain there for twenty-four hours coaling. We didn't turn out of our bunks, as we had given our passports and cameras to the captain the night before. 'The Japanese port authorities seal up all cameras while the ship is in port,' he had explained.

We were therefore unpleasantly surprised when there was a loud knocking on the cabin door and the captain shambled in, a harassed and ferocious grizzly.

'The Jap doctor insists that everybody on board has to be vaccinated at once.'

'But we were done in Hong Kong.'

'Have you certificates?'

We looked at one another blankly. We had no certificates.

'We can show him the marks.'

The captain tore his hair and disappeared, only to return presently followed by an undersized ape with protruding gold teeth and spectacles and a little round-faced nurse in a kimono bearing a glass slab and some instruments.

'He says nothing makes any difference. It is an order. He has already done the entire crew and he is going to vaccinate you girls, or the ship does not sail from here and we can continue to pay harbour dues for as long as we like.'

We argued and showed our scars and said we would remain on board and make no attempt to go ashore, we became very angry, but the Japanese doctor only sucked in his breath, rubbed his hands and said, 'Welly solly for you,' and prepared to go into action. It was clear that if Sunny and I remained obdurate the ship would simply stay in Keelung until we thought better of it, which would put our Norwegian benefactors into an idiotic position. There was no help for it.

'All right!' I said furiously. 'Go on, then!' And I shot a long, indignant leg out of my bunk at the doctor. He seized it and got busy. Sunny suffered the same fate. The instrument that was used for us had already done duty for sixty Chinese crew and had not once been sterilized. We both had septic legs for a month afterwards. But we also took good care to get our certificates from the doctor.

That afternoon we decided to have our vaccination's worth and go ashore. Mr. Mikimoto, the agent of the company, a very agreeable little man, offered to accompany us as the authorities refused to allow us to go alone. And the shy red-haired engineer came too. We drove up a hill in a ramshackle taxi, but when we wanted to get out on the summit and admire the view our escort became restive.

'If we go near that gun emplacement Micky Mouse will have a stroke,' I whispered. 'He's petrified that we may be spies.'

'He has only risked coming with us because he is wild to practise his English,' murmured Sunny. We had noticed that all the conversations between the ship's officers and the port authorities had been conducted in a queer brand of English, and I learned later that all Japanese are anxious to learn the language, which is the Esperanto of trade.

We were not impressed with our surroundings. Keelung was scarred with coal seams, a dirty squalid little port. But after supper on board, which Micky Mouse had with us as the captain's guest, we went ashore again.

'I take you go see pictures,' he beamed. 'Welly good film.'

The cinema was a large corrugated iron shed with narrow benches. These benches were so low that when we sat on them our knees hit our chins. The were also very hard. Micky sniggered and sucked in his breath. 'Sss, people here welly simple. No sit.'

We looked around and saw that it was indeed a case of 'no sit'. Everybody had a little cushion and they removed their shoes, placed the cushion on the benches thus and kneeling thereon, squatted back on their heels. They remained thus for the whole four hours of the performance. The main picture was Japanese, all about the amorous adventures of an emancipated young lady who had been to America and whose honour was eventually imperilled to such an extent by her wild Western ways that only an earthquake could save it. Fortunately, earthquakes are frequent in Japan, and after she had been duly shaken to her senses she reformed.

'No keezu,' observed Micky daringly. 'Ladies no commit keezu in Japanese picture.'

For, low as the heroine had sunk in Occidental depravity, she had not fallen so far as to surrender her rosebud lips to her would-be seducers. The film was silent inasmuch as the vox humana did not emerge from the screen, but from a gentleman in a sort of prompter's box, who spoke everybody's part with an amazing range of inflexions, from a shrill falsetto for the lady to a deep-throated roar for her father. The supporting picture was an American farce, but, alas! the censor had slipped up and a keezu had got by. The result was pandemonium, and we took the occasion to leave the cinema in well-feigned high dudgeon at such moral laxity, for we were both in extremis with violent posterior cramps. We looked hopefully at Micky Mouse. What now? It was only ten o'clock.

'P'rops ve can dance, or take some beer?' suggested Red tentatively.

Mr. Mikimoto scratched his head with a rasping sound. He was at a loss to know what to do with us, and he was quite determined not to give in and admit that Keelung had nothing other than the cinema to offer us.

'Sss, no dance,' he said at length. Then seized with a brainwave: 'I tell you, we go Yoshi-Wara!'

We tailed after him like lambs through the dark deserted alleys, and it was only when we were actually in the Street of the Red Lights that we realized where he had brought us.

'Good heavens!' I gasped to Sunny. 'This is the Red Light Quarter, or whatever you call it. Now we *are* seeing life!'

The face of evil in that out-of-the-way Japanese port was very young and gay under the rice powder, and it had a candour that was little sister to innocence.

We ordered green tea, and Red drank beer, in a cheerful jangling café where a crowd of girls in painted kimonos flocked round us with high-pitched laughter and chatter. They had never seen European women before, and my wavy fair hair was a source of amazement and interest. They stroked it and exclaimed over it to one another, and they made us feel their own smooth, top-heavy coiffures stiffened with wax and highly polished. They turned out the contents of our bags and examined our compacts and lipsticks with shrill exclamations, and Mr. Mikimoto, who was evidently on the best of terms with all of them, translated their questions for us. When we left they followed us to the door like a cloud of butterflies, and their regretful 'sayonaras' echoed down the narrow street.

The houses on either side were open-fronted, and in the wide entrance of each sat two old crones. Just inside was a picture gallery showing the portraits of the inmates, and we were lured into one to look at the photographs. Suddenly we heard the shuffle of soft quick steps on the rush mats and light laughter as a paper screen slid away and revealed the originals of the pictures peeping round it, all their heads close together like a bunch of flowers.

'How old are they?' asked Sunny.

Micky Mouse knew them all. Little Miss Snow-Flake was eighteen and little Miss Pear Blossom twenty-one. All were under twenty-five. Their profession was, like everything else in Japan, honourable. In that country the household cat is 'the honourable cat' and the camera is 'the honourable camera', and these little ladies of the Yoshi-Wara were no exception to this excellent rule. Later, should they marry, no stigma would attach to their names; in fact, it is considered that their experience would equip them for becoming the mothers of sons without delay.

'Sayonara! Sayonara!' The soft singing syllables pursued us.

Just as we were going back on board Red remembered that he had left his wallet in the café. Sunny and I tactfully forbore to make any comment on his loss, and Mr. Mikimoto instantly offered to go back with him to find it, and so we wished our little Japanese guide 'Sayonara' ('Farewell') with many good wishes.

So it was that Sunny and I came face to face with vice in Formosa.

CHAPTER THIRTY-ONE

SHANGHAI NIGHTS AND DAYS

As we steamed up the racing yellow Whangpoo River to Shanghai we looked eagerly for Bertie's cruiser and Richard's destroyer. Sure enough, both were at their appointed buoys, and as our little black coaling ship weighed anchor our husbands came on board to meet us. We were limping by then, as our legs were badly infected, and Sunny had a really wretched time with hers.

The *Kent* was lying opposite the Bund, that great façade of imposing buildings and banks – the temples of commerce – and the high gold dome of the Cathay Hotel glittered in the sun like the spire of a carnal cathedral.

There were other foreign warships in the river – French, Italian, American, German – and ten Japanese to one of any other nation.

Shanghai was the mouth of Moloch, sucking in and vomiting forth the great wealth of the China trade. It was dangerous and exciting. It had none of the colonial self-satisfaction of Hong Kong, none of the aloof culture of Peking, and none of that sweet set-apart peace that made sanctuary of Wei-Hai-Wei. It was wild and pleasure-bent, and like Johannesburg, the City of Gold, it lived at a feverish pace. All one's standards went haywire. Delirium was in the air.

Oh, the nights and the lights of Shanghai! Multi-coloured and whirling, dizzy under the stars, and rocking upon the bosom of the fast-flowing river! We knew that there were shadows on the waterfront where gangsters lurked ready to kill a man for the price of a meal, and shivering figures coughing out their lungs between the lowered shafts of their rickshaws, and hunger and cruelty and vice; but we forgot these things because we were caught and blinded in the dazzle of the lights. We were intoxicated on jazz, luxury, and glamour.

We ate caviar and frogs' legs and danced on the fourteenth floor of the Park Hotel. At midnight we went on to the 'Little Club', where a white Negress sang 'Dat Man o' Mine' in a deep throaty voice that pulled at one's emotions; then on to the 'Blue Danube', where a Viennese man and woman played two grand pianos, the man big and fair with a sensitive angry face, and the girl dark with a jealous mouth that twisted into haunting little love-songs. Sometimes a young thing, slightly shot, would leave her party to go and sit on the stool beside the man and sing with him, her cheek against his. Then his partner, at her piano, gulped and smiled, and there was black hatred beneath the smile. Last of all we went to Del Monte's for eggs and coffee – queer place that, a dance-hall with stained-glass windows you might have found in a mediaeval church. The Russian taxi-girls sat in a sulky row or danced with men half seas over. Haggard they were, with weariness starting through the paint, disillusion in their eyes and metallic laughter on their lips. A stern old woman went about among them, scolding and admonishing, cracking an invisible whip. Her face was mean and pinched, and I remembered Rum-tum-tum nagging the model-girls at Collette's. Dawn stole through the stained glass, and the frogs, croaking in the pond outside, fell silent. We went home and I leaned my head sleepily on Bertie's shoulder in the taxi. We were staying with Mrs. Cooper. The milk stood on the doorstep and the house dogs barked perfunctorily to announce our return.

As we crept upstairs I saw that Shirley's door was ajar and the light still on. I peeped in. Shirley was asleep. Her hair flowed over the pillow to frame the Greta Garbo profile, an open film magazine lay under her hand, which was chubby like a child's, a half-smoked cigarette had burnt a hole in the carpet and smouldered out. I switched off the light.

'Thank goodness she didn't set herself on fire!'

We little guessed that eight years later, to the day, April 16th, 1941, known ever afterwards to Londoners as 'the Wednesday', Shirley and I would be standing together on a London pavement watching our respective flats burn like the fires of hell while bombs rained down all round us. She was John's wife then, an M.T.C. driver, one of the many who showed her quality in the blitz. It was the seventh anniversary of their wedding day. They were still living dangerously, for that was their way. To them the blitz was 'just another thing'. John was at the Admiralty, and it did not occur to Shirley to evacuate. Mrs. Cooper had a flat nearby because she had to 'keep an eye on Shirley'. That was *her* way. And, anyhow, mother and daughter had seen cities bombed and burned before. They had lived in China.

In our room there was the incense perfume of the mosquito coil. I opened our windows wide to the sunrise. The birds were twittering in high sweet voices and the air was fresh and cool as the heart of a rose. We inhaled it deeply. A smile passed between us – delighted, incredulous. 'Can this be you and me – *here*?'

Mrs. Cooper was my Scheherazade, and from her I heard tales of a thousand and one nights – Shanghai nights. She knew all the 'characters' of that cosmopolitan city, and through her we met them too. There was 'Nunkie' Sassoon, universally beloved, and Victor Sassoon, grey-faced, lame, and powerful. And there was a certain kind, dark woman with the features of Arabia, a house like the mansion of Citizen Kane, and two most unprepossessing sons. Mrs. Cooper was acquainted with everybody and their history, and everybody was acquainted with her. She had been through all the 'troubles' and 'incidents' that are part of life in China, such as famine, flood, war, and the regular anti-foreign risings that were fomented as diversions whenever a temporary government was in difficulties. In the 1922 'Shanghai Incident' she had seen the Japanese shell Chapei from the river, bomb it from the skies, and shoot at it from the street that divided the International Settlement from the Chinese city, and she had seen, too, the influx of dazed refugees from the inferno that reddened the heavens and turned the Whangpoo to the colour of blood. The strange and the terrible were to her the normal. She was indomitable.

Jay, Mrs. Cooper's Number One, regarded Shirley as his child. When she was going to a dance, Jay, in his long white gown, could usually be found doing up her dress or fastening her shoes while she made him laugh rather sourly at her absurdities.

'You no savvy fasten my dress more quick I call Amah,' she threatened, carefully brushing mascara on to her eyelashes.

'Me savvy,' muttered Jay. 'This fashion can do.'

We were going to a dinner-dance at the Cathay in a party with Shirley's sister Gay and her husband.

Gay had a very white skin, washed, I sometimes fancied, by the milk of human kindness. She had great vitality, tempered with abundant charity. She rattled off wisecracks and little jokes like machine-gun fire and danced till the small hours, but I knew that she spent many of her days engaged on unobtrusive good works. The Roman Catholic nuns at the convent hospital looked forward eagerly to her visits. She was not a Roman Catholic, but in Shanghai it made no difference; every denomination recognized the splendid work done by the nuns, who stayed in the city throughout the hot weather and the epidemics, when most other Europeans sought respite in the hills or farther north along the coast. Outside the city limits there was a sinister place known as the Baby Tower; where ignorant peasant mothers used to get rid of unwanted baby girls. The nuns used to rescue these foundlings and bring them up in the convents, educating them, teaching them Christianity, equipping them with a trade of some sort, and even marrying them to suitable husbands. Eligible young men were glad to marry convent-trained girls, who were reputed among the Christian Chinese to make the best wives. Often, when I went to see Gay in her charming house, I found her sitting pale and exhausted after hours of serving at a sale or charity bazaar, with Amah massaging her blue-veined feet or her aching head.

'Amah's hands have magic in them.' She would smile and pat the little yellow fingers affectionately. Amah would have died for her young mistress. Gay was not the only one who made a habit of burning the candle at both ends. Nearly all the British girls in Shanghai seemed to dance all night and do full-time jobs all day, whether it was an economic necessity or not. They were typists and secretaries in business firms and clerks in travel agencies, or they taught in schools or served in foreign-owned curio or lingerie shops – and lost no 'face' thereby.

The prettiest and most seductive women in Shanghai were the Italians. They were at the Cathay in full force the night we dined there with Gay. They had a slightly different status from the other foreign communities – just a shade more elegance – due perhaps to the fact that Mussolini's son-in-law, Count Ciano, had been given some abiguous diplomatic appointment in Shanghai, and the presence there of Edda Ciano, the dictator's daughter, shed its reflected glory on her compatriots.

I have since seen photographs of Edda Ciano disguised as a platinum blonde, but in 1933 she was dark.

'She's heaven!' groaned a love-sick young man called Shrimp, who was sitting beside me at dinner. 'Have you ever seen anything so good-looking, so full of fire?' He took a long draught of champagne (it was always champagne in those days) and toyed idly with his chicken maryland as his eyes followed her round the ballroom.

I gave the matter my attention. Edda was certainly striking and easy to pick out among the other dancers. Neither tall nor short, but wide-shouldered, with a kind of peasant strength evident under the revealing gown. Strong features, flaring nostrils, a discontented mouth; and, yes, a sultry flame burned in her restless eyes. She looked bored, but then she was dancing with her husband. His jealousy was a legend in Shanghai. He was still obsessed with Edda, and she drove him crazy. He was handsome enough in a smooth dark way, and he had not yet thickened into early middle age, but his expression was hostile and frustrated. Their quarrels were public knowledge. I never remember seeing them together where one or the other hadn't got the sulks. Nobody in Shanghai took Ciano seriously, except, of course, Ciano. The shadow of his abrupt and tragic doom was still far off.

Shrimp sighed. 'All the Italian girls are wonderful. Look at the Cieris.'

It was no effort to look at the Cieris. They were three sisters who acted as sort of unofficial ladies-in-waiting to Edda Ciano. Laura was petite, raven-dark, and brittle, with a fine little nose that turned down at the tip when she laughed. She wore very close-fitting white satin and her figure was sharp and inviting. Mats was a Renaissance picture and floated on billowing clouds with her Titian head in the air; while Itala was Rachel carrying her pitcher to the well – sturdy and immortal. They all spoke English, French, German, and Mandarin Chinese as fluently as their own tongue.

The British Admiral, who had a cynical liking for putting other people out of countenance, was once rash enough to challenge Laura down the length of a dinner-table.

'Why aren't you married, Laura? You must have passed the age of consent some time ago.'

Her black eyes flashed a quick danger signal.

'I'll tell you why, Admiral. The only men I meet worth marrying are English and Italian. If I married an Italian he'd be unfaithful to me in a month – and if I married an Englishman I'd be unfaithful to him in a week.'

So she married a Frenchman.

But Shanghai was not all night life. Bertie and I often played tennis at the Country Club in the cool of the evening, and in the mornings Mrs. Cooper enjoyed what she called 'a quiet nine holes', so we used to go to Hung Jao and play desultory golf across a network of creeks and ponds. We used floater balls, and scarlet-clad elves with fishing-nets recovered unfortunate drives and iron shots from the lotus pools and bulrushes. On one occasion, as we were putting, an elf, sprawling by the stream which fringed the green, cleared his throat in the traditional Chinese fashion and made some pert remark to our caddies. Mrs. Cooper stopped putting and drew herself up to speak very severely to the boy in his own language. He looked sheepish.

As we walked to the next tee she said: 'I know that I have a well-developed chest, but I object to being reminded of it when I'm putting.'

The Chinese always make personal, and often obscene, remarks about foreigners when they think they will not be understood. 'They have filthy minds,' said Mrs. Cooper, and told me about a friend of hers who was afflicted with an outsize in mouths by any standards. 'Whenever Blanche went into a shop the merchants and their various relations, who all help behind the counter, never failed to make the most disgusting remarks about her mouth. She spoke fluent Chinese and understood every word they said, but she never batted an eyelid. Then, when they discussed among themselves what price they were prepared to accept for an article as opposed to the price they were asking, she always knew exactly where she was.'

Twice I borrowed a pony and went out with the Riding Club. I still blush to think of those rides. A kind man called Kenneth Cummings lent me a horse on each occasion, and I wounded the first and murdered the second. In extenuation I must plead that the terrain needs knowing. For instance, the bridges over the slimy creeks were no more than stone slabs about two feet wide and without any rails. As my pony clattered across one of these his hoof slipped and down he went, head over heels, into the filthiest creek in China. My pony cut his knees, but I, who fall like a cat, was undamaged apart from the inconvenience of swallowing a mouthful of newts and tadpoles. We rode home with the others – together and apart – for we smelt to high heaven and no one cared to come near us.

The next time, my horse, a mangy worn-out beast with a wall eye, got the staggers at the end of the run, leapt high into the air, fell down in a fit, and died. Luckily the man behind me saw what was happening and yelled, 'Jump for your life!' which I promptly did, thereby narrowly averting being overlaid and kicked to pieces. I told the tale, with lively embellishments, at Hung Jao a couple of days later. Lou Andrews, to whom I told it, was not amused.

'Kenneth isn't such a fool as he looks,' said Lou. 'That wasn't his horse he lent you. It was mine.'

CHAPTER THIRTY-TWO

HAPPY SHIP

WEI-HAI-WEI that summer was idyllic. Our bungalow consisted of two bedrooms, a dining-room and verandah, and a little garden which we planted with snapdragons, zinnias, sunflowers, sweet-williams, cornflowers, and hydrangeas – all, in fact, that the police-station nursery could afford us. From the verandah we could see the harbour and the mountains of the mainland through the feathery branches of the acacias. There was no roar of a city here, only the twitter of birds, the monotonous note of the cuckoo, and the drowsy swish of the breeze in the leaves. Close at hand there was the tap, tap of Goo's 'lily feet' crossing the courtyard and the brusque voice of Ah Lin bullying the coolies.

Ah Lin was our Number One. We paid him a comprehensive wage and he employed and paid (or didn't pay) the rest of our staff – the house-coolie, the water-coolie, and a 'makee learn', a moon-faced stooge who, I gather, actually paid Ah Lin for the privilege of doing all the most menial jobs of house and garden. He was said to be gaining experience and face.

We had got Ah Lin through the ship's wine-steward, Ah Po.

'What are his references?' asked Bertie.

'Master no wantchee leflence,' said Ah Po. 'Ah Lin b'long no good I lose face. Ah Lin b'long good I gain face. He b'long good.' It was as simple as that.

Ah Lin was a haughty-looking northerner with a sulky mouth and it went very much against his grain to serve me before 'the master'. I was even a little afraid of him, chiefly because I never had the faintest idea what he was thinking. He was the inscrutable Oriental of melodrama, except that he was not at all obsequious. Chinese servants seldom are, off the stage.

273

They bring great natural dignity to their work. Ah Lin was subject to malaria, and whenever he felt an attack coming on he sent for his uncle, who immediately took over the management of my household. His uncle was a mild-mannered but competent man, and I would like to have kept him instead of his arrogant nephew, but both Ah Lin and Ah Po would have lost face had I even mooted such a notion, so the fancy was still-born.

'Two people, three rooms, and five servants, I said to Bertie. 'It's mad.'

'It's face, darling. It's China.'

When I arrived at our new bungalow two men were still painting the walls. The one was very old, with a face like crinkled vellum. Grey stubble sprouted on his square head. His hands, though filthy, were sensitive, more like those of a painter of portraits than of houses. The thumb-nail was long and the fingers tapering and surprisingly steady. He smoked a tiny clay pipe as he squatted to paint the base of the wall. His mate, a callow youth with a pock-marked face, a head like a dusty doormat, and a pair of incredibly holey socks hanging down over his ankles, ran nimbly up and down a ladder to all the less easily accessible corners. As they worked they jabbered in their extraordinary language full of deep-throated gutturals. Chinese is an angry language, and the Chinese seem to talk among themselves more volubly than any other race. We were always shouting to Ah Lin to shush the coolies. 'No so much walla-walla [chatter].'

I suggested to him now that we hang a wet-paint notice on our verandah in English and Chinese. His Adam's apple danced as he tossed his head.

'No puttee Chinese sign. Chinese man see, he smell, he savvy. Only puttee English sign.'

'Moskee [No matter],' I murmured, sorry I had spoken.

Every morning, just before sunrise, Ah Lin brought us our tea, his slit eyes still swollen with sleep. The Chinese sleep till it is light and then their day begins, so that it was no hardship for our Number One to bestir himself with the birds. Across the water we heard the bugle notes of the Reveillé, and so still was the summer dawn that orders given out at sea carried clearly to our bungalow on the hill.

Sometimes I tumbled out of bed and flung on a pair of slacks and strolled down to the waterfront with Bertie in the pink light of the early morning. Boats were already out on the water and the crews were away training for the Fleet regatta.

The *Kent*'s motor-boat was chugging alongside the wooden jetty, and the Captain and the Paymaster called a greeting to us. They, too, were going away boat-pulling. And I happened to know that they, like my husband, had bad broken blisters on their behinds. We wives worried more about the universally raw state of our husbands' seats during the training season than they did themselves.

'Can't you row just as well sitting on a cushion?' we wanted to know. It seemed they couldn't.

Quite often I walked up to the Signal Station on the hill before the heat of the sun enervated the freshness of the new-born day. From there I could see the cruisers and destroyers swinging to the tide, and the *Medway*, heavy and maternal, with her submarines close to her flanks. Sometimes the thunder of their dynamos charging, or the roar of *Hermes*' seaplanes overhead, broke the enchanted silence of the island.

The look of the *Kent* always pulled at my heart. She was so pretty! My grey rival. Little men were suspended over the side, painting ship, giving her a new summer dress, pale as the sky before nightfall.

It is a strange relationship that exists between the woman and the ship. Other men go to their offices and do their job, and then they go back to the intimate human side of their life, and the worries of the office can be set aside in the comfort and relaxation of the home. But his ship keeps a man on a leash. He is never free of her. This is specially so of the commander, who is even closer to her than is her captain. I used to try to visualize my husband's life on board – but I soon had to give it up: I knew so little about it. There would be the 'Petty Assizes', of course, when defaulters would be brought before him on the quarter-deck, and he would administer the simple justice of the sea, fairly and without prejudice. If he needed guidance he could find it in the King's Regulations. The labyrinth of legal loopholes and quibbles had no place in a warship. If any one of his ship's company was in trouble, that man could apply to see the Commander, and his problem – no matter how personal it might be – would receive full and sympathetic consideration. The men's comfort and happiness was his first care. Out of some seven hundred and fifty of the ship's complement there were not more than a score who had their wives on the Station. Here and there we, who were fortunate enough to be near our men, touched the life of the ship, but our impact was light as that of a honey-bee in the chalice of a lily. We drew much sweetness from the contact, but we made little impression upon the dance of the flower.

To me, my husband's cruiser was 'the pretty ship'. To her ship's company she was something far more important. She was a 'happy ship'. Ships have a subtle character of their own. They may be lucky or unlucky, slovenly or efficient, good or evil, happy or unhappy, depending upon the spirit of those who serve in them. An unhappy ship casts a long shadow which reaches out to engulf the homes ashore, but a happy ship sails the seas as a summer cloud rides the heavens, and we wives who watch her White Ensign fluttering in the sun are light-hearted and proud, because, in a way, we too belong to her. The *Kent* was such a ship.

Sometimes, of a morning, the marines passed by our bungalow for exercise ashore or on their way to the rifle range, and then perhaps the Major of Marines stepped on to my verandah for a well-earned glass of beer. In the afternoons there was the tramp of feet and the sound of talk and laughter as the men went past to the sports ground for a football or a hockey match. Or those training for the Wei-Hai-Wei marathon loped up the hill with the easy, tireless rhythm of runners in good condition. Twice a week there were inter-ships matches, and I went with my husband to cheer on the 'men of *Kent*'. There were sports and regattas and shooting competitions. And there was the anxious morning of the Commander-in-Chief's inspection, when sailors stood by with guns loaded ready to scare away importunate seagulls who might be tempted to sully the well-polished decks. There was never time for the men to get bored. They had more work and play than schoolboys, and that was a good thing because their hours ashore had little else to offer them. They had no homes to go to and no girls to take to the pictures. The officers had the Hong Kong and Shanghai 'lovelies' to take picnicking or sailing, but for the sailors there was no one. So it meant a great deal to them to belong to 'a happy ship'.

On Sunday mornings all the wives put on dresses instead of

shorts or slacks, and they wore hats and stockings and went on board to church. I loved church on the quarter-deck. It has always seemed to me the best way to praise God – out in the open, with the crisp, clear tang of the sea, and the sun slanting through the awnings. The ship's company sat on the wooden benches in front of the long grey guns, their hair sleekly brushed and their faces shining. The sermon was honest man-to-man counsel – serve God and honour the King – and the Captain read the lesson while the breeze played in the canvas overhead and the cries of the gulls were hoarse above the hymns.

'O Trinity of love and power,
Our brethren shield in danger's hour;
From rock and tempest, fire and foe,
Protect them whereso'er they go;
Thus evermore shall rise to Thee
Glad hymns of praise from land and sea.'

In the evening the scene was transformed and there were pictures on the quarter-deck. The great guns were trained upon the screen – voices of wrath benevolently silent – and there were expressive sounds from the sailors during the love scenes, and apt Cockney quips, for many of the *Kent*'s company had been born within sound of Bow Bells.

Often there were dances on board one or other of the war-ships. Music and laughter floated across the harbour, and coloured lights were reflected in the water. Motor-boats chugged back and forth from Narcissus Bay and Half Moon Bay, and Shanghai Shirley's speed-boat was a silver rocket in the moonlight, while the cardboard mountains of Shantung looked down upon the little pantomime of peace that was drawing so swiftly to its close.

CHAPTER THIRTY-THREE

TINKO AND THE BANDITS

THE heat of Wei-Hai-Wei was damp, and if Amah did not put out our clothes in the sun every few days they grew whiskers and began to smell mouldy. Fog swathed the island from time to time, and then the junk-bells sounded mournfully through the mist, deceptively near.

At other times clouds of long typhoon-flies materialized out of nowhere, and then the sampans ran for shelter and Bertie stayed on board. The cicadas fell silent and the wind rose with a sinister whining note and shook the white acacia blossoms from the trees; the 'pretty ship' strained at the leash like a hound that hears the hunter's horn, and the guardship stood by with steam up ready to dash to the scene of a wreck or a piracy. For that was the way of the China coast. A typhoon seldom died down before it had exacted human sacrifice.

It was my second summer in Wei-Hai-Wei. My rickshaw runner was still the earless one who could run faster than any other coolie on the island, and yet I did not really believe in bandits any more than I believed in ogres and dragons.

It was Tinko Pawley who changed this comfortable outlook for me.

Tinko was in Wei-Hai-Wei to recover from an experience that would have left most girls nervous wrecks for life. She had just been six weeks in the hands of Chinese bandits.

We met her at dinner one night on board a destroyer, and, though she was at first reluctant to speak of her adventures, she warmed to the subject in response to our interest.

Afterwards I said: 'Why don't you write the whole story? It would make a book.'

She laughed ruefully. 'I can't. I'm pen-shy. But I've often wished I could find someone to do it for me.'

'Then you've been looking for me. I'll write your story.'

That was how it came about that I spent that summer writing 'My Bandit Hosts', which was published by Stanley Paul in the following year.

Tinko used to come up to our verandah and talk. She didn't tell me her story in any proper sequence. It just came out bit by bit as the mood took her, and when she had gone I made my notes and later I strung them together.

Although she was married, she was little more than a school-girl. She was eighteen years old, with a firm healthy body and a clear fair skin. Her hair was red-gold and her features were childlike. She was extremely naïve and entirely lacking in im-agination. Tinko hadn't a notion of how to dramatize herself, and it was this shortcoming which had saved her sanity through those weeks of alternate hell and boredom. That and her faith. She was the daughter of a missionary doctor and she believed implicitly in a God who was concerned with the personal fate of each and all of His creatures.

She had only been married a few weeks when she was cap-tured while out riding on the racecourse at Newchwang in company with Charles Corkran and Duncan Macintosh. Ma-cintosh subsequently escaped, but Tinko and Corkran were held captive for forty-three days.

Their capture caused a great outcry in China and even in England, where the *Daily Mail* took up the case and offered to pay a fat ransom for the prisoners. Missionaries and travellers had been kidnapped often enough and portions of their anat-omy sent to their relatives; many had disappeared altogether, their demise leaving little impression upon the public im-agination; but the plight of this girl-bride and the young man who was her fellow-prisoner was what Russell Stannard would have called 'sure fire human interest'. Tinko was young and pretty, and everybody wanted to know, *would* the bandits or wouldn't they? And later, when she was returned to her parents and her husband complete with fingers, toes, and ears, people asked one another in hushed whispers. '*Did* the bandits, or didn't they?'

When she spoke to me of Pei Pa-tien the bandit chief, Tinko's voice dropped and she shivered in the sun.

'He was a hideous monster with a huge purple underlip that hung down and showed his stained teeth like the fangs of an old dog.'

For seven hours this brute and his fellow-criminals had whipped their captives through the kao-liang, the tall sorghum that the bandits use as cover; and when at last she and Corkran were able to rest for the night and remove their riding-boots, the torn and bleeding skin came away at the same time. The scars on Tinko's feet will bear witness to the sufferings of that day for the rest of her life. And when I knew her her arms still carried the marks of the halter that had bound her to her body-guard day and night.

In spite of their lame and septic feet, bandaged with any old rags they could come by, the prisoners were kept on the march through the desolate Bad Lands, and at nights they shared a rough Chinese kong (bed) with nine of their captors. Luckily both Corkran and Tinko could speak fluent Chinese, and they understood the curious, sarcastic humour and boastfulness of the illiterate bandits. They understood, too, their superstitions and their greed, and they were able to play on their ignorance to save Tinko from rape and disfigurement.

'Pei Pa-tien used to come and threaten us,' she said with that little tremor in her voice that revealed something of the dumb terror she had felt for this loathsome beast. 'He loved to de-scribe tortures to us – the slicing process, slow strangulation, and torture by fire – and he said he was going to chop off our ears and send them to our people at home. Charles used to laugh at him and call him a fool. Charles had pluck and nerve! He used to tell Pei Pa-tien that if I was in any way spoilt my husband wouldn't want me back and I wouldn't be worth so much as a string of copper cash to my own people or to the bandits. It was lucky for us that we could talk Chinese and argue with the chief.'

As she spoke her toes wriggled in her open summer sandals and the great white welts on her insteps rose like cords.

From Tinko I learned much about the ways of bandits and their cruel, stupid urchin mentality. She told me how they kept whole areas under a reign of terror, torturing villagers and peasants whom they suspected of disclosing their whereabouts to the military authorities, and how they passed through hamlets like destroyers, commandeering food, billets, clothing, and even women. What they wanted they took, and their advent was the cause of dread and despair to the hard-working peasants.

Tinko and Corkran never knew one moment's privacy in those six weeks. They were creatures in captivity, continually on display. They were filthy and verminous, but even when they were most humiliated and brutalized they kept their heads high, and in their dreadful wanderings they managed to find and enjoy rare moments of beauty. There was a night trek across country, when they marched two hundred strong in single file on stealthy cloth shoes in the great unbroken silence of the night, with only the stars and here and there a swaying lantern to guide them. And there was a gusty morning when the cotton-wool clouds scurried across the cobalt sky and the dirty, ragged little captive felt the spirit of eternal life stir in her weary, fearful heart. Far away there was a range of blue hills, soft as velvet, and the words of the Bible gave her comfort: 'I will lift up mine eyes unto the hills from whence cometh my help.'

'Flocks of wild duck and geese rose out of the reeds at our feet that day,' she said with her blue eyes tranquil, 'and when we reached a wide stony river storks flapped out of the rushes and soared away with their long thin legs trailing foolishly behind them.' She had been allowed to paddle, and the memory of the cool water refreshing her aching, wounded feet was a strangely pleasant one.

Brave little Tinko, with her dauntless heart of a child and her child's inability to express herself or do justice to her own sufferings and experiences, is part of the pattern of my China years – a gold thread of courage and faith against a turbulent background.

The *Kent* returned to England in the following spring to pay off and recommission.

She gave passage to an Amoy tiger destined for Whipsnade Zoo. 'There is nothing the Navy cannot do,' and tending a young and lusty man-eating tiger for several weeks was just another thing in a sailor's life. The animal arrived at Chatham in excellent condition, highly polished from whiskers to tail.

Not being a fortunate tiger, I sailed for England by P. and O. On arrival I heard with mixed feelings that my husband had been reappointed to the China Station with the new commission. So once again I arranged to go back to South Africa on my own.

Imperial Airways had recently opened up the Empire Service, and I wanted to save time by flying. I asked Charles te Walter about it.

'If I could fly to Cape Town and then later from Cape Town to Singapore, it would save me weeks of sea travel, and I could spend a longer time at home with the family and Piet. Anyway, it would be a new adventure.'

'It's very expensive. Have you thought of that?'

'Yes, it would cost the earth. Financially I can't look at it. But I wondered if it couldn't be done on some compromise basis. I believe I could make it worth their while for Imperial Airways to send me at a considerably reduced rate.'

Charles laughed and shrugged. 'I don't know about that, my dear child. There may be some way you could make yourself useful. The service is still very new. I'll give you an introduction to the managing director, and then if you have any intelligent suggestions to make you can put them up to him.'

Flying tens of thousands of miles from one end of the earth to the other was not an everyday occurrence in 1934, and no woman had covered more than a small portion of the Empire route. I proposed to cover all of it – as far south as the Cape and as far east as Singapore, which was then the terminus.

The managing director sat in a very fine office and said with a kindly smile: 'What can I do for you?'

I put all my cards on the table.

'. . . and if I could pay you the same as it would cost to do the whole thing by sea, perhaps I could make the surplus good in publicity and in suggestions – anything I can think of that might increase the comfort of passengers, and especially women passengers . . .' I concluded lamely.

But the managing director was interested in my rather vague proposition, and before long we had come to an agreement that was satisfactory to both of us.

CHAPTER THIRTY-FOUR

SKY ROAD AND WILL-O'-THE-WISP

NOWADAYS Imperial Airways African Service is all by flying-boat, and the route has been changd in consequence, but we went by Paris, Brindisi and Cairo and then straight down the spine of the Dark Continent from top to tip.* We were a mixed bag and I was the only through passenger. There were a few business men to whom time meant money, a young cotton-grower returning to Uganda from home leave, two Belgian nuns bound for the Congo, and the wife of the governor of one of the Sudan provinces. The business men were frankly bored and blasé, and the young cotton-grower was a real Dismal Desmond who had left his heart at home.

'Why didn't you marry your girl and take her back with you?' I asked.

He sighed. 'Because the climate isn't fit for a white woman to live in.'

'Nor is the climate of England,' I said. He looked deeply shocked.

The younger of the two nuns was as excited as a schoolgirl at this glimpse of life outside the convent walls. Her eyes sparkled and every now and again she had to fight down the laughter that bubbled up from sheer joie de vivre. She was a filly turned loose in a meadow. Not so her companion, a stern-featured female whose expression remained as bleak and unsmiling when she was ushered into Cairo's leading hotel – a very sink of iniquity – as when she gazed down upon the clumsy capers of a pair of amorous young elephants.

The little lady returning to the Sudan was the best value. She had lovely humorous brown eyes and a tired face lit by a mischievous smile.

We arrived in Cairo after dark, and the lights of the city winked at us as we coasted down a flare-path on the Nile. Imperial Airways did things well, and on landing we were

* *BOAC is, of course, the product of these early beginnings.*

always whisked off to the best hotel with our dressing-cases for the night. We were to leave next morning at two o'clock, and the wise slept, but the foolish – Dismal Desmond and I – went to the Kit-Kat Cabaret and observed among other things that the professional partners were uniformly platinum. Egyptian gentlemen evidently preferred blondes.

Two a.m. Heliopolis in the light of a setting moon, and a long dragon-fly with a Roman name – Hadrian, our biplane – awaiting us. A cool wind on our faces, the drumming of the propellers, a little jackal fleeing, wraith-like, across our path, and for me a sense of elation. This was Africa and we were heading south – straight for home. Presently I dozed, and when I woke it was daybreak in the desert, a flat shell-pink world threaded by the blue ribbon of the Nile.

We came down to fuel and lunch at Wadi Halfa, and as the door of the cabin was opened to let us out I recoiled in alarm. A blazing breath of air rushed in at us as if from a blast-furnace.

'Something is on fire!' I exclaimed. But Brown-Eyes only laughed. 'That's the desert wind. A bit warm, isn't it? Do you wonder we all dry up out here?'

The two nuns had put on topees over their coifs. It was 110 degrees in the shade. 'A hundred and ten is nothing,' Brown-Eyes assured me. 'It's only beginning to hot up now.' She was a grand companion and her stories of life in the Sudan bid fair to surpass Mrs. Cooper's sagas of Shanghai. That night our stop was Khartoum, but we had to stay there for thirty-six hours, as a whirlwind sprang up during the night and damaged Hadrian, who had been sleeping out (there was no hangar for him on the flying-field), and his brother Hannibal had to be sent from Cairo to take his place.

Brown-Eyes had friends in Khartoum and she took me to dinner with Colonel Barker, the Game Warden of the Sudan. Colonel Barker lived in a zoo, and after dinner we went and admired his rare Sudanese beasts by torchlight. Then we sat in the garden and drank beer. Suddenly we heard a weird grunting from behind the fence that separated the lawn from the menagerie – an impatient adenoidal snorting such as I have never heard before.

'That's Horace. He wants his sugar,' remarked Colonel Barker, fishing a lump out of his pocket.

'Who is Horace?'

'The hippopotamus.'

There is in Cape Town Museum a stuffed hippopotamus with his mouth wide open. You could without difficulty put a couple of young babies into the yawning cavity.

'That lump of sugar you've got there would do nicely for a canary,' I said. 'What possible use can it be to a hippo? He won't even notice it.'

'That's all you know about hippos! Come along with me.'

We followed the snufflings and gruntings to the fence, where we met the monstrous bulk of Horace waddling along in the starlight with his vast mouth expectantly open. Colonel Barker threw him the sugar and Horace pounced. Now, one might well be excused for thinking that a hippopotamus would naturally be a crude eater, but such was far from being the case. Horace used his sugar like chewing-gum. He sucked it noisily, spat it out, licked it, and sucked it some more.

'He'll keep on at that for hours,' said Colonel Barker. 'He knows how to spin out a good thing. He's very intelligent and the best-natured animal in the zoo. Mind you, he did once eat a three-year-old child, but only under severe provocation.'

Next day we parted with Brown-Eyes at Malakal, but not before some of us had enjoyed a delicious cold luncheon with her and her husband in their cool oasis residence on the banks of the Nile. A dozen Berberine servants were lined up waiting for her when we arrived, each holding a bunch of flowers which they were too embarrassed to present.

'They know I love flowers,' she smiled. 'I've planted out quite a pretty garden here.'

Wherever Englishwomen go — whether it is the desert, the seashore, or a barren mountain-top — they call forth a garden. Flowers grow for them.

After Malakal we were flying over big-game country. Hundreds of Horace's relations wallowed in the green swamps of the Sud. Lumps of sugar they lacked, but liberty was theirs and the right to enjoy the spring as nature intended, two by two. Their surprised black faces were to us so many stout black boots neatly arranged in pairs. Giraffe cantered fantastically through the scrub, their necks, tree-high, like swaying masts in a heavy swell; shy buck stood transfixed to listen to Hannibal's roar and then bounded away as his dragon-fly shadow caught up with them; the Bor herd of elephant, about a hundred and fifty strong, grazed pastorally beneath us, wearing a halo of white tick-birds about their heads, but love was in the air, and as we wheeled down to within about seventy feet to take photographs we saw a pair of enterprising young jumbos seize the opportunity to give the old folk the slip and make a quick get-away on their own.

That night at Juba our nuns left us.

The flight down Africa was tremendous – over the vast primeval lands of the wild beast and the wild man. There below us lay the Great Rift Valley, which was part of the old slave route to the sea, and equatorial volcanoes towered into Kenya's azure air with bonnets of snow upon their lofty heads. I am not an early riser by habit or inclination, but it was no hardship to get up in the dark those mornings. In that immense scenery little Hannibal, picked out in pin-points of light on the aerodrome, seemed smaller than a mosquito on a postage stamp in mid-Atlantic. Dawn broke in bands of silver, sunrise flooded the immeasurable landscape with light and colour, horizons were blue with the pale mist-blue of untold distance, and each day I felt with awe and a sense of intrusion that I was witnessing the miracle of creation.

The Khartoum whirlwind had cost us a day, and that was why we had to spend a night in Kimberley instead of pushing straight on to Cape Town. I shall never forget the impatience and frustration I experienced in that sordid little hotel. And then, after dinner, the manager found me in the lounge. 'Mrs. Packer? A telephone call for you. From Cape Town.'

My knees went weak and my inside turned to water as I took up the receiver. It was two years since I had spoken to Mother. She said: 'Peter is longing to talk to you. He is here beside me.' Dimly I heard her murmur, 'There, darling, here you are,' and then over the wire came the thin, far-away little voice: 'Is that you, Mom? When are you coming home? Come soon, Mom . . .'

I was at Tees Lodge in time for lunch next day.

For the first time in nearly ten years something vital was missing from my home-coming.

My parents and little Piet were at the aerodrome – Peter clasping a whole bunch of carnations this time – and they told

286

me that I would see my brothers and their wives at lunch: the Senior Aunt had made a great effort to come to meet me – a little frailer and a little older – and Arend, waiting at the car, had grown broader and was inclined to be self-conscious about yet another increase to his family. And there on Tees Lodge stoep was dear Teena with her grand-piano smile playing a rhapsody for my benefit. And there was a young fox-terrier who was a stranger to me. 'My dog Gyppy,' said Piet with infinite pride and affection. At mention of his name 'my dog Gyppy' looked up at the child with devoted eyes, eager and questioning. Kismet, the airedale, slobbered amiably and jumped up on me with his huge paws rasping my skirt. But where was our little Cookie with her brown hands wringing out her apron, and her giggles and her high-pitched greeting.

'Cookie?'

Daddy said: 'Cookie is all right, old chap. She is in the Somerset Hospital. Norman operated on her last week for appendicitis, but he is quite satisfied with her.'

Mother and I went to see her that afternoon. She looked tiny in her hospital cot in the big ward where the other brown faces turned inquisitively towards us on their white pillows. I saw that her frizzy black mop was sprinkled with silver, that her cheeks were shrunken, and the little cold paw I took in mine was very light. But her smile was just the same.

'Welcome home, Miss Yoy, darling.'

'This is a nice thing, Cookie! We can't do without you at Tees Lodge.'

'Did Teena roas' dose pigeons nicely today?'

'Beautifully, but I'd have known the difference. Nobody can do them quite like you can.'

We didn't stay long. Not too much excitement, my brother, her surgeon, had ordered.

Mother sighed. 'She is growing old – like all of us.'

'Not you, darling. You'll never grow old.'

She smiled a little sadly. 'How do you find Daddy?'

'A bit quiet, sort of tired.' I had noticed how bowed his shoulders had grown, and he had said: 'Joytje, old chap, the wheels are running down.'

'Well, there it is,' she sighed. 'Darby and Joan are getting on.'

That day, as Mother and I drove home from the Somerset

287

Hospital, I was aware that my feeling towards my father had gone from the purely filial to the protective. This happens to all sons and daughters whose parents live into old age. It is a bitter-sweet moment and brings its own tears in the night. It is one of the poignant fundamental experiences of human growth, and as such it is better recognized and accepted.

And for me how quickly 'the lost years' were streaming away! Already 'our child' was eight and we were buying him his school outfit. He was to go to Diocesan College Preparatory School as a boarder – his first step into the world of men. He took it in July, after the winter holidays, and he took it boldly.

The special torments a small boy endures when he comes from a home where he has been king of the castle and has to find his own level among the cruellest little animals in the world, the boy-pack with their law of tooth and nail and tongue, is something only to be guessed at by mothers.

We know as little of those pangs and humiliations as they know of childbirth, but we can guess a good deal, and if there is a mother who doesn't agonize over her eight-year-old son's first term she is a woman of sawdust and iron.

When Piet had sailed through that ordeal with the flag still flying and the holidays had come and gone and he had expressed himself ready, albeit reluctant, to return to the prison-house, I knew that I could go back to China and my husband.

Six in the morning at Wingfield Aerodrome, the summer breeze scented with the mimosa that clothed the flats, a silver bird lost in a bank of clouds, and my face buried deep in the roses Fred had brought me from his garden, the dew still on their fragrant petals. Dew and tears and good-byes. Always good-byes.

In Cairo there were two days to wait for the eastern connection, which had met bad weather over the Mediterranean and been delayed. A friend met me there and we dined at Mena House in an open palm court where a little fountain played its crystal scales, and we saw the Pyramids by moonlight. Next day we went to the Museum and admired the gold death-mask of Tutankhamen – perennially young, broad-featured, symmetrical, and serene. But I am not one of those who is deeply affected by things Egyptian (Egypt can never have figured in any far-back incarnation of mine), and deserts have no allure for me, which may account for the fact that the flight east seemed dull to me compared with the African sky-road. There is a surfeit of deserts. But Baghdad upon the Tigris had the inevitable glamour of a city built upon a river, and we stopped one night at a romantic fortress in the midst of nowhere, like the Hollywood conception of the fort in 'Beau Geste'. It was protected from marauding Arab bands by barbed wire entanglements and patrolled by ferocious Arab guards. A tame deer dwelt amicably in the courtyard with an amber-eyed cat. Next day there was the lonely Air Force station of Sheiba, where the R.A.F. had their base, a 'bachelor station' swept by the hot desert wind that put a merciless cant on the spindly trees they tried to grow round the Mess. And it was there that I heard a name that came as an echo from my flapper days in London. Prendergast. I remembered a photograph on my cousin Cicely's dressing-table of a naval officer with a fine open face. Archer Prendergast had left the Navy and was now a pioneer for Imperial Airways. He was flying ahead of us in a new plane opening up the route to Australia.

'Prendy passed this way yesterday!' We heard it at every airport we touched after that. On the shores of the Persian Gulf, in Karachi and Delhi, and at Akyab, between the Burmese jungle and the grey silk sea. And then we heard it no more. Prendergast had crashed – lost in the Timor Sea. I had never known him except as a name and a photograph on a young girl's table, but somehow I felt very sad for him.

Rangoon was a night stop. Bankok was another, and their gold-leaf temples burned in the sun. At last, thirteen days out from Cape Town, we landed in Singapore by the light of flares.

I caught a Japanese ship the same night and slept most of the way to Hong Kong. Our flying hours had been long and exhausting and my impressions were bewildering, kaleidoscopic. I felt rather as most people do when they come out of 'Gone with the Wind' – drained of all vitality. There had been no time either for that all-important switch-over from looking back to looking forward. That, perhaps, is the worst of air travel when the journey is not just a business trip. On a sea voyage there is peace and leisure, in which emotions, raw from parting, heal and adjust themselves and the mind has time in which to take control and bring forth whatever philosophy it may need to meet the altered circumstances of the future. But an air journey is swift and bright, as clean and impersonal as a modern operating theatre, and it amputates time and space with callous efficiency. The operation can be too drastic, and the limbs that are cut away go on hurting.

This time I was not disappointed when I looked eagerly for the *Kent*. She lay at her buoy in Hong Kong harbour, so light and graceful, with her fastidious feminine air, that I felt tears of pride and affection prick my eyes. The square, corrugated sails of junks, like patchwork quilts, stood against the stiff winter breeze, and the sun shone brightly. We docked alongside Kowloon wharf under the massive block of the Peninsula Hotel, and I heard again the raucous shouts of the coolies and smelt once more those indescribable aromas of the East.

My husband was the first on board.

'It's been too long this time, Joy-Joy. Seven months.'

'Let's never be parted again!' I tried to laugh, knowing full well the foolishness of my words.

That evening we had dinner in our sitting-room, the same in which Hong Kong's leading golfer had stippled the walls with a well-driven lemon. A fat-faced young Chinaman in a trim uniform, who rejoiced in the appellation 'Room Service Captain', supervised our meal.

We had spent the afternoon together, but there still seemed everything to say. We had a long way to catch up. Bertie had given me little disconnected scraps of news and gossip. Shanghai Shirley and John were married and they had gone home to England. Gay and her husband had gone home too, but Mrs. Cooper was still in Shanghai. Did I remember Ah Lin's stooge in Wei-Hai-Wei? Well, he had attempted to murder Mrs. Poland's Hong Kong amah last summer. Mrs. Poland was the wife of the captain of the *Medway*, and she had taken our bungalow and our staff during the summer I was in South Africa. She had also taken her South China amah, who could not get on with the North Chinese.

'But I can't believe that that dull-looking water-coolie, who paid Ah Lin for the privilege of doing all our dirty work, had the temerity to knife anyone!' I exclaimed.

'He had, though. And when Phyllis Poland rushed into the kitchen quarters in answer to Amah's yells she found the little woman lying in a pool of blood and the water-coolie at the sink calmly washing the carving-knife under the tap. Moral: never mix northern and southern servants. It doesn't work.'

'Did Amah recover?'

'Oh yes, in time. But she'd been pretty thoroughly hacked about.'

Sunny had had a fine baby boy in a Shanghai hospital and she too had gone home. Few of the naval people who had been with us last commission were left. It was always that way. That, of course, was why folk ashore found us so 'unsatisfactory'. 'You no sooner get to know naval people than off they go!' How often I have heard that said! But those who say it seldom realize that it is a state of affairs which irks us even more than it does them.

'What's the new captain like?' I wanted to know.

'Ian Tower? He's marvellous. Sharp as a needle, and leaves everybody to do their own job. Encourages initiative.'

'And Mrs Tower?' This was important.

He smiled. 'She really enjoys life. Is always well turned out, and does us all credit. And then there's Evelyn Tufnell, whom you knew in Malta. She's just arrived. You remember Tuffy? He's our Japanese interpreter, among other things.'

But it was I who did the lion's share of the chattering. There was so much to tell about Tees Lodge and Piet.

'He's a real schoolboy now! None of your toddler any more, but a skinny little fellow covered in scars – knees like battlefields. You wouldn't know him at all. Boxes, plays rugger, and goodness knows what all.'

There was a great deal of 'Did I write to you about the time when he . . .?' and 'Did you hear about his fight with . . .?' and so on. But after a while I fell silent, oppressed with the inadequacy of words and phrases to bridge 'the lost years' between father and son.

The Room Service Captain pocketed his tip and cleared the table. From the harbour we heard the sad, beautiful notes of the Last Post. It was nine o'clock. We went to the window and looked out upon the lovely sight of Hong Kong at night. Lights garlanded the Peak and swayed on the water. The Peak tram crawled upwards like a glow-worm reaching for the stars, and the red and green of the ferry-boat shuttled gaily back and forth between the island and the mainland.

'You've had nothing of him,' I said with my thoughts still far away. 'Nothing at all of Piet.'

'You haven't had so much yourself.'

It is not what is said that counts, but how it is said. There was such a burden of sympathy in the brief sentence that my heart swelled and melted within me. The ghost of our little son clasped his arms about my neck and laid his smooth child's cheek against mine, and there was a heaviness in my throat that made it difficult to answer my husband. Indeed, it seemed to me that this marriage of ours was founded upon the poignant words 'forsaking all others'. And I thought also that we who lived in this manner, homeless and with empty places in our hearts, had greater need of love and kindness between us than other men and women.

Presently I said: 'How pretty she is – your *Kent*! Picked out in lights, she is a will-o'-the-wisp of the sea.'

'The will-o'-the-wisp you've followed across half the world.'

'She'll dance ahead of me yet.'

'Quite soon, I dare say.'

She lay, long and narrow, between the lights and stars, this ship so close to my heart and so remote from my understand- the 'grey mistress' whose claim upon my man would for ever come before my own.

'Dear enemy,' I said aloud, 'are you still a happy ship?'

My husband was filling his pipe. When he had pressed the tobacco well down and lighted it, he said: 'She is still a happy ship.' And his voice was warm with his feeling for her.

Early in the year my will-o'-the-wisp of the sea led me south to Malaya.* She was motivated by the will of the new Commander-in-Chief of the China Station, Admiral Sir Frederick Dreyer, a veritable giant of the Navy, both physically and mentally.

Lady Dreyer was white-haired and gentle, with a fragile leaf-in-a-storm personality that aroused the chivalry of men and the tenderness of women. She followed her husband's flagship, the *Kent*, in the sloop *Falmouth*, which was used as the Commander-in-Chief's yacht. The Captain's wife and one or two other friends went with her.

* *Now Malaysia.*

The rest of us learned, with gratification and surprise, that we could avail ourselves of a passage south in a naval oiler with the delicate name of *Pear Leaf*.

I shared a tiny cabin with Eileen Walker, the wife of the commander of the *Falmouth*. We had one peg and a drawer between us. But Eileen was like a wraith in the cabin. Her possessions were invisible, and, while my powders and face creams littered the narrow shelf we used as a dressing-table, her face was kept tidily tucked away in a Hong Kong basket under her bunk. It came out twice a day to point the shy woodland charm of her features and was pushed back out of sight. Eileen was a writer and she had published several novels. When she was silently observing and recording what was going on around her she reminded me of a doe standing motionless on a kopje, a part of the earth and the leaves, apparent only to the trained eye of the hunter. Like Evelyn Tufnell, she had three children in England, and was only in China for a few months to be near her husband for a little while.

Evelyn and Sheila Findlay were cabin mates, and the Flag-Lieutenant's wife shared with Janice Kyall, the wife of a young gunner. Evelyn was a Walt Disney thrush, with a comical way of fluttering her eyelashes and making mischievously disconcerting remarks. Sheila was very diffident, and inducing her blushes was a sort of game among us. The Flag-Lieutenant's wife had a true, sweet singing voice, and sometimes in the evenings she sang softly to us on deck and we listened enthralled. Janice, who before her marriage had been a Wimbledon star, was as full of grace and high spirits as an alsation puppy.

The Captain had a family of Siamese cats on board, wild creatures with hard, egotistical blue eyes and knots in their tails. And although we were five days in the *Pear Leaf*, we talked as little scandal as did those four-legged cats. One evening at sunset Evelyn called us to the rail.

'See!' she cried. 'The green ray!'

There it was! A funnel of luminous jade, cutting clear through the banners of the sunset. As we watched it, marvelling at the other-world purity of its colour, a vagrant breeze came to us from the distant outline of the land. On its breath was the perfume of sandalwood, burning leaves, and night-scented flowers.

'Malaya!' said the Captain, inhaling great draughts of it.

Evelyn fluttered her eyelashes at him. 'Leave a little for us!' she said.

CHAPTER THIRTY-FIVE

SOUTHERN CRUISE

In Singapore we scattered. Some wives had friends ashore and the rest of us went wherever our husbands deemed suitable.

Bertie had taken a barnlike room for me in a ramshackle hotel conveniently placed opposite the Tanglin Club. I shared it with a swarm of bees who had settled on the window-sill, two amorous bats who pursued each other round and round after dark (until I caught them in a basin of soapy water as Marjorie and I had learned to do with Onrust bats in days long gone by), and a score of cheechaks – small nocturnal lizards who ate the insects that settled on the electric light globe. One evening a cheechak fell from the ceiling into my lap. His beady eyes cast me dumbfounded glances as his tail came off and bustled across the floor-boarding all by itself and before I had uttered so much as one yell the truncated reptile was hot on the track of his nether parts. His expression of shock and embarrassment made me laugh.

'Like Piet', I said, 'when he took a high dive and his bathing pants came off with the impact of the water.'

In the pond, outside, a concourse of highly vocal frogs gave tongue every night. They had in their midst one who went off with the pop of a champagne cork, and we named him 'Daddy' Wallem.

Singapore swarmed with tigers and Japanese agents. The tigers were as harmless as the mythical beasts of my childhood, whose excursions into the jungle had always coincided with my interruption of a grown-up conversation. As I gazed at the fearsome brutes on every poster and hoarding advertising TIGER BEER, TIGER BALM, and TIGER OATS I heard a distant echo of my mother's cautious tones as she cleared her throat, with a meaning look at my father, and said: '. . . so the tiger went into the jungle.' There were tiger cocktails too, and young officers were wont to go to the Tanglin Club and fling out magnificent orders such as 'Just bring me two Million Dollars and a couple of Tigers'.

The Japanese were less innocuous. They were barbers, photographers, masseurs, storekeepers, business men, and travel agents. And the young ladies of the Land of Smiles adorned the Red Light Quarter in their thousands and added their quota of information to that which swelled the files of the widest and most sinister espionage system in the world.

A day or two after we arrived a prominent Japanese resident was arrested. On the way to the police station for questioning he took poison. No one was even interested. 'Everybody knows the place swarms with Jap spies,' they said. 'Why worry. Tidapa.'

Tidapa. Let it alone – who cares? That was the spirit of Singapore. The French expression for that attitude of mind is laissez-faire; the Malays say tidapa.

When I went up-country to Kuala Lumpur to stay with our friends Peter and Vera Wallis, I was glad to leave the colony. It had little charm for me.

In Kuala Lumpur people were genuine and kind, and when Bertie got an unexpected three days' leave and flew up in an R.A.F. bomber they could not do enough to show their goodwill towards him and towards the Navy.

The Wallises had a pretty house on Marlowe Hill, like a villa in Biarritz. But it was built to allow through draughts everywhere, as Kuala Lumpur is on the Equator and the moist, perpetual heat is intense.

Every afternoon it rained, and after the rain we played tennis on perfect grass courts. In Malaya it can deluge on one court and be as dry as a bone on another. You walk out of the rain into the sun as if passing through a gateway.

Vera had a light Wendy look, as if she might fly out of the nursery window, over the jungle tree-tops and far away. The Wallises were living for their leave. It was the beautiful mirage ahead. Peter was rising fifty and he had earned the long leave for which they were making so many plans.

Vera looked after her husband as if he was the child she had never had.

'Don't forget your scarf, Peter! Put on your blazer, darling!'

And then to me she'd add: 'One's blood gets thin out here. Peter has been in Malaya too long already.'

In the mornings the Chinese cook's baby woke us with his lusty yells that penetrated the convolvulus hedge dividing the servants' quarters from the house. Vera leaned out of her window then and shouted 'Deum!' which, we gathered, was the Malay for 'Shut up!'

'If Mrs. Cookie doesn't learn to control that brat we'll have to sack Cookie,' she grumbled insincerely. 'There is no excuse for it. That baby is the healthiest youngster in Malaya!'

Presently Ah Fong, the Chinese houseman, would bring our breakfast to our room, and later we'd go down and find Allighan, the little Tamil butler, flicking a duster round the cool green living-room and loggia. Allighan wore an emerald sash and turban, a wide, coy smile, and no shoes. When he rode his five-shilling Japanese bicycle his toes clasped the pedals like the prehensile digits of an ape.

One afternoon, when the rain had soaked every court in Kuala Lumpur, Vera took me for a drive round the residential part of the town with its attractive houses standing back in lush tropical gardens. Near the Chinese Quarter she pointed to a piece of waste land.

'The Letter House used to be there,' she said. 'You've probably read Somerset Maugham's famous short story, "The Letter"? Well, that plot was based on fact. Many years ago there was a bungalow here and Mr. and Mrs. Dash lived in it. Mrs. Dash had a lover who jilted her for a Chinese girl. So she shot him. She was sentenced to death, but the Sultan of Selangor found extenuating circumstances and she was deported instead. When Somerset Maugham came out here he was interested in the case and he examined the scene of the crime with the lawyer who had defended Mrs. Dash. Later he wrote the short story which was afterwards produced as a play in the West End with Gladys Cooper in the lead. Now, it happened that the lawyer was in London at the time and he went to the first night.

'I don't know if you remember the beginning of the play, but it is very dramatic. The stage is in darkness, a shot rings out, and then you hear a woman's voice screaming: "He attacked me and I killed him!" The lights go up. Well, you can imagine how the lawyer from Malaya felt at that point when he saw that Somerset Maugham had transferred the real setting of the real crime to the stage down to the last chair and table-lamp. The scene was identical with that of the murder in Kuala Lumpur.

'In the interval the lawyer decided to go out and get himself a much-needed drink. As he went towards the foyer his eyes roamed casually over the audience. All the usual first-nighters were there. Then he stood stock-still in the aisle. There in the last row of the stalls, white-faced and tight-lipped, and looking none too sure of herself, sat Mrs. Dash herself.' Vera paused. Then she added: 'It was never possible to let the house after the murder. So they pulled it down. Now, as you see, it is a playground for children.'

I looked at the children romping there. One mite was Eurasian, pretty as a picture, with the slanting eyes of China. It amused me to think that she might be a descendant of the victim of what was a true *crime passionel*.

There is no winter in Malaya. But there is Frazer Hill. When Bertie had returned to Singapore the Wallises took me there for the week-end.

We drove out of the steaming plains into the jungle-clad mountains. From the spine of the peninsula the world fell thousands of feet into an abyss of leaf and flower which rose again and undulated over hill and vale into the smoke-blue distance. The jungle.

'Nature gone mad,' said Peter. 'Fighting for the light.'

Spring trees grappled with one another and were wound about with the hungry tentacles of parasite plants, all striving into the sun. Here and there a fiery wild orchid lit a torch in the leafy twilight or waxen blooms glimmered like stars in the night. On the dark, hidden floor of that mighty madhouse the tiger stalked the shy jungle deer and the wild pig dwelt side by side with the black panther. Monkeys swung from strong liana ropes and were only stilled in their capers when the lidless eyes of a snake mesmerized them into shivering immobility. Brilliant birds shrieked in the rustling tree-tops. Such was the green hell in which our troops had to fight the Japanese in 1941–42. Long before the attack on Malaya new paths had been cut through the jungle to all important points the invaders intended to take on their advance down the peninsula. While the white man was ordering his gin-sling at the club the Japanese fifth column was working antlike in the interior as well as round the coast of the doomed peninsula.

Frazer Hill, 'our English village', as Vera called it, was backed and flanked by jungle, yet its cottages stood in English gardens and bees hummed busily in lavender and heliotrope hedges. All the big firms had their own bungalows there, and employees could book them, fully staffed, for a few days at any time. Maur Cottage, allotted to us, was typical. The Chinese houseman had arranged cut flowers in the vases and a fire crackled in the hearth.

Vera went and warmed her thin hands.

'What heaven!' she said. 'Playing at winter. There should be muffins for tea!'

A fire. Healthy cold. A night's profound, restful sleep under two blankets. These things were wonderful – a foretaste of home for Vera and Peter.

Next morning, after a game of golf on the little course scooped out of the jungle, we went along to the dairy for glasses of fresh, foaming milk straight from the cow.

The Chinaman who served us said that last night a tiger had got into the pasture and stolen a calf.

'What happened to him?' I asked. 'Was he caught?'

The boy shook his head, and before he could give it, I knew the answer.

'Miskee,' I said. 'I savvee. The tiger went into the jungle.'

The boy smiled. 'Mem savvee,' he said.

A few days later the Wallises drove me down the Malay Peninsula to Penang, through the rubber plantations and tin-mining country to the coast. And there I parted with these kind friends. I next saw Vera and Peter on their precious leave in England nearly two years later. Fate had played them a bitter trick. On their first night out in London the taxi driving them home from a restaurant crashed into a high-powered car. They were taken unconscious to Middlesex Hospital, and for weeks they hovered between life and death. Vera's injuries were the more severe, and when she recovered it was Peter who said: 'Don't forget your scarf, Vera-Vera. Put on your coat, darling.'

They returned to Malaya soon afterwards. The longed-for

holiday had turned out to be nothing but many months of sick leave.

The *Kent*'s next port of call was Belawan Deli,* and the British residents of Medan, the little Dutch Capital of Northern Sumatra, a few miles inland from the port, had very generously offered to put up any of the officers' wives. So I and my companions of the *Pear Leaf* embarked on the Straits steamer *Kedah* at Penang. We were as excited as children plunging their hands into a bran-tub for a lucky dip.

'I wonder what Sumatra will be like,' speculated Eileen Walker that night at dinner on board. 'It'll be interesting to see a Dutch colony after Singapore.'

'It's very nice of the British community to offer to put us up,' said Sheila Findlay. 'After all, there is a hotel in Medan.'

'Indeed, yes,' said I. 'It's called the Hotel des Boers.' I felt that if anyone ought to be staying there I was that one.

At nine next morning three ships lay in the Belaway River – the *Kent*, the *Falmouth*, and the stocky little Straits steamer.

The young Dutch passport officer looked at us and smiled.

'You ladies belong to the man-of-war?'

We replied with pride that we did. He stamped our passports without further ado.

Meanwhile my unknown host and hostess, who were friends of the Wallises, had come on board.

'I'm Macdonald, and this is my wife. You must be Mrs. Packer. We had your description from Peter Wallis, and you answer it perfectly.'

I wondered a trifle nervously what the description had been.

Mr. Macdonald was tall and amazingly fresh-complexioned for one who had lived many years in the tropics. His wife was an energetic little Londoner with the sharp black eyes of a city sparrow.

I saw that Eileen Walker had been appropriated and was already being swept down the gangway. Evelyn and Sheila were still peering expectantly at the jetty.

'Will you introduce me to Mrs. Tufnell and Mrs. Findlay?' said Mr. Macdonald. 'Their hosts have already gone to call on the *Kent*. I am going myself presently, but my wife will take

* *Now part of Indonesia.*

you three ladies to Medan and settle you in, so to speak.'

When I introduced him to Evelyn and Sheila, who appeared relieved to find that they had not been overlooked, he said, with a twinkle: 'You are going to stay with two reliable bachelors. No objection, I hope!'

Evelyn's eyelashes danced with amusement, and Sheila ran true to form and blushed to the roots of her brown hair. 'I'm sure it will be quite all right,' she said with her shy laugh.

'My word!' exclaimed Mrs. Macdonald, as her husband left us to join the other gentlemen who were calling on the wardroom thus early in the day. 'We've never had a ship this size at Belawan Deli! Mmn. The last British warship to come here was the *Caradoc*. That was seven years ago, and we've talked about it ever since. But the *Kent* is bigger. Yes, this'll certainly impress the Dutch!'

We were gratified. In Singapore 'the pretty ship' had been just another warship. Here she was an event.

Being part of an event is always very moving to me. I felt now as I had done many years ago when the backveld Boers rode in commando to meet the Nationalist leaders in the Orange Free State. They, too, had gathered in the dorp for the occasion, riding and driving many miles from lonely farms to do so and bringing their wives and families with them. Just so had these British planters and their wives travelled to the little town of Medan from remote up-country plantations to be present at the celebrations to welcome this grey ambassadress of their distant homeland. For weeks in advance the plans for this four-day visit of the flagship of the China Station had been made. Nothing had been forgotten. Officers on forty-eight hours' leave could be accommodated in Medan or they could go to tea plantations in the interior to get some shooting. There were sports matches, water polo, and excursions for the ship's company. There was a grand ball at the Hotel des Boers and another at the mansion of the Dutch Resident.

Medan was white and green and tidy. I found here the same order and prosperity that characterized Batavia. The Dutch East Indian colonies had none of the haphazard 'just growed, like Topsy' air of the British possessions east of Suez. Their public buildings were air-conditioned and modern, their medical services and educational facilities were magnificent, the natives were contented, and there seemed to be little of the dreadful poverty evident in Hong Kong, Singapore, and Ceylon. Up in the cold, healthy air of the mountains, 4,500 feet above sea-level, was Brastagi, where many of the Dutch settled when they retired, and where there were good schools for the children of Europeans in the Straits Settlements. There was very little colour bar, and there was consequently a certain amount of intermarriage between brown and white, but such unions were not encouraged.

Yet the British women in that model tropical colony were homesick, just as a city urchin pines in the green fields of the country.

I realized how homesick they were when I walked over to the tennis club with Mrs. Macdonald. Sailors were strolling along under the oak trees of the little town. They carried tennis shoes or bathing trunks and towels. They were laughing and joking, and their voices and their speech were of London town. Their caps were pushed far back on their perspiring foreheads, their faces were young and fresh, and there was a healthy tan on their fair skins.

The little woman beside me halted in the dappled shadows to watch them go by. Her bright black eyes were wet with tears, and I knew that Bow Bells were ringing in her heart.

'Not Dutch or Malay,' she whispered chokily, 'but Cockney! To see our own boys in blue, and hear them – in Medan! Can you think what it means?' As we walked on she mopped her eyes and then, defiantly, her brow. 'Fairly rolls off you here,' she said, changing the subject abruptly. 'You should see my poor husband! How that man can sweat when he's working! Sheer concentration.'

'It fairly rolls off you' was Mrs. Macdonald's pet expression, and I had to admit that she had good reason to use it that night at the dance at the Hotel des Boers. When she returned to our table after a waltz her new dress, made specially for the occasion, was saturated, and her partner's collar was as limp as a sick cat's tail.

At supper I sat next to the Sultan of Deli – a stout, elderly gentleman who wore a black-and-gold cap, a glittering diamond watch-chain, and fine diamond rings and studs. Later I danced with his favourite son, a tawny youth, somewhat bejewelled, who spoke French, the language of his Parisian mother. When we rejoined our party we found that the Sultan had repaired to a high chair at the bar, there to drink many a contemplative toast to the lastest addition to his large family. Despite his advancing years, he was the father of a new-born man-child of whom he was moderately proud. Eileen and Sheila, who had that morning attended the bathing ceremony of the royal infant, declared it a masterpiece, but the Sultan was blasé. They had many strange tales to tell us of the ritual wherewith the Sultan's last-born held court in his bath, an exclusive levée to which they were only admitted through the good offices of Eileen's influential hostess.

I observed that Evelyn had made a hit with a good-looking Dutch baron. It was impossible to ignore them because the baron, who was clearly a great individualist, disobeyed all laws of a ballroom rotation and leapt against the stream like a salmon, using Evelyn's slight little form as a buffer.

'He always does that,' explained Mrs. Macdonald. 'Sort of left-handed idea – can't help himself. Mmm.'

Evelyn brought him to our table to introduce him to me, and he bowed his dripping face low over my hand.

The baron was very kind and he lent Evelyn and me an enormous Mercédès Benz and a Lilliputian Tamil soupère (chauffeur) and sent us up to Brastagi, where we spent a cold and refreshing night under the lee of the twin volcanoes, Sibajak and Sanabang.

The roof of Sumatra is not unlike an exotic version of Dartmoor, and it is peopled by a mountain race whose forbears would have had much in common with those who will see no other view. For their hobby, too, was homicide. The Bataks are fairly recent descendants of cannibals. They still file their teeth, and their mouths, stained with betel-nut, are vast bloody gashes. The women are but little concerned with dress, except for their headgear – a huge black oblong turban – which in life contains their worldly goods and in death becomes their winding-sheet.

These lazy, uncouth, and alarming individuals are first-class chess players. In every Batak village, in the shade of the primitive, deep-roofed huts on stilts, a chessboard is marked out on the ground in order that the elders of the tribe may beguile their endless leisure poring over that game in which time is no object. Chess was bequeathed to the hill-folk by an early Portuguese invasion of Sumatra.

On our way to Medan we stopped our little Tamil soupère so that we might dart down the jungle path which led to a hidden waterfall.

We stood at the side of the horseshoe precipice, where monkeys hooted among vagrant rainbows and flung themselves madly from bough to bough above the flying spray.

Evelyn said: 'All these lovely things! How can we keep them?'

'We can't,' I said. 'Not altogether. But bits will cling. And some day, when life seems all one colour, we'll be able to shut our eyes and see bright things again. . . .'

'A golden oriel with the sun on its wings, or a monkey springing through a rainbow.'

We fell silent and listened to the song of the waterfall and the wild inconsequent conversation of the grey monkeys.

Meanwhile, down at the port, the *Kent* was receiving homage suitable to a sea goddess as lovely as she.

The natives, in their gaudy, glittering sarongs, encamped on the wharf, and for three days hundreds of them simply squatted there and observed the habits and activities of those whose privilege it was to scrub and polish, to pad hither and thither at the double, to blow whistles and bugles, to run flags up and down, and to man the motor-boats that made free of the muddy Belawan River. Cars bore officers back and forth from Medan, and buses fetched teams of cheerful sailors. Special trainloads of Straits-born Chinese from all over Sumatra were permitted to ravish the grey goddess. So also were more trainloads of arrogant British Indians, who, as they stalked up the gangway, expressed themselves displeased at seeing so many 'black people' on the quay. (The British Indians, themselves a dark chocolate, referred contemptuously to all other persons of sombre hue as 'black people'.) On the afternoon of the third day the worshippers on shore observed that preparations for a feast were in progress and that sailors ran here and there to array the goddess in red, white, and blue bunting and that they jewelled her with coloured lights. And presently the Lord High Admiral himself, in all his glory, stood on the quarter-deck to receive his guests. A Marine band played the wild, thumping music of the West and there was a mighty sound of swishing as if the wind were rising in the jungle tree-tops. This was the feet of many dancers. There was, too, a simian jabbering, a shrieking as of gleeful parrots, and strange echoes of hyena laughter, which was the collective voice of the white race making merry.

But at last, on the morning of the fourth and last day, the patience of those who had only squatted and waited was rewarded and the *Kent* was thrown open to them. The phalanx of brilliant sarongs surged forward, regardless of the bottleneck produced by the gangway, and men, women, and little children were precipitated nonchalantly into the ditch. Swift as thought the goddess asserted her objection to human sacrifice, and her fire-hoses were turned on to the ardent worshippers, whose eager stampede was thus reduced to order.

That afternoon, as 'the pretty ship' sailed, under the admiring gaze of the natives and the hungry, homesick eyes of the British community who had gathered to see her go, she took with her as an unoffered memento most of the pier. The audience raised a feeble cheer. And soon the Belawan River was empty once more of the symbol of Empire and majesty.

'Well, there now,' said Mrs. Macdonald a little shakily, and her black eyes were suspiciously bright. 'She's gone again, and I s'pose it'll be another seven years before we see a British warship in Belawan!'

Planters and their wives turned slowly away, to go back to lonely estates in the interior. It was all over – the weeks of happy planning and the brief burst of emotional excitement with its backlash of nostalgic memories and longings.

The *Kent* had shown the Flag.

And now Evelyn and I set forth on the road which the fall of France was to open to the Japanese a few years hence, thereby sealing the fate of all South-Eastern Asia.

The International Express bore us from Penang to Bangkok. It was a sort of triumphal procession. The express ran twice a week and was cheered upon its way and pelted with flowers by the populace of every hamlet.

In the small hours of the morning I had occasion to visit the loo, where I tumbled over two large full sacks in the dark.

'Evelyn!' I cried when I got back to the sleeper. 'Wake up! There are two dead bodies in the lavatory!'

'Forget it,' she replied drowsily. 'They are probably bales of something or another, and even if they are dead bodies I'm not interested.'

In the morning, when we were dressing, she said: 'You must have been dreaming last night. There are no corpses in the loo this morning.' And upon further investigation I had to admit that she was right.

Near Bangkok a Thai passport officer came into our compartment. He was very polite, spoke surprisingly good English, and apologized for 'investing' our time. When he had done with the usual formalities he said: 'Do you know about last night?' It was obvious that he was bursting with news. 'At two-thirty this morning this train went over two men – took their heads off. They were asleep on the line and they did not hear this train until it was too late.' He seemed rather proud of our stealthy iron monster for catching the two poor coolies napping.

'Did the train stop?' I asked.

'Yes, the men were put in bags and put out at the next station. . . .' He sighed. 'But we could only find one head.'

I looked pallidly at Evelyn. She fluttered her eyelashes and said: 'Do you always have bags ready for – emergencies?'

'Yes,' replied the passport officer. 'We have bags for men and bags for buffaloes. Last week we killed a buffalo. When we kill a buffalo the farmers all run away across the fields as fast as they can because they do not want to own the dead animal. We make them pay damages to the train for – *obstruction*.' He was manifestly pleased with both the word and the sentiment.

Evelyn turned to me as he bowed himself out of the compartment. 'All right,' she said. 'You win!'

We discovered later that about fifty coolies a year were decapitated by the bi-weekly juggernaut. They were neither drunk nor desirous of committing suicide. It was only the coolness of the rail they sought, and they relied upon the thunder of the approaching train to wake them, instead of which the vibration lulled them into deeper slumber.

Bangkok was full of its own curious enchantment.* Wedding-cake temples and tiled palace roofs reminiscent of Peking clustered on the banks of the Menam River. The city was built upon a Venetian network of lily-choked waterways, and the Thai children stripped off and sprang naked into the water whenever and wherever they pleased. So did the water-buffaloes, only they did not find it necessary to strip.

* *Siam now Thailand.*

The *Kent* lay many miles down river, but Bertie took forty-eight hours' leave, and we stayed with a charming grass-widower called Mr. Adams, who lived in a vast wooden house with several hundred cheechaks and a score of tockais (lizards resembling baby alligators, who wind themselves up with the sound of a air-raid warden's gas rattle and then call out 'Tockai! Tockai!' like the harsh cry of a bird of the wilderness). To bear him company Mr. Adams had three dalmatians and a bull-mastiff. The bull-mastiff had a habit of padding softly up behind people and then jumping at them so as to plant his forepaws neatly and heavily against some unsuspecting posterior.

'He has the rarest gift in any animal,' explained Mr. Adams, 'a sense of humour.'

'Must have had a fairy godmother at his christening,' I said without enthusiasm as I performed a contortion the better to observe the extent of the animal's spoor on the back of my clean white dress.

Mr. Adams, who was nothing if not a man of taste, had also an exquisite maiden in the house to attend to our needs – a sort of sublimated amah.

'She answers to the name of Moon,' he said. 'Whatever you want, shout for it – washing, pressing, a bath, or a drink.'

It was evening as Bertie and I stood upon our wooden balcony and stared out at the garden, which was a go-as-you-please affair girdled by a klong (canal). Flowers of unbelievable brilliance were poised upon the boughs of trees motionless in the heat. Dusk fell. The sky was mother-of-pearl, the water-lilies folded their petals, and on the lawn the night-watchman, who came on duty at sunset, bowed his monstrous turban over his toenails as he pared them laboriously under the indifferent eyes of the four dogs. The chirping of the cheechaks sounded from dim corners of the balcony, and presently the raucous cry of the tockai repeated itself seven times, which was supposed to be lucky. A faint breeze lifted the veils of heat. We looked at one another and smiled.

'A gin-sling might be a good idea,' said Bertie. And, lifting up his voice, he called 'Moon!' The sonorous bellow was as the mournful lament of a cow at milking-time.

On the following day there was a thé-dansant in honour of

the *Kent* at the house of the Senior Regent, whose son, an alert young officer in the Thai Navy, had received his training in the British Navy.

The Regent was a charming old gentleman who had long since scored up his three score and ten. He was attired in bright blue satin breeches and a khaki uniform tunic and a Panama hat such as my father wore when he pottered about the garden.

Refreshments were set out of doors, but there was dancing in the big reception-room, which led on to a wide wooden verandah. And the *Kent*'s band had been borrowed for the occasion.

Round the french windows there clustered posies of golden daisy-faces – the children. At first I thought that the regent, like the Sultan of Deli, carried his years lightly and that these were his youngest-born, but his eldest son disillusioned me.

'My nephews and nieces,' he smiled, as a burst of whispered chatter broke out among the daisies. 'They are very excited about the party. They have never seen anything like it before.'

Nor, for that matter, had I.

The Thai young ladies of society, who had been invited to meet and dance with our officers were as light and pliant as bamboo wands. They had the liquid almond eyes and beautiful features of the women of South-Eastern Asia and a languid grace of movement.

I gathered presently that the house of the Regent had many courts, since his innumerable grandchildren and their various parents evidently dwelt with him. Soon after dusk a large grey-haired English Nannie bustled out to gather her nosegay of daisy-faces. But first they had to make their curtsies to Captain and Mrs. Tower. Their frilly Western frocks quivered like flower petal as they dipped their knees, and their round black orbs were dewy and mischievous. The Nannie caught my eye and smiled.

'It is early for Thai children to go to bed, but, as you see, we are bringing these little ones up like English children.'

The Thais were very well disposed towards the British; and Western innovations were fashionable. But not all were popular. For instance, the Minister for Defence had recently been wounded by a revolver shot, and he now sweated profusely under a bullet-proof waistcoat wherever he went. The Thais were not shocked at the attempt on his life, but they heartily detested the crudity of the method. Shooting! A foreign habit, lacking all subtlety.

On the other side in the scales were the life-saving advantages of the Pasteur Institute, a magnificent building where I assimilated food for nightmares for years to come. We saw attendants there, wearing neither gloves nor leggings, scoop deadly banded kraits and king-cobras out of their hives like macaroni and milk them of their venom, and there were tanks full of bloated poison-fish with beaks and whiskers, whose bite was death.

'In the rainy season hundreds of coolies working in the fields are bitten by snakes every day,' said the Paris-trained Thai doctor who was showing us round. 'If they can get here within three hours we reckon to save them. But we need to know what type of snake has bitten them because the serum for cobra-bite is different from that used against krait venom. Of course, if the snake's fangs have been partially emptied by biting a mole or rat first, so much the better for the patient.'

There were hutches full of rabbits waiting to be injected with the serum from a mad dog's brain. Later their brains and spinal columns would be used to make anti-rabies serum. In the bright laboratories smallpox vaccine was being made of buffaloes' glands. We went to the out-patients' department too, where we saw long queues of people who had come for treatment. A baby was screaming as the life-saving needle pierced his little belly.

'He has been licked by a mad dog. But he will be all right,' said our doctor-guide as he led us to the research laboratories, staffed by Thai doctors and students. 'We have great opportunities for research here,' he added, 'and we hope to do good work for future generations.'

Evelyn Tufnell and her husband and another officer, whose name was John, were my companions on the road to Cambodia and the ruins of Angkor. We went to the railhead by train, and there we hired an obsolete car to convey us to the lost world of the vanished Khmers.

We had not rattled far into the jungle forests before Desmond Tufnell expressed an urgent desire for the car to stop. We were too tactful to protest or to question his intentions, but we were not best pleased when it transpired that his sole object was to rush about catching butterflies, for which purpose he had seized his wife's hat from her head.

'One has to make allowances for Tuffy,' said John. 'After all, he is an artist, something of an entomologist, and also a Japanese interpreter.'

So we bore with him. Towards evening the crenellated stone turrets of the ruined temples of the Khmers wavered like a mirage above the jungle trees. A thousand years ago they had been tipped with gold, and elephants had paced six abreast upon the giant causeways or had borne their regal masters into the parks and pleasaunces under the gateways of four-faced Sivas.

We felt that we were lost in time. Here amid the ruins of a vanished civilization we were in the presence of one of the strangest mysteries of history. The Khmers, who had wrought this magnificence from the forest with the labour of millions of conquered slaves, had disappeared without a trace, no one knew why or how or when. We discussed the various theories and preferred the one most in tune with the sentiments of our modern age. The slaves had revolted, slain their masters, burned the wooden cities, failed to demolish the massive sacred precincts, and in time had reverted to the primitive type of the present-day Cambodian.

Grey gibbers scampered along the crumbling parapets and terraces, already clasped in the hungry arms of the jungle, and naked brown Cambodian children with elf locks and cigarette stumps behind their ears shouted at them: 'Thwark maow! Thwark maow!' ('Monkey! Monkey!) The gibbers chattered back at them Thwark maow! Thwark maow!' ('Monkey yourself!'), and presently the human monkeys got bored and drew their bows and arrows against a swarm of wild bees in the trunk of a giant bo tree. Emerald parrots and bluebirds flitted in the branches, while golden pheasants and arrogant peacocks strutted in the park. Snakes sunned themselves upon the Naga balustrades, bats clung squealing in the deserted towers, and at night the tiger roamed in search of food. Evelyn deplored our car and begged Tuffy to hire an elephant for her to do her sightseeing.

'I want to be saturated in atmosphere,' she said. But Tuffy, no doubt feeling that it would be less convenient to stop and start the elephant for butterfly-catching digressions, would have none of it.

I disgraced myself by scaling the steep worn steps of the Khmers to the dizzy summit of Angkor Wat and then announcing myself unable to descend.

'You must come down,' said John 'You can't stay up there till your bones are picked by the vultures.'

I peered giddily over the towering conical dome and shuddered.

'We had a cat at home who did this sort of thing constantly,' I said feebly.

'How do you mean?' said John a trifle impatiently. The heat of the noonday was shimmering between the leaves and on the surface of the moat, and he was thirsty.

'It climbed the highest tree in our garden and was too scared to come down.'

'What happened to it?'

'The gardener used to get a ladder and go up it, and then he caught the cat and carried the poor animal down.'

'Well, I can't carry you down. But I'll go first and hang on to your ankles if that'll give you confidence.'

I deduced from that nightmare descent that the Khmers must have had remarkably small feet and a fine sense of equilibrium.

That night, by the light of the full moon, the past and the present met and merged while the troupe of palace dancers from Bangkok performed the ageless ritual dances that are depicted ever and again on the weather-worn friezes of the Wats. High, glittering headdresses and painted masks appeared tiny under the mighty shadow of Angkor Wat as the dancers paced and postured and bent back their double-jointed hands and turned their inscrutable eyes this way and that. Their audience was composed mainly of Cambodian children whose small paws clasped resinous flares. Behind their ears they carried half-smoked cigarettes, and when they weren't smoking, giggling, shoving, and milling, they dozed as they squatted on the ground and all but cremated one another with their flares.

In the morning our battered car swept us through many miles of half-hearted jungle to Saigon.* A myriad white

* *Saigon is now the capital of South Vietnam.*

butterflies rose in clouds from under our wheels. Tuffy spared them. He liked his butterflies gaudy.

When Bertie met me at the hotel he looked concerned.

'What is it, Joy-Joy? Aren't you well?'

I said, not too confidently: 'Oh, I'm all right. It's just the heat and all this running around. I haven't felt so wonderful just lately.'

'Take it easy when we get back to Hong Kong.'

I nodded. 'Mmn. I'll knock off hunting.' That was easy. The season was nearly over.

Saigon was – oh, so French. We sat on the boulevards after the great heat of the day and sipped dubonnet under the trees. We heard French all round us, real French and pidgin French, and even the taxis said 'Pip, pip' in high, impatient Parisian voices.

The terrain was flat as a pancake, and the rickshaw coolies, described in the guide-book as 'human horses', behaved in most unequine fashion and rode on bicycles to pull enormous rickshaws full of white people, near-whites, and Anamites.

There was no colour bar, and we met high French officials married to Anamite wives. There was a good deal of opium-smoking among the Europeans, and many of the women were addicts.

The Governor, a charming and amusing little man, gave a grand dinner in honour of the Commander-in-Chief, and we were included in the party. His Anamite servants wore gorgeous brocaded tunics, and presently his six-year-old son invited himself to dinner and was given a seat and a glass of wine. Like most French children, this infant had never even heard of a nursery. Afterwards, in the moonlit garden, the Governor confided to me that he would not be sorry to get home when his time was up, as Indo-China was really too hot for love.

The French Admiral gave a luncheon on board his flagship, and over coffee and liqueurs in his red plush quarters he asked me if I could guess how many garments a Japanese girl wore. I confessed myself baffled by this riddle. His little goatee beard tossed merrily into the air as his chin went up in laughter.

'Chère Madame, when last I undressed a Japanese girl I took off twenty-one vestments before I got to rock-bottom.'

Saigon was the gateway to Siam and thus to Malaya. But

when France collapsed the French colonists in Indo-China agreed to co-operate with the Japanese end of the Axis. It was only to be expected. There was no precedent for European resistance to Japan in Asia.

CHAPTER THIRTY-SIX

PEOPLE OF THE SUN GODDESS

IN the spring the *Kent* turned her slender nose northwards towards the Island of the Rising Sun, and somewhat wearily I prepared to pack and follow. I had been feeling extraordinarily tired for some time.

For that reason, perhaps, I was particularly vulnerable to the Japanese habit of baiting foreigners. The Japanese love to make a European feel like a horse with his tail docked, attacked by a swarm of bees from the rear. When a Japanese is angry he only smiles with his teeth clenched and sucks in his breath a little harder. But the white man in a temper makes noises and turns red. Thus he appears ridiculous, and to the Japanese, who is always a trifle nervous lest he himself may seem absurd, the discomfiture of a European is extremely satisfying. It confirms his belief in his own superiority over all other races. Japan is always right. What anyone else can do the Japanese can do a little better. It is this point of view that makes them the world's best copyists and adapters.

We now had the good fortune to be invited to spend a few days in Tokyo with the Assistant Naval Attaché and his wife Alice.

George Ross was the most unusual naval officer I have ever met, which is saying a good deal, because naval officers are far from being all of one pattern, as people are apt to suppose. He was the son of a Scottish father and a Russian mother, and a nephew of the famous linguist the late Sir Dennison Ross. Languages presented no difficulties to George, and he spoke several fluently. He had considerable charm, a versatile mind, and a liking for abstract discussion. We often argued far into the night, 'getting nowhere' as Bertie complained. Alice was German, an eager, attractive personality who never hesitated to speak her mind. They lived in the House of the Wrestler.

The House of the Wrestler was, of course, a flimsy wooden house, but it was one in which Europeans could move and breathe, since it had been built specially to accommodate its owner. Japanese wrestlers are a breed apart – Brobdingnags amid the Lilliputians – and this one had evidently commanded that his ceilings be lofty and his rooms spacious.

'The doors are only paper and they slide,' explained Alice. 'They don't lock, so you never know when they won't just slip open and a face look in. Nothing is soundproof, so when George and I get involved in an argument you'll know all about it. The rope outside your window is an earthquake escape. You fling yourself down it in an emergency. Then you'd better come and see the bath and how it works.' She took us to the basement, where we found a large wooden box divided into two partitions. Planks covered it. 'You soap yourself outside the bath here, where there's a hot tap. Then when you've washed off the soap you just sit in the bath and cook. This side of the partition is extra hot and the other side is just the right heat for most people. The water is changed every couple of days. It's the Japanese system, and it's really very good.'

There was a lovely sunk garden with an azalea shrubbery and a pool, on the edge of which Alice's two white samoyeds, Sergei San and Boris San (the Honourable Sergei and the Honourable Boris), sat and gazed at their own reflections like white lions with Narcissist tendencies.

Alice had a little maid with bow legs, a painted kimono, and a most insipid smile.

'She's a darling,' said her mistress. 'Japanese women are so different from the bumptious little men.'

'They have centuries of submission behind them,' explained George. 'Their task in life is to make the world a pleasant place for men.'

'Good little Japanese girls are brought up on the notions of the Chinese sage Kaibara,' said Alice. 'He wrote a most reactionary tome called "Greater Learning for Women".'

'It teaches them to be good wives,' added George with a smile. 'And there's a great deal of sound common sense in it.'

Alice pouted.

I read portions of Kaibara's notable work later, and was interested to discover the Oriental conception of a perfect wife.

> '*A woman should look upon her husband as if he were heaven itself, and never weary of thinking how she may yield to her husband, and thus escape celestial castigation. She must fold his clothes, dust his rug, rear his children, wash what is dirty, be constantly in the midst of her household, and never go abroad but of necessity.*' I learned also that '*the five worst maladies that afflict the female mind are: indocility, discontent, slander, jealousy and silliness ... and the worst of them all is silliness*'. Furthermore, it is written that '*A woman shall be divorced if she fail to bear children, the reason for this rule being that women are sought in marriage for the purpose of giving men posterity*'.

Woman's place in the Islands of the Rising Sun was certainly a humble one. It was quite in order for a father to sell his daughter into a brothel to pay for the education of his son!

One afternoon Bertie and I played golf on the most expensive course in Japan. Acres of turf had been imported from America, and the club house was a cubist monstrosity of concrete and glass. The caddies all looked like the direct descendants of Mr. Toad, of Toad Hall. They wore long black tights, short flaring jackets with a sort of skull and cross-bones patterned on the back, and mushrooms on their heads. They bowed low before taking our clubs, because, in case I have not mentioned it before, the Japanese have very beautiful manners. Even while they are driving one demented with their 'Velly solly for you – no do this, that, or the other', they are also hissing, smiling, and bowing – oh, so politely.

We found, before long, that we had got behind a sevensome. These seven dwarfs, clad in exotic plus fours of lengths varying between knee breeches and ski suits, were golfing along earnestly in front of us, accompanied by the seven toads, who staggered under a weight of glittering clubs. We panted with impatience on the fairway while the seven putted, and we caught up with them on every tee. But their good manners did not extend to letting us through. It was, as usual, a case of 'Velly solly for you'.

Afterwards we happened to meet one of the Embassy staff, and we told him about the seven dwarfs.

He laughed. 'Probably aspiring young diplomats. They take their golf terribly seriously, and they often go out like that in gangs. They are getting their handicaps down in the hopes of being appointed to London.'

'What on earth has their golf handicap got to do with being appointed to London?'

'A great deal. It must be twelve or under if they are to be appointed to the London Embassy. You see, their Intelligence has informed them that a good handicap at golf is essential to the English week-end, and that more information is given away at the nineteenth than between any closed doors. So the little men are applying themselves to golf.'

'And if they lose a match I suppose they'll commit hara-kiri?'

'Not at all. Their opponent will be in a better humour at the all-important nineteenth.'

On April 23rd we helped the Emperor of Japan to celebrate his birthday.

A very gorgeous invitation card with the dynastic chrysanthemum stamped upon it in gold bade us attend the Imperial Cherry Blossom Tea Party, and this we graciously did.

The party, which was more or less equivalent to a garden party at Buckingham Palace, was not held in the actual grounds of the palace, but in a special imperial garden set aside for such occasions.

Foreign clothes were 'the rig of the day' for the men, but the traditional kimonos were worn by the women. The shape and length of the men's tails was a matter of personal taste. Some gentlemen fancied them angle-length and others elected to wear them just above the back of the knee.

But if the masculine element was, as usual, somewhat ludicrous, the feminine was entirely picturesque. The faces of the little ladies were whitened with liquid powder, their hair was simply done in a knot at the nape of the neck, and their ceremonial kimonos were held in place by gorgeous embroidered obis. Everybody, male or female, carried a common black cotton umbrella such as Chinese amahs always use.

I had never dreamed of so much cherry blossom – the real

thing this time. It drifted across the lawns and streams and flower-beds with every gust of wind, soft and rosy as snowflakes at sunset. There were little vermilion *tors* and stone lanterns, and grottoes where goldfish with trailing skirts swam self-consciously. Trees were trained to graceful shapes and ruthlessly dwarfed for the pleasure of these little people who prefer the thin 'song' of an insect to the carolling of the lark.

Japan was ruled by the military clique, the only sector which had direct access to the Emperor. This privilege was a hang-over from the Shogunate. From the seventeenth to the nine-teenth century the Emperors were mere figure-heads under the dominion of a dynasty of military Prime Ministers (Shoguns) belonging to the powerful Tokugawa clan, who for two hun-dred and thirty years succeeded in isolating their people from the rest of the world. During that time it was death for a foreigner to enter Japan or for a Japanese to go abroad. The only Europeans who retained any trading concessions were the Dutch, and they were virtually interned on the tiny islet of Deshima.

I have often thought about those Dutch traders content to live like pariahs on Deshima for the sake of the huge profits they derived from rich cargoes of gold, silver, copper, and other treasures of the East. They must have been men of very different calibre from the early settlers of South Africa. The Dutch who came to South Africa, exiles for ever from their own country, were colonists, not traders. They were agricultur-alists whose toil and joy was to make the wilderness fruitful. They were builders of homes and founders of families. They lived by their bibles and theirs was the dignity of the man who is close to the earth and the sky and who fears only his God. They did not seek gold. And when it was found on their land the old President, pensive on his stoep, was sick at heart and fearful of what must now befall his people.

It is interesting to consider how differently China and Japan reacted to the hated impact of Western civilization. China ab-sorbed it reluctantly into herself and was exploited, whereas Japan, the more virile nation, turned it into a boomerang. No sooner had the foreigner appeared in any numbers in Japan than the Japanese sent their scouts westwards. California and the South Seas were flooded with Japanese emigrants, and the little yellow students flocked to Paris, London, Berlin, and the United States to suck the brains of the Occident. These presently took their new-found knowledge back to their own country and soon warriors and peasants found themselves transformed into capitalists and factory workers, and the fields and shores of Nippon began to sprout tall chimneys and mushroom industrial towns where thousands of men, women, and children worked long hours for starvation wages under conditions approaching slavery. Then a new word came into being – Bushido.

Bushido, like everything else in Japan, is an adaptation. It has been grafted on to the Samurai code, which had to be widened to include the entire nation, even the contemptible merchant, whose importance in this new economic scheme of things had to be taken into account. It is a form of patriotic fanaticism in which the end justifies the means. Acts of suicidal courage are committed in the name of Bushido, and so also are outrages such as the attack upon Pearl Harbour or the sale of millions of cheap heroin-doped cigarettes to Chinese coolies 'to weaken the enemy'.

When the *Kent* went south I travelled into the countryside and mountains of Japan. I saw peasants in the fields planting the young rice by hand, and the gentle kindness of the little maidens who looked after my wants in humble inns, and a busdriver who stopped his bus upon a mountain pass to allow his passengers to get out and bow to the sacred volcano, Fuji San – the honourable Fuji. I saw smiling rosy country mothers with their babies strapped to their backs, and crocodiles of schoolchildren being taken to visit historic parks and temples and beauty spots. But I saw these things through a haze of smoke. The Dragon, Industry, crawled across the land, devouring the green pastures and the white sands and the bodies and souls of a pastoral, nature-worshipping people, sapping their life-blood that Japan might swamp world markets and make enough money to carry out her long-term policy of aggression.

'Back in the Garden of Eden,' I said, as Bertie and I dined together in our bungalow on our first evening back in Wei-Hai-Wei.

Ah Lin, in his long white gown, brought us our coffee on the verandah. The cicadas shrilled in the trees and the bugle notes of the Last Post came to us across the water. Nine o'clock.

'And now for a few months you can sit back and relax,' said Bertie as he filled his pipe. He himself would be busy with the summer routine of 'Working up.'

'It's lovely here,' I said. 'Not in a hotel, but all on our own in a bungalow. One day we'll have a real house – with Peter in it . . .'

There is no human heart without its empty corners, and, as we sat in the tranquil darkness watching little flurries of white acacia petals shower on to the paths in the night breeze, my thoughts went home to the house under the mountain, and for a while memories peopled the desert spaces within me.

'He'll have changed since I saw him,' I said. 'Even in these few months. They change so quickly at his age.' And as I spoke it seemed to me that the lost years brushed past us on the ghost footsteps of a child.

We had not been long in Wei-Hai-Wei before it became evident that the weariness which had overtaken me in Saigon and Japan had been, in fact, the unheeded prelude to a severe illness.

Illness had no place in the Garden of Eden. There was no hospital except the naval hospital, staffed entirely by sick-bay stewards; and the naval surgeon in charge had no facilities for performing emergency operations on the wives of the officers. Wives were not expected to fall ill on the island. However, luckily for me, it happened that the *Kent* was going to Tsingtao, and after several signals to and from Their Lordships it was decided to give me a passage in view of the emergency. The next thing I knew I was tucked up in the Captain's cabin and one of my greatest wishes was coming true. I was on board my husband's ship when she was actually under way! But, as is so often the case in this contrary world of ours, my good fortune left me unmoved. I was scarcely even aware of it.

It was terribly hot in Tsingtao. There were pepper trees outside my window at the German hospital, and they had a queer resinous smell. Their fine stringy leaves were transparent gold-green against a hard blue sky, and watching them hang limp in the sun I was reminded once more of Val's little monkey at Brandkop. Almost I saw him chasing about the pale branches, clutching a hairy black caterpillar every now and again, munching it greedily and flinging away the head and tail, or at noon squatting in the lacy shade, defleaing the patient dogs with restless energy.

The boots of the German doctor squeaked, and he operated on me at six o'clock one morning before the great heat of the day. Bertie was given a week's leave to see me 'out of the wood' while the ship went on without him, for the Navy is not as inhuman as one might suppose from the excellence of its discipline. He knew no one in Tsingtao, and that week, which was extended to a fortnight, must have been hell for him. It wasn't much fun for me.

When I began to get better I came to know a little about my doctor. He was by no means young – sixty-five, perhaps – and he had been a naval doctor in Kiel.

'That was a long time ago,' he said. 'After the war – in 1919 – I came to China.'

'But how is it that you are a gynaecologist? Did you specialize after you left the Navy?'

'Aber nein. We have women's specialists in our Marine. After all, the men marry, the wives get ill, and babies are born.' He smiled. 'Is it not so with you?'

'Yes,' I admitted with a wan grin. 'As you see, the wives get ill. But our naval doctors are not supposed to look after us. We are not part of their job.'

He raised his eyebrows and wagged his square shaven head. '*Soh?* With us it is different.'

He had been brought up in Garmisch in the mountains of Bavaria and soon he intended to go back.

'To go home, to see snow deep on the ground and to breathe air that is keen and strong! That will be good!' he said in his heavy accent, and sighed deeply. He was short and thick-set, overworked and extremely thorough and conscientious.

'Next month I return to Germany – to end my days in my own country.'

He took off his spectacles to wipe them. His hands were square and blunt and the perspiration stood on his clean-shaven upper lip and his lined forehead. 'I have lived so long in China that I sometimes think I have developed the Chinese way of thought. I want to die among my own people in my own land. A Chinaman may spend most of his life in America or Singapore, but when the end of the journey draws near he likes to know that his bones will lie with those of his ancestors.'

'I understand.'

A brief silence fell between us. For a moment it was as if that bare hospital room were empty of our presence. The old German doctor's halting words had taken him back to his snow-clad mountains and had spirited me far away to the little cemetery at Brandkop where my friend and her father lay in the golden-warmed earth of their own land – their beloved veld – side by side with those of their family who had gone before.

He stood up and braced his shoulders.

'*Also,*' he said, 'one dreams of home. But the years pass and there are many changes. When I go back I may find that I am Rip Van Winkle' (he pronounced it Vinkle), 'and perhaps then I will suffer heimweh for Tsingtao. Who knows? ... You are getting on well, gnadige Frau. You have much determination.'

'I too want to get home,' I said, and smiled.

'Auf weidersehen,' he said gravely, as he stood up to go.

'Auf wiedersehen.'

I heard his boots creak down the corridor and soon a white-faced overworked German nurse came in.

'Your medicine,' she said. She never smiled. She was always too tired to make the effort.

Soon after I was well again my little German doctor went home. I fear he must have found himself Rip Van Winkle indeed.

In the New Year my husband was promoted to Captain and relieved.

We took a Japanese ship to South Africa, where we intended to spend his foreign service leave.

As we steamed out of Hong Kong harbour, past the grey cruiser, the *Kent*'s ship's company gave their late commander a hearty cheer.

'You're goin' the wrong way!' they called.

There was the spasmodic cackle of a string of Chinese fire-crackers for good joss. No ship sails from Hong Kong without those attendant explosions.

The best view of all – from the stern of a liner homeward bound.

Well, now that view was mine. The Peak with a coif of cloud. Kowloon spreading away towards the vast hinterland of

China. 'The pretty ship', light and purposeful, dwindling in the distance. The grey mistress. We two, she and I, had known good and evil times. We had shared this man who stood at my side with his blue eyes upon her as if he grieved to leave her. Many times she had taken him from me and left me to weeks and months of loneliness. And yet, in my extremity, she had shown herself generous. I knew that I owed her my life.

I felt my eyes fill with tears. For I had loved my rival. She had been of all things the best and finest – a happy ship.

Part Four

'DAY THAT I HAVE LOVED...'

CHAPTER THIRTY-SEVEN

'AS IT WAS IN THE BEGINNING ...'

My newly promoted Captain had to wait a few months for a job, and we spent the time in South Africa, staying at Tees Lodge with my parents.

The Chinese 'greater family system' worked very well, and, if daddy occasionally chafed when we were late for a meal, Mother urged upon him the wise counsels of Chang-Kung-yi, of the Tang dynasty – he who had found that many generations could live successfully under the same roof if they all practised *jen* (forbearance). Mother had weakened in her fidelity to Culbertson and a new name was often upon her lips. This was Carnegie, an exponent of *jen* rather than of bridge. On Thursday morning Peter no longer cried aloud from his porridge, 'No bridge talk! No Culbertson!' and my father did not exclaim impatiently, 'Acht! what! *Culbertson*. I use my common sense.' For only by ignoring Carnegie could Mother have maintained her allegiance with the inexorable Culbertson. And Carnegie's star was in the ascendant. This gentleman had written books about how to win friends and influence people, and my mother professed to be one of his most ardent students.

'Why your mother wants to read Carnegie I can't imagine,' said my husband. 'She does all that tactful stuff by instinct, without having to worry why she's doing it.'

But I, who knew her methods, was not deceived. 'It's part of the system,' I said. 'By quoting the fellow she's getting us to read him because she thinks we could do with it. Especially Norman.'

But I was a little injured to hear later from Norman's wife, Molly, that Mother had confided in my brother that Carnegie would 'do dear Joy such a lot of good'. We all had to admit that my elder brother Fred got on very well without him. And Peter was, of course, the experimental rabbit.

'Now, darling,' Mother would say to me when 'our child' was being obstreperous, 'don't flare up. Just try a little Carnegie on him, and you'll see how wonderfully he responds.'

So Carnegie spent the Easter holidays with us, and Mother and he strove to teach me how to manage my little schoolboy wisely. But I learned more from watching my husband with him than I did from all their gentle lessons.

One member of the household scored greatly from Mother's application of *jen* every day and in every way. This was Gyp, Peter's terrier and Kismet's successor. He was even allowed to bring his fleas into the house and warm them by the fire.

'I'm not as fussy as I used to be,' said my mother. 'So long as I don't have to pat him I quite like him about the place.'

Mother could never touch an animal without feeling that she must immediately go and wash her hands. Nor could she tolerate wet dog kisses.

There were few changes at Tees Lodge. Cookie's daughter, Chrissie, had grown up and was now established as our parlourmaid. So it was she who brought the sherry tray on to the stoep at twelve o'clock when the gun went. 'The General,' who, like Gyppy, enjoyed new privileges since household rules had been relaxed, now came regularly to Sunday lunch with his family in the kitchen.

Teena had moved into the 'outside room', facing into the dog kennel, which had once been the stronghold of my brothers and their hottentot gods, silkworms and tarantulas; and on Saturday mornings Gyp retired under her bed, whence he was invariably dragged by Arend's deaf boy, David, for his weekly bath in the yard.

David was a sunny, eager-eyed lad whose disability made it difficult for him to get a job, so my father's carnations became his special care. He worked all day among the rows of tins, and the lovely blooms followed one another under his sensitive diligent fingers. The smoothness of the stalks, the crisp fragrance of the petals, with their dusting of silver or gold, were softer, sweeter, and brighter to him because he did not hear the wind as it swept through our garden or the doves in the firs. To touch, to see, and to smell. To David these things were the essence of life.

I had forgotten how good it was to walk down a street where every second person smiled a greeting or stopped for a chat. 'Good gracious! Joy Petersen – I always forget your married name – back again after all these years! Where've you been this time? China! Well, what next?'

'What next? I don't know yet myself.'

I had forgotten that at eleven o'clock every shop and office was littered with teacups, or that if you wanted a yard of ribbon you'd probably have to wait while the young lady behind the counter finished her private conversation with the young lady from 'the stockings' or 'the gloves'.

'Man! You'd have fallen flat on your back if you'd seen her face then. Daggers wasn't in it! . . . Oh, good morning. What was it you wanted? A yard of pink baby. Righteeo, I think we've got some – satin finish. This do? One yard? Okay.'

In the sunshine and showers of April, good days for 'a monkey's wedding', my husband and I often walked with our son over the mountainside to Kloof Nek. The squirrels, already active with their winter hoarding, were blue-grey as the ring-doves, and their movements were swifter than thought.

One day we met a little coloured girl with a bush baby on her shoulder; a tiny creature, half monkey, half squirrel, with enormous round golden eyes that took up all its face, and the hands of a very old person – thin, nimble, little fingers, hairless and black, with incipient finger-nails. We stopped to talk to her, and she told us that her uncle had brought her the little animal from Potgietersrust in the Transvaal.

But the bush baby was impatient of our conversation and he began to cry like a human child.

She laughed. 'Foei tog, hy es hongerig! Ek moet hom huis-toe neem.' (For shame, he is hungry. I must take him home.)

The sobs of the bush baby ceased as the child walked on, and his golden cartwheel eyes stared after us as he rode with his sharp little face against her frizzy black mop.

Sometimes we visited one or another of my various cousins. Doreen had a fine new house between Wynberg and Constantia.

'It has the views I love,' she said. 'The mountains, the vineyards, and the sea.'

A Gwelo Goodman of arums in a meadow and another of my

grandfather's birthplace, Nectar, hung in her lounge – bits of South Africa I would have given much to possess.

'You are lucky,' I said. 'Your own home, a wide outlook on every side, and things you have chosen with your husband all around you – things you both really love. It must be wonderful to gather your own background about you bit by bit through the years.'

My cousin looked at me speculatively.

'Would you swop your life for mine?' she asked. 'For land of your own with a house on it and a garden? There is no end to such interests, you know. Collecting things you find pleasing and living with them, so that your furniture, your pictures, and your books become part of you. And then there's the garden. A garden is a constant delight. There is always something to be done to it.'

We were sitting on the lawn. The mountain was a violet buttress behind us and our eyes followed the long line of the flats to the sea and the distant blue range cupping the bay. Piet and Doreen's little girl played under the silver trees with the clumsy springer spaniels. There were good nurseries in this house and later there would be more children to romp in them.

Land of my own, and a home. These were deep longings – the heritage of a settler people. And yet those forbears of mine had not hesitated to tear up their roots and move on when restrictions on their freedom, or man's inherent wanderlust, had driven them forth. I had chosen the way of my life as they had. And I was content.

'No,' I said, 'I wouldn't swop.'

My husband looked up and smiled.

'One day we'll settle here,' he said. 'I'm in love with South Africa too.'

When the snows were deep on the Drakenstein Mountains, and the high white rollers on the Atlantic seaboard crashed at the base of the mist-swathed cliffs, we took 'our child' from those who had cherished him throughout our long absences.

'Can I take Gyp with me?' begged Piet, clinging a little desperately to the curly neck of his fox-terrier. 'You know he's my friend and my brother as well as my dog.'

But when we told him of the six months' quarantine Gyp would have to endure he couldn't bear it.

'He must stay in Tees Lodge,' he said with his voice choked. 'He couldn't be kept like that – in prison.'

Teena packed his things with her brown face grey with misery. And for the first time in many years I saw my mother weep.

'Be patient with him always, darling,' she said. 'Remember that here he has known only sympathy – and love. . . .'

So the day came when 'our child' sailed for England with his stranger parents, and in Tees Lodge a thin little ghost ran and laughed and whistled, and a black and white fox-terrier with haunted eyes sought in vain for his friend and his brother.

When spring walked the mountains in South Africa, scattering gold-spangled disas in the kloofs and sprinkling the krantzes with velvet suiker-bossies, it was autumn in England and time for our son to go to his new preparatory school at Oxford.

The lanes were carpeted with ruby and amber beech leaves; old-fashioned inns were covered in Virginia creeper, the colour of old port and brandy, and towards evening there was a bloom on the countryside soft as the down on a blue Constantia grape.

These things were beautiful. But the small boy beside us in the car did not notice them. He was unfamiliar in his new school suit, and silent. His fingers twisted his handkerchief into a grubby ball, and because his action twisted also my heart I put my own hand over his.

'You'll like this school,' I said. 'And you'll make friends there.'

He answered, not looking up: 'It can't come up to Bishop's. And nobody will make up for my friends Hans and Ronnie . . .'

It was as if his homesickness entered into me then to join forces with my own misgivings. He had more to fear than his ten-year-old debut at a new school. For we had just heard of his father's appointment as Naval Attaché to Greece, Turkey, and Yugo-Slavia. Soon we would be on our way to Athens, and Piet would be left alone and uncertain of himself in this strange land so far from the only home he had ever known. Already for him the world was widening, and the wind blew cold.

But the months slipped by and we did not leave. Great events turn the wheel of destiny for Strube's little man in the street, so far removed from their source, and the drama of Edward VIII and 'Wally' Simpson kept us in England.

The appointment of a naval attaché has to receive the personal approval of the King. And this was near the close of 1936. The world's greatest romance was rocking the nation to its foundations, and we waited, breathless, our small affairs in abeyance.

In Fort Belvedere Edward VIII was taking one of the most difficult decisions in history. I think that was when the beast Suspense first got its fangs deep into the flesh of the Empire. Afterwards we got accustomed to wondering, What next? and to never being sure of anything except the integrity of the British race and its love of its land. Grumblers and agitators there might be, but the heart of the people was sound. I had seen that in 1931 when the country went off gold, I saw it now in 1936 when a popular and well-loved King abdicated in favour of his brother, 'who has one matchless blessing . . . a happy home with his wife and children'. And I was to see it in 1939 when a heartsick people went to war. There was never excitement or panic when the inevitable crisis had to be faced, but there was the curious deep quiet peculiar to an island race – a gathering together and concentrating of power and determination within the encircling sea.

Edward VIII stepped down from the throne and George VI took his place. The people felt a little piqued at being jilted and rather anxious and sad, but they were helped towards the rebound by the Press, and soon an affectionate tenderness enfolded the family who had succeeded him. Already the shape of things to come was a grim shadow upon our time, and there were few of us who did not wonder what heavy responsibilities waited the new Sovereign. Perhaps, even, in a fey moment, there were those who saw the little lady with the sweet smile treading the wreckage of a beloved city with head held high and sorrow in her eyes, stooping here and there to say a few words to the homeless and the bereaved – her fellow-sufferers.

Peter displayed the glorious egotism of childhood towards the whole affair, thereby reducing it to what must surely have been its lowest denominator.

'Good old Mrs. Simpson!' he exulted. 'But for her you would have been in Athens by now and you'd have missed my Christmas hols.'

So, while Bertie remained in London to do certain special courses, Piet and I spent 'my Christmas hols' in Liverpool with my sister-in-law and her husband. They had a tall house overlooking Prince's Park and a terrier called Toby, who, according to Peter, compared unfavourably with Gyp.

Dorothy and her husband had no children of their own, but they understood boys a great deal better than many parents of large families. My sister-in-law knew at once that this little nephew from South Africa badly needed something treasured and familiar about him to make him feel at home.

'While your mother and I unpack,' she said, 'how would it be if you set out your electric railway? You'd probably rather have the rails here in your bedroom with you than up in the attic playroom. Uncle has managed to get a transformer, so you can run it off the power plug.'

Piet flushed and gasped with pleasure. This was friendship indeed!

'And I thought of a new lay-out just as I was going to sleep last night,' he said. 'Thank you, Aunt Dee!'

She did not call him Peter, but dropped straight into Piet. She even spelt it in the South African way, as he saw when he was greeted with the princely gift of a leather wallet. 'To welcome Piet', suitably inscribed with his initials and filled with a crisp pound note.

'I think,' said his uncle, 'that it would be a good idea if you were to open a Post Office Savings-Bank account, don't you?'

'Oh yes,' agreed the boy, green eyes gleaming. In Grannie's safe at Tees Lodge there reposed a number of Post Office Savings-Bank books. There was Cookie's and Teena's and Chrissie's. Arend, David, and Peter were also in the habit of entrusting my mother with their small savings, and it was her habit to note these insignificant sums as she received them in a tome known as THE BOOK. Then, if Arend wanted 'five bob to take de wife to de football' or Peter wanted a 'ticky' for sweets, they had only to ask for it. 'Yus, put it in de book, please, Madam,' Arend would say, as the ever-ready bag was opened and the five shillings disgorged. In Peter's eyes a

Post Office Savings account was a decided step-up on the more convenient BOOK kept by his grandmother, and the prospect of opening one filled him with a sense of his own importance as being a man of means.

His uncle was a doctor, and this, too, seemed to Peter right and proper. Both his South African uncles were doctors, and so he naturally assumed that all the most satisfactory relations were in the medical profession. Mary, the cook, was an aged crone, and this also was fitting. For, to Piet, it implied that she had been in his aunt's employ since the dawn of time, like Cookie.

One thing in this admirable household surprised him. Toby, the terrier, was allowed to jump on to couches and chairs whenever he felt so inclined.

'A dog getting up on things!' he remarked to me, much puzzled. 'Gyp was never allowed to do that. And Toby eats *biscuits*. He has them in the kitchen with Mary.'

Gyp, who had never heard of biscuits, devoured his 'scraps' in the yard, rain or shine. And even on those rare occasions when he rode in the car he would not have dreamed of elevating his fleas on to the seat.

'English dogs are different,' I explained. 'They usually sit on chairs, and quite often they have their meals in the dining-room with the family.'

'Trick dogs?'

'No, ordinary dogs.'

'Seems cissie, doesn't it?'

'Oh I don't know. It's not such fun being an entirely outdoor animal here. The weather, you see.'

Peter looked out of the window at the December fog. He saw.

One day Dorothy came to me with a curious look on her face.

She said: 'I took Piet's jacket to clean a dirty mark off it. But he's got something *dead* in the pocket. Shall I throw it away?'

'Where is it?'

Gingerly she handed me something wrapped in a piece of paper. I burst out laughing as I recognized what it was.

'If you throw that stringy piece of old shoe leather away you'll make an enemy for life!'

'What is it?'

'Biltong. Sun-dried buck's meat. Or it may even be baboon or ostrich biltong. It's the mainstay of a Boer's diet. When the old Boers went hunting or rode in commando they always had a hunk of this stuff in their pockets and they gnawed it when they were hungry. It's about all a lot of them lived on in the Boer War when they were carrying on their guerilla warfare in the mountains. But for biltong we wouldn't have kept you English on the hop for three years, my dear.'

'Oh, well, in that case . . .' She laughed.

Just then Piet appeared, with Toby at his heels.

'There you are, Mom! I've been looking for my biltong. Somebody's pinched it out of my pocket.'

'We have it here.'

'That's good. Would you like to try some, Aunt Dee?'

Dorothy blenched. 'No, thanks, not just now.'

But Toby had other ideas. With a quick leap he grabbed the sun-dried meat from Piet's hand and made off with it.

'Hey! You can't do that!' My son was after him in a flash. But by this piece of impertinence Toby established himself in Peter's affections.

'It's funny,' said the boy. 'Old Toby's the only person here who appreciates biltong. He's a jolly smart dog, if you ask me.'

Early in the New Year my husband received his appointment, officially signed and sealed by King George VI. He was to go as Naval Attaché to Turkey, Greece, and Yugo-Slavia, with headquarters in Athens.

'How about holidays?' I asked. 'Can we get Piet out to Athens?'

'Yes. We'll have him out in the summer and for Easter. Dorothy will take him for Christmas.'

'Can we afford to let him fly out this Easter? It'd be so much quicker and safer.'

Bertie nodded. 'This job is paid on Foreign Office rates. We'll be quite well off.'

When we took Piet back to school after the holidays we bade him farewell. At the door of School House he summoned all his bravado for the benefit of a few scrubby contemporaries hanging about on the lookout for new arrivals.

'So long,' he said in an offhand but suspiciously brittle voice. 'See you again in Athens!'

The contemporaries affected to be deaf.

CHAPTER THIRTY-EIGHT

ROMAN ROAD AND MIXED DOUBLE

So now a new bubble was swelling from life's soap-bowl. How bright was my Mediterranean bubble! There was music within its opalescent walls, lost echoes of pagan laughter and the heartbreak song of the nightingale. And here was light and colour too, the metal gleam of the Bosphorus and the ripple of Homer's wine-dark seas. How lightly it danced from the pipe of time, through sunshine and rainbows into the bloodstained darkness that was war! And there, against those walls of night, my bubble burst in a shower of tears.

But they were wonderful, the two and a half soap-bubble years that led into such harsh reality. During that time we lived the privileged life of diplomats, whose ambiguities are phrased in many tongues, and who move and have their being in a fourth-dimensional world of their own making, where rude, forthright men of war are strangely out of place.

My husband had, of course, attempted to fit himself for the rarefied atmosphere of diplomacy. During the months waiting in London for the matrimonial destiny of a King to be settled he had taken a special course at the Admiralty, had brushed up his French and German and made himself acquainted with some of the labyrinthine ways of the Foreign Office.

Before January was out we were on our way. We sent our luggage by sea and we drove as far as Brindisi by car. There we took ship to Athens. But we had to break our journey for a few days in Rome to enable my husband to take over from Captain Bevan, the Naval Attaché there, whose 'parish' had hitherto included Greece and Turkey.

Captain and Mrs. Bevan lived in a spacious modern apartment with a fine view of the city. As we entered we stumbled over two baby dachshunds who had their kennel in the hall. They welcomed us with squeals and a frantic scrabble of claws on the polished floor. The way in which their feet went unexpectedly from under them reminded me of our son on the rink at Liverpool.

Mrs. Bevan was tall and slight and possessed of the rare gift of being efficient while appearing dreamily helpless.

Next morning, while my husband was at the Embassy with Captain Bevan, I asked her to give me an idea of what my part of this new job involved.

She was sitting at her writing-desk by an open window, and she turned round, put down her pen, and gave me her attention. The sun shone on her wavy fair hair, and her slender figure was clad in a well-tailored grey flannel costume. She looked English to the tips of her unpainted finger-nails. Beyond her, outside the window, I could see the roofs of the city spreading away to the Seven Hills. The Tiber was a golden thread through the heart of Rome, and the air was keen and bright.

'Margie,' I said, 'do give me some idea of what it's all about – this Attaché business. What does an Attaché's wife have to do about it?'

She smiled in her charming vague way.

'The Attaché business, as you put it, has always seemed rather nebulous to me. But as far as I can gather a Naval Attaché is supposed to advise his Ambassador or Minister on all naval matters and procedure, and he has to keep in touch with the navies of the countries to which he is accredited. The wife looks after the social side of the game. And there's plenty of that!'

'What form does one's entertaining take? I've no experience of the diplomatic merry-go-round in a foreign capital.'

'All sorts. Attachés' luncheons are the dullest. Long meals with too many wines. But the most popular form of entertainment in Athens is the "mastika". That is five-to-nine cocktail party with a good variety of hors d'oeuvres, and if possible a few tables of cards. You go from one mastika to another during the season, as many as two and three in one evening, and you meet the same people at each. You smile till your face feels like a mask, and then you go home and relax.'

'A bit wearing, I should think.'

333

'It is, if you aren't brought up to it. But it is a necessary evil. When you take your house and your servants, bear it in mind that you'll need to compete with giving those mastikas.'

'Sounds like the sort of shore job where a wife might come in useful.'

'Now, another thing you'll need to know about is the Bag', said Margie. 'The Diplomatic Bag rules our lives.'

'What exactly is it?'

'A grey canvas sack. But its comings and goings are of the utmost importance to our comfort. It carries letters quickly and uncensored, and there's a parcel bag too, so that you can have library books sent by it and also parcels of certain dimensions. As diplomats get everything duty free, it's an economy to order a good many of the more expensive groceries from London. I'll make out a list of things you'll find useful.'

As she took up her pen a yapping and slithering of puppies in the hall heralded the appearance of our husbands.

'Margie's been turning over to me,' I said. 'And I gather that this job is in the nature of a mixed double.'

'That's right,' agreed Captain Bevan. 'The woman keeps the ball in play and makes opportunities for her partner.'

That afternoon we played golf on a rather amateurish little course just outside Rome.

Margie said, as we strolled over to the ladies' tee: 'This game used to be played in English. But when we applied sanctions all the English terms were quickly translated into Italian. Bogey is too complicated to remember, but, as you can see, "Ladies' Tee" has been painted out on the tee-boxes, and we go from Battadore per Signore.'

'Very euphonious, anyway.'

'There used to be a restaurant called "The Garden of Eden", but that had its named changed too. Nobody wants to hear the word "Eden" here.'

Anthony Eden was a painful thorn in the side of il Duce. He represented British opposition to the power politics of the dictators. Mussolini envisaged the revival of a great Roman Empire, and he resented any interference.

That night there was a ball at the Embassy to celebrate the engagement of the Ambassador's daughter to an American archaeologist. It was my first experience of an important diplomatic function and I was suitably impressed. In accordance with some charming Latin custom, almost everybody who had been invited had sent white flowers; and against this snowy background gorgeous men, studded with medals and orders, preened like peacocks, except that they did not wear their medals on their tails. The women wore gloves and diamonds, but little else, and their fashionable perfumes mingled incongruously with funeral parlour fragrance of the white lilies through which we waded to the ballroom.

When the dance was in full swing a face and a figure suddenly swept me through time and space to far-away Shanghai.

'Have you met our young Foreign Minister?' asked my partner, a dashing cavalry officer. 'He is over there in the doorway talking to the Ambassador. See how he holds himself. He is the image of his illustrious father-in-law, il Duce.'

'Where is his wife? I remember her as a very good-looking woman.'

'She is not going out at present. You understand?'

I understood. Edda Ciano was no longer able to lead the free and easy life of Shanghai. Here, under her father's eye, it was necessary for her to give her attention to the important business of securing the future of the Mussolini-Ciano combine. It was common talk in Rome that Mussolini had great hopes of Edda's children. It was even suggested that he aimed at a dynasty of dictators of this line running in double harness with the House of Savoia, just as the Tokugawa Shoguns had once ruled Japan for two and a half centuries side by side with the puppet Emperors.

Count Ciano was not yet forty, but he had thickened into premature middle age. He stood in the entrance of the ballroom now, patronizing the Ambassador, lord of all he surveyed. I was amused to watch him. He had aped many of his father-in-law's attitudes. He too, spread his legs, braced his shoulders, and thrust out his chin. This was not the jealous, glowering husband of a handsome passionate woman, but an actor playing a part written exclusively for him. It was evident that he little dreamed how short was to be the run of the play or how pitiful the climax: dawn, with his back against a wall and a Nazi bullet through the heart.

Ciano's presence at the Embassy that night was in the nature

335

of an olive-branch. It was the dictator's sign that the British need no longer regard themselves as hopelessly beyond the pale.

On our way out of Rome a few days later we ran into a battalion of boys of Peter's age. The Ballilla. They marched singing down the street, very smart and cocky in their military uniforms with swinging capes and wooden guns. Every lad in Italy, from eight to eighteen, was a little toy soldier. Poor little toy soldiers. Their day has been brief.

Cities, like people and ships, have their own personalities, good or evil.

Athens took hers from the goddess whose name she bore. She was wise, beautiful, and ageless, a virginal white city dreaming between the barren Acropolis rock and the fir-crowned hill of Lycabetus. She was guarded by marble-bearing mountains where once the outrageous gods sported, squabbled, and vied with one another in wizardry and magic. Her cypresses were threaded with the silver voice of the nightingale, her gardens and cloistered courtyards were sweet with the scent of jasmine and gardenia, and her summer stars sped across the sky like the winged heels of Hermes. And when, at sunset, Apollo drove his flaming chariot into the sea behind the island of Salamis, the Parthenon was splashed with amethyst and gold, and, at other times, in the dark of the moon, you could hear the little owl of Athena hooting mournfully from the ruins of her mistress's temple.

I was no Greek scholar and no worshipper of Byron; if I had any pagan tendencies they were entirely unconscious; and the only Greeks I had ever met were the swarthy good-natured sweet and fruit merchants of Cape Town; but the movement we arrived in Athens I knew that here we would be happy.

Perhaps the mountains and the sea, the cream-coloured houses and the pepper trees, green-gold in the sun, had something to do with that feeling of home-coming, or maybe it was just the knowledge that at last there was no ship to share my husband with me. His job would take his brain and his time, but a ship can take a man's heart also. Now we were going to live like other people. My husband would go to his office after breakfast and come home to lunch with me. In the afternoons his work would be over at a reasonable hour; and if a storm blew up in the night he would not wake uneasily from his sleep and say: 'I'd better get off to the ship while the boats can still run!' For a spell there would be no loneliness. And when the holidays came we would have our son with us. No wonder, then, that Athens grew dear to me. She wore the face of my own country and she gave me a home. To take a house for two years! In all our married life we had not known such permanence.

It was an enchanting house we found for ourselves – a furnished villa by the sea at Glyfada, seven miles out of the city. It had a pretty garden with three graceful pines in it, and french doors led on to a wide terrace where we would dine on summer nights. Behind this villa rose Hymettus, the honey mountain, and from the bedroom windows we could look across the sea to the Island of Ægina and Salamis. Inside, the house was pure Hollywood, which was not surprising in view of the fact that its owner was a young Athenian actress living in London. Her brother-in-law, our next-door neighbour, acted as her agent. His name was Agammemnon, and he was the most exuberant personality I have ever met. There was animation in every fibre of his little dark moustache and in every nerve of his eloquent hands. The Greeks can look tremendously alive and vibrant when they are happy, but when they are sad they wilt. Their eyes fade, their shoulders droop, and they dwindle and die like the meadow flowers children pluck and throw away.

'Everything will be ready for you next week,' said Agammemnon, as we stood on the terrace, having satisfactorily settled the terms of our tenancy. 'If there is anything you require you have only to tell me what it is.'

'The garden,' I said, with a glance at the empty flower-beds. 'Could you perhaps find us a gardener and advise us what to plant? Your own garden next door is so lovely that I feel you must know a great deal about flowers.'

Agammemnon sprang to his feet, and before we knew what was happening he had leapt lightly over the garden wall dividing his property from that of his sister-in-law. In a few seconds he vaulted back, and hot on his heels hurdled a fine young fellow with a scarlet flower behind his ear.

'Madame,' said Agammemnon, who was not even out of breath after his impromptu steeplechase, 'I exist only for flowers! Leave this matter entirely in my hands. My own gardener here will attend to it. Only wait until the spring and you will see all the blossoms in creation in these flower-beds.' And he bunched up his fingers and kissed them into the pellucid air. 'I will give all instructions immediately.' With which he poured a torrent of temperamental Greek into the flower-decked ear of his minion.

When the gardener had nodded a vigorous equivalent of the Chinese 'Can do, can do', Agammemnon dismissed him brusquely and promised, with his black eyes flashing: 'Everything you shall have here! A thousand different blooms – a million!' An upward spiralling gesture of his hand indicated the mounting floral glories we might anticipate. To Bertie he added, as man to man: 'With flowers and women, Captain Packer, the eye and the soul can best be refreshed by variety.'

As we drove back to the Hotel Grande Bretagne, where we were staying till our villa should be ready for us, Bertie said: 'And now we must get a reliable team to run the place. We'll be away a good deal of the time, in Turkey and Yugo-Slavia, and we need servants we can trust. I'll speak to the steward of the British Club about finding someone.'

Finding servants in Greece was like finding them in China. There were no established agencies. The news just seemed to get around in those circles where it was of most interest. We did not lack applicants, for the British diplomats were known to be among the most gullible employers. The French and the Germans had far more difficulty when they needed domestic staff, as the French were recognized as the most cheese-paring and the Germans were considered interfering slave-drivers.

'The steward of the British Club is sending us a married couple called Slovakis this evening,' said Bertie, as we were dressing for a soirée at the French Legation. 'The man has experience as a valet-butler, but he is really a barman. He had his own little bar in the Pyraeus, but it was sold over his head and so he's out of a job. He is an Istanbul Greek, and they are supposed to be the best workers.'

I was putting the last touches to my toilet when the little couple were shown up to our room.

Slovakis was a wisp of a man in the early thirties, with very fair hair and blue eyes that, in moments of anxiety or concentration, squinted slightly, like a windy baby's. His neck was thin as a baby's too, but his hands were surprisingly strong and sinewy. His wife was a dimpled girl with bovine eyes, in which

338

lay unplumbed depths of naïveté, and a smile as soothing as a
kitten's purr. Slovakis did the talking and the girl stood silently
beside him with that soft smile on her lips and a 'this-is-going-
to-be-all-right' expression in her revealing orbs. Her name, it
seemed, was Ero.

We heard, with relief, that, though shaking cocktails was in
the nature of a vocation to Slovakis, he himself did not drink,
because, as he explained without embarrassment, he suffered
from a fallen stomach which reacted unfavourably to alcohol.
Nearly all Greek townsmen and women seemed to suffer from
peculiar maladies, which they unhesitatingly described to total
strangers.

'Have you any babies?' I asked the girl. The interview was
being conducted in French, which she understood well and
spoke badly.

She shook her head, and I noticed a wise, rather smug little
look pass between the pair.

I asked them what days out they would want. The little man
smiled and his shoulders shrugged forward in a gesture wholly
Greek, which meant, 'I hardly know, and it is really of no
importance'.

'A married couple do not seek amusements outside,
Madame. We can take our outings when it suits you.'

'Well?' said Bertie, as the door closed behind them. 'What do
you think?'

I sprayed some perfume on to my hair. 'Decidedly yes,' I
said. 'The little white monkey looks competent, and the girl is
sweet.'

So we moved into our new villa. And Slovakis and Ero came
with us.

Our 'little white monkey' appeared, at first glance, to be
anything but a typical Greek, yet we soon realized that he
exemplified the very spirit of that brave, independent land. He
and Ero made no secret of the fact that they were working
towards a definite objective. They wanted to save enough
money to set up in another 'little bar' and have a family. It was
the true Hellenic outlook. Every Greek is an individualist who
craves his own business, however humble, and his own sons
to inherit it. Better a street barrow that is your own than an
assured position in another man's grand emporium. Or, let us

339

say, better a proud, small nation struggling along independently than a flourishing unit in a New Order without freedom.

Heaven knows what fate our little couple met when war and famine laid their country waste and killed their hopes, if not themselves. But in those last two years of peace and happiness they gave us full value. They took a pride in their work, and it was a point of honour with both of them never to let us down.

Diki, our chauffeur, was a grizzled Russian of impeccable character, the son of a schoolmaster in the Ukraine. He had fought throughout the Great War and then fought on for two years against the Bolsheviks. He and his wife and eight-year-old son Basil were exiles who could never hope to return to their own land.

They lived in a two-roomed pent-house adjoining our garage. There was always some animal sharing their cramped quarters, and flowers cascaded from the narrow windows.

When Diki washed the car his open-throated dungarees showed a deep bullet-hole beneath his collar-bone, and there was an old wound in his leg which gave him trouble periodically. His upper lip was severely scarred, but a small grey moustache partially concealed it. As he worked he bumbled to himself in a sort of tuneless song without words.

In his spare time he sat in the sun with a book open in his hands and the longest cigarette holder in the world hanging from that scarred lip. His reading matter was surprising for a chauffeur, if not for the son of a Cossack schoolmaster. It included the classics of many languages.

His wife was always ailing. She was a highly strung woman of middle age, who must once have been extremely pretty. Sometimes she did a little sewing for me, but if it didn't go right her hands trembled, she almost swallowed her mouthful of pins, and her hazel eyes filled with anxious tears. Her road into exile with Diki was marked with the graves of their children, and now she lived only for Basil, the boy whose birth in the wilds of Macedonia had cost her her health.

This boy went cheerfully to school in the mornings, and if he met me as he passed through the garden he said 'Good morning' very politely and bowed low over my hand as he carried it to his lips. In the afternoons he played by himself near the sand fortress he had built outside the garage, attacking it frequently by air with zooming noises and much banking and gliding of his grubby little paws. A baby lamb teetered at his heels.

'A friend has given it to him for Easter,' explained Diki.

'But Easter is a long way off,' I said.

'I know. When it is Easter we will eat the lamb.'

'What a shame. To eat your pet!'

'Sentiment is a luxury the poor cannot afford, Madame.'

Diki's soul was steeped in pessimism. In his experience, all was for the worst in this worst of all possible worlds. I taxed him with his gloomy viewpoint upon occasions.

'When you expect nothing of life you are seldom disappointed,' he said. 'But you may often be pleased. That is philosophy.'

Apostoles, our cook, was a lively little man who suffered from recurrent malaria. But, like Ah Lin, he produced convenient relatives to deputize for him when he was laid low. It was his habit, when he had reason to believe that I might be displeased with him, to employ ostrich tactics. As soon as I appeared outside the kitchen he opened wide the oven door and plunged his head, starched chef's cap and all, therein, feigning ignorance of my presence.

This farce was usually conducted on Friday mornings when I had examined his weekly marketing accounts.

'It is always necessary to complain that they are too high,' explained Slovakis patiently.'He would think it odd if Madame did not do so.'

'Then get him out of the oven,' I said.

Slovakis, who was my interpreter in the kitchen, addressed the posterior of Apostoles sharply. And the little man emerged, flushed and reluctant, with a hasty 'Milles pardons, Madame,' as he straightened his cap. 'Milles pardons' was all the French he knew.

'Ask him why his bus fare to Athens and back cost him fourteen drachmae on Monday and twenty-one drachmae on Thursday,' I said severely.

Slovakis rattled off an aggressive query, and Apostoles beamed. A swift explanation followed.

'It all depends on the bus conductor,' said Slovakis with his face blank. 'Apostoles says the fare is seven drachmae each way. But when he returns from the market he sometimes has a large basket of supplies to carry and he has to put it on the seat beside him. If the conductor is in a good mood and the bus is empty it is all right. But if the bus is full and the conductor is in a bad temper Apostoles has to pay for the seat occupied by his parcel.'

Apostoles knew all the answers.

One day Bertie asked Ero to shift a button on his dinner jacket.

'It has been very professionally done,' he remarked to me afterwards. 'It might have been done by a tailor. Congratulate your Hebe for me.'

When I told her that the Captain was pleased, Ero's smile, soft as the bloom on a peach, spread from her gentle eyes to her lips.

'It is because I was apprenticed to a tailor when I was eight years old.'

'When you were *eight*?'

'Yes, Madame. That was in 1922 when the Turks chased the Greeks out of Asia Minor. My family lived in Smyrna. My father and eldest brothers were cut down by Kemal's troops, but my mother escaped with the rest of us in a little ship which came to the Pyraeus. When we landed with thousands of other refugees we had nothing except the ragged clothes we stood up in – no home, no friends, and no money. People were dying of starvation and typhoid in the streets. It was terrible. . . . We were glad to work for our food and for a roof over our heads. I was an intelligent child, and the tailor to whom my mother apprenticed me was a kind man. He was poor himself and he could not afford to pay me, but he fed me and housed me for two years. I worked twelve hours a day. It is a lot for a child.'

The words poured out in her weird French. But as I looked at my little maid more closely it was clear to me that she took her own hard childhood for granted. We could not guess then that those dark eyes were destined to see the hand of famine strike down her people yet again. The Greeks are a nation well used to suffering.

'Afterwards, when I was ten, I worked as a general maid in a boarding-house for students,' she continued. 'No one paid me and no one tipped me. I often had to sleep in the bath when the rooms were full, and I was always hungry. Sometimes I stole a

342

potato or a piece of bread – but it is not really stealing for a hungry child to take food. Now that I am happy and well enough off I go back to that house from time to time in case there may be a child working there again one day. If ever there is I want to give her a present.'

'But surely children are no longer permitted to work. They have to go to school.'

'By law that is so, but you cannot stop adoption. There are still people who adopt little girls on the agreement that when the child is grown up they will give her a suitable dot to enable her to marry. In the meantime she "helps" in the house. It is a good bargain. She may die before she is old enough to marry, and then there will be no need to pay out the dot.'

I thought of 'mu tsai' in Hong Kong – the 'adoption' of little children who work as slaves for the foster-parents who have bought them.

Ero's mother and young sisters lived in one of the pitiful refugee settlements that disfigure the environs of Athens, wretched villages of mud and tin cans like the native locations outside Johannesburg, or the birdcage houses of Chungking clinging to the high banks of the Yangtse Kiang. When the winter storms made rivers of the roads and tore up trees by the roots, the roofs of those flimsy abodes were swept away by the wind and there was desolation once more for a portion of the population which dwelt for ever side by side with hunger and want.

Such, then, was 'our team'. When we gave a 'mastika' one or two reserves were called in, and the party was enjoyed by all. The Greeks, like the Chinese, always had available relations.

CHAPTER THIRTY-NINE

ATHENIAN SKETCH

THERE were three distinct aspects of our social life in Athens.

First, there was the British community. It was not very large, but it was homely and congenial. With these English friends we were at ease.

The British community in Athens did not consist of a group of poets or artists seeking a spot in the sun. It was comprised of people holding essential positions in the city. A substantial amount of British capital was invested in Greece. For instance, all the electric light and power in Athens was supplied by a British company, and another big enterprise was the draining and development of Lake Kòpais, near Thebes. A slightly less important, but equally British, achievement was the creation of a golf club.

The golf club was the hub of our existence. It was a strip of dry mud in winter, sandwiched between mountains, vineyards, and the sea.

'Ought to make you feel at home,' smiled my husband.

'It does,' I agreed, with a glance at the wide stoep of the unpretentious clubhouse. Members could have tea there or play cards, and there was a little beach and a fine natural bathing pool right under the verandah. The golf club was the boating and bathing club too.

The course was the result of that dogged British spirit which never knows when it is beaten. The first professional imported to lay it out attempted to drown himself when he saw what his lightly signed contract really demanded of him. But some fishermen pulled him out of the sea just in time to frustrate his intentions. His successor, however, was a red-headed North-countryman called Farrar, who had campaigned with Lawrence of Arabia and who was undismayed by deserts or mud flats. He compelled this arid tongue of unproductive land to yield up nine quite reasonable holes, and before long he was busy giving lessons to the younger Athenians, who became nearly as keen on the game as the British.

The second, and most interesting, facet of life in Athens reflected the Greeks themselves. Both the Athenians and the country-folk. Each in their different fashion showed us true hospitality and kindness.

Greece is a country unique in the world, in that it has a genuine affection for, and appreciation of, the English. There are strong reasons for this. Of the three Protective Powers – Russia, France, and Great Britain – who helped to liberate Greece from four centuries of Turkish domination, it was England who unconsciously dramatized that all-important human interest which is always so much more memorable than the bare facts of history. Lord Byron, with his wicked reputation and his golden pen, was the greatest Hellenic propagandist of all time. In the dreary flats of Missalonghi he made atonement for the notoriety of his life with the piteous circumstances of a lonely fever-stricken death. With word and deed and his private fortune this English poet had backed the cause of Hellenic liberty. In Greece you dare speak no ill of Byron. Then, too, the victorious Greek Army was under the leadership of an English General, Sir Richard Church, and one of England's finest seamen, Lord Cochrane, commanded the Greek Navy in the War of Independence. Thus it is that the British Navy and the Greek Navy are closely linked by history and sentiment. They have fought together and conquered together in the name of freedom.

In the glorious months of the spring, when the poppies flung their blood-red patchwork on to the bright green of the rye, and asphodels were silver-pink under the pink and silver of almond blossom and olive bough, we went deep into that lovely countryside where every rock and cliff is permeated with legend and tales of gallantry. There in the superb mountain passes or in little fishing villages along the coast we met peasants and fisher-folk in whose eyes was the wisdom and serenity of those who have solved the mysteries of nature. Pagans these – rugged immortals who had seen Demeter give birth to the spring and Poseidon drive his gleaming harvest into the nets.

They greeted us with their grave kind smiles and deep voices; they offered us a share of their black bread and goat's cheese and a draught of retsina or of milk. They spoke to us of Byron, of the Royal Navy, and of Navarino. Every peasant knows the history of his country, and we found that these simple men had long memories. They were men of peace but well accustomed to warfare. For over a hundred years their land had been sporadically at war. Klephts – outlaws who carried on guerilla tactics against invaders or enemy occupying forces – had been the cave-dwellers of the mountains from time immemorial, and it was the way of the peasant and the shepherd to help them – just as they help the guerillas today at the risk of their lives. The peasant of Greece is the true aristocrat of his country. Nobility is written by the hand of time upon his features.

The third aspect of our new existence was that presented by the Diplomatic Corps. This facet never really came alive for me. As human beings I found diplomats more elusive than soap in the bath. The art of evasion seemed to be the crux of their training, and I felt sometimes as if we were a caste of clowns and midgets rehearsing a comedy of manners in a runaway circus train heading for an abyss.

It was the National Day of Greece.

My husband arrayed himself in all his glory of epaulettes, aiguillettes, and sword-belt, and I, like the drab little hen beside her golden pheasant, accompanied him to the Legation, where the staff of the British Minister, Sir Sydney Waterlow, was to meet before going in convoy to the Cathedral for the official church service.

The British Legation had once been the mansion of the famous Cretan statesman, the late Mr. Venizelos, who had brought Greece into the Great War on the side of the Allies, but whose personality and liberal policy had split the country in two factions, Venizelist and Royalist. In the basement of this mansion – once the servants' quarters – was housed the Chancery, and there my husband had a little office with the legend *ΝΑΥΤΙΚΟΣ ΑΚΟΛΟΥΘΟΣ* inscribed over his door. On the wall opposite his desk hung a calendar adorned with the portrait of the Chinese tiger which had been given a passage to England on board H.M.S. *Kent*.

'I'll just see if there are any letters or messages,' said my husband. 'The Bag came in this morning. Yes, here you are – something from Piet and one from Dorothy. And here's a message for me.' He groaned. 'It's another inventor wanting me to take up his invention with the Admiralty.'

Bertie suffered from inventors. 'The Greeks are as full of original ideas as Peter,' he said. 'Only they don't often bother to produce any models to demonstrate them, and Peter does.' (Model-making was our son's hobby.)

The Commercial Attaché put his head in at the door.

'Lady Waterlow wants us to assemble in the hall straight away.'

Lady Waterlow was in a fluster. 'My husband is still in his

shirt,' she said, glancing anxiously at her watch. 'We'll never be at the Cathedral in time.'

The wife of the First Secretary, a good-looking Croatian bacteriologist said: 'I feel a leetle faint, Lady Votterlow. I should like some brondy.'

'If you feel faint it's not the slighest use going to the Cathedral,' said Lady Waterlow. 'You know we have to stand all the time, as there are no seats, and you don't want to fall in a heap. You'd better stay here and wait for us.'

The wife of the First Secretary passed a tapering hand across her wide intellectual brow. 'It is all right,' she said. 'The feeling is passing over.' She gracefully waived the question of a stimulant.

Presently the Minister appeared, a magnificent figure heavily embroidered in gold. And we set off in a triumphal procession of motor-cars. Our Minister was invariably cheered as he drove through the crowded streets with their cordons of military and marine guards, and he bowed graciously to right and left. Of all the foreign heads of missions, only 'Sir Waterloo', as the Greeks called him, received this audible tribute as he bowled along in his vintage Rolls-Royce. (The British Government had bought, besides the house of the late Venizelos, his bullet-proof touring car, but tact forbade the use of this conveyance upon official occasions.)

The Diplomatic Corps entered the Cathedral by a side door and stood facing the members of the government in the position usually held by the choir in the Church of England. The body of the Cathedral was occupied by officers of the fighting services and officials of the Court and of the State.

To my amazement the diplomats were chatting to one another with animation and even laughing at little jests and compliments.

'Don't look so astonished,' smiled the wife of the Brazilian Minister, a handsome English blonde, with golden curls pinned high under a smart little Athenian hat. 'We all tell each other the latest gossip while we wait for the curtain to go up. Did you know that . . .' She lowered her voice. While I listened to her my eyes were dazzled by the spectacular uniforms all round us. Only the Turkish and American diplomats were in tails with top-hats.

But there was one Minister whose plain dark uniform was in

347

sombre contrast to the theatrical effects of the others. This was Prince Erbach zu Schönberg, the representative of Adolf Hitler. He was tall and lightly built, with finely bred features and a sharp clever face. Almost all the German diplomats we met were men of distinction and authority. The heads of missions were men of the old school, brought up in the ways of diplomacy and foreign affairs. But, for all their courtesy and breeding, they had to be good Nazis, and in every embassy and legation there was a Gestapo man to report on the behaviour and friendships of the staff, including even his chief.

Prince Erbach was talking to the Austrian Minister, Baron Wimmer. He seemed to be explaining something in his hoarse falsetto, and the Baron listened to him with his thin pale lips stretched in the tight archaic grin of an early Greek statue.

Wimmer was destined to be the first foreign diplomat to be compelled to hand his legation over to Erbach. And the little Czechoslovakian Minister, already nervously aggressive in his manner, would be the next.

Prince Erbach zu Schönberg was a descendant of Queen Victoria, and when we dined at his legation a few evenings later we observed with amusement the incongruity of a signed photograph of the old Queen cheek by jowl with one of Adolf Hitler on the grand piano. Princess Erbach was a Hungarian, a woman of considerable charm and personality with a perfect figure. She wore the simplest and most elegantly cut clothes in Athens as a background to her exquisite jewels.

Presently the Bishops appeared, and it was as if a light had flooded the dim Cathedral, so splendid were their gold brocade robes and their glittering mitres. They waited as the King walked up the aisle, followed by his sisters, the Princesses Irene and Katherine, and his brother, Prince Paul, the Deodov.

It was the first time I had seen the King. He was in profile to us, and his face was a cold lonely mask, arrogant and still. He was slight and compact and he had the habit of absolute repose.

George II of the Hellenes* had returned to the throne in 1935 after twelve years of exile, during which interval he had

---

*King George II's brother, King Paul, succeeded him and he, in turn, was followed by his son, King Constantine, who was dethroned by a military coup in 1967. The future of Greece is politically still uncertain.

made his headquarters in London. For him that must have been a decade of freedom. For Greece it was a turbulent period of internal strife with republics and dictatorships succeeding one another with lightning rapidity. But now it seemed that the country was heading for an era of peace and prosperity.

Across the church from where we stood was General Metaxas, the Prime Minister and Greece's 'strong man'. He had a small round body, but a formidable head, and his eyes, magnified by powerful glasses, were determined and ruthless. So were the tightly controlled thick lips under his stiff grey moustache. There was no lighter side to this man's life. Metaxas was a worker who drove himself hard. Many of his methods were those of a dictator, but until the revival of the monarchy was firmly established an arbitrary attitude was necessary. He had muzzled the Press and done away with all opposition in the Government by the simple expedient of dissolving the Chamber, and he now ruled the country in conjunction with the King and a Cabinet of his own choosing.

Metaxas was not popular, but the poor trusted him and looked to him to better their living conditions. Through him their hours were shorter, their wages higher, and their health improved. There were holiday camps and free hospitals, and child labour was abolished. His import duties had encouraged home industries and alleviated unemployment. At the instigation of the King he was bringing in widespread army reforms, and he inspired respect and admiration as well as fear.

He only inspired love when the hour of testing was at hand for his country and his own life was nearing its close. Then, at three o'clock on the cold autumn morning of October 28th, 1940, the gross figure of the Italian Minister appeared at his house. Metaxas, still heavy with sleep, was summoned into the presence of Mussolini's envoy to receive a monstrous ultimatum. His answer, on behalf of the nation, was an unhesitating 'No'.

For that his people loved him.

When in the following spring the more terrible ultimatum was handed to the Greek Government by Prince Erbach zu Shönberg, grave of face and suave of voice, it was not Metaxas who received it.

The little round dictator was dead. But the answer was the

same as before: one of the bravest and most defiant No's in history.

After the service in the Cathedral there was a military review, and the Diplomatic Corps stood at the side of the King for two hours to watch it. The Albanian Minister, who was very tall and weedy, swooned and was spirited away in an ambulance. I felt very sorry for him, and, at sight of his chagrin, shades of my schooldays gathered round me and I heard the voice of Sister Hildegarde: 'You are getting a lanky girl. We must put a weight on your head.' The Albanian Minister, too, appeared to have outgrown his strength, and, as he had been standing up, he could not even have resorted to Sister Hildegarde's method of putting his head between his knees.

The Albanian Minister was often a source of interest and concern. It was his habit to sit by himself in the old-fashioned 'dicky seat' of his two-seater car, with his head high above the wind-screen and his white hair blowing in the breeze, while his wife and the chauffeur sat comfortably in front. Whenever the Diplomatic Corps had to stand for any length of time he swooned. We grew accustomed to seeing him gathered up and pushed into an ambulance. But as far as we were concerned he fainted for the last time on Good Friday, 1939, when Mussolini attacked Albania. After that he disappeared altogether, the Italian flag flew over his legation, and he was seen no more stiffly perched in the old-fashioned 'dicky' of his two-seater car.

On the evening of the National Day there was a reception at the Military Club, which we attended.

My husband had already been received by the King in private audience, but I was presented to him at the reception. His stern, aloof expression warmed into animation as soon as he spoke in his deep, rather abrupt voice. When he gave his sudden laugh his monocle escaped his eye and his face was kind and friendly. His English was perfect with only the faintest foreign inflexion.

The present Greek dynasty is descended from the royal houses of Denmark and Russia. After the abdication of King Otho, who was imported from Bavaria and whose despotic ideas did not suit the democratic Greeks, the vacant throne was offered to the Duke of Edinburgh. It was, however, impossible for him to accept the offer, as the agreement between the three

Powers who had sponsored the War of Independence (Russia, France, and Great Britain) precluded all members of any of their reigning houses from occupying the Greek throne. So Great Britain undertook to find a Sovereign, and her choice, which was entirely acceptable to Greece, bound the two countries even more closely than before.

George I, who ascended the throne of the Hellenes in 1863 and who subsequently married the Grand Duchess Olga of Russia, was the second son of King Christian of Denmark and the brother of Queen Alexandra, the wife of Edward VII of England.

Unfortunately, these dynastic bonds with Great Britain and Russia were somewhat slackened during the Great War, when King Constantine, the father of the present King of Greece, found it impossible to throw in his lot definitely with the Allies. This was understandable, since he was married to the Kaiser's favourite sister and, like General Metaxas, had received his military training at the Kriegsakademie in Berlin. But the result of his hedging was to force the hand of Venizelos, the pro-Ally, pro-war Cretan statesman who became the leader of a powerful anti-royalist faction. This faction split the feeling of the country into two bitterly opposed camps, and eventually drove successive kings into exile.

But when at last King George II returned to the throne in 1935 he was determined, if possible, to reunite the country, and with this end in view he proclaimed a general amnesty which even included his erstwhile foe, Venizelos, who, with characteristic wisdom and generosity, advised the Liberty Party not to fight against the new régime.

In the following year Venizelos died in Paris. But many of his adherents continued to look with disfavour upon the monarchy.

This atmosphere complicated our social relations not a little. There were always the people who could not be invited to the same parties because they or their families had suffered at the hands of either Venizelists or Royalists. For instance, on a certain occasion I introduced one of my guests, whom I did not realize was an ex-naval officer, to a very pleasant naval captain.

'You have surely met Captain So-and-so?' I said with my best hostess smile.

'Yes, indeed,' replied the other with a cool bow. 'When last we met the captain sentenced me to three years' imprisonment.'

Only the perfect manners of the Greeks saved my face at such moments. And I appreciated their consideration. No one knew better than I did that old wounds heal slowly and that the flame of political hatred takes many generations to burn out. I had seen it in South Africa. For a time the fires may be banked down and then some incident, however trivial, will fan them into a blaze once more. In Greece, as in South Africa, the personal element is a powerful one, and so long as there are men and women alive to say, '*This* they did to *me*' or 'to my father', the bellows will be at hand for those who know how to use them.

Athenian women are the most amusing and sophisticated in the world, and I often felt gauche and clumsy in their company. But a good friend of ours was Mary Carolou. She and her beautiful sister Penny took me under their wings.

Mary and her husband, Chris, were sea-gypsies, and in the summer they lived in their yacht *Troll*. But during the winter months they made their home with Chris's mother, Mrs. Carolou, senior. The two sisters, Mary Carolou and Penny Vlangalis, both of whom had married Athenians, were American-born Greeks with the statuesque figures and regular features one associates more readily with the ancient than the modern Greeks.

'You are tall like I am,' said Penny one evening, as we sat on the roof garden of her lovely apartment overlooking the finest view in Athens. 'The same models will suit us both. We must take her to Eugenie's *exposition*, Mary. What about tomorrow morning?'

Mary nodded her dark Madonna head. 'That's a good idea.'

So they took me to Eugenie's.

Eugenie's was the Athenian version of Collette's. But how much more human and amusing!

There were no shop windows at Eugenie's. We rang the bell outside a massive door in a tall house and I followed Mary and Penny up a short flight of stairs. The rows of little gilt chairs surrounded the salon and already they were nearly all occupied.

There was Princess Erbach talking animatedly to the old Countess Capodistria, the acknowledged doyenne of Athenian society. We went over and spoke to them. The Countess's shrewd, humorous, black eyes twinkled up at us as she said in her deep voice: 'Mary, I shall expect you to bring Captain and Mrs. Packer to my house on Sunday morning for a mastika. It is some weeks since you have been to see me, you naughty girl.'

On Sunday mornings Countess Capodistria held court, and outside the old-fashioned mansion in Patisia there waited shining limousines flying the flags of the Ministers of many nations. The aged Count did not care about entertaining and he seldom put in an appearance, but punctually at a quarter to one his handbell sounded with peremptory insistence, and the guests smiled at one another and said, 'The Count wants his lunch,' as they took leave of their hostess.

Ellie Zaloucosta, the loveliest of all the Greeks, was sitting next to Madame la Baronne Peyronnet, the witty massive wife of the French Military Attaché. La Baronne's shrill laugh set the crystal tear-drops of the chandelier quivering and Ellie's enormous liquid eyes were moist with mirth.

Presently, after a good deal of fussing behind the scenes, the models were announced as the mannequins made their entry.

'Numero soixante-neuf de Molyneux. Quelques fleurs . . . Et numero quinze de Vionnet. Le Rêve.'

Suzie, the tall debonair mannequin, turned this way and that to show off the floral cocktail dress, and as she did so she answered little bursts of questions in French or Greek. Weenie followed her, a red-haired Aphrodite. She stopped in front of Penny.

'For cinq à sept heurs this négligée is lovely,' she said, speaking in English for my benefit. 'Look, this is amusing.' With a little chuckle she drew the long gold zip down the length of the gown and stood in her flimsy underwear. 'Pour l'heure d'amour, Madame Vlangalis.'

Penny's classic face was full of mischief. 'Show my Italian friend over there, Weenie.' She whispered lightly. 'Cinq à sept heurs – l'heure d'amour . . . is her speciality!'

There was laughter and back-chat between the clients and the mannequins. Here the girls were human beings, not mere dolls such as we had been at Collette's. I remembered the haughty women for whom we had modelled dresses, women who had seen us only as dummies, and I felt a sudden little flare of resentment. That was the trouble with England. There were too many women in England who saw only their social equals and superiors and were blind to anyone else. The democratic attitude of Greece was a frank assumption that everybody was as good as everybody else. There was no defiance in it and no hostility and therefore no impertinence. It was perfectly natural and very refreshing.

There were other signs than the *expositions* of the various model-houses to tell us that spring was at hand. The flower donkeys, who ambled drowsily through the bright sunny streets of Athens, were laden with the first almond blossom, and the panniers attached to their flanks were filled with violets, hyacinths, many-coloured anemones, and the tidy beauty of irises. And one evening, as Diki drove me home from a tea-party, we met a family of frogs hopping across the road.

'I thought we were having a false spring,' said Diki. 'But now I know it is the real thing. The frogs are on the move, and they never make a mistake.'

It was Carnival, and for three weeks there was a sweet madness in the air and the ghosts of Dionysus and Aphrodite haunted woods and gardens and cloistered courtyards. When we dined at tavernas in the country or by the sea, figures in masks and dominoes came in and sat down for a brochette or a glass of wine. Perhaps the violinist recognized a pair of lovers under the disguise, and then he strolled over to their table and played and sang of love. In Carnival time husbands and wives had their own latchkeys and night and day changed places.

One day, down at the golf club, I saw a slim stranger driving from the first tee. His thick curly hair was sprinkled with grey, he had a little brown moustache and heavy-lidded eyes. He wore a yellow pull-over.

'Who is he?' I asked Count Mercati. Bertie and I were playing a match against the young Count and his pretty wife.

'He is my brother-in-law, Michael Arlen.'

'The novelist who turned London into a village and glamorized British decadence?'

Young Mercati smiled. 'You seem to know who I mean.'

Afterwards Michael Arlen met us on the veradah for a cup of tea. And presently we were joined by his wife and family – a delicate-featured woman, with an exquisite figure, and two small children clinging to her hands. Atlanta Arlen was the daughter of old Count Mercati, who held a high place in the King's entourage.

When the children were introduced to us the boy bowed politely and the little girl's golden ringlets bobbed as she curtsied. Later, when we came to know Michael better, I said: 'Your children have perfect manners. I admire the way your wife has trained them.'

He smiled. 'Good manners matter more than most things. Good manners in living and in dying – and, of course, in bed.'

He was as outrageous and scintillating as his book. Thin ice was a challenge to Michael to attempt a conversational skating ballet. He was his most cynical at his own expense, and it amused him to refer to himself as 'another Armenian massacre' on the slightest provocation. He told me his unpronounceable Armenian name, but I cannot remember a syllable of it. He was at that time writing novels with a deeper meaning than those with which he originally made his name. He knew that London – the 'village' he loved – was in danger, and that the time for purely light-hearted romance, or even for 'The Green Hat', was at an end. But manners still made the men of Michael Arlen's fiction.

In this insistence upon good manners he was at one with the people of his wife's country. The Greeks set great store by behaviour.

I went to an Athenian tea-party one afternoon. My hostess was the wife of a wealthy cigarette manufacturer. She was a decorative little woman with lavender hair and well-cared-for hands, as sensitive as the antennae of a butterfly. With them she explored the texture of life. The Greeks use their hands as an auxiliary sense. They speak with them as do the dumb and see with them as do the blind, but they only work with them if it is absolutely necessary to their livelihood.

There were two or three others at tea. One was a young woman with hard brown eyes who had just divorced her husband.

'Please tell me,' I murmured to my hostess, 'how is it that so many Athenian women seem to have gone through the divorce courts?'

She raised her eyebrows and her slight shoulders. 'If people are not happy together surely it is sensible to part. After all, the relationship between men and women was scarcely intended by nature to be permanent.'

'I quite agree. But by our law it is not so easy to get free. With you perhaps it is simpler?'

'If there is good reason it is quite simple.'

'What do you call good reason? Infidelity?'

She tossed back her lavender head and gave herself up to mirth.

'Adultère good reason? Mais, ma chère, how can that be important? All men are polygamous, and a wise woman accepts that state of affairs. As for women' – the inevitable little shrug – 'a clever woman can always deceive her husband. In any case it is practically impossible to prove adultère.'

The girl whose divorce had recently gone through said thoughtfully: 'I think my grounds were best. My husband was attempting to gain control over my fortune. Now, that really is a serious matter.'

A good-looking young woman leaned forward, and the diamanté on her black afternoon dress shivered. Her crazy little hat swooped down to meet a quizzical lifted eyebrow.

'Let us be civilized,' she said. 'The best grounds for divorce are surely bad manners.'

'But those can't possibly be grounds,' I said.

'But yes! With us they are certainly grounds. If a man tells his wife to go to the devil in front of the servants, or slaps her face in the presence of a witness, it is sufficient evidence for her to obtain her freedom.'

'But if you can divorce so easily, doesn't it encourage you to go into marriage rather lightly?' I asked.

'No,' said my hostess, 'that is not so. Our Church looks after that. With us there is only one form of wedding, and that is religious. We do not differentiate between the Church and the legal ceremony as you do. And our Church only permits us to marry three times. If we can't make a success of marriage after three efforts we have to give it up as a bad job.'

Soon after tea people began arriving for bridge and other card games. The salons of Athens were always set about with card-tables. Little snatches of French, German, English, Italian, and Greek clashed lightly in the smoke-wreathed air. Most Athenians spoke excellent English, for the English

Nannie or governess had been an institution in wealthy families for close on a century. Narrow finger-tips drummed on the table and impatient high heels tapped on the carpet if anyone took too long over a call. 'Jouez mal mais jouez vite!' The Greeks played by instinct and flair, and my mother's ally, Mr. Culbertson, cut but little ice among these racy gamblers. But although they often expressed annoyance with each other, they always condoned and excused my mistakes or slowness. I was a guest, not only in the house, but in the country, and good manners demanded that they exercise patience towards me in all things.

Agammemnon leapt over the garden wall, closely followed by the gardener, who wore a purple anemone behind his ear.

'You are satisfied, Madame Packer?' he asked with a wave of his hand at the roses blooming in the flower-beds. Larkspurs, pansies, and daffodils grew along the walls, and the sweet peas nodded on the trellis behind the villa.

My husband and I looked at all these things and found them good.

'We are delighted,' I said.

'Pah-pah-pahp,' shrugged Agammemnon. 'I do not expect you to be *delighted* – yet. This is only the beginning.'

He made a brief tour of inspection with the gardener and rattled out a volley of instructions. The young man answered him with a quick 'Nē, Kirios; nē Kirios' ('Yes, Sir; Yes, Sir') and vaulted back whence he had come.

'You will have a whisky and soda?' suggested Bertie.

'Weeskee!' Agammemnon rolled his eyes heavenwards and made gestures indicative of approval.

Slovakis brought the glasses out on the terrace. The boy Basil came in at the gate with his lamb frisking at his heels and ran towards the garage singing to himself. The first swallows swooped and twittered with a gay flirting of forked blue tails.

'They have built their nest under our porch,' said my husband. 'That is a good omen,' said Agammemnon. 'Better the swallow than the stork in these hard times.'

'It all depends how you look at it,' I said. 'Are not children supposed to be an insurance against a destitute old age?'

He pushed out his lips in a dubious grimace.

357

'For the peasant perhaps. A peasant needs a family to work in his fields. But even then the younger son usually goes to America to seek his fortune – or did until the quota – because the farm cannot support the whole family. As for daughters. They are a liability, however you look at it. A daughter always needs a dot. Ask a peasant how many children he has, and, if he is the father of six sons and four daughters, he will reply simply: "I have six children." He may add "and four girls", or he may not bother to mention them. They do not count. Take, for example, the case of my father-in-law. That unfortunate gentleman was presented by my estimable mother-in-law with four daughters, one after the other. Beautiful girls!' He kissed his fingers into the pearly dusk. 'But what is the result? My father-in-law slaved in an office till the day he died in order that I and three other men should receive a substantial sum of money with his daughters. He has worked himself to death for us. Now Dora and I have one daughter, our little Marika, but we want no storks on our roof-top, Madame, because we might well have three more girls, and I do not propose to tie myself to a desk all my life in order to provide my daughters' husbands with fortunes!'

Agammemnon savoured his whisky. 'This is good,' he said. 'Poli kala. When do you hope to see your son?'

'We are leaving for Belgrade next week,' said Bertie. 'But we will be back before Easter to meet him. He is flying out for his Easter holidays.'

'By himself?'

My husband nodded.

Agammemnon gasped. 'But I believe he is not yet eleven years old!'

'That is right.'

'Oh, la, la! You British parents! My wife would fall into a fit at the mere notion of allowing a child of that age to make such a journey alone.'

The Greeks were always appalled at the 'callousness' of British parents. They thought it dreadful to 'get rid of the poor things to those barbarous boarding schools', and every time Piet came to us by air, sea, or train they threw up their expressive hands in horror.

Yet, even as Agammemnon exclaimed, a thrill of joy momentarily stopped my heart. For the first time we had a home

358

to offer our son for his holidays. The fact that he must cross Europe to come to it was immaterial. At last no great oceans lay between him and us. Peter's father looked at me across Agammemnon's shocked countenance, and all our deep contentment was in the look that passed between us.

CHAPTER FORTY

YUGO-SLAVIA AND THE REGENT

A FEW days later we were on our way to Belgrade in the Orient Express. For dinner we were served with a blue trout who carried a sprig of lilac in his mouth, and within two hours, replete with trout, we were driving through the streets of Belgrade to the British Legation, where we were to spend a few days as the guests of the British Minister, Sir Ronald Campbell, and Lady Campbell. The air was heavy with the perfume of lilac and night balsam, and a chilly little mist, like a shivering child, crept into the city from the broad grey-gold bosom of the Danube.

The Legation was a solid, comfortable Georgian house set back from an avenue of chestnuts. There was a walled garden and a wide lawn in the shade of plane trees, syringas, and, of course, lilacs. Roses and irises clustered around a lily pond, a herbaceous border grew along the wall, and regiments of tulips stood to attention.

Lady Campbell had that essentially English attribute, a true understanding of flowers. She had also a mass of lovely snow-white hair like whipped cream and more than the usual share of feminine intuition. Her ready wit was often spiced with a pretty flash of satire.

'I am sorry I cannot shake hands,' said Sir Ronald, as we were ushered in, somewhat travel-stained. And he indicated his thumb, which was swathed in bandages. He had just had a cyst excised.

Sir Ronald was to be our Ambassador in Paris at the time of the collapse of France, and later, as British Ambassador in

Portugal, he was largely instrumental in influencing Salazar to allow the Allies military facilities in the Azores. He was slight and fair with an easy manner and a dry humorous way of expressing himself. He was a keen golfer and tennis player, and played well but not too earnestly. He held the golf championship of Belgrade and had little difficulty in defeating the tall, dark German Minister, who was the runner-up. One had the feeling with Sir Ronald that he had powerful reserves of nervous energy to draw upon when necessary. It had been necessary during the General Strike, and this diplomat stood high in my esteem when I heard that during the national emergency he had worked as a fireman on the Southern Railway.

'And a very bad fireman I was,' he said. 'Stoking up my engine took me three times as long as it would have taken an experienced man.'

Later in the evening I said with a sympathetic glance at his bandaged thumb: 'Removing that cyst must have been very painful. Anything to do with nails—'

He made a wry grimace. 'Removing the cyst might have been painful, I suppose. But I'm sure it couldn't have hurt as much as administering the local anaesthetic! The doctor gave me six injections at the base of the nail, and they really were excruciating. But then the Serbs have no conception of pain. They happen to be the bravest people on earth themselves – almost impervious to physical suffering – and they don't understand its effect on others.'

'A general anaesthetic is unheard of here, even for a major operation,' said Lady Campbell. 'The Greek Minister had his appendix out under local and watched the whole operation in a hand mirror. And no one would dream of asking for chloroform in childbirth. From the Queen-Mother to the humblest peasant childbirth is treated entirely as a natural function.'

Sir Ronald, who proposed to play tennis next day, despite his inconvenient thumb, said: 'One has to remember that the Serbs are a stoical race of warrior peasants. In the war there were no anaesthetics to be had in Belgrade, and limbs were amputated without so much as the tot of grog our soldiers and sailors could count on a hundred years ago. Why, the late King Alexander had his appendix removed under far more unpleasant conditions than the Greek Minister. He was taken ill during the terrible retreat to the coast in 1915. An army surgeon operated on him in a tent in the mountains of Albania, and he was carried down those wild snow-covered passes on a litter, ill as he was.'

I think that was the first thing to strike one in Belgrade – both directly and indirectly – the extraordinary toughness of the Serbs, their fearlessness and powers of endurance, and their total indifference to pain or death itself. They were a swarthy people with hard black eyes, and practically all the men appeared to be doing their military service. The great barracks sprawled under the royal parks, and in the gardens of Kalamegdan, above the confluence of the Sava and the Danube, young soldiers walked with their wives and families and the toddler was tugged uphill hanging on to father's sword. And in restaurants there was always the tramp of heavy boots and the clatter of sword-belts being taken off and hung up, and later the deep voices of the soldiers were accompanied by the gypsy music of the Tsigane bands.

Belgrade, which was to suffer such devastation in the second World War, had already been razed to the ground in 1914, and had been almost entirely rebuilt, but where any place of historic interest remained, its associations invariably led me to the conclusion that to be a Balkan royalty was a far from enviable fate. The palace in the city had witnessed the assassination of the last King and Queen of the Obrenovitch dynasty. They were murdered in their bed and flung from the window into the snowy street to be eaten by cur-dogs. And in Kalamegdan, once a Turkish fortress, there is a museum where the visitor may view the gory relics of the late King Alexander, who was assassinated at Marseilles in 1935 by a Bulgar Macedonian terrorist. His bullet-ripped uniform lies in a glass coffin, and in a show-case is the death-car, a dilapidated old taxi with bloodstained cushions, which the French thoughtfully sent as a present to the Belgrade Government after the tragedy.

I had just been very much shocked by this exhibition when Bertie took me to lunch with Colonel and Mrs. Hanau.

Colonel Hanau was the representative of certain important British interests in Belgrade. He was also a South African Jew, and he greeted me as a long-lost sister.

'Your father brought me into the world,' he said, as he wrung my hand. And I marvelled afresh at the enormous number of people who appeared to have made their debut in this vale of tears under the supervision of my father. We told each other how small the world was and then I confided in the Colonel that I was really horrified at the Alexander section of the museum.

'It seems so crude and morbid that one should be able to pay to see all those pitiful things at Kalamegdan. The clothes the poor man wore, and that outrageous old rattle-trap in which he was killed. How must young King Peter feel with such dreadful reminders of his father's fate on view here in Belgrade?'

'My dear girl,' said Colonel Hanau, 'the Kings of Yugo-Slavia do not expect to die in their beds. Consider their history.'

As soon as I had the opportunity I did consider it. I found that young King Peter was the great-grandson of the first Black George, Karadjordje, the landowner-outlaw who gained the love of his people by his successful insurrections against the Turkish overlords. He was eventually betrayed by a rival farmer, Obrenovitch, who handed the head of Black George to the Turks on a silver salver. In gratitude the overlords allowed Obrenovitch to call himself the ruler of Serbia. From then on the Obrenovitch and Karadjordje dynasties have contested the throne of Serbia, and kings, queens, and pretenders have met with violent ends. But it is even more interesting, in view of this World War and its amazing history of resistance in Europe long after so-called defeat has overwhelmed a country, that King Peter's ancestors were really nothing more nor less than guerillas refusing to accept the domination of the Ottomans. They and their kind freed Serbia from the Turk, and the guerillas of today are living up to the traditions of those rebels of the early nineteenth century.

My countryman and his hospitable Scottish wife gave us an excellent luncheon, after which we played somewhat somnolent tennis on their very good hard court under the flowering trees. Far below, the Danube flowed to join the River Sava under the battlements of the old Turkish fort of Kalamegdan. And let me put on record that I have yet to see that famous river blue. In winter the Danube was steel-grey, in summer it was gold-grey, but as far as I was concerned it was only blue in the Strauss waltz, to the strains of which my parents fell in love.

A sentry with a gun over his shoulder paced up and down the street outside Colonel Hanau's house.

'Who is he there for?' I asked.

The little Colonel laughed. 'Not for me, happily! He is there for the Prime Minister, Stoyadenovitch. Stoya has many enemies. You see that island in the Danube? That is Gypsy Island. A bunch of his would-be-assassins are imprisoned there. But if they escape he can count himself out. They are after his blood. He lives opposite us. You ask Sir Ronald about the attempt made on Stoya's life in the Chamber of Deputies. The bullet very nearly picked off Sir Ronald instead. He was in the diplomats' gallery just behind the Speaker's rostrum. It was a narrow shave, I can assure you.'

When we asked the Minister to tell us the story he chuckled.

'The would-be assassin was exceedingly drunk,' he said, 'or he couldn't possibly have missed Stoya at point-blank range. That was the only reason why I didn't duck. It never entered my head that anyone could miss such an elephantine target.'

The rest of the Diplomatic Corps, who had acted by instinct rather than logic, had grovelled under their seats with amazing promptitude at the first indication of trouble. Sir Ronald alone had seen fit to keep his ringside place. Next day the Belgrade papers carried headlines extolling this example of British 'sang-froid'.

I saw Stoyadenovitch for myself a few days later at a ball. We dined with the Military Attaché, Colonel Stronge, and Mrs. Stronge, beforehand.

Jill Stronge was a champion of oppressed humans and animals, and since her arrival in Belgrade the horses of that city has taken on a new lease of life. Her round black eyes that glowed in her thin, attractive face and blazed at the mere mention of a lost cause were always mischievously amused at the social snobberies of Belgrade.

'Must I put on my gloves?' I asked after dinner.

'Most certainly. It's long gloves tonight, and tiaras for those who have them. Prince Paul, the Regent, will be there. And Queen Marie, the King's mother. You watch the women trample each other underfoot to get in the limelight.'

'What about the Regent's wife? And King Peter?'

'You won't see them. Princess Olga is away, staying with her sister, the Duchess of Kent. And King Peter* is still too young for official functions.'

The ballroom was long and narrow with a raised dais at the far end. The guests lined the walls, men on one side and ladies on the other. While we waited for the royal party we had time to look around at our leisure. I noticed that the swarthy Yugo-Slav women did not use depilatories, although they wore elaborate sleeveless gowns, and that their figures were distorted by stiff funnel-shaped brassieres that pressed their full bosoms abruptly outwards and upwards like horns. When I asked my Russian dressmaker about this afterwards she shrugged and groaned.

'I have implored my clients to wear brassieres that make some attempt to follow nature, but, no, they prefer these contraptions! Pour exciter les hommes, Madame, pour les piquer! What are the Yugo-Slav women, anyway? They are as Oriental as the Turks, who occupied this country for nearly five centuries. They eat, sleep, and pander to the desires of their men. That is all they are good for.'

They were sturdy women, over-painted, with heavy, stubborn faces, unimaginative and built to survive disaster. These women were Serbian, but later we were to see the young goddesses of Yugo-Slavia – the Dalmatian peasants of the fertile Konavle Valley, and tall fair girls in the mountains of Slovenia.

A hundred conversations in many different languages created a sort of roar that was broken suddenly by a sibilant *hist!* which ran down the waiting ranks. In the silence which followed, Queen Marie, the widow of the murdered Alexander and mother of King Peter, walked between the guests to the dais. She was in black velvet with a blue order across her chest – pearly skinned, plump, and pretty. Beside her was Prince Paul, the Regent, in military uniform – slim, younger looking than his forty-four years, with an intellectual, sharp-featured face full of sensibility. Behind them followed the other guests of honour, including Stoyadenovitch. The massive snake-faced Premier wore his tails down to his ankles. He was known to be as fearless as he was unscrupulous. His wife, who

* *King Peter, like so many Balkan royalties, is in exile and Yugo-Slavia is a Communist county.*

364

followed him, was a small-featured Greek from the island of Corfu, with metallic gold curls. Stoyadenovitch towered over everyone else. He was a giant among men. Yet it was said that his father was a dwarf and his only child deformed. He was bitterly hated by the Croats, who were actively opposed to the Belgrade Government. The people of Yugo-Slavia are divided into three groups – Serbs, Croats, and Slovenes. The Serbs, who were the core of the nation, held the controlling voice in the Government, and it was a stern one. The Croats chafed under it. Furthermore, the country had three different religious sects. The Serbs belonged to the Orthodox Church, the Croats were Catholic or Moslem, and the Slovenes were Catholic. The Croats, at the risk of their lives, worked unceasingly for an autonomy, and it was this Croatian problem that was the number one headache for Prince Paul and for his Prime Minister, Stoyadenovitch. It was known in Belgrade that Stoyadenovitch's policy was pro-German.

Later in the evening we were presented to the Queen Mother and the Regent.

When my husband told Queen Marie that we proposed to visit Dalmatia, she said in her perfect English: 'That coast is glorious. I had a villa at Split one summer, and my children loved it. Now I am building a house near Dubrovnik.'

'Is it finished yet, Ma'am?' asked Sir Ronald.

She laughed and turned her head so that the light made a ripple of gold in her pale brown curls.

'Is anything ever finished? When the villa is ready there will still be the garden. There is always something more to be done to a garden.'

What difference whether you are a queen or a naval wife? I thought. Your interests are those of any other woman. Here was a queen speaking of her house and garden just as my South African cousin had done, just as I hoped to do one day. A home where her children may be happy. That is the dream in the heart of every woman who is denied such a blessing. And then I shivered as the grim memory of a glass coffin in Kalamegdan Museum intruded. There, for all to see, lay the bloodstained uniform of this attractive woman's husband – a dreadful reminder that, no matter where she housed them, her children must live in constant danger of their lives.

I noticed that Prince Paul's expression was sad and

frustrated until he smiled. We talked about England and his two sons who were at school there.

'The elder boy is blissfully happy at Eton,' he said. 'He has a room of his own and complete independence, and he writes to say that he did not know such happiness could exist.'

Freedom from fear and surveillance, I thought, for I knew that in their own country Prince Paul's children never moved without police protection.

'And the younger one, Sir?'

The Regent's face clouded and his brown eyes seemed to withdraw into some shadow-land where ghosts walked.

'Ah, the younger one. When his brother left he was my constant companion and friend. I miss him terribly. Alexander has been away four years already, and I have learned to accustom myself to his absence – but Niki . . . it was awful to let him go! But he seems well content with school life in England.'

Prince Paul himself was educated in England at a public school and a university, and, whatever his subsequent political manoeuvres may have been, his sympathies were almost certainly fundamentally British. In fact, his elder son joined the Air Force as soon as he was of age to do so.

Prince Paul was a man who lived with fear at his elbow – an intangible yet inescapable companion. It is not easy for people brought up under normal conditions to envisage the life of a Balkan Regent in an extremely turbulent part of Europe, the very hatchery of wars. When the sons of the Regent were returning to Yugo-Slavia for their school holidays in 1938 there was a plot to murder them in the Orient Express. Fortunately, it was discovered in time to prevent the double tragedy. Sometimes they and their cousins, young King Peter's small brothers, went to play with the Strongs' little daughter Bridget, and then the Military Attaché's garden had to be surrounded with a cordon of police. The boys were used to their special detectives and called them 'peepers'.

'They regard them as sort of extra nurses,' said Jill Strong, and sighed. 'Poor children!'

A few days later we received an invitation to dinner at Beli Dvor (the White Lodge), the palace of the Regent.

There were about a dozen guests, and I found myself placed between Stoyadenovitch and Andritch, the Minister of Foreign

Affairs. General Neditch was opposite me, a heavy man with a face too stupid to be sly. He had a reputation for great gallantry in the field and he was a man trusted and respected, yet he became the chief Nazi collaborator. It is possible that, like the Regent, he sincerely believed such a course to be the only one open to his country. The power politics of Germany were not easy for a small nation to resist, and it needed a long view to see beyond the anguish of the crushing occupation resistance must inevitably bring in its wake. For the strength of the Allies took a pitiably long time to make itself apparent in Europe.

The palace was furnished in a light modern style and was comfortable and agreeable – very twentieth century. The long polished table was decorated with fluffy mimosa trailers and we ate off silver platters.

Stoyadenovitch sat like a mountain on my left and his curious flickering eyes seemed to be everywhere at once. His voice was thick and heavy. He was learning English, and we conversed in that tongue. We spoke of the great autostradas of Europe.

'Soon it will be possible to speed from the English Channel to the Bosphorus,' he said. 'In Europe we build the great auto-stradas. Why do not the British and the French construct the Channel tunnel?'

'Perhaps we feel safer with our British moat dividing us from Europe.'

'Yes, Madame, perhaps. "Over the border" is a term you have not fully understood in England since the wars with Scotland and Wales. But the air-roads are even more important than autostradas and Channel tunnels that can be destroyed or defended. From the air the British moat would seem thin as a thread.'

'That, too, could be defended, if not destroyed,' I smiled.

The narrow eyes of my neighbour regarded me with amusement. 'Many fighter planes would be needed to defend the wide sky-road over that narrow moat.'

I knew very well what he had in mind. There was an international aero exhibition in Belgrade at the time, and dangerous-looking German planes dominated all others with their numbers and variety. They were part of Goebbels's propaganda – a small part. Yet they had evidently impressed the Premier of Yugo-Slavia not a little.

After dinner we had coffee in the salon, and Prince Paul said: 'I have just received a new Marlene Dietrich film, and I thought it might be amusing. We are going to show it tonight. It is called "Nuit Sans Amour", I believe.'

The picture, far from being 'Nuit Sans Armour', turned out to be 'Knight Without Armour', a depressing tale of the Russian Revolution. Marlene floated through snowy wastes and fearful escapades clad only in a chiffon nightdress. He pale hair seemed to have receded off her vast bulging forehead into the remote middle distance of her scalp.

'Is she going bald?' asked Prince Paul with interest. It was his sole comment on the film.

In the interval between the main picture and a Disney cartoon to cheer us up the Regent told me that he was learning to drive a car.

'It seems absurd at my age,' he smiled. 'But I love it. I find it most exhilarating.'

That he found it exhilarating was hardly surprising, since he was learning on his supercharged Mercédès.

'My car is the same as that of Paul of Greece,' he said. 'Perhaps you know his?'

I laughed. 'I've often seen him escape his detectives in it. First you see a silver streak and a cloud of dust on the road to Athens, and you know that is the Crown Prince. And then, miles behind, the wretched bodyguard rattle along at full speed trying to keep up with him. I am told they have applied to the Government for a faster car.'

'Yes, shaking off the detectives is a sort of game.'

'Prince Paul of Greece has a reputation as a dare-devil driver,' I said. 'And they say he is a very fine pilot.'

The words had no sooner left my lips than I realized that I had made a gaffe.

Prince Paul buried his face in his hands. 'Don't!' he said. 'Don't talk about the air! I cannot endure to think of it since that horrible crash when the Hesse family were killed.'

I was appalled. For the moment I had forgotten the terrible catastrophe that had shadowed a famous London wedding.

Prince Paul's dread of the air was to be further justified by our own British tragedy of 1942, when the Duke of Kent lost his life in a plane crash on active service. The Duke of Kent had not only been married to the Regent's sister-in-law, but the young couple had actually become engaged under his roof in Dalmatia.

When the entertainment was over the Regent said a few words to each of his guests and then he bade us goodnight. We watched him ascend his wide staircase – a sensitive, solitary figure, hemmed in by fears and shadows. And then we went our separate happier ways.

Next day we played golf on the hill which is part of the Royal Park. Tame pheasants trailed across the greens and fairways. The caddies were decorative boys in national costume, and the bunkers were overgrown shell craters in memory of 1914. Across the wooded valley, on Dedinje Hill, we saw Beli Dvor at which we had dined the night before. Below us, at the meeting-place of two great rivers, lay the city of Belgrade. The sunset played sinister prophetic tricks with the scene. Windows flamed up suddenly as if the city burned, the rivers were molten, then the fiery glow melted into a murky red. Belgrade and the Danube seemed flowing with blood. I looked towards Dedinje and saw that Beli Dvor was lurid in the afterglow.

'Prince Paul's palace is on fire,' I said.

'Looks like the fifth of November,' agreed my husband.

We stood for a while to watch the city on the river fade into the long lavender twilight.

Poor Belgrade! When the wings of war beat over the capital in June, 1941, over ten thousand men, women, and children were blown to bits in two days. Such a death-roll over so short a period was never known even in battered London. Those summer days and nights when Hitler, thwarted, struck at defiant Belgrade the flames were no sunset illusion. A human shambles was devoured by fire. But somewhere from the wholesale cremation there rose the spirit that lives on when the shell of man is consumed.

Each man works for freedom in the way to which he is best fitted, and my fellow-countryman, Colonel Hanau, after a hairbreadth escape from Belgrade, quickly got back into uniform, and when last I saw him he was just about to fly many thousands of miles in a bomb-rack on a hazardous mission. And he is more years past military age than it would be tactful to state.

CHAPTER FORTY-ONE

EASTER LAMBS

WE travelled back to Athens in a very small Yugo-Slav ship in company with some German tourists, fifty Yugo-Slav students, and a large flock of sheep. The women tourists wore trousers and blouses, but their blouses were too short, and when they leaned forward we were treated to unappetizing expanses of soiled pink corset. The men wore curious plus fours and white American sailor caps.

The sheep only joined us at the dusty little Albanian port of Durazzo. We saw, heard, and smelt them a long way off. They were accompanied by a fat merchant, who ran an amber chaplet continually through his podgy fingers, and two handsome shepherds with white skull-caps, long black jodhpurs, and (very appropriately) sheepskin boleros. The hold was opened to receive the animals and they were driven into it through a hole in the ship's side. Alas! the hold was very little better than a booby-trap, specially designed for the undoing of simple sheep. It was shaped like a large platform with a deep hole on three sides. The sheep milled on to the platform and those in front, pressed upon by those behind, overflowed into the abyss. As legs were broken and several layers of sheep suffocated, the gaps between German trousers and blouses widened like horrified pink mouths, and we heard 'Gott in Himmel!' interspersed with frenzied bleatings and savage Albanian curses. Within ten minutes forty-nine out of the four hundred who had charged into the valley of death were slain. The shepherds brandished their knives and threatened to murder all the ship's officers, but these had wisely made themselves scarce, so the shepherds sheathed their knives once more and set about slinging out the carcases. The mound of dead animals piled on the quay numbered fifty-three. The survivors were driven out again, the hold closed down, and what remained of the flock was parked aft among the winches and capstans.

As we sailed I said: 'There'll be mutton in Durazzo for a week.'

'On the contrary,' said Bertie, 'that's what the merchant is wringing his hands about. The Albanians are Moslems and won't eat anything that hasn't had its throat cut. The merchant told me that if only he hadn't lost his head he'd have slit their throats as they died!'

The master of our ship was himself a mutton-faced man with a glum and dumb demeanour.

'Well,' I said lightly at dinner (which was described on the menu as 'Roost beak' and which turned out to be beef), 'are we embarking more sheep at Valona tomorrow?'

'Yes,' said Mutton-face stolidly. 'A thousand.'

We laughed heartily at the unsuspected humour of the man.

'I suppose the passengers take them into their cabins?'

He shook his heavy head. 'I do not think that will be necessary. We will put them on the deck outside the saloon and keep the door locked.'

We beamed upon him, and the captain looked gratified at the success of his little joke.

But at Valona two enormous lighters were towed out to meet our ship. One was piled with goats and the other with sheep, and everything came to pass as Mutton-face had said. We had sheep and goats fore and aft and all along one deck. The other was left clear for the students. But iron bars had to be unloaded, and the operating of the winches caused the demise of several more of the flock. This time the merchant, seasoned by bitter experience, did not lose his head.

The students, who had brought their own food and blankets, lived on deck like Chinese coolie passengers. They had their guitars with them too, and at night they sang their folksongs in clear young voices. They were poor, shabby girls and boys, but very happy. For many years they had saved up every dinar they could come by for this jaunt and they meant to enjoy it. Whenever we left port they cheered, 'Ra! Ra! Ra!' and the sheep and goats took up the refrain in a nasal key and sang, 'Ba! Ba! Ba!' It was very hot, and I fancy our arrival anywhere must have been heralded by our smell. The crew could not clean the decks, as there was no room to move, and they carried sheep dung all over the ship on their bare feet.

The German tourists were very angry about the sheep and

the students. They said that Yugo-Slav shipping lines would be better managed if Herr Hitler had control of them.

The students had come to Greece for Easter and so had the sheep. So also had our son Peter, who landed in Old Phaleron by Imperial Airways two days later. He was wildly excited, though he confessed that he had not enjoyed every aspect of the journey.

'We slept at Rome last night, and my room was very big and awfully spooky. But I felt safe because I had my knife.' He tapped a sheath-knife at his belt with pride.

'That's a new knife! And where did you get the snakeskin sheath?' said Bertie.

'We came across the snake – my pal and I – and we killed it and skinned it ourselves. The cobbler sewed the sheath for me. I don't think we salted it quite enough, 'cos it stinks. Here, smell! But the knife is a real bargain – a swop.'

The Customs' officer, however, viewed the bargain with disfavour.

'No knives or weapons can be brought into the country,' he said. 'If people carry knives you never know what they mightn't do with them.' Then, relenting at the sight of Peter's despairing countenance, he added, with the inevitable Greek shrug: 'No matter, I haven't seen your knife.'

As we entered our villa I said: 'Well, how do you like our new home?'

Piet looked round him and considered.

'It's nice. But not so nice as Tees Lodge. Tees Lodge was kind of homey – and this isn't.'

I laughed and hugged him.

Ero's bovine eyes were bright with pleasure as she greeted Piet.

'Now Madame is content,' she murmured, patting my arm with her soft little hand.

'You must ask Ero for what you want in French,' I explained. 'She does not understand English.'

'That's all right,' said Piet. 'Any noises will do for the sort of things I want.'

'And Apostoles, the cook, only talks Greek. How about that?'

'I can explain ice-cream and jelly and chocolate cake in any language,' said our son. And he could.

Chris and Mary Carolou lent him a dinghy and he learned to

sail it. Sometimes the thirteen-year-old son of the Italian Naval Attaché sailed with him.

He struck up a firm friendship with the golf pro, Farrar, who had a clumsy old caique called *White Elephant*. Peter became first mate, and he and Farrar sailed far and wide in *White Elephant*. Only recently I heard that when Greece was overrun Farrar, at the risk of his life, sailed his old caique into the bays and coves of the mainland, taking off anyone he could find who had been left over from the main evacuation.

Sailing was Peter's keenest delight. We often went out in the *Troll* with Chris and Mary, and usually Penny and her husband, Niko, came along too. The *Troll* was a fifty-ton ketch with ample living accommodation for six passengers. The Greeks are born sailors – the girls as well as the men – and we sailed in the path of Ulysses with the sea purple-blue beneath our heeling keel, and the wind singing weird songs in our high white sail.

One sparkling day we anchored off Corinth and bathed from the yacht. Penny wore no cap, and her long black tresses trailed on the water like a naiad's. Afterwards Chris told us tales of the Peloponnese, where vendetta still exists.

'The law cannot stamp it out,' said Chris, 'because it is as natural to the people as their religion. As soon as a man has earned his first fiver he goes out and buys himself a gun. Men shoot each other there for an ancient grudge without thinking twice about it.'

'It's a distorted form of family loyalty,' put in Penny. 'We Greeks are very tied by our family obligations – especially the peasants and the fisher-folk.'

'You see that sailor over there,' said Niko. 'He is a Greek from Albania. Fifteen years ago he left his home town and he has never been back. Now he has received a letter from his mother telling him that his father is dead and his youngest sister is of marriageable age and must have a suitable dot. So he has sent his mother all his savings. He doesn't feel virtuous about it. He takes it for granted.'

Mary smiled her slow sweet smile. 'Brothers in Greece are very devoted to their sisters,' she said.

'And very jealous of their honour,' added Penny. 'If Chris were to find some man playing fast and loose with his sister he would be entitled to shoot that man.'

'Would he suffer the death penalty for such a crime?' asked Bertie.

'Certainly not. It would be a crime for the honour of the family. The family is all-important.'

'Would a husband be justified in killing his wife's lover for the same reason?' I asked, recalling with amusement that Athenians more often contented themselves with slapping the faces of the importunate lovers of their wives.

Chris laughed.

'My dear Joy, where is your sense of proportion? A wife is not fundamentally of a man's family. She is an import. If she misbehaves herself he can get rid of her in the divorce courts one way or another. But a man's sister is quite another matter. She is of his own blood. She is himself.'

Mary's dark eyes, so much less cynical than most Greeks', twinkled tolerantly.

'In spite of the fact that we are the world's greatest individualists, we hang together,' she said. 'If ever we went into a Greek hotel when we were in America, the proprietor would practically give us the place just because we spoke his language. . . .'

'We have heaps of Greeks in South Africa. They seem to emigrate a good deal.'

Chris said: 'The country is too poor to support its own population. The youngest son is generally a sort of Dick Whittington who goes in search of his fortune. Before the quota it was usually to America, where the streets are paved with gold! He probably signs on with the crew of a ship going to San Francisco or somewhere and deserts the moment she gets into port. Like as not he falls in with some fellow-countryman who is selling popcorn on the quay and who passes him on to a Greek restauranteur. He works at the restaurant for nothing but his board and lodging until he has learn to speak English. After that he is good for a wage unheard of in his own country. You get the same thing with the Yugo-Slavs.'

'But do these emigrants settle permanently in America?'

'Some do. But most of them come back, and then they do something for their town or village. Perhaps they donate a library or a school or whatever is needed. Most public buildings, and even roads, in Greece are given by private individuals; even warships sometimes – like the *Averof*.'

'We quarrel among ourselves like cat and dog,' said Penny, 'but we love our country.'

'The Greeks and the South Africans have a lot in common,' I laughed. 'Maybe it's climatic.'

And now Easter Day drew near and the flocks began to assemble in Athens. In Orthodox countries Easter is more important than Christmas, and the Easter lamb means to them what the Christmas turkey does to us. Sometimes in the fresh, mysterious hour before the dawn we woke to hear the muffled sound of a flock passing, a bleat or two, and the rough cries of the shepherd driving them towards the city.

'It must be getting near zero hour for Basil's lamb,' said Bertie.

On Good Friday all the flags flew at half-mast, and when Peter asked Diki about this the Russian looked at him reproachfully.

'Jesus Christ died today.'

Next evening Bertie and I were dining with friends at Psychico. At midnight, on our way home, we stopped the car outside a village church. The people were all coming out and embracing one another with the words 'Christ is risen' and the response 'He is risen indeed'. At the same time volleys of firecrackers, such as celebrate the Chinese New Year and our fifth of November, announced that the time for rejoicing had come.

When we arrived at the villa we found lights burning and Peter's bed empty. Slovakis was waiting up for us with Ero. He smiled as he said: 'Master Peter woke at midnight when the fireworks began next door. He ran out on to the balcony in his pyjamas, and the little Marika saw him and called out to him to join them. So he is over there now.'

As he spoke Agammemnon appeared with Marika and our son at his heels. Peter's head was still tousled from sleep and he was in his pyjamas and dressing-gown, but his eyes were wide awake and shining.

'Such wonderful fireworks!' he cried. 'Catherine wheels, and rockets that blew Pontius Pilate sky-high!'

Pontius Pilate was evidently a sort of Guy.

Agammemnon wished us the season's greetings. 'And tomorrow you must share our Easter lamb with us,' he added generously. 'There are two ready for the spit, and at five o'clock tomorrow morning I shall be up to superintend their cooking. Ah, how tender they will be by noon! You must come early to see them roasting.'

We demurred at intruding on his family party, but he waved away our objections with hospitable gestures. Those lambs! He kissed his fingers into the air and smacked his lips in anticipation, while Marika's limpid black orbs endorsed her father's invitation.

'Oh, Mom, we must go!' said Piet, unable to resist them. So we smiled and agreed to accept our neighbour's kind offer.

That night, when we had tucked Piet in and kissed him happy Easter, we went and stood on the balcony for a while.

There was moonlight on the sea, and here and there a chain of lights put out from the shore – the fishing caiques. A torchlight procession of children passed our house, laughing and singing, and we observed one little figure disengage itself and come into the garden. It was the boy Basil, whose parents joined him at the gate.

'They've been to the midnight Mass at the Russian Church in Athens,' said Bertie

At last the sporadic fireworks ceased and a fragrant silence enfolded the night. The lights in our neighbour's house were out, and presently Bertie laid his hand lightly on my arm.

'Listen!' he said. 'Our nightingale is getting up steam.'

The tenuous song was soft at first, just a tentative phrase or two. And then the little bird poured forth his crystal madrigal and we listened breathless to the high, thrilling coloratura. Suddenly, for no reason, it was cut off.

'Tantalizing little wretch,' I whispered. 'He always does that. It's as if he had just remembered something terribly important that must be done immediately.'

From the darkness we heard the low crooning of his mate.

'He'll tune up again,' said Bertie. 'His love-song is only interrupted. It is not over.'

We stood together in silence, with the soft spring scents of the night about us, as the nightingale resumed his serenade. From the dark branches of the cypress came trills and bubbles of melody and quivering silver ladders of sound. This was the rhapsody of all time. It was the very soul of ecstasy soaring to the stars on a stream of glittering song.

At daybreak on Easter Sunday the people of Greece began their preparations for feasting and merry-making. It was their custom to spend the whole day out of doors. 'The pagan element,' the Legation parson would say crustily. In woods and gardens, in the mountains and on the seashore the Easter lambs turned on the spits over the embers, and friends gave one another hard-boiled eggs dyed red or gaily speckled.

Next door Agammemnon and his wife and daughter and the servants grilled the two lambs under a pergola of roses, and the garden was set out with little tables.

Marika came early to fetch Peter, and when Bertie and I went over a little later we found our son already a trifle pale.

'I've eaten red eggs and cake,' he said. 'And brochettes. I'm a bit sorry about the brochettes.' (These were the innards of the lambs grilled on skewers.)

Presently the combined families of both Agammemnon and his wife Dora began to arrive. They greeted us warmly, and the ladies kissed Peter, while the gentlemen pulled and pinched his cheeks affectionately. He took these signs of good feeling in his stride.

At noon Greek champagne was poured into the glasses and the lambs were carved, and we partook of them. Many toasts were drunk. Soon after lunch Piet came over from the table where he was playing ludo with Marika and her cousins. He was bright yellow.

'I must go home,' he said. 'Quick!'

We took a hasty departure, only delayed by an old gentleman who, little realizing his peril, enveloped Peter in a bearded embrace. When the boy emerged from the bird's nest he had turned from yellow to green.

We made it in the nick of time.

'Gee!' said Peter with relief, when he and his Easter lamb had parted company. 'Gosh! that's better. It was all that cake did me in. And the brochettes. Sorry.'

In the woods behind our house the Diki family feasted with their Russian friends. It was evening when we saw them return. And – strange, delightful, unexpected sight – the lamb still frisked at the heels of the boy!

'How is that?' I asked Diki later. 'I thought you were going to eat the lamb for Easter.'

The Russian juggled with his double spectacles, and his mild

377

blue eyes, exposed for a moment, were half ashamed. He grinned a little ruefully.

'Our appetites and our necessity would make monsters of us, Madame. But in the end it is we who are devoured by our affections. Basil could not part with his pet. We ate today with friends. Later we will give the lamb to a farmer near Kefisia. He is getting too big to share our ménage.'

It was dawn as we watched *Coriolanus* take off from the rosy waters of Old Phaleron, smooth as a gull. She circled three times over the city and presently she was a mosquito in infinity. My heart sank.

'It's your turn to see him go, Joy-Joy,' said my husband gently. 'It's always been the other way round.'

I was glad that we were sailing with the Carolous that day. As we walked down to the landing-stage at Glyfada after an early breakfast we met a fisherman beating out an octopus on the rocks to make it tender. Octopus is a great delicacy in Greece.

When our row-boat arrived alongside the *Troll* we saw that Chris and Mary had a bigger party than usual. And as we stepped on board we were presented to two of the King's tall old uncles, Prince Andrew and Prince Christopher.

Prince Andrew had a sad austere face. His life had been dogged by tragedy, which culminated in the terrible air crash in which his beautiful daughter, the Archduchess of Hesse, and all her family, except one small son, were killed.

Prince Christopher had a funny round face, very pale, like an india-rubber doll, and he was a very amusing raconteur. He had small, white, lazy hands with a sapphire cabouchon ring on each third finger, and he told us tales of the magnificence of St. Petersburg, where he had been brought up at the court of the Tsar.

'I took it all entirely for granted,' he said. 'The jewels, the dresses of gold and silver and priceless brocade. The long embroidered trains and the corsages sewn with precious stones such as one never sees any more.'

He was a great admirer of Queen Mary.

'A truly fine and good woman,' he said. 'She always behaves with faultless taste and perfect dignity. She is shy and recoils from people until she knows them, when she is the most agreeable of companions.'

His American wife was in Rome, about to have her first baby. 'I hope it won't be a boy,' said Prince Christopher. 'This is no world for kings and princes these days. No more pomp and imperial glitter. More like a shot in the back.'

I saw him again several months later. He had a photograph of his new-born daughter in his pocket. 'Isn't she adorable? But I had a terrible time when she was born. Oh, it was awful! Men shouldn't have to go through such things! When my wife said, "I think we'll have to get the doctor now", I fainted dead away. I have never been so scared in all my life.' And his funny india-rubber face puckered with smiles. He had little joy out of the baby princess, as he died soon afterwards.

We sailed over to the island of Poros and bathed in the lee of a big white mansion in which Prince Andrew lived as a child. Like all Greek islands, Poros was bare of foliage, and one's eyes flinched from the arid mountainside and dazzling white houses.

Penny was at the helm when we set our course for Athens in the sunset – a figure out of the Heroic Age. The wind filled our tall white sails and we sped before it over Homer's 'wine-dark' Ægean. Chris lounged on deck and sang to us. He had a full rich baritone and he sang the songs of the islands while Mary's narrow fingers plucked softly at her guitar.

After dinner, when it was quite dark, old Prince Andrew came and sat beside me. He told me about his 'little place' in Monaco and his Siamese cat, who was more like a watchdog, and about many a campaign in the Balkans and Asia Minor. Prince Andrew was a seasoned warrior. He had fought three wars – the Balkan War, the Great War, and then the unlucky war against Turkey. Even then he had proved himself a determined foe, and I knew that when Ismet Ineunu had visited Greece he had asked that he might be presented to Prince Andrew. 'You, Sir, gave me some bad moments in Asia Minor,' he had said when they met.

My companion sighed and smiled as he leaned back in his deck-chair and stared up into the luminous heavens. 'Look at those stars! In other lands they seem far away. Here they lie in one's lap.'

And, indeed, it seemed that we might reach up and brush them from the sky.

CHAPTER FORTY-TWO

ROAD OF THE INVADER

IT was June and the pink oleanders were in bloom along the road to Glyfada. There was often mirage, and ships seemed to float above the water, or they appeared like an X-ray photograph, skeletons without substance.

'Very difficult to shoot at them when they look like that,' said my husband, who was first and foremost a man of war.

Life had moved out of doors and we dined on the terrace at night and slept on mattresses on our back balcony under the shoulder of Hymettus. All day long the shutters were down to keep out the heat, but at night we opened them wide to let the cool air circulate through the house.

A man with a bottle of tiny mosquito fish came round from the Health Department and told us to put them in our goldfish pond. These tiny transparent creatures, which, like ships in a mirage, appear to have no outer covering, have a wise safeguard against malaria. They devour mosquitoes voraciously.

The diplomatic merry-go-round had slowed down, but our warships were coming into Athens regularly from Nyon Patrol, and this meant a great deal of work for the Naval Attaché, and a great deal of pleasure for both of us. I found, to my surprise, that I had hungered for the sight of an English warship.

Towards the end of June we went to Turkey. Colonel Ross, the British Military Attaché to the Embassy at Istanbul and Ankara, was going to London for a military conference and taking his wife with him, so he had very kindly written and offered to lend us his flat in Pera if we could bring our own staff with us. The arrangement suited us admirably. '*Don't worry about a cook,*' he had written. '*Ours will stay on. But you need your own maid and valet.*'

We decided to go by car and to send Slovakis and Ero by sea with the heavy baggage.

Slovakis was delighted when he heard our plans. Only

through diplomatic channels could he ever have revisited the country of his birth, as Greeks expelled from Turkey were not permitted to return. And Ero, her dewy eyes swimming with pleasure informed me that the next few weeks would be 'a holiday for all of us'.

Diki, ever pessimistic, shook his grizzled head when he heard that we proposed to go without him.

'You will certainly require me to mend punctures and broken springs,' he grumbled. 'I know Macedonia. I drove a lorry there for seven years.'

He was disgruntled when we laughed at his warnings.

'At any rate,' he said dourly, 'you are unlikely to lose your way. Owing to the formation of the country, there are few roads and passes. The road to the north is self-evident. It is the road of the invader.'

The journey took us several days. It was, as Diki had said, the road of the invader. Many conquerors, from the noble Æcheans and the Macedonian hosts to the Bulgars and the Turks, had crossed those mountains and plains, and still more were to thunder south to the white city under the temple of Athena.

We spent our first night with Jack Bailey, the manager of the Kopais Estate, just beyond the pretty little town of Thebes, where once a wicked virgin-devouring Sphynx had thrived on his unseemly diet till Perseus came along. Perseus had guessed the feeble home-made riddle of the Sphynx, after which he was eligible to meet the creature in mortal combat. First taking the precaution of eating a dish of Kopais eels, the hero slew the Sphynx, and the virgins of Thebes breathed freely once more. Kopais eels were to the Thebans what spinach was to Pop-Eye. The vitamins these reptiles contained were of a highly belligerent nature, and no Theban or Athenian warrior ever went into battle unfortified by eels. It was therefore with some misgivings that we heard from Jack Bailey that Adolf Hitler had recently arranged to import several thousand Kopais eels into German rivers.

Kopais, once a wide lake hemmed in by mountains, had been drained and irrigated by a British engineering company, and was now one of the richest areas under cultivation in Greece. The company farmed the land and the tenants were thrifty Greek peasants. On the shores of this lake Alexander the Great, as a mere youth, had won his spurs against the Thebans – eels or no eels – in the Battle of Cheronea, and a huge white stone lion marked the spot.

But if Hitler had taken the bellicose eels out of Kopais, Jack Bailey, running true to traditional British form, had brought the racehorse in. Derby winners, having earned their leisure, now grazed in Greek pastures and mated with local mares, and the progeny of these unions won and lost us many a drachma at the Athens Racecourse.

We left on the next stage of our journey early in the morning. We had a picnic basket with us well replenished by Jack's cook. The plains, cut off from one another by tortuous mountain passes, were amber-gold with a rich harvest of wheat, or fluffy white with the cotton crop. The women worked in the fields, picking the cotton into their aprons, or cutting down the grain with curved sickles reminiscent of Millais' 'Reapers'. The men sat in the shade and talked politics. They seemed well satisfied with their lot.

'It is a good harvest,' said Bertie. 'That means the King-Metaxas régime will be popular. They will say the King is lucky for Greece.'

At noon the peasants hoisted squares of cloth on poles to shelter them for the hour of the siesta – little white sails riding a golden sea.

The nomad shepherds were grazing their flocks in the mountains, and often when we paused for our picnic lunch we could hear the thin tinkle of the goat-bells near some mountain spring that chuckled out of the rock.

There are few manufacturing areas in Greece and no chains of towns or suburbs. There is a city, a town, or a village, and the olive-groves, vineyards, and wheatfields flow right up to the white walls of the first houses. The people are still essentially pagan and pastoral at heart. Their religion stresses the glory of regeneration, and that is why Easter is more important to them than Christmas. It is the resurrection of Our Lord. And their festivals are of nature – the blessing of the waters and of the crops. Every year they watch the rebirth of nature and it is the spirit of the Earth-Mother which stirs in their grateful hearts.

Something of the same spirit quickened in my veins too on that journey north alone with my husband. A warm, bountiful sense of fulfilment, of rich harvests reaped, and of the spring that would blossom again in its appointed season. There is no death, I thought, only a time of lying fallow – whether for months, years, or centuries.

We made Larissa towards nightfall.

Our humble Greek hotel was on the Square, and opposite our window a minaret was silvered by the moon, for Northern Greece had been longer under the Turks than the south. On top of the minaret a stork was poised like a weathercock, and we saw that there were storks on every housetop.

Larissa, at the cross-roads of Thessaly and Macedonia, was a garrison town, and the cheerful Greek soldiers sat out in the gardens to drink a glass of oozoo or retsina and to eat their evening meal. Every land invader of Greece arrived at Larissa sooner or later, and it was there that the forces of Germany and Italy were to join hands and that earthquake was to add its horrors to those of war.

We went to bed early, drugged with sunshine and fresh air, and fell alseep instantly. I was awakened at about four in the morning by what I took to be machine-gun fire. Again and again there was a loud volley out in the Square.

I leapt out of bed and ran to the window.

'What's the matter?' asked Bertie sleepily.

'Machine-gun fire!'

'So it is!'

'It must be a revolution!'

He was beside me in a flash. But Larissa was sound asleep. Only the leaves in the gardens stirred, and a nocturnal feline prowler. And then we saw a great winged shadow obscure the moon as a stork flew across the silver disc and alighted on a roof. Once again the harsh mechanical rattle stammered into the night.

Bertie laughed and patted my shoulder.

'It's not a revolution. It's the clappering of the storks!' Their mating cry. Watch that chap up there! He's just raising his bill for another innings.'

'I prefer the nightingales', I said, as I crept back into bed.

When we paid our bill the manager presented us each with a white gardenia.

Small delightful gestures are never forgotten in Greece, for the people are gay and kindly and like to give pleasure. That is why they are so apt to promise things they know they cannot do. The pleasure derived from the giving and receiving of the empty promise, in their opinion, justifies the disappointment caused by its subsequent non-fulfilment.

Next evening at sunset we rumbled over the cobbles of Salonika to the house of the British Consul, with whom we were to stay the night.

We had dinner on the loggia, which faced seawards across the bay to the humpy outline of Mount Olympus, who still wore her white carpet of snow for the feet of Zeus and Hera and their merry company of boisterous pagan deities. The bay was uninviting and discoloured.

'The result of last night's vardar,' said the Consul. 'All through the summer we get the vardar, a wind which howls down the Vardar River valley from Serbia and churns up the bay and drenches the houses. That's why your bedroom window has double glass.'

Up to 1910 Salonika belonged to Turkey, and it was there that Mustapha Kemal was born and that he, Ismet, Enver, and their fellow-conspirators hatched the Young Turk movement and planned to overthrow Abdul Hamid, the Red Sultan.

'I suppose this is really Macedonia?' I asked the Consul.

'Yes,' he said. 'This is Greek Macedonia. But it is difficult to define Macedonia at all. After the war it became a sort of dumping-ground for unwanted populations, and at present it is part Greek, part Bulgarian, part Yugo-Slavian, and a small part Turkish.'

'Is it really a hotbed of terrorist activity – or is that just a legend?'

He laughed. 'It certainly isn't a legend. Political secret societies thrive there. The Bulgars are the most active. They are aiming for an autonomous Macedonian State under Bulgar "protection". In days gone by Macedonia's greatest export was leeches. They were used all over Europe for blood-letting. Well, blood-letting is still her chief stock-in-trade.'

The night was very still after the vardar, and out in the bay we could see the lights of little fishing caiques and row-boats, and we heard the fishermen singing in deep melodious voices, and from time to time they stamped their feet rhythmically in the bottom of their boats to frighten the fish into the nets.

The road up the Stuma Valley and over the mountains into

Bulgaria was, as Diki had warned us, unspeakable. Most of those Macedonian highways had been constructed by our troops during the first World War, and since then no one had troubled to keep them in repair.

'Blood-letting,' I said with a glance at the turbulent red-brown Struma River crashing through the hot green funnel of the valley, shot here and there with the blue flash of a kingfisher's wings. 'Blood of our troops, maybe!'

'More of them died of malaria and dysentery than in battle,' said my husband.

There was an ugly crunch as I took the car over a stone which turned out to be a tortoise.

My husband sighed. 'Difficult to avoid the mad rush of a tortoise!'

'The valley bristles with them.'

'The French soldiers used to tickle their tails, and when Mr. Tortoise put out his head they cut it off. Then they made soup of him, and they used his shell as a guitar – so he had his uses.'

'But that was Hermes' first action when he toddled out of his mother's cave!'

'A precocious infant,' said my husband.

The only difference between the operation as conducted by the infant deity and the adult poilu was the charming manner in which Hermes addressed his victim before disembowelling it.

' "Hail, darling and dancer, friend of the feast, welcome art thou! Whence gatst thou the gay garment, a speckled shell, thou a mountain-dwelling tortoise? Nay, I will carry thee within. Living shalt thou be a spell against all witchery, and dead then a right sweet music-maker."

'So spake he, and, raising in both hands the tortoise went back within the dwelling, bearing the glad treasure. Then choked he the creature, and with a gouge of grey iron he scooped out the marrow of the hill tortoise. He cut to measure stalks of reed and fixed them in through holes bored in the strong shell of the tortoise, and he fitted the bridge and stretched some harmonious cords of sheep gut. Then took he his treasure and touched the strings of the plektron, and wondrously it sounded under his hand, and fair sang the god to its notes.'

What the poilu said to the tortoise is unrecorded, and I doubt if he sang very fair to the notes of his 'right sweet music-maker'.

When we emerged from the valley into the meadows I was, for a spell, taken back to China. Here, as in Szechwan, the opium poppy bloomed, and the papery petals of the second crop fluttered in the hot wind.

We drove to the British Legation in Sofia towards evening. We felt as if our bones had been rattled and flung about like the contents of a witch-doctor's bag.

We had never met the British Minister and his wife before, but they put us at our ease immediately.

'We are dining early tonight,' said Lady Peterson when we had had tea. 'We have to go to a concert. An infant prodigy is going to punish the piano. We knew you wouldn't want to go after such a long hot journey, so you must just make yourselves at home.'

'We have some German friends coming to dinner,' added the Minister. 'A bit awkward, as we are not too sure what our relations are with Germany at the moment. However, the Von Bülows are charming.'

But there was another guest for dinner, and for the second time that day I was transported back to China to a moment on Peking Station when three kind friends had come to see me off – Jane, with her Tibetan lion-dog under her arm; Jack, with his kind, tired smile; and Charles, who was the only one left of those three. The sight of him now, detached and wise behind his glasses, and quite unchanged, eliminated time and space in a fashion even more satisfactory than that of Mr. Priestley.

I woke early to the sound of wooden wheels on the cobbles. That is the voice of a Balkan city – the deep, primitive rumble of a bullock-drawn farm-cart rattling over the pavé.

After breakfast in bed I washed my hair in the amazingly soft snow-water from the Vitocha and dried it in the garden. The sun on the rose-bushes filled the air with perfume. Lady Peterson, in gardening gloves and a huge straw hat, was busy replanting a flower-bed, and her youngest son, Colin, played chattily in a sand-pit near her.

Later we went for a drive and Lady Peterson pointed out a

not very impressive church where the usual Balkan tragi-comedy had been enacted.

Macedonian anarchists had taken it upon themselves to do away with King Boris, and, as a few lives one way or the other were of no account, they hit upon a not particularly subtle plan. First, they did away with a harmless and extremely distinguished old General – one whose funeral the King would be bound to attend. Then they planted a time-bomb in the church where the funeral service would take place. The bomb duly exploded at the scheduled time and some thirty celebrities were blown to perdition. When the bits and pieces were sorted out the King's were not among them. That sixth sense which is so necessary to European monarchs had warned him to keep away. But Boris was destined to die violently, and in 1943 his fate caught up with him.

Before we left Sofia we asked Lady Peterson to tell us a few words that would help us to ask our way if we got into difficulties.

'I'll write them down,' she said. '*Levo* means left, *desno* right, *praho* straight on, *dada* O.K., *molier* please or hi! and *duvish-denai* is good-bye.'

'What about "thank you"?' I asked.

She smiled. 'There is no Bulgarian word for "thank you". You might say the French "merci" if you feel inclined – but they say that in a country where the word does not exist the sentiment does not exist either.'

We could believe that when we saw the swarthy, heavy-featured Bulgarian peasants, so surly and truculent after the friendly good-natured country-folk of Greece, who always called out a greeting and quite often added the blessing, 'Whoever you are, good luck go with you!'

We stopped for our picnic lunch in the fir-forested heights of Cham Korea, where the swift mountain streams were alive with trout and grayling and where, in 1941, the German Military Staff set up their headquarters for the attack on Yugo-Slavia and Greece. Sometimes in the wild passes we had to stop to let a bullock-wagon convoy go by. Everybody in the long wagon-train slept except the leader. It was nearly nightfall when we came at last to the plain of Thrace and to the city of Adrianople* on the Maritza River. Adrianople, once the capital of

* *Now called Edirne.*

the Sultans in Europe, had long been in Bulgarian hands, and it was Mustapha Kemal who helped to regain it for Turkey in the Balkan War of 1912. Here we saw the first land fortifications of Turkey against attack through Bulgaria.

The domes and minarets etched their Eastern picture against the darkening sky as we crossed the glimmering river into the outskirts of this tumble-down city of gardens and avenues and ramshackle dwellings. The windows were stuffed with old rags and bits of brushwood and tin, and the worm-eaten, out-jutting porches looked ready to disintegrate at any moment, an appearance which was not even deceptive, as it was quite a common occurrence for people to fall through their over-hanging balconies into the road.

The squalor evident all round us was in odd contrast to the healthy high spirits of the boys and girls who stampeded our dusty car.

The hotel of Madame Marila, to which we were directed, was an ancient wooden Turkish house in a side street. Marila was a middle-aged Austrian woman, plump and blowzy, with a pale pretty face and wistful eyes. She showed us up the rickety stairs into a barn-like room, and when she opened the wooden shutters a cloud of dust flew in to join that which we had brought with us.

'My husband will bring you hot water to wash in. There is no bathroom. Will you dine here? I advise you to.' She smiled and added: 'I am the only person in Adrianople who understands the foreign cuisine. I could give you a nice steak and you could have some local wine with it. It isn't bad.' She spoke in French, and we were glad to accept her suggestions.

When we went down we found that dinner had been set for us in a little courtyard open to the stars and surrounded with plants. An aspidistra hobnobbed with a cactus *serpente*. The night was balmy and the meal delicious. The stiff weariness of the long drive fell away from us and we felt relaxed and re-freshed.

It was Bertie's country-bred eye which first picked out Micky.

'Look!' he whispered. 'What d'you make of that?'

The dark leaves of the aspidistra had parted to reveal a tiny inquisitive wide-browed face. The sensitive pointed muzzle quivered, red-brown eyes gleamed, and pointed russet ears twitched nervously.

'What is it? It looks like a bush baby, only its eyes aren't big enough.'

'It's a fox cub.'

Bertie is good with wild things, and presently he coaxed the little animal to take a bit of toast from his hand.

Marila smiled as she brought us our Turkish coffee. 'You are making friends with Micky – the impertinent one. Mookie is shy and timid. He is the wild one. You would never induce him to come to your hand.'

And then we saw the second cub gazing at us, bright-eyed, from behind the plants.

'Where did you get them?' asked Bertie.

'They sell them here,' she answered carelessly. 'Micky! Tsck, tsck, tsck! Come here, Mookie!' She called to them softly and threw them scraps of food. 'They know me already, and I have only had them a week. They are a month old. Soon they will be quite tame.'

'They are strange pets,' I said. 'What will you do with them when they grow up?'

She laughed. 'I will wear Micky and my daughter will wear Mookie. They are males, and males make the best furs.'

A tall, fair girl came into the courtyard. She had her mother's prettiness and a certain languor, derived, no doubt, from the handsome, charming, but indolent-looking Austrian who had brought us our hot water.

'Will you stay in Adrianople always, Madame?' I asked.

She shook her head and made a small frustrated gesture with a work-worn hand. 'Ah no. How can we do that? Our daughter is fifteen. Soon she must marry, and there is no match for her here. Even if we were willing that she should marry a Turk, the Government would not permit it. A new law has been passed forbidding Turks to marry aliens. No, we hope to return to Trieste next year. My husband came from Trieste, but it is not like it was. Trieste is Italian now.'

'Wonderful tank country,' remarked my husband as the car plunged over the flat Thracian fields in a cloud of thick grey dust. 'And there'll be a good crop of baby boys coming along

389

next year,' he added with a glance at the storks, thick as flies on every haystack and thatched roof.

The peasants believe that a baby boy will be born under any roof on which a stork has nested. The storks are not only a world-wide emblem of a fertile marriage, but they are themselves the most respectable of birds.

The Turkish Minister in Athens, Unayden, was a poet and something of a naturalist, and one afternoon he told me a story that amused and interested me. As he spoke his long narrow fingers played idly with a chaplet of shark's teeth.

'One summer when I was in Ankara a pair of storks nested on the roof of our house. There were some naughty boys who lived next door, and one day they succeeded in changing the storks' eggs for hens' eggs. When the chickens were hatched there was a great commotion. The parents were appalled at the little yellow fledglings scrambling about on the roof, and when Aunt Stork came to see the new babies she was shocked to the backbone. Within a few hours the scandal had spread far and wide among the bird community and the sky over our roof-tops was white with angry storks going into committee. The dupes were hauled out of their nest and publicly tried and condemned. Feathers flew like snowflakes as sentence was carried out, and our poor storks were pecked to death by the others. Nature accepts no excuses, Madame, and she suffers neither cheats nor fools.'

Bertie, who was driving, slowed down.

'The sea!' he said.

Beyond the ruffled golf of the wheatfields was the dazzling blue of the Marmara, and presently we saw the great turreted walls of old Constantinople with the history of Byzantium in every stone and crevice. In front of them were wide, deep moats, now transformed into market gardens, and behind them rose a dark fringe of cypresses and the shining spires of the minarets above the clustering cupolas of the mosques.

'Please stop! I just want to look – and think. . . .'

This was where Mahommed the Conquerer had come with his hordes five centuries ago, in the spring of 1452 – across Thrace from his capital at Adrianople to the walls of the city by the sea.

There was very little Mahommed didn't know about the policy of encirclement, and it couldn't have been much fun for the Byzantine Emperor, Constantine, to wake up one April morning and see the encampments of the infidel all along his land fortifications from the Marmara to the Golden Horn. The Turks were already the masters of Asia as far north as Ankara and of Europe from Athens to Hungary, but Constantinople still defied them. She lay within her impregnable walls, infinitely desirable, 'gleaming with gold and porphyry ... like a robe woven to the very fringe'.

For six weeks Mahommed bided his time, and every night the camp-fires of the infidel under the walls were reflected on the burnished dome of St. Sophia in the beleaguered city. It must have been a teasing 'war of nerves'. There were thirty thousand of Mahommed's janissaries waiting for Der Tag, and there were a mere seven thousand defenders on the battlements. Throughout the expectant nights the sentries called to one another from the towers, striving thus to keep awake and vigilant. At last, on the night of May 28th, Mahommed heartened his troops for the great effort of the morrow, and in the city there was the fatalism of the doomed. The people of Constantinople knew what had happened in other occupied Christian territories – men killed or worse, women raped, girls sold into slavery or into the harems, and boys enslaved or brought up in the barracks of the janissaries to become the most bloodthirsty of all the Conqueror's soldiers.

Incense was burned in the churches and prayers rose into the summer night. Men prepared to defend their city to the end, and women clung fiercely to their children, as mothers will when the hour of peril is at hand. Up on the moonlit battlements the Emperor Constantine went about among his men and urged them to fight to the death.

Next day when the sun was high in the heavens the great wall was pierced at the Gate of Romano and the dark tide of Islam surged into the city by the sea over the dead body of the last Christian Emperor of Byzantium.

I slipped my hand into my husband's.

'And now Istanbul!'

CHAPTER FORTY-THREE

PASHA'S PALACE IN PERA

As Colonel and Mrs. Ross had not yet left for England, we spent our first few days in Istanbul at the Park Hotel, which was very modern and commanded a superb view of the Bosphorus and the Marmara. There was dancing there every night, and it was a favourite haunt of the dictator, Mustapha Kemal Atatürk, the President of the Turkish Republic.

Just as Hitler had put a veto on jazz for Nazi youth, so Atatürk had forbidden the caterwauling of the Orient and imported instead the hottest jazz he could find to train the reluctant ears of his subjects to the syncopation of the West.

We arrived on a Saturday evening, and we were unpacking a few things in our room when Colonel and Mrs. Ross were announced.

'I'll go down and have a drink with Ross,' said Bertie, 'and Mrs. Ross might like to come and have a talk to you here. You'll want to fix up about moving into the flat and one thing and another.'

A few minutes later there was a knock at the door and a sleek dark head looked in.

'Is thees Mrs. Packer's room? Good. I am Mrs. Ross.' She pronounced it 'Rorse'.

'Do come in. I'm sorry about all this muddle, but my husband has just changed.'

Tania Ross waved away the apology with a thin nervous hand and perched on the end of the bed amid a confusion of half-packed garments.

'Don't worry. Alick is same. Men never hang up clothes. May I smoke?'

She was Russian, with all the temperament and tragedy of her race in her tawny eyes. Tania's eyes! I can see them still — those hurt, fighting eyes under level brows, screwed up and staring through the thin blue haze of her inevitable cigarette. Eyes are the mirrors of the past, and those who have seen violence and endured fear and despair can never erase the reflection. Look into the eyes of a man or a woman and you will know how they have lived.

Tania, as a young girl, had escaped from Red Russia with her sister through Vladivostok and China, and the experiences of which she never spoke lay at the back of those eyes of hers.

'I have a message for you,' she said. 'You are dining weeth Ambassador tomorrow night.'

'But my hair! I tried to set it in Sofia and made a mess of it. Can I get it done here tomorrow?'

She dilated her fine sensitive nostrils and allowed a stream of smoke to escape them. Her voice was deep and husky and she had a harsh little smoker's cough.

'Tomorrow is Sunday.'

'But does that make any difference in a Moslem country?'

'Certainly it makes difference.' (Tania never used an 'a' or a 'the' in her conversation, for there is no article in the Russian language.) 'Sunday is holiday in Europe, so it must be holiday in Turkey. Kemal wants European Turkey. But I weel ring up wife of American Military Attaché. She has man comes to her house to do her hair. Perhaps we can get hold of him.'

She seized the receiver and asked for a number in French.

'Is that Mrs. Washington? Yes, Tania speaking. Listen. I have friend here – wife of new Naval Attaché. She is dining weeth Ambassador tomorrow night and must have hair set. . . . Yes, I know it is too late today, but what about tomorrow? Can I find your man? . . . Not on Sunday. Are you sure? That is peety. Then there is nothing to be done? . . . Oh, has *everybordy* heard that I danced with Atatürk last night? Yes, ma chère, I *deed*! He is nice comfortable dancer, like rorking-horse. . . . No, he *deed* not! But then he has been sick for long time and I don't think he is well yet. . . . Yes, we weel come round for cocktail tonight. Sure! Good-bye.'

'Did you dance with the dictator?' I asked, completely awed.

She laughed. 'I had honour to be his partner for two dances at cabaret last night.'

'Is he really as wicked as he is made out to be?'

'He has been very ill and he does not make so many scandals.' She coughed and lit another cigarette. 'I am sorry you cannot have hair set tomorrow. On Monday perhaps. There is Russian here can do it. Deed you have good journey?'

'Yes, very, on the whole. The roads are incredible, of course, and jangled my bones like a bunch of keys. And I've been bitten by bugs.'

Tania gave her short husky laugh. 'You must not worry about bug. Bug is everywhere in Turkey. He is in wooden house, in train, in bed, in lavatory. You weel get used to bug.'

I shuddered, but she was right. I got used to bug. Like the poor, he was ever with us.

Presently, when we had made suitable arrangements about taking over the flat, we went down and joined our husbands.

I would have known Alick Ross anywhere by the likeness of his brother George, who had been Assistant Naval Attaché in Tokyo. He had the same Slav cast of countenance and the same attractive speaking voice. When he cared to exert it he had his brother's charm, but when he was angry he could look sullen and dangerous. But one didn't get angry in Istanbul. The climate was relaxing and kind to tempers. It was Ankara that set people's teeth on edge and made them snappy as evil-natured dogs.

Next evening we made the acquaintance of Sir Percy Loraine, the Ambassador.

A gorgeous Montenegrin in a scarlet-and-gold bolero and black satin knee breeches admitted us into the palatial Embassy. His smile, under a pair of black moustachios like antlers, was so dazzling that I reeled.

Lady Loraine was in Rome, staying with her mother, and so Sir Percy was alone. The only other guests were Colonel and Mrs. Woods.

Colonel Harold Woods, the Commercial Attaché to the British Embassy in Turkey, was a cadaverous man, no longer young, with melancholy light green eyes and a hushed way of talking as if he were visiting a sick-room or telling a secret. He had lived most of his life in Turkey and had fought through the Dardanelles campaign with the Australians. His wife, who was small and plump, was one of the kindest people in the world. They owned a lovely old Turkish house in Istanbul, but in the summer they moved to the island of Principo in the Marmara.

I have known Sir Percy Loraine in various circumstances and many different settings, but my first impression is still the most vivid.

We were ushered into a pleasant sitting-room which had none of the stiff formality one expects of an official establishment. The valuable Persian and Turkish rugs, the pictures and ornaments, and the carefully arranged flowers, combined to create an atmosphere of culture and luxury. There was a fire crackling merrily in the grate and the room had a human lived-in feeling.

Then we heard the Ambassador's step, unhurried and deliberate, with a characteristic little drag in it.

Sir Percy came of a long line of baronets from the north of England, and there was a look of race in his clear-cut features and penetrating speculative blue eyes. His close-clipped moustache and thick wavy hair were iron-grey, and all his words and actions were informed with fastidious deliberation. He was a man so accustomed to assert authority that he wielded it without effort or ostentation. It is the man with small beginnings who feels the instinctive need to impress others.

We dined in the 'miniature room'. Here again the bleak comfort of the Embassy had been warmed by the touch of a connoisseur, and the ambassador's collection of exquisite Persian miniatures adorned the walls. Those delicate, elaborate little pictures satisfied some highly evolved instinct in their owner, who sought after perfection in all things.

Sir Percy had been British Minister in Persia and High Commissioner in Egypt before he was appointed to Turkey. His knowledge of Near Eastern problems was immense, and he had a strong flair for reading an alien mind. His personal friendship with Atatürk will one day find its place in history as a turning-point in world affairs.

Atatürk, who was himself a strange inspired hybrid of heaven and hell, recognized in this tall elegant Englishman a rare suppleness of mind and a sympathetic understanding that accorded well with his absolute integrity. And the two men had in common a love of gambling. There were many nights when Sir Percy played poker till dawn with the Turkish dictator, and then sat up till breakfast-time discussing foreign policy. Atatürk drank his countless glasses of rakia, and Sir Percy never touched anything but an occasional whisky. Two wedges of red appeared in the broad high cheek-bones of Kemal, while the mind of the Abassador functioned with perfect clarity, recording every detail of the conversation, guiding it dextrously, and sensing when a flash of sentiment, humour, or anger would shift the uneasy weight in the scales more favourably.

During dinner the talk turned on war and diplomacy.

'What is war?' asked the Ambassador, fixing my husband with a steely eye.

'Surely,' smiled Bertie, 'it is the failure of diplomacy?'

There was a characteristic hiatus while Sir Percy selected the best verbal weapons from an imposing armoury.

'Not at all. War only follows the breakdown of diplomacy, which is usually caused by the hasty and ill-considered action of the man with the sword. Acting on his own initiative, he frequently creates a situation which nullifies all the patient efforts of the diplomat to keep his country in the way of peace. Let me quote an instance.' This he did and proved his case conclusively.

'I think, sir,' said my husband, 'that the case you have just mentioned shows a lamentable lack of understanding between the diplomatic and the fighting Services. If the Army and the Navy abroad knew more about the Foreign Office, and if the Foreign Office had greater sympathy with the C.-in-C. who is expected to keep order on the spot, there might be fewer of these inflammable incidents.'

Sir Percy agreed that this was so. 'The left hand and the right are too often in ignorance of each other's activities. But there is one thing you should know about diplomacy, N.A. The duty of a diplomat is not so much to avert war at any price as to ensure that, if war is inevitable, his country will at least have the right allies. It takes many years of persevering peace-time effort to accomplish as much.' He spoke earnestly and with emphasis, and I guessed that he was thinking of his own task in Turkey, where the German influence had been paramount for close on half a century. If the pendulum was now swinging over to friendship with Great Britain, it was because the unremitting efforts of the Ambassador had set it in motion.

The Rosses' flat in Pera had once been the women's quarters of a pasha's palace. It was high, airy, and spacious, and pigeons nested on the window-ledges.

Hélènie, the cook Tania had left for us, said that the pigeons were sacred birds and gave them some of the straw in which

Slovakis had packed various ingredients for cocktails. The pigeons, like all privileged classes, proved themselves lazy and improvident, and the nest Hélènie had built for the young couple on my window-sill was misused to accommodate a Bohemian ménage à trois. One of the ladies laid two eggs, the other sat on them, then everybody got bored and flew away on pleasure bent. When they returned, obviously the worse for wear, father clumsily rolled one of the eggs off the ledge, while the other addled from lack of pre-natal care.

A host of cats watched the antics of the sacred pigeons wistfully, but the days of the cats were numbered, for there was a pogrom in operation against them. Just as the stray dogs of Istanbul had once been taken wholesale to a barren rock in the Marmara, now known as Dog Island, and left there to die of thirst and madness, so now the stray cats were being liquidated by order of the Government. All except the rare Ankara cats. And these long-haired snow-white aristocrats with their curious two-coloured eyes were rapidly becoming extinct on their own. They were stone-deaf and most of them found an untimely end under the hasty wheels of Istanbul taxis.

Hélènie had a small daughter to whom she was deeply devoted. The child was all eyes like a bush baby, and it wore a red-and-blue bead on its pinafore against the evil eye.

'Do you really think that charm helps?' I asked Hélènie, recalling that Greek horses wore bead necklaces for the same reason.

'Oh yes, Madame!'

'What would happen if somebody put the evil eye on the child?'

'She would become pale and listless and she would pine away . . .'

The fat Turkish woman's heavy brows drew together and she made a quick protective gesture towards the child. 'It is wise to wear a talisman.' She spoke in French.

We found on the golf course a tame lamb similarly adorned. He wore his beads rakishly over his left ear.

Our borrowed flat was full of the strong exotic personality of its owners. The large rooms were attractively furnished and they were comfortable and unusual, though rather bare. The atmosphere was very pleasant. Most things I wrote up my diary in Alick's study. On his big desk was a little bookstand of dictionaries – German, French, Italian, Turkish, Greek, and all the Slav languages from Russian to Bulgarian. The Military Attaché was an exceptionally versatile linguist.

Every morning the soldiers went by to drill on the hill. The steady tramp of their feet and their deep, stirring marching songs were part of the rhythm of modern Turkey. Their faces were rough and brutish, but young and healthy. And they laughed readily. Like the children of Adrianople, they looked happy.

Mrs. Woods took us sightseeing. She knew every inch of Istanbul. As a little girl she had lived there in the days of purdah and eunuchs and harem slaves. She knew all the stories and legends of the city and of the Bosphorus, and she could tell them well. With her we saw the bazaars and the palace of the Byzantine Emperors on the water-front, which was later used by the Sultans as the seraglio. Attached to this palace, like a long narrow pent-house, was the kafess (which means 'cage'), where the heir to the Sultan's jewelled throne had invariably been imprisoned in the exclusive and corrupt company of eunuchs and sterile odalisks, so that when he finally came to power he was generally as addled as the unhatched egg of our sacred pigeon. It was by incarcerating the heir that the Sultans made sure that no usurper would threaten their power. And they had an agreeable little habit of making assurance doubly sure by personally strangling all their brothers the moment they ascended the throne.

Religion had suffered in Turkey, as is always the case after a revolution, and the ill-attended mosques were falling into disrepair. One afternoon, as we were passing by the Blue Mosque, we heard the muezzins on the minarets calling the faithful to prayer. Several people bowed down, some took no notice, and others went into the mosque. We followed these last after removing our shoes.

D. H. Lawrence has said that blue is the colour of wind and of atmosphere, of distance and of thought. Sunlight filtered through the violet stained-glass windows and cast blue reflections upon the white marble pillars and intensified the colours of the precious turquoise tiles on the walls. At the far end a plain glass window was open to the Bosphorus and the blue sky. A priest was conducting a service in front of it, and a number of men knelt before him. Women were not allowed to approach more than half-way down the mosque. Here they were not yet regarded as the equals of man. We noticed that the men were all very curiously hatted. This was a repercussion of Kemal's order that the fez be abandoned on pain of death. Some wore skull-caps, others had pulled handkerchiefs, knotted at the corners, over their heads, and still more wore caps with the peaks at the back. The abolition of the fez had incommoded the faithful. A good Moslem must wear a head-covering in church and must also touch his forehead to the ground in performing his devotions, an exercise to which the intransigent headgear of the West does not lend itself.

Afterwards I said to Mrs. Woods: 'The Moslem religion permits polygamy. Is it still allowed in Turkey?'

'No,' she said. 'Polygamy was made illegal in 1926.'

'But is woman really regarded as man's equal here?'

Mrs. Wood's plump little hand disclaimed such a ridiculous notion. 'You can't alter the mental attitude of centuries in a day. But Kemal has done wonders towards their complete emancipation. Women are no longer the toys and prisoners of men. They are being educated to recognize their duties as citizens.'

'I read somewhere that a woman was publicly hanged on Galata Bridge to prove that there was perfect equality between the sexes.'

Mrs. Woods said, rather firmly: 'Mightn't it be more to the point to consider that in 1932 the first woman was appointed to the Turkish Diplomatic Service? We haven't got that far ourselves.'

Of all the weird, mysterious tales of the Byzantine Emperors and the Turkish Sultans, none were more strange and bizarre than those told of Mustapha Kemal Atatürk.

Kemal, like Stalin and Sun Yat Sen, was the born revolutionary and reformer. As a young Macedonian Turk in Salonika he and his confederates had plotted against the degenerate Red Sultan. As a soldier in the Great War he had fought a losing battle on the barren cliffs of the Dardanelles and turned it into a victory, and when, after the Great War, the Greek forces occupied Asia Minor he had mustered his war-weary troops and made them into an army strong enough to clear the Greeks out of Asia Minor altogether. Kemal's goal was to modernize and revitalize a nation that had long been oppressed and demoralized under the rule of decadent Sultans. And he had to work quickly. That is the trouble with dictators. The time factor is heavily against them. The evolution of a national creed and a new form of government has to be compressed into the limited span of one human being's maturity.

Kemal had lived wildly. He knew that he would never reach old age, and he was going to put new Turkey on the map before he went the way of all flesh.

Bertie is an indulgent husband, and one day he came home with a present for me.

'I bought him from a taxi-driver who was taking him to the lethal chamber. Hell's delight! He's covered me with white fur.'

He was a beautiful example of a dying race – a Sultan among cats. His fur was soft and snowy, his feet were large and so were his ears, with a sharp lynx-look about them – deaf ears lined with pink satin to match his delicate little nose. He stared at me with two hostile jewels, one blue, one gold.

'Miaow,' said our Ankara cat. 'Miaow-aow.' And his voice was husky and uncertain, now loud, now soft, as is the way with those who cannot hear.

We gave him a saucer of milk and he thought better of us.

Slovakis' blue eyes squinted a trifle. 'What about the sacred pigeons now?'

Hélènie, pouring a little more milk into the saucer, said: 'Turkish cats respect pigeons.'

'I shall call him Mustapha,' I said.

Hélènie pursed up her lips. She did not approve.

Mustapha was no ordinary cat. He went daily down our five flights of stairs into the garden, apparently intent upon stalking the humble birds, who were not sacrosanct. He was a white tiger, low on the ground, stealthy and without mercy. But we soon discovered that bird-catching was only a blind. He had other, more important, business in the garden. We knew this when he came back exhausted and dishevelled, disguised in a harlequin suit, black on the underside.

'He has been sliding down the coal-shute on his stomach,' said Ero.

Mustapha fell into a coma and slept all afternoon. In the

gloaming he woke, stretched, collected himself, and strolled into the kitchen for an aperitive. Then he undulated haughtily down the white marble stairway of the pasha's palace.

We watched him from our window, over the restless blue-grey heads of the sacred ménage à trois, as he stepped into the garden.

He was an animal with rare powers of concentration. The evening twittering of the common birds did not disturb him, for he heard them not. He sat outside the coal-shute and washed his face with his big hands, fiercely and with determination, and no sooner had he pressed down a sharp lynx ear with the damp camber of his elbow than up it went again.

Presently we saw half a dozen sly, low shapes slink out of the shadows. Tabbies, black cats, white cats, and ginger-haired girls. One by one they approached the coal-shute. Mustapha desisted from his ablutions long enough to motion them in, and each in turn they slithered down into the dusty black maw of the coal-cellar.

'I'll venture to say he is the leader of an underground movement,' remarked Bertie. 'All those beasts down there have a price upon their heads.'

'It's his harem,' I said, profoundly shocked.

'He's a Turk,' said my husband. 'In any case, it seems to me that he is qualifying for the title of Atakat – Father of all the Cats.'

One night, at a dance, the Spanish Chargé d'Affaires came to speak to me.

'Madame,' he said, 'I hear you have an Ankara cat of great beauty and personality.'

'That is so, Monsieur le Chargé.'

'Well, it happens that I have three such enchanting creatures myself. A lady and two young boys. The lady has reached years of indiscretion and seeks a husband, and unfortunately the boys are too callow and slumsy to respond suitably to her charming advances. Dare I suggest, chère Madame, that your excellent animal spends a few days in our keeping?'

'But certainly, Monsieur. Our cat is of an enterprising disposition, and we have reason to believe that he is also an animal of experience – though young.'

So a glittering Hispano Suiza, flying the Spanish flag, drew up at the palace of the pasha on Pera Hill, and two footmen, gorgeously attired and bearing a large basket between them, climbed the white marble stairs.

Mustapha Atakat was called forth and placed therein. The gold and the blue light flickered for a brief instant of astonishment before being extinguished by the lid.

When I told Bertie what had come to pass, he said: 'A diplomatic faux pas, my Joy. Our policy with regard to Spanish affairs is strictly non-interventionist!'

CHAPTER FORTY-FOUR

MARMARA MEMORIES

I SAW Atatürk for the first time at Modhur Regatta.

The Ambassador had invited several of his staff to go out in his steam yacht *Makook II* for the afternoon's regatta, and in the evening we were to change and dine on board and then go to the dance at the Yacht Club.

Modhur Bay was crowded with scores of yachts, sailing-boats, motor launches, speed-boats, and row-boats, all gaily beflagged, and the afternoon was already waning when a plume of smoke was sighted on the beautiful skyline of Istanbul over in the west. And then as the dictator's long white yacht *Ertegrül* – English-built on the lines of *Victoria and Albert* – entered the harbour everything that could make a noise made it, and for a full minute and a half the bay resounded with the penetrating notes of hooters, whistles, sirens, and bells.

The *Ertegrül* took up her station alongside the *Makook* and we saw the dictator standing bareheaded on the after-deck. His thinning grey hair was stirred by the breeze, and there was a certain nobility and command in the way he held his head. He was a little over medium height, a compact well-knit figure. For once he was not in the tails and white tie which he had affected as a sort of uniform for all occasions, suitable and unsuitable, and his white sports shirt, under a blue blazer, was open at the throat. He was surrounded by his staff and guests – the women standing a little apart. Most of them were pretty and smart in gay printed dresses that bore the hall-mark of Paris.

But three women were singled out to take their places near the dictator. On his right was Afet, who was said to be his favourite and his confidante – a heavy masculine-looking woman with a dark powerful face, the historian of New Turkey. Next to her was Makbule, his sister, to whom he was devoted, and on his left was Sabiya Gokcen, the aviatrix. She was very small and slim with an attractive little face, somehow fey, yet determined. She was nineteen years old and an officer in the Turkish Air Force. Sabiya had already been on active service. She had raided a rebel encampment, and the insurgents had done their best to shoot her down. She had been promoted to squadron leader after that, an example to girls who hoped to become amazons of the air. She had trained a corps of girl parachutists, and was, in her own way, one of Kemal's most spectacular 'adopted daughters'.

Atatürk's 'adopted daughters' were girls of particular talent and personality who were educated at his personal expense and sent abroad to study whatever their special subject might be. They were trained to be the pioneers of Western culture in Turkey. An aura of glamour and notoriety surrounded these girls, a lurid reflection of the strange fires that leapt and crackled round the private life of the dictator. It was even whispered that the younger ones, still in Ankara, were guarded by eunuchs, and that one girl who had been studying in Paris had thrown herself from the window of the Orient Express on her way back to Turkey. Such were the rumours. The facts were self-evident. The 'adopted daughters' of Atatürk were the leaders of the new womanhood that was struggling out of the terrible soul-destroying bondage of purdah. Sabiya was not the only one among them with wings. Her sisters, like herself, were no longer earth-bound chattels to be sold like cattle into the harems, there to be for ever subordinate to the carnal desires of man. They had grown into entities with the right to think, to learn, to live, and to love in freedom. They were indebted to Atatürk beyond price or measure.

Presently the dictator sat down and we saw a child clamber on to his knee, a wild little thing with black elf locks blowing across a precocious gypsy face.

'That is his mascot, Ülkü,' murmured Harold Woods at

my side. 'She goes everywhere with him – even to the cabarets.'

I heard the full story of Ülkü later from a Turk. The little one was the daughter of a servant who had worked faithfully for Atatürk's mother in Salonika and who was now married to a railway employee at Chiflye, the dictator's model farm near Ankara. One day he had visited the woman and her husband, and the child, then aged two, had played so agreeably in the room and had so delighted Atatürk with her engaging ways that he had staightway adopted her and taken her home, much to the gratification of her parents.

It must have been a strange upbringing for the child – to be the pet and plaything of a dying man, half god, half devil. Sometimes it amused him to give her rakia to drink and to dress her as if she were a doll-woman of London or Paris. He always treated her as if she were grown up, and she never knew what it was to be with other children or to play childish games. So now, at five years old, she had acquired a queer unnatural sophistication. She adored her benefactor, and when she saw that he was tired and jaded she would nestle into his arms and say: 'Atatürk, you are tired. Let us have some music so that you may relax.'

The music was red-hot jazz.

Kemal had no children of his own, though for a brief period he had been married to Latife Hanum, who was the rich, beautiful, highly educated young woman in whose house he had elected to set up his headquarters during the occupation of Smyrna, when the Greeks were driven into the sea. But the love which was born against a background of flame and death did not endure, and three years later, in 1925, they were divorced.

The races were over and the afterglow of the sunset washed the dancing water and the white-winged yachts with rose, while the clustering domes and thin minarets of Istanbul were silhouetted against the painted sky.

We changed and dined on board and went ashore later to the dance at Modhur Yacht Club.

During the evening Aras, the Minister for Foreign Affairs (later Turkish Ambassador to the Court of St. James), came to our table to talk to Sir Percy.

Aras was a bird-man – bald and heavy-beaked, with a too big head that pecked this way and that. His nervous fingers were never still, his knee twitched under the table, and his foot tapped softly on the floor. His protruding red-rimmed eyes darted all over the room.

'Excellence,' he said suddenly, 'I wish to present a most beautiful lady to you. I will fetch her if you will excuse me.' And he disappeared with quick short strides and returned presently with a young woman of the goose-girl type at his heels. She was very young and her voluptuous curves strained against the restrictions imposed upon them by her tight-fitting taffeta dress. She sat, stolid as a suet pudding, while Aras, now less agitated, talked to the Ambassador with his thick lips close against Sir Percy's ear.

That was one of the interesting things about parties in Turkey as compared with Athens and Belgrade. There was less diplomatic fencing and more getting down to business. Members of the Turkish Cabinet, following the example of their leader, were at their most voluble and receptive between midnight and breakfast-time.

Soon after midnight we left.

The *Makook* slid gently out of Modhur Bay to a little inlet round the corner, and there we bathed in the moonlight, and the cool refreshing water banished the stickiness of the hot, crowded ballroom.

Harold told me the stories of the Marmara and the Bosphorus as we sailed past dreaming islands.

'See that islet near Dog Island? That's Bulwer's Island, named after the British Ambassador who built a mansion on it for the Turkish princess with whom he was madly in love.' And later, when we came in sight of the white lighthouse that marked the entrance to the Bosphorus, he said: 'That's Leander's Tower. There was once a pasha who had read in his daughter's horoscope that she would die of a serpent's tooth. So he built a tower in the sea where no serpent could come near her. But one day a handsome pirate captain called Leander sailed past under her window, and their eyes met and they fell in love. Every night he swam secretly to her tower and by day he sent her baskets of fruit and flowers, which she drew up to her window on a piece of rope. And one sad day a tiny snake like Cleopatra's asp crept into the lover's gift, and as the pasha's daughter put her cheek to the petals of a rose the asp bit her, and the fate foretold for her came true. So you see, my dear, no one can escape their destiny.'

We disembarked at the little pier by Dolma Bagtché Palace and drove home.

A few cats, taking their lives in their paws, prowled stealthily. Over fifteen thousand had already demonstrated that even nine lives are not proof against the lethal chamber. All the dogs in the world seemed to be howling to the moon.

'Listen to the ghosts from Dog Island,' I said.

'Those are no ghosts. You can't stamp out dogs and cats any more than you can stamp out human beings, as Herr Hitler will find out one of these days,' said Bertie.

Next morning we heard that soon after our departure the President had appeared at the dance in great form and one of his most mischievous moods, when it amused him to cause everybody the maximum amount of embarrassment. He picked on a pretty English girl who had been brought up in Turkey.

'Do you speak Turkish?' he asked in French.

'Mais oui, Monsieur le President.'

'Splendid! Then you will stand up and sing for us in Turkish!'

The girl had a charming voice and, in spite of her shyness, she was able to comply with Atatürk's command.

The President then proceeded to demand turns from all and sundry, selecting the fattest and most ungainly for dance numbers, regardless of age, rank, or nationality.

Modhur Yacht Club. Strange that it meant nothing to Kemal to go there and amuse himself so well. Surely he must have remembered, if only for a moment, that its last president had been Dchjavid the Jew, his erstwhile friend.

Dchjavid had been publicly hanged in Ankara one hot August night in company with a dozen others in one of those purges that seem so essential to dictatorships. And, by order of Kemal, a ball had been given at Modhur to celebrate the occasion.

Lady Loraine had returned to Istanbul, and soon afterwards the Third Secretary rang us up to say we were expected to lunch at the Embassy next day.

'We are going out in the *Makook* in the afternoon, and in the evening the Prime Minister, Ismet, is coming on board, and also Fethi and Madame Fethi.'

Lady Loraine was tall and dark with a small queenly head well set upon her slight shoulders. Illness had set shadows round her eyes, but that afternoon she was at her best and gayest.

We left the sticky heat of Istanbul behind and a couple of hours later the *Makook* was anchored under the lee of one of the islands. A ruined monastery was the only habitation in sight, deserted except for two mad old monks.

'This was a favourite bathing-place of the Russians,' remarked Harold Woods, and added a little wistfully: 'They wore no bathing suits.'

Tales of 'the Russians' were many and various. The Revolution had chased them all over the Balkans by way of the Crimea just as it had let them loose on China through Vladivostok and Manchuria.

'The bazaars in those days were worth visiting,' put in Mrs. Woods. 'There were wonderful bargains to be picked up.'

'Yes,' said Harold. 'When the Russians flooded Istanbul in 1920 they were homeless and destitute, with nothing but their furs and jewels. They had to sell their heirlooms to live for a few days, and the bazaars overflowed with treasures to be bought for a song. Archduchesses and princesses – real ones – wandered about the streets starving. They sang and danced in the cabarets if they had the talent. If not they haunted them in the hopes of finding someone to give them a meal. Women of royal birth were marrying Tommies of our army of occupation as a means of getting a roof over their heads. Others were forced by necessity into the oldest profession of all.' He sighed. 'Yes, that was the time to pick up a bargain.'

I laughed. 'You refer, of course, to jewels and furs?'

A pale gleam of amusement crept into his light green eyes and his grey moustache twitched. 'Of course.'

We bathed from the yacht. Lilos were flung into the water, and we lay on them and were rocked on the sparkling sea. I took off my cap and let the sun and breeze play through my hair. The air was fresh and clear with the taste and odour of salt in it and drifts of resinous pine perfume from the wooded slopes above the cove.

At sunset we sailed round to Principo to pick up Fethi and

Madame Fethi, and then to Halkis for Ineunu, who came on board with his secretary.

Fethi Okyar was then Turkish Ambassador in London, and he was on leave for a few weeks at his island home in the Marmara.

General Ismet Ineunu, now President of the Turkish Republic, was then its Prime Minister. He was also Atatürk's closest friend and disciple. He alone among the dictator's satellites was never afraid to disagree with his master. He was a man nearing sixty, stubborn as a mule, honest and forthright, exceptionally brave, and reputed to be quite without mercy. He was a man of undeviating purpose and his national aims were those of Atatürk. Both men desired, above all else, the peaceful internal development of their country and the education of their people. Kemal's methods had been surrealist. By shock he had emptied the Turkish mind of its preconceived ideas and by violence he had implanted new ones. The fez and the veil had gone, so also had the flowing Arabic script, the amenities of polygamy, and the ancient Turkish titles. Every man had been compelled to take a surname. Kemal's own was significant and apt for a dictator. Mustapha Kemal means 'Perfect Choice', and Atatürk is the patriarchal title 'Father of all Turks'. Ismet means 'Honest', and Ineunu was the place where the little General had fought his most famous battle. To educate his Ministers to a sense of historic proportion Atatürk had insisted that they all read Wells's 'History of the World'. He commanded also that they learn French. It was a sign of the times, however, that Ismet, in spite of his deafness, had set himself the task of learning English, and that the grandchildren of the Foreign Minister, Aras, had an English nurse.

Night was falling as we dropped anchor in a quiet bay. A sombre forest loomed over a silver strip of beach. The moon rose, enormous as only a harvest moon can be, and the *Makook* lay in solitude and beauty, wearing the shimmering Marmara like a sequin robe.

After dinner we played bridge on deck. Bertie, Tommy Elmhirst, Fethi, and Mrs. Woods at one table, and Sir Percy, Ineunu, Madame Fethi, and I at the other.

Ineunu was short, stocky, and sallow, with a small moustache and a predatory hooked nose. He was deaf as an Ankara cat, and his brilliant brown eyes were suspicious and alert – listening eyes, dramatized by short, thick, black eyebrows, winged like the eaves of a Chinese temple. Every now and again the breeze lifted his thin crest of silvery hair and then he wore the remote bird-deity look of a stone Pharaoh. His voice was husky and harsh, now too loud, now too soft, as if his deafness had thrown its timbre out of gear. His courage over his disability was extraordinary. He refused to allow it to isolate him, and in some strange way he transformed it into a distinguishing mark. He could lip-read Turkish, Greek, French, and a little German and English, and men feared those listening eyes that pierced the walls of silence and heard their thoughts.

It was after midnight. Ineunu was my partner. Madame Fethi opened the bidding. She had a dreamy intellectual face and spoke perfect English, French, and German. Her bridge was excellent.

'One spade,' she said in French.

I called 'One no trump', and Sir Percy passed. The other game had broken up, and Fethi stood behind the Prime Minister's chair, his broad Tartar countenance and hooded eyes expressionless.

Ineunu slapped his hand down on the table, face downwards, and looked round at us with defiance and merriment.

'Grand slam in hearts!' he cried in his thick uneven French.

Fethi's slow smile congratulated the gambler who is playing his luck.

As I put down my cards Ineunu laughed aloud like a delighted child and stretched his hand across the table to clasp mine and shake it.

'We have it!' he exclaimed with gusto.

Afterwards Madame Fethi turned to me and murmured in English: 'Just as well you won that rubber, or we'd have been here till morning. The Prime Minister never goes home till he has won.'

CHAPTER FORTY-FIVE

ANKARA, WHERE MEN GO MAD

JULY was nearly over and in England the children were scattering for the summer holidays.

Bertie had arranged that Peter should join a party of school-children coming out to Istanbul by train. I was tormented by maternal misgivings.

'I know he'll get out and look at the engine.'

'Of course he will.'

'And then he'll look at other engines and the train will go without him. He'll be stranded somewhere in the heart of Europe all by himself!'

'He'll be all right, you'll find.'

We met the train at 7 a.m., and when I saw a cheerful, mischievous, filthy, and beloved small face at the window I could not help shedding a few furtive womanish tears of sheer relief.

'Here, Dad! Catch!'

His suitcase came hurtling out of the window before the train had stopped, and a second later the boy hurtled after it.

'*Must* you fling yourself out of windows?'

'Why not?' he said. 'I'm here!'

He hauled a crumpled itinerary out of his pocket.

'Look! That's how we came.'

'London, Paris, Zurich, Milan, Belgrade, Sofia, Istanbul,' I read. 'Seven countries! Not a bad trip for eleven years old.'

'I had a water-pistol. I squirted everything from cows to the Fascisti on the stations in Italy.'

'I wonder you weren't picked off the train and put in a concentration camp.'

'I squirted them on the way *out*, not in, with ink, 'cos we'd run out of water.'

'Where did you get the ink?'

'I brought it with me from school. We are s'posed to keep a diary of our hols. What's for breakfast?'

'Lots.'

'That's good. I'm hungry.'

A week later we returned to Athens by sea, taking Mustapha Atakat with us. He had returned from his honeymoon, and he beguiled the brief voyage in slumber.

We passed through the Dardanelles in the evening, and the barren cliffs were chill in the dying light.

They were scarred with British war graves and the skeletons of British ships lay under our keel. Flights of little white birds skimmed madly up and down the surface of the water. We call them the lesser shearwater, but the Turks say they are the spirits of those who have been drowned in the Dardanelles.

Greece had become a land of heat and mirage, and Athens was often veiled in a cloud of golden dust put up by the batthi that blew all day and dropped at sunset suddenly as a kitten ceases its play and falls asleep.

The opium-incense smell of the mosquito coils burning beside our mattresses at night and the shrilling of the cicadas reminded me of Shanghai. The Greeks called August 'the season of shooting stars', and I used to stare up at the firmament while I lay sleepless in the heat. Sirius, the Dog Star, resting on the shoulder of Hymettus, was brilliant as a spotlight, and there were streaks of radiance across the heavens as if star fragments had been brushed over them by a silver broom. One night a star with a golden heel sped across our red-tiled roof to lose itself in the sea. Perhaps it was Hermes, messenger of the gods and link between this world and the hereafter.

Our garden was parched and empty, and Agammemnon shrugged at it when he sprang over the wall. 'Wait until September and the second spring,' he said. 'This is the dead season.'

September came and the countryside burst into flower in a brief rally before the winds and snows of winter, and Agammemnon kissed his hand to our rejuvenated garden.

The holidays were over, and one night we saw Piet off by the Orient Express. He was to join up with the Istanbul children's party at Nish next day.

'So long! See you soon!' His voice was a little too high-pitched, and his face at the window seemed very small and alone with that queer bright bravado in his eyes that meant he was not too sure of himself.

A little square hand waved wildly as the wheels gathered

411

their rhythm and their thunder and the engine flung a bouquet of sparks into the Athenian night.

My husband and I turned away from the empty platform.

The Turkish National Day, which celebrates the birth of the Republic, falls on Ocotber 29th, and we were to go to Ankara for it.

Ero was packing for me. Her small dimpled hands placed black tissue paper deftly between the silver folds of my best evening gown.

'When Madame wears this dress Mustapha Kemal will summon you to speak with him.'

'I doubt it. I am told that he prefers ladies to be fat and dark like Madame Afet.'

'Oh,' said Ero, disappointed. 'I wonder why? He can buy any number like that in Turkey.'

The Turkish Minister and poet, Unayden, was on board the same ship and we shared a table with him.

'Will you join us in a gin and French before dinner?' said Bertie.

'I have not tasted that. But I will try it.'

He sipped it thoughtfully. 'This is good. It is strong, and I like everything that is strong.'

The Minister was a grand Oriental. One could picture him turbaned and bearded, eating, drinking, and loving in a big way. His soulful heavy-lidded eyes were alight with expression and humour, and his magnificent height, high forehead, and cleft chin lent him a memorable appearance. His moustache was hennaed, his voice was deep and full of shadows. He had been brought up in a palace in the manner of Old Turkey, in the days when a mother, observing her son attain manhood, personally selected her loveliest slave to initiate him into the ways of love.

'All experience expands the soul, Madame,' said the poet. He gave much thought to the soul.

We took the night train to Ankara, and I woke in the morning to see the wide Anatolian table-land rolling away to far blue mountains. Here, once more, were the pastel colours and the empty sense of light and space of the South African veld. But this was a harsher land. Jagged escarpments, gashed with orange, chrome, and violet, rose sharply from the arid plain,

intersected with deep ravines which had been wrought by cata-
clysms, for Anatolia lay in the great Cradle of Humanity and
was rocked from time to time by the dread hand of earthquake.
Elma Dagh, the Apple Mountain, snow-crowned, rose in majesty from the plateau, and in winter, when the bitter winds
blew thin sleety snow across the landscape, wolves ranged down
those slopes to attack the sheep, and fought to the death with
the huge white dogs that guard the flocks. In summer the light,
beating back from volcanic rocks, was a blinding pain, and a
hundred thousand struggling, hand-watered acacia trees pet-
itioned the rains with brave green leaves.

Foreigners went crazy in Ankara.

When Kemal gathered his experts and built his modern
capital in the heart of Anatolia the Diplomatic Corps threw up
its hands in horror at the idea of being buried in the midst of
nowhere for the better part of the year. Istanbul, yes. But
Ankara? Mon Dieu!'

As the wife of the American Military Attaché said: 'In
Ankara everything goes out and nothing comes in. We are like
squirrels in a cage, running round in circles, and all to no purpose.'

'You need resources within yourself to keep on an even keel
in this place,' said my husband. 'Otherwise everybody just
drives everybody else mad.'

There was little for those who lack such resources. No culture in the way of operas, theatres, or music. No good shops or
sports clubs. There was only the city, bare and cubist,
dumped down in the middle of the plain, and the foreign em-
bassies and legations that grew up on Chan Kaya Hill, each after
the fashion of its own country like national pavilions at a world
fair. And there was only the hectic social round of the Diplomatic Corps.

The Third Secretary of a certain Embassy attempted to
hang himself and fortunately failed. The wife of one of the
Ambassadors went out of her mind and had to be sent home,
and there were several outstanding scandals. Pavillon and Karpitch's, the two Government subsidized cabarets, were the
scenes of many grotesque incidents when Kemal put in an appearance in one of his sportive or malevolent moods.

We stayed at the Ankara Palas Hotel, and we were lucky to
get a room because, as the Hungarian Minister pointed out in

his picturesque English, 'All the hotels are entirely fulfilled'. There was a great gathering in Ankara for the National Day, and most of the Balkan Governments had sent distinguished representatives. So also had the Near Eastern nations.

Most days we lunched at Karpitch's.

Karpitch was a hunched lame old Russian with a shaven bullet head and a pair of sharp black eyes, bold and cunning as a wharf-rat's. When the Military Attaché and his wife were with us, Karpitch often came to our table to join us in a vodka, and presently he and Tania would be deep in Russian reminiscences, and then suddenly there'd be some weird Slav oath from Alick and a spurt of flame from the black rat's eyes as a quarrel broke. They always quarrelled sooner or later – Karpitch and the Rosses. Then Karpitch would stump away in high dudgeon, muttering to himself. But before long he would be back with the thick Turkish coffee, and a bottle of Napoleon brandy under his arm, which he produced as a peace-offering.

'This is the real thing,' he said as he poured it into the thin globe glasses. 'This I do not bring out for everybody – only upon occasions.'

Karpitch and his tall, melancholy head waiter, Sergei, were among Atatürk's imports, as was the Argentine jazz band that played in the restaurant.

On our first afternoon in Ankara we went for a walk with the Ambassador. The British Embassy was on the summit of Chan Kaya, facing across a ravine to the rose-coloured mansion of the President. The view was wide as eternity.

As we rounded the brow of the hill we saw the scaffolding of a series of gibbets silhouetted against the snowy slopes of Elma Dagh. Hanging figures swayed in the cold wind.

'Targets for bayonet practice,' remarked Sir Percy.

And then, to complete the illusion of menace in the wilderness, two shaggy brown Caucasian bears lumbered towards us out of a gulley. Their pigeon toes, hanging heads, and little eyes, peering up from under lowered brows, suddenly and absurdly reminded me a certain South African medical student with whom I had been wont to dance in days long gone by – so mild was their expression, so incongruous their gait. 'Doesn't know his own strength,' was the cliché that leapt to mind. Yet, in spite of these amiable associations, I was far from pleased when the leading bear made straight for me.

'They belong to Atatürk's bodyguard,' said Sir Percy, and shouted something in Turkish to some soldiers who were laughing at my discomfiture. To my relief the soldiers called off the bears, who shambled back into the valley whence they had come.

But if the Ambassador had treated the appearance of the bears with somewhat surprising calm, he was less laconic when he saw a few sheep grazing on a hill in charge of a huge white dog with a spiked collar round its neck. He stooped and picked up a stone, and so did Harold Woods, who was with us, and they took care to make a wide detour to avoid the dog.

'Now, these animals *are* dangerous,' explained Harold. 'They are trained to fight the wolves – that is why their collars are studded, to protect their throats – and they will attack anyone and anything approaching their sheep. I have even known them rush at the tyres of a car and bite at them, and they can easily kill a man.'

Here and there little Armenian houses with jutting porches were scattered about the valleys among the beeches, poplars, and willows that were at the height of their autumnal beauty. On the twin ridges overlooking the new city, and cleft asunder by some act of God, we could see the stubborn outline of the Old Fortress. Under its battlements crouched the ancient city that dated back to the Hittite period. There on market days rough men with sheepskin coats and shaggy caps bargained for a wolf pelt or a mule saddle, and there the women still covered their faces quickly at the approach of a stranger.

Sometimes I went riding with the Air Attaché and his wife, Tommy and Katharine Elmhirst. The Anatolian ponies had all the qualities and disadvantages of Chinese ponies. Their mouths were made of iron and their staying-power was immense, as I found when I tried to stop my animal galloping over the plateau for ever. The only hope was to put him up a 'kopje' or to take him to the lip of a ravine, which usually brought him up neatly on his hind legs.

A dominating but shadowy figure in Ankara was that of Marshal Fevzi, the granite-faced Commander-in-Chief of the Army, who kept himself hidden somewhere in the vast grey block of buildings that was the Ministry for War. We seldom saw him or any of his officers. All day long there was the tramp of marching feet as his soldiers drilled. They wore the ankle-length field-grey coats of the Prussian Army, but when they were off duty these fierce fellows walked about arm in arm giggling and calling one another 'my lamb'. Officers were not allowed to accept invitations to foreign houses except in special circumstances, and then they were expected to write a report of the entertainment afterwards for the benefit of their senior officer.

The Diplomatic Corps was wildly gay, as if it feared to stop and think.

The small group of foreigners on Chan Kaya danced as senselessly as a cloud of autumn leaves caught in a whirlwind. And sometimes I felt that if the whirlwind chasing these human leaves were to abate they would flutter to the earth, there to reveal themselves as dead as the era which had bred them. Meanwhile the childish merry-go-round revolved noisily in the desolation and silence of the Anatolian plateau. Once Ankara had been the grain centre of Asia, once it had stood at the cross-roads of the rich caravanserais that travelled from the city on the Bosphorus to Persia, India, Arabia, and far Cathay. Now it was only a nucleus in space, the embryo of one man's vision. Atatürk saw the wheat golden on the plain once more and the railroads linking his city with the capitals of Europe and Asia. He saw her strategically safe, a great junction and a great power – the link between East and West. The rest of us saw only the wilderness, the grey wolves, and the ghosts of the past.

One afternoon the Ambassador took us to see his English racehorse Sire, a Derby winner. It was Sir Percy Loraine who introduced the English racehorse into Turkey. All Turks are natural horse-lovers, and, at the Ambassador's suggestion and with his help, arrangements were made to import £20,000 worth of brood mares from Great Britain. And on Saturday afternoons we went to the races at the Hippodrome, which was laid out on the same lavish scale as the rest of the city.

I also went and saw for myself a little of what the dictator had achieved in the brief life of the Republic.

It was interesting to watch the way in which this Eastern nation was flinging itself headlong at a Western mode of existence. Not as Japan had done – in ape-like outward imitation with adaptation as the mainspring of the transition – but systematically and with a revolution in thought as the basis of reform.

Sukuru Kaya, the Minister for the Interior, gave me facilities for visiting the schools and institutions of Ankara.

One of Kemal's 'adopted daughters' took me over the Girls' School.

She was a trim little person who had studied dress designing and cutting in Paris.

'It is not enough that our girls learn their lessons,' she said in French. 'They have to learn a whole new way of thought and behaviour. They are very keen on dress designing, and we teach them how to make their Western clothes, how to launder them, and how to wear them. Girls who show special talent in designing will have their own workrooms and shops. Our industries are developing and we are making our own textiles in Anatolia, and soon we hope to be able to manufacture Paris dresses out of Turkish materials.'

Most of the girls were boarders and their curriculum was both academic and domestic.

In the Institute of Agriculture I saw how a neglected land was being revitalized and cultured. Apart from the modern laboratories, there was a sort of 'out-patients' department' to which the farmers and peasants came for free advice. They brought samples of their soil and were told how best to exploit it. Many of them were entrusted with Government land to farm, and if they tended it well it became their own property. Over a thousand students worked there.

But the People's Palace was the most remarkable institution of all. Its purpose was both cultural and advisory, and it had over two hundred branches all over the country. At the People's Palace you could learn anything from syncopation and dramatic art to modern languages and social welfare. There were lectures on all subjects, and a special health section, from which young women trained in hygiene toured the country teaching the peasant mothers how best to care for their babies and for themselves. A war was waged against vermin, and for the first time in hundreds of years Bug himself trembled in the wooden houses.

Bertie went over the Military Hospital and came back surprised.

'Very revolutionary,' he said. 'Atatürk insists that the finest surgeons in Turkey must be employed for the Army. He considers his soldiers better worth preserving than his civilians. Quite a new notion – but not a bad one.'

Kemal was making a fine job of Young Turkey, but he needed two things if this child of his was to prosper. He needed time and peace in which to develop the internal resources of the country.

We were lunching at Karpitch's with the Rosses.

Tania said: 'Are you going to Persia for tea this afternoon?'

'Yes, and then to Germany for dinner.'

'Tomorrow there is attachés' luncheon at Yugo-Slavia.'

We sighed. Those long attachés' luncheons, with endless courses and wines, were a bitter trial to us.

Fourteen guests were crammed into a very small room adorned with all the impedimenta of the chase and of warfare – a suitable setting, no doubt, for the Military Attaché of a fierce Central European State like Yugo-Slavia. There were daggers and swords, duelling pistols, stuffed beasts, and even a stuffed baby bear. The walls were studded with enlarged photographs of our host and his friends standing over regiments of dead boars.

'But this little fellow you did not shoot,' said Boglione, the Italian Military Attaché, stroking the suckling. 'You just walked up to him and breathed on him, so – pouff! And he fell down dead.' Boglione was amusing and might have been attractive had he seen fit to use a razor more often.

I was sitting next to the German Military Attaché, who had a faded little Aryan wife and six children who were all being educated at the school attached to the German Embassy. The Colonel was one of the dapper sort, with fair hair close-clipped, and very good manners. He seemed always at attention. He had never been to Japan, but he was a qualified Japanese interpreter, and translated German military manuals into Japanese. He had also learned Turkish, so that now he could, if necessary, translate them into Turkish too.

I told him about our encounter with Atatürk's bears.

'Our First Secretary has a pair of bear cubs,' he said. 'He brought them back when last he went shooting in the Caucasus.'

'What will he do with them when they grow up?'

'He will kill them. They become unsafe after a certain age. It is a pity because they are charming pets now.'

I thought of Basil's lamb and Micky and Mookie in Adrianople and sighed.

Afterwards I said to Tania: 'My knowledge of French must be even worse than I thought, because I really couldn't understand a word our host said.'

She shrugged and laughed. 'His French is not much better than yours, my dear, but you would not understand him in any language. His tongue is too big for his mouth and he makes porridge of his speech.'

We went to Poland for tea. The Polish Embassy was the finest in Ankara. It was built in the traditional style of an old Polish country house, and all the wood and stone and marble used for its construction had been brought from Poland regardless of expense. The little Ambassador with his anxious pug face was a collector of all manner of treasures – china, silver, furniture, and pictures. As he showed me a Del Sarto on an easel in his study he said in his curiously thin light voice: 'I love my possessions too much. I wish I could be liberated from this passion. Was it not your English writer Oscar Wilde who said that man was never really free until he ceased to be fettered by possesssions?'

There was a lovely mirrored room in which we danced. The best dancers were the young secretaries of the German Embassy. Very tall and Aryan they were, and obviously of good family. Hitler chose his samples of the Herren Volk well.

It was there that we met the German Counsellor, poor ill-fated Heinz Marschall Von Bieberstein, and his charming, frail, ashy-haired wife Vela.

Heinz was the son of the old Baron Von Bieberstein, who, as German Ambassador to the Sublime Porte, had been mainly instrumental in bringing Turkey into the Great War on the side of Germany, and Heinz and his brothers and sisters had spent their childhood at the German Embassy at Therapia on the shores of the Bosphorus. The young Baron was exceptionally tall and his long, thoughtful face and blue eyes were sensitive and sentimental. He liked the English and was at home with them, but sometimes we teased him about Hitler and the Nazi world, and then he flushed and smiled unhappily and changed the subject. But wherever we met Hitler's diplomatic representatives we met also the representative of the Gestapo – a rough uncouth type; the Embassy spy.

I was dancing with the Chargé d'Affaires of a South American State. He was a handsome fellow with a reputation for candour – a rare trait in a diplomat.

'Our German friend had better be careful,' he remarked. 'His liking for your countrymen is under observation.'

I laughed. 'The Gestapo would hardly call him to account for his personal friendships!'

He raised his thick black eyebrows and smiled cynically.

We came to like Heinz and Vela immensely, and in the following summer when we were in Istanbul they made up a party with the Elmhirsts and ourselves to spend a week-end at Brusa, the birthplace and burial-place of the first Osmanli Sultans. It was a gay and happy time. But looking back upon it in the light of after-events, certain expressions that crossed Heinz's long aesthetic face wore a new significance. When we used to joke about the possibility of our two countries being at war the smile in his blue eyes was tolerant and sad, and he was forbearing with Katharine and me as a grown-up with some dark knowledge and prevision is patient with children who laugh about things they do not understand – terrible things.

We were back in Athens when we heard that Heinz had been recalled from Turkey and sent to Tunis.

And then we read a brief paragraph in the paper to the effect that Baron Marschall Von Bieberstein and his beautiful wife had been killed in a car crash near Tunis.

It seemed difficult to account for the accident.

CHAPTER FORTY-SIX

ATATÜRK – MIDNIGHT TO MORNING. FAIRY TALE WEDDING.

IT was 10.15 on the morning of October 29th, the Turkish National Day.

My husband much disgruntled, plunged under the bed and drew forth a tin case.

'And now I must get this garbage out,' said he, wallowing in the case for his full-dress uniform.

'Why are you getting into it so early? Atatürk isn't receiving the Diplomatic Corps till twelve-thirty.'

'Because we all have to be photographed at the Embassy at eleven.'

He pulled out the stiff navy-blue coat, resplendent with epaulettes, aiguillettes and sword-belt. 'No pockets,' he grumbled. 'Where can I put my money and cigarettes? I need a handbag, like a woman.' He fumbled wildly with his coat-tails, which had recesses in them like the folds in a Japanese kimono sleeve. 'Hell's delight! I appear to have laid half a dozen eggs!' A clutch of mothballs flew out in all directions.

'Come here! You need brushing.'

'Of course I do. No man should have to put on a navy-blue uniform in his wife's bedroom. When I laid out my coat on that chair I found it covered in powder, when I put it on the bed it picked up the blanket fluff. What I need is a nice plain man's cabin and a good capable marine servant.'

'In spite of the camphor, the moths have been at your tails – one flap.'

'That's comforting.'

'When you bend forward I can see the whites of your tail pockets.'

'That's comforting too.'

At last he was ready, prowling impatiently back and forth, waiting for the taxi that was to take him to Chan Kaya.

The telephone bell rang.

'That'll be the taxi,' I said.

He took up the receiver. When he put it down he wore on his face the look of one who has endured greatly and in vain.

'Harold says there'll be no photograph this morning.'

All morning there was a strange intermittent roar in the city. Somewhere the dictator was out in his car with the motor-cycle outriders, and the people were uttering their deep-throated cry of greeting: 'Varol Atatürk!' ('Long live Atatürk!').

In the afternoon there was a military review at the Hippodrome, and we saw the bomber squadrons dropping parachutists on the plain, many of them girls like Sabiya Gokcen. In the President's box the strong profile of Atatürk was silhouetted beyond the soft white plumes of the diplomatic hats. He was, as usual, in evening dress.

My neighbour, the South African Chargé, leaned towards me.

'The Ancient Greeks used to say that a man's adult life should fall naturally into three phases. First he should be a warrior, then a statesman, and finally a philosopher. The President used to be called Gazi (Conqueror) and he dressed the part. Now he has abandoned his uniform and he is Atatürk the statesman.'

'Isn't he something of a philosopher too?'

'I think perhaps his illness has made him so. The doctors have given him a year to live.'

'What will Turkey do without him?'

'Turkey will be all right. He has created a system that will continue when he is no longer here, one that will lead to a constitution. You will see. When Atatürk has gone there will be another President of the Turkish Republic to succeed him, but there will be no dictator. It will not be necessary.'

That night Atatürk gave a ball in the huge Exhibition Hall. Five thousand people were there. A special room and buffet was set aside for the Diplomatic Corps.

Bertie and I wandered into the main hall. At one end there was a stage on which stood Atatürk and his party. Celal Bayer, spectacled and dark, who had succeeded Ismet Ineunu as Premier, was on his right, and on his left was Marshal Fevzi, the Commander-in-Chief of the Turkish Army, grim as the Anatolian rocks. The old soldier's stubble of grizzled hair was en brosse, and his shaggy black brows dominated a pockmarked, weather-beaten countenance. He was one of the few members of the Government to be a devout Moslem, and he – like Ismet – was abstemious and almost austere in his behaviour. Aras, the restless, ugly little Foreign Minister, was there too, limbs twitching, swollen eyes darting here and there behind his strong glasses. And near him stood Makbule, the dictator's sister, and Afet, the heavy dark woman historian. But we missed the hawk features of Ismet Ineunu, who had retired from politics and gone into a sort of seclusion. Some said he was 'being kept on ice for the Presidency' (a forecast which proved to be correct).

The band was playing a slow waltz, but nobody danced.

Instead a crescent of humanity pressed round the stage. But now someone up there was dancing a pas seul – a midget of a woman in a cyclamen satin evening dress. Her face was round and wise and ageless, flowers clung in her black elf locks, and her body was tiny as a child's.

'It *is* a child!' whispered Bertie. 'It is Ulkü, the mascot!'

The music stopped. Somebody gave her a bouquet. She presented it to the President with a curtsy. He smiled and fondled her, patting her cheeks and her hair. Then a nondescript female in black stepped forward and the little woman of five years old was led away by her nurse. At midnight the dictator's party came into the room set aside for the Diplomatic Corps and we formed a circle.

And so began my first and last close-up of one of the most remarkable men in history.

Mustapha Kemal was fifty-six years old and very well built. His famous evening suit fitted him perfectly and he carried himself with confidence and authority. His features were strong, the forehead wide and deeply lined, the lips thin and flexible, but it was the eyes, under their winged, tufted eyebrows, that left an undying impression. As he shook hands with me he looked directly at me, and it was as if two grey flames burned into me. His eyes were compelling, inspiring, and frightening too. There was no tolerance or compassion in their depths, but they held a vision – the vision of a nation growing to maturity under his guidance. His handshake was limp, as is often the case with foreigners, and I noticed that his hand was as small and fine-boned as a woman's.

The dictator did not greet everybody personally, and someone near me murmured: 'Not even a handshake for the Belgian Minister this year, and last year he was kissed on both cheeks!' The tall fair Belgian Minister overheard the remark and a flush mantled his lean sabre-scarred face.

Chairs were placed in a horseshoe facing three large fauteuils, and the South American Chargé groaned: 'A conference! That means an all-night sitting.'

Unayden, the Turkish Minister to Athens, called Bertie and me to sit next to him on the outer fringe of the semicircle where we could see and hear all that was going on.

Atatürk had beckoned Sir Percy Loraine and Tatarescu,

the visiting Roumanian representative, to take their places on either side of him, and the other chairs were occupied by other notable guests and ambassadors who came forward at the invitation of Aras, the Foreign Minister.

Afet, massive and immobile, was near the dictator, and so was the beautiful wife of the German archaeologist in charge of the excavations of the old city. The archaeologist, who was far from beautiful, had not been included in the magic circle and was consoling himself at the buffet with more than a reasonable share of Turkish champagne.

That was a queer night.

Having settled his audience, Atatürk began to lecture them in French on all manner of subjects – educational, industrial, and even sentimental – before opening up on his foreign policy. They listened, attentively at first, but as the night wore on into the small hours a great weariness overwhelmed them. A blue haze of smoke hung over the lofty room and strains of jazz from the main hall accompanied the dictator's voice. Champagne flowed into the glasses of those who wanted it; diplomats not in the privileged circle talked softly among themselves; women yawned and painted faces sagged. The only two who did not drink champagne were Atatürk and Sir Percy. The British Ambassador drank whisky and water only, and the President's small glass was filled again and again with rakia. I counted over fifty refills in those seven hours during which he talked and talked.

Never, even in China, have I seen a face as inscrutable as that of Tatarescu.

Papagos, the Chief of the Greek Military Staff, sat pale and rigid, his fine aristocratic features drawn by toothache. Marshal Fevzi was rugged as granite. Aras dozed, his mouth agape, lids and fingers twitching. Ponsot, the podgy little French Ambassador, waited for a chance to speak. Atatürk was now broaching the vexed question of Alexandretta. Ponsot's opportunity came when the President was afflicted with a sudden and violent attack of hiccoughs. But he was sufficiently ill-advised to mention the word 'defeat' with regard to Turkey. At that the dictator, shocked out of his hiccoughs, cried out, with his grey eyes burning: 'I am never defeated! Either I win or I die!'

Aras woke abruptly, jerked upright in his chair, took out a

large coloured handkerchief, held it in front of his face, and spat accurately.

It was five o'clock in the morning. Dawn was seeping in through the long curtained windows. The German archaeologist was breathing alcoholically down my neck. I looked up at him and murmured that I would like a sandwich. He stared at me vaguely.

'I wish you would get a waiter,' I said hopefully.

He drew himself up with the exaggerated dignity of one under the influence of wine. 'You wish I would get away? Zat is not at all polite!' And he stalked away, stepping unduly high.

Every now and again Atatürk swayed towards Sir Percy and said: 'What do you think, my friend?' And the Ambassador replied in his exquisite French.

At last the dictator called for his confidential secretary, a venerable man who had been one of the great Turkish Generals of the war. Atatürk addressed an agreeable little speech to Sir Percy in his own tongue and the aged one translated it somewhat freely into medieval English.

Kemal patted Sir Percy's arm. 'You are my friend,' he said in all sincerity. 'And you too,' he added to his old comrade-in-arms, who stood behind him, bending over his shoulder. His narrow fingers reached up to stroke the other's lined cheek. And suddenly he drew the white head down and embraced the old gentleman, who kissed his master's hand.

It was seven o'clock.

Chairs were pushed back and the circle widened as Atatürk summoned his troops of Anatolian dancers who had been waiting all night for this moment. Clarionettes and drums throbbed as the performers leapt, cat-like, in savage folk-dances, uttering hoarse cries as they did so. Many of them went unapplauded, as only if the President showed his approval did anyone else dare to follow suit.

At last, rubbing our sleepy eyes, we followed the dictator into the full sunshine of a frosty morning.

A year later, on November 10th, 1938, Atatürk died in Dolma Bagtché Palace on the Bosphorus.

My husband was in Ankara at the time. I was not with him but he wrote and told me what happened in the capital on the day the President died.

He described the vast crowd that assembled in Ülus Square when the news came through – their tears and despair and the deeply moving moment when 'everybody took off their hats and sang. I suppose it was a hymn of the Revolution or something. It was then that I was sure that the passing of Atatürk had gone as he would have wished, and that the wonderful things he had done without any roaring or ranting had really sunk into the souls of these sullen illiterate people that he had ruled with a rod of iron and an enlightenment that comes to few.'

And he wrote of the dictator's funeral: 'It was gloomy and drizzling. Every now and again a burst of wailing broke from the crowd, lasted about three minutes, and died away. I did not know what it was at first. I had never heard wailing before, a sound effect impossible to describe. Everyone was crying their eyes out, men and women. But the most extraordinary thing was the soldiers lining the route. Those stolid Turks. They stood at attention, did not move or sob, but tears were just pouring out of their eyes, running down their cheeks, and falling on to the road with the raindrops.'

Thus a well-loved leader who desired only peace and enlightenment for his people went his way deeply mourned.

In the eyes of foreigners it may be that the spotlight will rest for a while upon his strange and bizarre private life. But his own people will be his ultimate judges and his justification. In looking inwards at themselves they will see in their own growth and emancipation the work of Kemal.

Atatürk – Father of all the Turks – is dead. But the vision behind the burning eyes has passed into the soul of a nation and is imperishable.

The year 1938, in which Atatürk died and Ismet Ineunu* succeeded him in the rose-coloured house on Chan Kaya, in which Austria and the Sudetenland were absorbed into the Reich, and in which the war clouds gathered heavily in Europe, was ushered into Greece with a royal wedding.

Prince Paul, brother of the King of the Hellenes and heir to

* *There have been several Presidents of the Turkish Republic since Ismet Ineunu, and certain conflicts between the politicians and the Generals but the Kemalist philosophy of Democracy is still very much alive.*

the throne, was married to the Princess Frederika-Louise of Hanover.

It was a fairy-tale wedding.

Fifty-two royalties from all over Europe visited Athens for the occasion, and there was a week of dazzle and glitter which flared up like a bouquet of tracer before the shell-burst.

A Cinderella coach with six white horses bore the bride and bridegroom through the streets of Athens. In the Cathedral they were awaited by thirty-one bishops in mitres and cloth of gold and seventeen priests in purple and gilt, their black locks curled and pomaded.

Jewels and tiaras sparkled at concerts and soirées, and we saw that princes could be tall and handsome and princesses lovely to behold.

Yet a chill breath of what was to come whispered through the frosty air.

There was a reception at the British Legation. The Minister, Sir Sydney Waterlow, was imposing amid his illustrious guests. His magnificent flowing moustache lent him a noble air. Old Prince George of Greece, the uncle of the King, twirled his own superb whiskers thoughtfully, and cast an appraising eye upon those of the Minister.

'There are only two moustaches worth seeing in Athens,' he said. 'Yours and mine.'

Sir Sydney, much gratified, bowed from the waist with infinite dignity.

The King of Greece, always a little apart, stood talking to his sister, Princess Helen of Roumania – a lovely woman whose life had been wrecked on the red waves of Lupescu's hair. She was happy tonight because she was with her son Michael, a fine-looking lad with deep-set eyes and an obstinate mouth. He fidgeted with his uniform as if he had outgrown it, which, indeed, was probably the case. Every now and again Princess Helen made her brother give one of his deep sudden laughs that dislodged the monocle from his eye and lit up his pale aloof features.

Prince Paul of Yugo-Slavia, who had brought his special guards and armoured car from Belgrade, drank a glass of champagne with Princess Irene, the King's second sister. She was tall and slender with her brother's rather arrogant profile. The Regent of Yugo-Slavia could hardly guess that the time was not far distant when she would marry the Duke of Spoleto and become the puppet queen of his number one headache, Croatia.

Princess Katherine, the third sister, was laughing and joking with everyone. She was young and fair, as princesses should be, and her small expressive hands reached out for life. Too soon they would be tending the wounded in the military hospital of Athens.

Three other beautiful sisters were there that night, Princess Olga of Yugo-Slavia, the Countess of Törring-Jettenbach, and the Duchess of Kent. A diadem of sapphires and diamonds rested on the light brown hair of Princess Marina, and every now and again she put up her hand and raised the tiara a little as if the weight worried her. She bestowed her crooked smile here and there, and her black velvet dress whirled as she danced, feather-light, in her partner's arms. The Duke watched her with narrowed gaze. So brief a space was left to these two of happiness.

And there, by the wall, was the King's Chamberlain, with his broad Slavonic face smoothed out with pleasure and his secret joy. He was himself to be married soon to a young lady much admired in Athens. He did not dream that three years hence his duty to his Sovereign would compel him to bid her farewell a few days before the birth of their son – that he would walk with her one summer night through the rooms and terraces of the home they had built together, talking of trivial things as men and women do when their hearts are breaking.

'Will you freeze if you come outside?' the King asked me.

We went on to the terrace. It was very dark and moonless. Suddenly we heard a fearful wail.

'Was that somebody groaning?' said the King in alarm.

We saw a lean white cat sneak across the lawn in the direction of the sound.

'A love-call,' I said.

Our eyes had grown accustomed to the gloom, and as we stared across the parapet on to the grass we made out the forms of men there – still as statues and strangely silent. The collars of their overcoats were turned up and the brims of their hats pulled down. Their right hands were ready in their pockets grasping revolvers. I felt sure they were there for the Regent of

Yugo-Slavia, and I shivered, remembering the fate of the late King Alexander.

There was the scent of honeysuckle in the air. In Greece there was always some soft flower perfume under the sun and under the moon. I remarked upon it.

'When I was in London I was sent some flowers from your country – South Africa,' said the King. 'Little green buds they were when they arrived, but before I left they had blossomed into starry white flowers, several growing on one head. They were still blooming when I left, so I passed them on to somebody else. They were very pretty, but quite scentless.'

'I know them well. Chincherinchees we call them at home.' I had a fleeting vision of fields near Onrust starry with chincherinchees – white and orange. Marjorie and I had gathered great bunches of them, or we had gone into the water meadows to pick arums – pig-lilies – more than we could hold. 'Few of our wild flowers have any scent. It is a pity. They are so lovely to look at.'

'I would like to transplant some of those whatever-you-call-thems to Greece. All our flowers here have a strong prfume, and these others might develop one in this country.'

'I'll get my mother to send me some bulbs, and I'll grow them in my garden and we'll see what happens.'

'Tell her to send one specially for the King,' he smiled. 'I want to make this experiment.'

So in due course a starry white South African flower was planted near the cypress avenue in the palace garden, where swallows swooped and twittered and nightingales sang their madrigals to the moon. But when the King looked down at the pale flower face, still obstinately scentless, he could not know that one day the invasion of his own brave land would send him forth upon the long, hazardous journey to London to carry on the bitter struggle against the Axis, or that he would find on that journey a moment of respite in the country of the little white chincherinchee.

CHAPTER FORTY-SEVEN

CORFU AND SEPTEMBER CRISIS

THE next time we saw the King was in the summer, in the enchanted island of Corfu.

We were his guests at a small informal dinner-party in his villa on the hill above the olive-groves and the sea.

We dined on the balcony. The light of the rising moon washed the stars from the sky, the cypresses were tall and solid against it, there was the soft polished clash of magnolia leaves in a shy breeze, and the tuberoses in a silver bowl on the table filled the moon-drenched air with sweetness.

The King was on holiday, a light-hearted and amusing host with a quick and cutting wit. He was exceptionally widely read and well informed – a man of the world with the tastes of a hermit of the hills.

All was peace.

Peter was with us in Corfu that summer. The sea was deep cobalt and transparent as blue Venetian glass. The orange-flowers drugged our senses with their perfume. The women were queens borrowed from packs of cards, and the horses, disguised in flowered and feathered straw hats, with holes for their ears, passed themselves off as English dowagers coiffed for a garden-party at Buckingham Palace. Wasps shared our breakfast under the peach blossom on the hotel terrace, and Peter discovered that a long-ago occupation of the island by the British had left its mark in the shape of a cricket pitch and a ginger-beer factory.

Then, one morning early, a man with a bell clanged through the streets, pausing ever and again to shout: '*Warspite* arriving! *Warspite* arriving!' And Peter tumbled out of bed and pulled on his clothes and dashed down to the breakwater.

'I was just in time to see her anchor!' he said as he returned to the hotel. 'Gee! What a ship!'

So once again we saw the *Warspite*, the temporary flagship of the Commander-in-Chief of the Mediterranean Fleet,

Admiral Sir Dudley Pound. Admiral Pound was later to be our First Sea Lord during World War Two until his sudden death in October 1943 (so soon after that of his wife), left the Navy doubly bereaved.

We had known Admiral Pound in Malta – indefatigable, vital, forthright and fearless, with intense brown eyes and a lean, fit figure.

One day he took us in his barge across the narrow strip of water that separates Corfu from the Albanian coast, up a jade-green river to a lonely lake cupped in the mountains.

The Commander-in-Chief lowered a little skiff over the side of the barge, stripped to the waist, and rowed away by himself to explore every inlet. He was a keen shot, and these Albanian marshes were as rich in birds as the rivers were in fish.

Lady Pound, the kindest and most lovable of women, watched her energetic husband pull briskly across the lake. The Flag-Lieutenant, who was courting the Admiral's daughter, was getting out his water-skis under the limpid black eyes of his lady.

'We came up here last winter,' said Lady Pound. 'And the whole lake was black with duck. I can't tell you how lovely it looked in the dawn – for we were here very early, before day-break. The light was pink and gold on the hills, those blue mountains were snow-covered, and the water was opalescent. But oh, how bitter cold! Sometimes I walked with the men for hours, wading through the marshes and trudging over the mountains, and other times I waited for them here in the barge, wrapped in rugs and hot bottles. We never got near enough to the duck to bring any down. They always rose off the surface and flew away before we were within range. The wild pigeon was an easier shot.'

Admiral Pound told us that he had two rafts built in the ship weighing about eighty pounds each. 'We brought them here to this lake intending to have them carried overland on muleback to another lake farther on. They were usable on the marshes – just what we needed. We therefore arranged for mules to meet us. But when we tried to strap the rafts on to the mules it couldn't be done, and at last the muleteers gave it up as a bad job. We asked them what we could do, and one of them brought his wife forward. She was a wiry little brown woman spinning her raw cotton on a wooden hand distaff, like a child's top. He turned her round and strapped the raft on to her back. *Two* men took the other raft. The little woman was quite unconcerned. She plodded along for over ten miles to the second lake. Then, when her burden was taken from her, she squatted down and went on with her spinning.'

Balkan peasant women, like the Chinese, are accustomed to act as beasts of burden.

When we left Corfu we took our car across to Albania, and from there we drove over the Pindus Mountains to Thessaly and so to Athens.

The road over the Pindus range had not yet been completed and was essentially a military route. Ours was the first private car to attempt the journey, and it was far from plain sailing. There, in those snowy heights, the soldiers of Greece were to throw back the picked troops of Mussolini and drive them back over the border into Albania.

It took both ends of the Axis to subdue that little country of South-Eastern Europe which is Greece.

May we never forget it.

September came, and the end of the holidays. Piet and a dozen other children returned to England by sea, and soon afterwards private affairs took me to London.

I flew by Luft Hansa on September 17th because it was the quickest and cheapest way of making the journey. But when I saw the huge swastika on the tail of our air liner I was assailed with misgivings lest I should find myself interned in Germany, for the Munich crisis was coming to the boil. My husband reassured me. 'They won't keep you long. After a day or two they'll be glad to exchange you for a bag-load of monkeys.'

It was bitterly cold as we took off in the dawn, and the cabin looked and smelt like an operating theatre. Our passengers were few. A lymphatic blonde in a mink coat, a young man who was evidently her husband, and a Greek Jewess with a bunch of last night's jasmine pinned to her collar. The second pilot showed us how to use our oxygen apparatus. He was tall and grave with a deep voice and he spoke good English.

The vardar shrieked over Salonika and whipped the bay into muddy waves. In Sophia there was rain and sleet and the Vitocha sulked under a pall of cloud. Belgrade was turbulent too, and the Danube and the Sava were churned into a fury at the base of Kalamegdan. The autumn wheatfields of Hungary lay stripped of their crops in the driving rain.

Suddenly the door from the controls opened and the second pilot went into the back of the plane and murmured something to our newest passenger, a little Czech with a smooth guinea-pig face. His manner was serious, but there was a twinkle at the back of his eye that led me to believe that the Germans must have a sense of humour after all. The second pilot was certainly amused in his own restrained way. The little Czech was not. He sprang to his feet with an exclamation of horror and the colour drained from his pink cheeks.

'But that is terrible!' he cried in German. 'You cannot do that! No! No!'

The second pilot merely shrugged his broad shoulders and returned to the controls.

Guinea-pig wrung his hands and began to rush wildly up and down the cabin pouring out his troubles to the other passengers, who heard them unmoved. Then he came and addressed himself to me, fastening imploring, desperate eyes on mine.

'She doesn't understand German,' said the lymphatic blonde laconically. The little man switched readily into English.

'Madam, I beg you to help me! The pilot says we have engine trouble and that we cannot come down at Budapest. It is not true. It is a plot to carry me on to Vienna! Madame, I am booked for Budapest. We *must* come down there!'

'But surely the pilot knows best? If you go on to Vienna, Luft Hansa will send you back. It is only a matter of two hours.'

He glanced at me frantically. 'It is not a matter of two hours. It is life and death! Luft Hansa will never send me back.' His face was working and his lips were white. 'Don't you understand, I am a Czech? I am of military age. Our country is in imminent danger of war. This is a German trap to carry me on to Vienna, where I will be interned – or worse.'

'But what can I do?'

'You must speak to the pilot. You must insist that we come down in Budapest. These others will do nothing; they are German.' He was pleading for his life, his pink nose quivering. I felt sorry for him and quite helpless.

'That would clearly be absurd. He knows I have to make the

connection for London at Vienna and we are late as it is. But you can go and tell him I want to come down at Budapest if you think it will do any good.'

He rushed into the control cabin. When he returned his shoulders sagged, his eyes were dull and despairing, and his face was pinched. He looked as if he had been vivisected.

'We have passed Budapest already,' he said. 'They have signed my death warrant.'

Half an hour later we landed on a very fine aerodrome.

The little Czech crawled out of the plane last, and the second pilot stood over him as he emerged.

'Well, here we are – at Budapest,' said the big German. 'I hope you enjoyed your flight.'

Guinea-pig turned crimson and his eyes shot hatred at the other. He did not appreciate the Teutonic sense of humour.

We had engine trouble all right and I missed the London connection in Vienna, where a red-haired Yorkshireman befriended me. Vienna was alive with troops waiting to cross the border into Czechoslovakia if necessary. The shops in the broad avenues had lovely clothes in their windows, and, as decoration, always a bunch of flower and a gas mask.

I think that was when I first began to get really scared of war.

I arrived in London next day and went to stay with Charles and Maisie te Water, and the scared feeling got worse. Charles and the other Dominion High Commissioners all looked deeply troubled. London was in the grip of a queer lethargy, as if peace and happiness were doomed and those who might save our security powerless.

There were sandbags against the buildings and men were digging trenches in Hyde Park.

On Thursday, September 22nd, Mr. Chamberlain flew to Godesberg for his second conference with Hitler, and hope ran high. But that night Charles came in late with lines of weariness round his eyes and lips, and we knew by his step and bearing that the talks were not going well.

Friday was 'Black Friday'. Folk went about their business with a curious mechanical detachment. No man, woman, or child appeared to have any initiative left. It seemed to me that the people of England were marching towards disaster like sleep-walkers. Late that night Maisie came into my room.

434

'Charles has been called to Downing Street. What is going to happen? I am afraid for all of us – for the whole world.'

She shivered and drew her dressing-gown more tightly about her slight figure. Her golden eyes were dark with anxiety.

At breakfast Charles looked drawn and tired.

'I don't want to alarm you,' he said to me, 'but this is a week-end for decisions. By next week we may be at war. If that happens communications will be difficult. If you want to get back to Athens I advise you to go while you can, or do you propose to stay here with Peter? You could wait and take him to South Africa in the event of war. You must have some plan. You must think things over well.'

'There isn't any thinking to be done,' I said with a sick sensation in my chest. 'I must go back to Bertie as soon as possible.'

That day I went to Oxford to bid my son good-bye. He was apprehensive too, and I knew that his poor little heart was heavy as lead. We walked in the park and gusts of wind shook the bright leaves from the trees.

He kicked at a stone. 'Take me back to Greece with you,' he said, not looking up. 'We don't want to be separated if there's a war.'

'Don't let's be panicky.' I tried to smile, but the tears were stinging the backs of my eyes. I knew full well that the storms of war might blow us far apart. The clouds were gathering and they were heavy over our parting that day.

Maisie was alone when I got back to London. She was sitting in front of the fire and the little green love-bird was on her shoulder. It said 'Peter – peter – peter' as it ran its beak along her soft pale cheek.

She looked up at me, enquiring and understanding. 'Some tea might help,' she said.

I sank into a chair, tired to the marrow of my bones.

'Peter – peter – peter,' chirruped the love-bird on my cousin's shoulder as she bent to put the electric kettle on.

'The Prime Minister got back from Godesberg this afternoon,' she said. 'Charles is with him now.'

When Charles came in we greeted him with eager question: 'Well? Is Chamberlain hopeful?' We feared the answer.

He did not reply directly, but ran his long nervous hand through his hair. He said: 'It often strikes me as pitiful – this utter inability of human beings to understand one another. Chamberlain and Hitler, for instance. Chamberlain said to-day: "I found it very difficult to speak to Hitler. He was so hard and unapproachable." I don't suppose it occurred to him that he himself can appear aloof and forbidding at times – in his own way unapproachable too. . . .'

He told us that the Prime Minister looked broken with fatigue and strain, as if he had expended every jot of his vitality in his effort to save the world from war.

'We all appreciate your efforts so much,' Charles had said to him. 'We know that you have done and are doing everything in your power to keep us from this ghastly disaster. Keep on, Sir! Keep up your heart and fight on!'

He had touched Chamberlain's arm with a gesture of sympathy, and the Prime Minster, with a movement of infinite weariness, had put his hand on the younger man's shoulder and dropped his grey head. In that moment he had seemed very old and defeated. But almost immediately he had raised his head and braced his shoulders, and his eyes were courageous as he said: 'I will!'

Only Hitler has ever doubted Chamberlain's sincerity.

I flew back to Athens by Imperial Airways on Thursday, September 29th.

In Rome they told us, with Italian optimism and confidence in their leader that now all would be well because Mussolini was going to Munich. He would arrange everything satisfactorily with Hitler and Chamberlain.

So it was to be 'Peace in our time'! And everybody was overjoyed.

In Athens they called Chamberlain 'the second Christ'.

CHAPTER FORTY-EIGHT

'NIGHT IS HERE!'

THE mountains of Greece drew their fleecy winter shawls about their shoulders; the flowers slept, and the sand fortress the boy Basil had made for himself in our back garden was frosted over as if with icing sugar. Bertie had lost much of his sunburn and my freckles had paled to the colour of Hymettus honey. Many of our friends were skiing on the upper slopes of Parnese or in the mountains of Eubea, and the diplomatic social roundabout was in full swing.

And then one day Bertie came home from the Legation with a cable for me. I was needed in the house under the mountain. My father was very ill.

My husband's eyes were grieved and troubled.

'This is the first time your mother has ever asked anything of us. You must go.'

A week later I stepped out of a plane on Wingfield Aerodrome.

Table Mountain was hidden under its cloth of cloud, and the South-Easter tore across the Flats. My mother's hands, when I took them in mine, were icy cold. The strength had gone out of them, and I could feel that her rings were loose upon her fingers.

Arend stood by the car, waiting for us, as he had done so often before, but this time there was no little jest between us when he greeted me.

'My Oubaas is very sick, Miss Yoy,' he said sadly.

Cookie and Teena had tears in their eyes as I ran up the little flagged path between the green lawns, and there was a stranger in uniform on the front stoep. She had a pleasant face and her smile was kind. Her nurse's veil blew back from her face in the wind.

'You must not expect him to know you,' she said gently.

Perhaps because all was sorrow in my home the beauty of the peninsula enfolded me as never before.

The mountains yearned towards the sea with proteas and silver-trees in their arms; the summer winds ruffled the young vines in the green Constantia valley, and the Dutch homesteads stood, white and enduring, under the great oaks. The sea birds wheeled and cried above Cape Point, where two oceans met and merged. The sands were silken and the spray rose in thin salt walls that towered and dissolved as the waves broke upon the rocks. And all these things were a solace to set against the twilight in my mother's eyes.

It was the close of the year. For three days the trees were tormented by the South-Easter, and the roar of the wind thundered down the face of the mountain with the Niagara of cloud.

Then at last the leaves of the fig trees lay limp in the summer dusk. Devil's Peak was amethyst and the evening star glimmered above Lion's Head. In the house under the mountain he who had suffered was quiet as the aftermath of the tempest – one with the abiding peace that stole over the face of the land.

They gave him back to the earth he loved on the sweep of the mountain within sight of the bay. The Jovian voice of the wind, the eternal murmur of the sea, and the melancholy cooing of the doves were all one to him now. So also were heaven's rain and human tears. Sleep was his.

In Tees Lodge little was changed.

My mother sat at her writing-desk of a morning and the same bar of sunlight slanted daily through the french windows on to her silver hair. Arend's deaf son, David, tended 'Daddy's carnations' in his world of silence. When the twelve o'clock gun boomed and we set our watches, Chrissie carried the sherry-tray on to the stoep. Every Monday Teena turned out the drawing-room, and on Fridays Cookie made bobotie, 'in case Doctor Fred comes up to lunch – Doctor Fred likes his bobotie'. Once a fortnight Nannie came to morning tea and once a week we visited the Senior Aunt. And every Saturday Gyppy betook himself to the sanctuary under Teena's bed in the vain hope that David would suddenly change the habit of years and seek him elsewhere for his bath.

The ghosts of my childhood haunted my last days at home. Every corner of the house under the mountain held its own poignant memory. Here I had been happy, here sad, here jubilant or ashamed. There, under the vine, my father had made me jump out of my skin and stamp my foot by sneezing at me suddenly, and there, by the loquat tree, I had hidden a baby-tooth and the Mouse had exchanged it for a bright new three-penny bit. Over in that tub my brothers had held me head downwards with my long yellow pigtails dangling in the water, and Nannie had rescued me with a flow of outraged German. In the woods above our house Marjorie and I had walked with the scent of pine-needles in our nostrils and the spring in our blood, discussing life's untried problems. Under this very oak we had sworn to 'tell each other everything, always'. There were other trysting-places and other memories. I sought them all. Somehow I felt that this next parting with my home would be a long one.

So the hour came upon us when my mother held me in her arms and said in her quiet voice: 'When will we two meet again?' And I turned quickly away from the sad new loneliness in her eyes.

The propellers were whirling and the engines gathering power. My mother's figure became small and far away, the mountain dwindled and faded, and the long lines of foam were narrow and frail as Valenciennes lace. There, behind and beneath me, lay all that was dear and safe; ahead was a long rocky road losing itself in the mist.

Before we left Greece my husband and I made many excursions into the lovely countryside.

We went to Delphi, Apollo's great sanctuary in the heights of Parnassus. But the Oracle had long since fallen silent. It did not warn us that one day the Allied guerillas would operate from those caves and fastnesses that were once the lairs of legendary monsters and the strongholds of far from legendary bandits.

We drove through Eubea and saw the peasants standing in their doorways, their bare feet stained with the trampled grape, and the carters lifting the swollen goatskins and drinking from them as if to drown with unfermented wine the fear of what was to come. We went to Sparta, the grim little town of the brave, in its mighty mountain setting, and to Epidaurus, the place of healing, where solitude and beauty are balm to the spirit. From the hill of Mycenae we looked over the plain of Argos, and we stayed a week-end at Nauplia in a castle built in the sea.

Argos. It meant wild irises and anemones to us, silver-pink asphodel and the warm, aromatic scent of thyme and sage. It was the land of ancient heroes and of drama – of Agammemnon and Clytemnaestra, of Menelaus and Helen of the Fair Hands, of Jason and the Argonauts. Pan frisked on the mountains and Artemis hunted there, silver-footed. Poseidon, the Minoan sea-gold, raised his hoary head from the purple sea, and Demeter clothed the plain with cloth of gold. But to many thousands of our soldiers, Argos will mean only the bitterness and horror of a terrible evacuation in which ships and men paid the price of unpreparedness.

439

We did not know that even then Greece was facing towards her Hill of Calvary as now she looks towards the Day of Resurrection. We only knew that the sands were running out and that soon our time in Athens would be up.

Ero's dimpled hands packed my things. She wept a little and said: 'I feel that we will never be so happy again . . .'

'When Slovakis has his little bar and you have a baby you will be happiest of all,' I assured her.

But she shook her head and her lip trembled.

'Those blessings are still far off, Madame – and the good God knows what may not lie between.'

That evening Agammemnon sprang over the garden wall for the last time, and Dora, his pretty wife, tapped round by way of the gate on her high narrow heels. Apostoles cooked our final dinner, and Slovakis shook his last martini for us on the terrace, and his blue eyes squinted a little like a windy baby's as he poured it. And presently we were sitting in the scented darkness of the August night watching the ghostly antics of Mustapha Atakat in the pine tree. He balanced a sickle moon alternately on his pink satin nose and his white plume of a tail.

'Mrs. Diki will be good to him,' I said. 'She loves all cats, and especially Mustapha.'

Bertie nodded and drew silently at his pipe.

A host of reflections crowded in on us. The kindness and gaiety of the Greeks, the beauty of their land, so like South Africa, the tranquil faces of the peasants, the fortitude of the people in their poverty and adversity, and their unfailing generosity.

On our balcony, where our mattresses awaited us, the summer jasmine was starry and the pale acrid smoke of the mosquito coil filtered into the darkness. We could put up our hands to pluck the stars from the sky. 'In other lands they seem far away. Here they lie in one's lap!' I saw the white sail of the *Troll* billowing to the wind and the gaunt features of old Prince Andrew as he had spoken those words. Other recollections followed. The pinewoods above the sea on a spring day and the King playing truant to go on a picnic; a shepherd of the hills with eternity stamped upon his rugged features, and the girls of Megara in all their finery dancing the ancient dance of the waves on Easter Day. I saw the evzones in their starched fustanellas standing guard at the palace gates; the boy with his strings of coloured balloons outside Hadrian's Arch; the flower donkeys sleep-walking in the white streets of Athens, and the fishermen drying their nets in the sun at Old Phaleron.

The lights of the fishing-caiques and row-boats garlanded the waters, the song of the fishermen floated to us across the silver sea. A star slipped its moorings and fell from the heavens, and Sleep stepped softly to my side. *Day that I have loved, day that I have loved, the Night is here!*

August was drawing to its close when we arrived in London, and we rented a small service flat in Chelsea until we could get away for Bertie's foreign service leave.

Piet's summer holidays had begun. A mellow beauty, warm and serene, held London in thrall – the calm before the storm. And between families a new gentleness was apparent and a clinging close together, not so much in fear as in hunger for the kind and tender things that were slipping away so fast.

Piet and I went rowing on the Serpentine on those golden autumn mornings, and one day he carved his name and the date on a willow bough overhanging the stream.

It was August 30th, 1939.

Next morning, while we were at breakfast, there was a ring at the door.

Piet jumped up and answered it.

'A telegram for you, Dad!'

My husband read it in silence. Then he turned to us with a queer bright look in his eyes.

'Leave is off,' he said. 'I am to go to my war station.'

His 'war station' was a little anti-aircraft cruiser in Hull. He was to bring her forward for active service. Piet and I packed up the flat and went with him. We stayed at the Station Hotel.

The newsboys in the streets of Hull were crying: 'HITLER ATTACKS POLAND!' 'GERMANY AND POLAND AT WAR!' A thin layer of ice formed round my heart and chilled the palms of my hands.

So it happened soon afterwards that Piet stood by my side on a wooden pier to watch that little anti-aircraft cruiser sail. She looked old and small and tenacious. 'Like Gyppy,' said our son, who could pay her no higher compliment. She passed so near to us that we could see her Captain on the bridge. We could have spoken to him. He turned and smiled at us — a crooked, reassuring, looking-forward kind of smile. Peter stood to attention and saluted, and his father returned the salute. There was an officer beside him on the bridge who wore a white cockatoo like an emblem upon his shoulder.

So many times I had watched a warship sail! But this was different. This was the real thing.

What sailor's wife does not know the quickening of fear in her breast when her man puts out to sea in time of war? What sailor's wife does not learn to accept that fear as a woman accepts the fluttering movement of the unborn child within her body? I, too, accepted it. Fear and I. From now on we two must dwell together. So be it.

The little cruiser was headed into the sullen North Sea. We could no longer distinguish the familiar figure of her Captain. He was proud that day. All his training had led to this privilege — to be given command of a ship at sea when his country was in peril. And suddenly I knew that I too was very proud, that my training too had brought me to this hour, that 'the grey mistress' was as dear to me as to him.

My head went up a little higher. The wind whipped through my hair, the gulls mewed and wheeled, and the chill, salt tang of the sea was on my lips as I said in my heart: 'God bless this ship and all who sail in her!'

THE END

NOR THE MOON BY NIGHT BY JOY PACKER

For two years they had written letters to each other – Alice Lang, the English nurse, and Andrew Miller, the Game Warden of Velaba. And now Alice stood in a Pretoria garden listening to Andrew's sister . . .

'You'll hate me for this,' said Meg. 'But Alice, don't marry my brother! You don't know Andrew . . . what can you possibly know about a man with the wilderness in his blood. I know the men of my family, and what they expect of their women . . . they've broken the hearts and the health of their wives for generations . . .'

It was sound advice – but Alice was a young woman keen for life, longing to love and be loved, wanting desperately to meet and marry the man whose letters had sustained her for so long . . .

552 09305 X   40p

THE HIGH ROOF BY JOY PACKER

When she was fourteen she had been shattered by the news that her mother, who was beautiful, soignée – and thirty-eight years old – was to marry again. The marriage, to a man twelve years her junior, completely destroyed any relationship between Kirsten and her mother.

Four years later, returning to the lush Cape Peninsular from school in Europe, a compromise was effected – a compromise helped in some degree by Kirsten's own marriage to a young and gentle man who adored her.

The two marriages, one so young and confident, the other based on the nervous love of an ageing woman for her young husband, moved side by side in a mounting crescendo of tension. The 'High Roof' of marriage was steep and slippery indeed for the two couples who were moving irrevocably towards a dramatic crisis . . .

552 09306 8   40p

GREY MISTRESS BY JOY PACKER

Joy Packer writes:
'In peace-time it is possible for a woman to share her man with his ship. But in time of war the Grey Mistress takes full possession. Her needs are inexorable. Women yield their men – not readily or easily but with the courage of understanding . . .'

And in *Grey Mistress*, the second volume of her autobiography begun in *Pack and Follow*, Joy Packer relates her life as a naval wife during the war years when she needed a great deal of that understanding. 'It is,' said the *Scotsman*, 'an exciting story, full of human interest, all infused with the kind of courage and good humour under trying conditions that the Navy likes to associate with its wives.'

552 09449 8   50p

APES AND IVORY BY JOY PACKER

Apes and Ivory – the third volume in Joy Packer's autobiography – is concerned with her travels during the period when her husband, the late Admiral Sir Herbert Packer, K.C.B., C.B.E. was Commander-in-Chief of the South Atlantic (Africa) Station.

'It catches the burning colours, the heady scents. The seething steaming Africa of today is inescapable.' – *Daily Telegraph*

'She is observant and enthusiastic, nothing fails to interest her. A racy and revealing book, uninhibited and fresh.' – *Sunday Times*

552 09450 1   50p

THE GLASS BARRIER BY JOY PACKER

The four of them grew up together, sometimes in Cape Town, sometimes in the lush countryside of the Paarl Valley. They were days of sunshine, and shared confidences and future hopes.

And then the two girls discovered that they wanted the same man. Maxie Lamotte, sensitive and vulnerable was too shy – or proud – to fight for Simon. Rima, who was vital and determined, had no such scruples. She wanted Simon, her adopted brother, and would do anything to get him. Maxie's brother Claude wanted a girl too, but here the barrier was tougher than merely defeating a rival suitor. For Claude was white, and Fara, the girl he loved, was coloured . . .

552 09316 5   40p

DINNER AT ANTOINE'S BY FRANCES PARKINSON KEYES

Antoine's was New Orleans' most exclusive and gracious restaurant. The men who dined there were rich and successful, the women beautiful, vivacious, and talented. Orson Foxworth's party on 2nd January, 1949, was as glittering a company as any the restaurant had seen.

But the evening, on the surface so gay, was fraught with tensions and jealousies . . . all centering around Odile St. Amant, the young bride with the handsome but inattentive husband . . . the bride in the white dress. And when the dress was suddenly stained with the mark of red wine, it seemed a foreboding of the passion and death and drama that was to follow . . .

0 552 08834 X   40p

A GEORGIAN LOVE STORY BY ERNEST RAYMOND

Set in London during the Edwardian and Georgian years, Ernest Raymond's novel relates the simple and moving story of a young boy and girl separated by background and birth but joined by a deep love.

Stewart O'Murry, whose family lives in respectable Hollen Hill, longs to know what goes on in the disreputable Hollen Dene area a few streets away. In his search for the unknown, he follows a seductive girl into a tobacconist's shop, and there the first of many great surprises awaits him . . .

552 09125 1   40p

THE INVITATION BY CATHERINE COOKSON

When the Gallachers received an invitation from the Duke of Moorshire to attend his musical evening, Maggie was overwhelmed. Naturally, she did not see the invitation as the rock on which she was to perish; nor was she prepared for the reactions of her family. Her son Paul, daughter Elizabeth and daughter-in-law Arlette were as delighted as she was but the effect on Sam, Arlette's husband, was to bring his smouldering hate of his mother to flashpoint. Maggie herself, however, was to be prime mover of the downfall of the family she loved too dearly . . .

552 09035 2   35p

A SELECTED LIST OF FINE FICTION FOR YOUR READING PLEASURE